Above Politics
Bureaucratic Discretion and Credible Commitment

Economic development requires secure contract enforcement and stable property rights. Normal majority-rule politics, such as bargaining
over distributive and monetary policies, generates instability and frequently undermines economic development. *Above Politics* argues that
bureaucracies can contribute to stability and economic development,
but only if they are insulated from unstable politics. A separation-of-
powers stalemate creates the conditions for bureaucratic autonomy. But
what keeps delegated bureaucrats from being more abusive as they
become more autonomous? One answer is the negotiation of long-term,
cooperative relationships that – when successful – typically bind subordinates to provide more effort in exchange for autonomy. Even more
compelling is professionalism, which embeds its professional practitioners in professional norms and culture, and incidentally mitigates corruption. Financial examples are provided throughout the book, which
ends with an analysis of the role played by professionalized bureaucracies during the Great Recession.

Gary J. Miller is Professor Emeritus of Political Science at Washington University in St. Louis. He taught previously at California Institute
of Technology, Michigan State University, and Washington University's
John M. Olin School of Business.

Andrew B. Whitford is Alexander M. Crenshaw Professor of Public Policy in the School of Public and International Affairs at the University
of Georgia. His research centers on strategy and innovation in public
policy and organization studies. He is an elected fellow of the National
Academy of Public Administration.

Political Economy of Institutions and Decisions

Series Editors
Stephen Ansolabehere, *Harvard University*
Jeffry Frieden, *Harvard University*

Founding Editors
James E. Alt, *Harvard University*
Douglass C. North, *Washington University of St. Louis*

Other books in the series

Alberto Alesina and Howard Rosenthal, *Partisan Politics, Divided Government, and the Economy*

Lee J. Alston, Thrainn Eggertsson, and Douglass C. North, eds., *Empirical Studies in Institutional Change*

Lee J. Alston and Joseph P. Ferrie, *Southern Paternalism and the Rise of the American Welfare State: Economics, Politics, and Institutions, 1865–1965*

James E. Alt and Kenneth Shepsle, eds., *Perspectives on Positive Political Economy*

Josephine T. Andrews, *When Majorities Fail: The Russian Parliament, 1990–1993*

Jeffrey S. Banks and Eric A. Hanushek, eds., *Modern Political Economy: Old Topics, New Directions*

Yoram Barzel, *Economic Analysis of Property Rights, 2nd edition*

Yoram Barzel, *A Theory of the State: Economic Rights, Legal Rights, and the Scope of the State*

Robert Bates, *Beyond the Miracle of the Market: The Political Economy of Agrarian Development in Kenya*

Jenna Bednar, *The Robust Federation: Principles of Design*

Charles M. Cameron, *Veto Bargaining: Presidents and the Politics of Negative Power*

Kelly H. Chang, *Appointing Central Bankers: The Politics of Monetary Policy in the United States and the European Monetary Union*

Peter Cowhey and Mathew McCubbins, eds., *Structure and Policy in Japan and the United States: An Institutionalist Approach*

Gary W. Cox, *The Efficient Secret: The Cabinet and the Development of Political Parties in Victorian England*

Gary W. Cox, *Making Votes Count: Strategic Coordination in the World's Electoral System*

Gary W. Cox and Jonathan N. Katz, *Elbridge Gerry's Salamander: The Electoral Consequences of the Reapportionment Revolution*

(Continued after the Index)

Above Politics

Bureaucratic Discretion and Credible Commitment

GARY J. MILLER
Washington University in St. Louis

ANDREW B. WHITFORD
University of Georgia

CAMBRIDGE
UNIVERSITY PRESS

CAMBRIDGE
UNIVERSITY PRESS

32 Avenue of the Americas, New York NY 10013-2473, USA

Cambridge University Press is part of the University of Cambridge.

It furthers the University's mission by disseminating knowledge in the pursuit of education, learning, and research at the highest international levels of excellence.

www.cambridge.org
Information on this title: www.cambridge.org/9781107401310

First published 2016

Printed in the United States of America by Sheridan Books, Inc

A catalog record for this publication is available from the British Library.

Library of Congress Cataloging in Publication Data
Names: Miller, Gary J., author. | Whitford, Andrew B., author.
Title: Above politics : bureaucratic discretion and credible commitment /
Gary J. Miller, Washington University in St. Louis; Andrew B. Whitford, University of Georgia.
Description: New York, NY : Cambridge University Press, 2016. | Series: Political economy of institutions and decisions | Includes bibliographical references and index.
Identifiers: LCCN 2015039155 |
ISBN 9781107008755 (hardback) | ISBN 9781107401310 (paperback)
Subjects: LCSH: Administrative agencies – United States. | Executive departments – United States. | Bureaucracy – United States. | Separation of powers – United States. | Civil service ethics – United States. | Public administration – Moral and ethical aspects. | United States – Economic policy. | BISAC: POLITICAL SCIENCE / History & Theory.
Classification: LCC JK421 .M458 2016 | DDC 352.20973–dc23
LC record available at http://lccn.loc.gov/2015039155

ISBN 978-1-107-00875-5 Hardback
ISBN 978-1-107-40131-0 Paperback

Contents

Preface

From the redistributive societies of ancient Egyptian dynasties through the slavery system of the Greek and Roman world to the medieval manor, there was persistent tension between the ownership structure which maximized the rents to the ruler (and his group) and an efficient system that reduced the transaction costs and encouraged economic growth. This fundamental dichotomy is the root cause of the failure of societies to experience sustained economic growth.

(North, 1981, 25)

The state, like Janus, has two faces: one benign and one malevolent. The creation of the state facilitates the provision of public goods that would otherwise be absent, but it also allows a degree of hierarchical exploitation that would have been impossible before the existence of the state. Trying to design a set of governmental institutions that will encourage the benign aspects of the state while limiting its capacity for exploitation has been a persistent puzzle throughout history.

The state was the first form of social organization, of ten thousand people and more, for the purpose of supplying public goods. The action of the citizens under the coordination of the state generated benefits that would otherwise never have existed. The defining good for the emergent state was food storage. When food could be stored to tide people over in difficult times, social organization could exist on a scale otherwise impossible. However, any state that is strong enough to protect a large store of food and to direct the productive activities of the many also has the capacity to direct the benefits toward (or impose costs on) the few. Individuals did not come to build large irrigation systems or serve in the army by a happy coincidence of individual self-interest and the needs of the state.

It is not hard to understand why humans were reluctant recruits to the new state. It is not because they had no interest in the alluring goods and benefits made possible by the creation of states. Rather, it was the quite obvious realization that most citizens of the state were not going to be significant beneficiaries of the new regime. The creation of the state did not follow the invention of a perfect incentive system that made everyone better off than they had been in the pre-state systems. The state came to be when stored food and other resources were distributed in the form of patronage to a bureaucracy. Thus, for most citizens, the state means imposed "crop quotas, taxation, labor conscription, and other coercive and asymmetrical forms of redistribution" (Marvin Harris, 1989, 385).

The bureaucracy played a critical role in the new state. The size and sophistication of the bureaucracy no doubt grew with the size and sophistication of the projects attempted, such as dams, roads, and navies. For the most part, the benefits of these public goods went first to the elites who controlled the machinery of the state.

Douglass North claimed that the rent-seeking behavior of the elites was at odds with the requirements of greater efficiency. Grants of monopolies to reward key members of the elite, the sale of judicial decisions, the targeting of wealthy citizens for "loans" to the king – all of these are examples of North's notion of inefficient regimes at odds with more welfare-enhancing regimes.

Modern times have brought complex governance problems for the state: the subprime mortgage crisis, credit default swaps and derivatives, and quantitative easing are examples. These problems have helped us better understand the role of the state – and in particular the role of expertise, located in independent agencies, wielded by professionals with labels like "economist" and "lawyer." These problems have also helped us better understand what those organizations can do that cannot be done by the primary institutions of modern advanced industrial democracies: legislatures, executives, and courts.

Of course, academics have long debated the power and promise of independent regulators. Foundational books such as Marver Bernstein's *Regulating Business by Independent Commission* (Bernstein, 1955) have thrown light on dilemmas that such organizations experienced over their lifetimes – of how they would need to be diligent to maintain their independence from both politicians and the industries they regulated. The lexicon of study of these organizations soon centered on "capture by industry" and "iron triangles," and this lexicon shaped how we saw these organizations as part of the developing societies Douglass North sought to understand. For a state that was strong enough to direct the benefits to the few was certainly one worth lobbying.

In a classic statement of our knowledge about these organizations, historian Thomas McCraw clarified the long-running debate about the difference between "pursuing the public interest" and "being captured by industry" by pointing out the problem for scholars of regulation: "Regulation in America has been a multi-functional pursuit, a circumstance that has offered scholars a choice, when they generalize about the regulatory process as a whole, between extreme caution on the one hand, and extreme likelihood of error on the other" (McCraw, 1975, 180).

Our hope in this book is to add to this lexicon by focusing on North's contribution to understanding the long-run development of states and markets. For personal and professional reasons, we believe that the bureaucracy remains an understudied and misunderstood player in this game. We see its role as helping navigate fundamental dilemmas in the operation of modern states and markets. Like McCraw, we see the world of these agencies as a "shadowy zone" worthy of study in academic political science and public administration. We hope that our observations help move the study of that zone forward, knowing that our perceptions are necessarily fraught with error, though tempered by caution.

Acknowledgments

Bureaucracies can contribute to stability and economic development, but only if they are insulated from unstable democratic politics. Our greatest intellectual debt is to Douglass North, who demonstrated how economic development depends on a stable political regime of property rights and contract enforcement. The contribution this book makes is to look at bureaucracy through a lens of Northean commitment rather than political accountability. Bureaucracies, especially when known for their professional expertise and stability, make credible commitment possible.

We owe a large debt to Jeffrey Frieden and Kenneth Shepsle of Harvard. They spent the final weeks of a graduate seminar discussing the manuscript and generating a list of criticisms that were the basis for the final revisions. Just as important to us, Jeff and Ken were generous in their encouragement during those final weeks.

In addition, we thank Robert Dreesen, our editor at Cambridge, for shepherding the manuscript through the publication process. All of this started, however, with Scott Parris during his time as editor-in-charge of the Political Economy of Institutions and Decisions Series, and we are grateful for the vision he showed in encouraging the writing of this book.

Over the years, other scholars have made a lasting contribution to the conception and implementation of the manuscript. First and foremost was Terry Moe; Terry enriched his own ideas about bureaucracy by studying schools, unions, and the National Labor Relations Board. His understanding of these organizations gave him the footing to generate powerful theoretical advances – advances that will last for generations.

Since about 1980, a group of scholars have constituted a pool from which productive teams continue to generate new ideas. The path-breaking research of Tom Hammond and Jack Knott comes to mind; their research on bureaucracy and stability was central at key moments in the development of the book. More recently, Tony Bertelli and like-minded scholars of public administration have pushed the boundaries of our knowledge of agencies operating in polities.

Gary Miller thanks the members of the Washington University Political Science Department for contributing to a productive and invigorating transition from the business school. He thanks Geoffrey Brennan of the Australian National University for giving him time in 1996 to explore the emerging literature on moral hazard and budget balancing that ended up in this book. Andy Whitford was both a workhorse and an inspiration for our laboratory experiments on principal-agency theory. And thanks to Katy and Ethan for asking several clarifying and challenging questions – and for letting a perfectly good babysitter go out the door to work on the book.

Andy Whitford thanks his colleagues at the University of Georgia for their generous support during the writing of this book. He thanks Gary Miller for his enduring commitment to a research enterprise that dates to years spent at Washington University in St. Louis in the 1990s. Most importantly, Andy thanks his family – Jan, Anna, and Max – for their long suffering during years developing and delivering this project. Without them, none of this would have been possible.

I

Introduction

Many public officials regard U.S. senators as powerful individuals – especially so mid-level bureaucrats whose agencies are subject to oversight by those senators. On April 9, 1987, when four bureaucrats from the Federal Home Loan Bank Board (FHLBB) were summoned from their San Francisco office to Washington, DC, to face five U.S. senators, it should have been a simple matter of those elected officials flexing their senatorial muscle. Once the senators made their wishes clear, they would obviously expect the bureaucrats to defer readily to their requests on behalf of a constituent.

Moreover, the FHLBB, responsible for regulating savings and loans, was in an especially vulnerable position as the scope of what came to be called the "savings and loan (S&L) crisis" became clearer. Ed Gray, chairman of the FHLBB and the boss of the four summoned bureaucrats, had shown a great deal of deference to the same group of U.S. senators during a meeting held a week earlier. When asked later why he had accommodated the senators by flying the bureaucrats across the country for a second meeting, Gray answered simply, "Because they were senators. And I considered senators to be pretty powerful people" (Goldin, 1990). A close examination of the context reveals numerous reasons for the bureaucrats to be at least as deferential as Gray had been.

CONGRESSIONAL WEAPONS

> *The congressional dominance approach assumes that congressmen – or, more specifically, particular congressmen on the relevant committees – possess sufficient rewards and sanctions to create agencies that pursue policies of interest to the current committee members; those agencies that fail to do so are confronted with sanctions.*
>
> – Weingast & Moran (1983, 768)

1

First of all, the senators were in a position to control critical funding for the FHLBB. The agency had sought funds from Congress for recapitalization of the Federal Savings and Loan Insurance Corporation; in the face of unprecedented thrift failures, the FHLBB would be hamstrung if Congress did not replenish the fund. To guarantee passage of the recapitalization bill, Chairman Gray had recently agreed to House Speaker Jim Wright's demands that Gray force bene-ficial S&L debt restructuring for a bankrupt borrower named Craig Hall. Gray acquiesced, and Wright, in return, allowed the recapitalization to come to a vote (Black, 2005, 96–97).

Funding limits could also prevent the FHLBB from hiring enough staffers to identify problem thrifts. Individual deposits at savings and loans, or thrifts, were federally insured up to $100,000; if the agency could not hire enough bank examiners to find out which thrifts were going under, then the tax-paying public faced the real prospect of having to pay a huge bill to compensate depositors for the loss of those deposits as the thrifts went under. Yet neither the Reagan administration nor Congress had been responsive to what the FHLBB leaders saw as a crisis. Staffing was still short.

Through the confirmation process, the senators were in a position to have enormous influence over appointments to the three-person Bank Board, which ran the FHLBB. The senators could choose to approve board members who could make life miserable for the bureaucrats. This was not just a possibility; the most recent board appointee had been Lee Henkel, a business partner of Charles Keating Jr. Keating, the owner of Lincoln Savings and Loan, along with its parent company American Continental Corporation (a major development firm based in Ohio), was the constituent being discussed with the five senators, and he had used his political influence to obtain the appointment for Henkel. (In fact, just two days before the meeting with the bureaucrats, Henkel had been forced to resign when it became apparent that he had proposed rule changes to favor Keating.)

Furthermore, because Chairman Gray's term would be up in two months, the five U.S. senators would be in a position to influence the appointment of the bureaucrats' new boss. In fact, the Senate *did* later confirm someone who undermined the bureaucrats. The new head of the Bank Board as of two months after the meeting was Danny Wall, a "creature of the Senate" (Goldin, 1990) who had worked on the Senate Banking Committee. After being confirmed as chair, Wall proceeded to cut the San Francisco bureaucrats off from access to some of the cases of S&L fraud that most concerned them.

As members of Congress, the senators at the April 9 meeting also had the authority to call any of the bureaucrats to testify in hearings. Bill Black, one of the four bureaucrats, frequently testified before Congress about the actions of the FHLBB. Black's relationship with Speaker Wright had deteri-orated; in the preceding February, Black and others were called to a meet-ing with Wright about the FHLBB's investigations of Texas thrifts. This meet-ing had ended with Wright calling Black a liar and screaming profanities

(Black, 2005, 128–129; Riccucci, 1995, 40). A summons to Congress could be a painful experience.

Nor were the senators at the April 9 meeting there simply as individual legislators; several held key committee positions that came with official oversight for the FHLBB. Political scientists argue that members of senate oversight committees have more influence, compared to committee non-members, on bureaucratic behavior. "The congressional committee system provides the key institutional link between interest groups and the provision of benefits. Committees and subcommittees dominate policymaking" (Barry, 1989, 149). The senators at the April 9 meeting had the committee connections to expect deference from the FHLBB bureaucrats. Both Alan Cranston (D-CA) and Don Riegle (D-MI) had seniority on the Senate Banking Committee, and Riegle was soon to become its chair

Ultimately, of course, the senators were also in a position to legislate a change in the statutory authority of the FHLBB. In fact, that was in the cards as well: the FHLBB was eliminated by an act of Congress within a few years and its responsibilities given to the newly created Office of Thrift Supervision (OTS). In contrast to the FHLBB, the OTS was located within the Department of the Treasury, thereby decreasing its political independence.

So all of the weapons that the U.S. Senate could hold over federal bureaucrats – budget, staffing, leadership, statutory authority, and committee power – were very much in play at the meeting in 1987. The senators had a few tasty carrots and many painful sticks with which to induce the bureaucrats to give them what they wanted. And what the five senators wanted was fairly simple: they wanted the four bureaucrats to back off in their investigation of a constituent – Charles Keating Jr. – in exchange for Keating's promise not to engage in further wrongdoing.

CHARLES KEATING PULLS A "FIRE ALARM"

One question, among many raised in recent weeks, had to do with whether my financial support in any way influenced several political figures to take up my cause. I want to say in the most forceful way I can: I certainly hope so.
– Charles Keating, Jr. (quoted in Goldin, 1990)

The legislators requested that meeting with the bureaucrats in response to what McCubbins and Schwartz would characterize as a "fire alarm" from Keating (McCubbins & Schwartz, 1984). "Fire alarm" oversight consists of legislators waiting for constituents – like Keating – to vocalize concerns about the actions of bureaucrats. It contrasts with "police patrol" oversight, in which legislators actively spend resources to find bureaucratic practices that they find objectionable and wish to change. The latter type of oversight is costly indeed; that kind of close scrutiny requires that more congressional staff be devoted to oversight than Congress could possibly afford. "Fire alarm" oversight, in contrast, allows legislators to respond directly to expressions of concerns from constituents, thereby building support for reelection without the expense of close monitoring. The possibility of effective fire alarms supports the case made by congressional scholars that legislators have the capacity, as well as the motivation, to shape bureaucratic decisions to enhance their own reelection chances (Weingast, 1984).

Keating's was a classic case of "fire alarm" oversight. He had brought his own case to the attention of the senators – and the senators were in a position to reap significant electoral benefit by responding favorably to him. Charles Keating argued that the FHLBB was harassing him and threatening actions that could bankrupt his companies.

In particular, Keating was trying to get the FHLBB to change a rule, called the *direct investment rule*, which it had promulgated in the face of excessively risky investments from S&Ls across the country. In the wake of the deregulation of the S&L industry in the early 1980s, more and more S&Ls were putting more and more of their depositors' money directly into risky investments such as shopping malls and hotels, rather than loaning it out in the form of safe, 30-year mortgages. Because the depositors' money was federally insured, this strategy put the taxpayers at risk; in response, the direct investment rule required S&Ls to constrain the proportion of their funds put at risk in this way so as to forestall bankruptcies and reduce taxpayer expense. In search of the greatest possible profits, the financial institutions that Keating controlled had far exceeded the limit of risky investments as specified by the rule.

Keating not only alerted the senators to his problems but he also emphasized the economic significance of the case by making large campaign contributions. One of the five senators at the April 1987 meeting was Alan Cranston (D-CA), who had been a party whip since 1977. He could claim Keating as a constituent because of the California location of Lincoln Savings. He had met with Charles Keating 12 times and had received from him campaign contributions of $889,000 (Pizzo, Fricker, & Muolo, 1989, 290).

Both senators from Arizona – Democrat Dennis DeConcini and Republican John McCain – were in the meeting room. Keating was a constituent of theirs as well, because American Continental Corporation, the parent company of Lincoln Savings, was developing "The Phoenician" – a luxury resort of unprecedented cost in the Phoenix region. DeConcini and McCain had received campaign contributions of $55,000 and $112,000, respectively, from Keating (Pizzo et al., 1989, 290).

The American Continental Corporation was originally based in Ohio, which explained the presence of yet another senator, John Glenn (D-OH), who had received $200,000 in contributions from Keating. Keating also owned the Hotel Pontchartrain in downtown Detroit; hence the presence of Don Riegle (D-MI).

According to an influential theory of congressional-bureaucratic interactions, generally referred to as "congressional dominance," the senators in this case should have had, through fire alarms, the information necessary to alert them to a constituent-serving opportunity, and they should have had both the motivation and the means to set the FHLBB bureaucrats straight on the subject of Charles Keating and enforcement of the direct investment rule. As Weingast and Moran point out in a landmark first paper on the subject, congressional oversight is of interest to members of Congress because of their reelection motivation: they can enhance their reelection goals by the efficient shaping of bureaucratic behavior. "The congressional dominance approach assumes that congressmen – or, more specifically, particular congressmen on the relevant committees – possess sufficient rewards and sanctions to create agencies that pursue policies of interest to the current committee members; those agencies that fail to do so are confronted with sanctions" (Weingast & Moran, 1983, 768). The confrontation with the Keating Five (as they came to be known) should have been an easy test of congressional dominance and a lopsided success for the senators.

The Nature of the Meeting

The only thing we have as regulators is our credibility. We have to preserve it.
— Michael Patriarca (quoted in Pizzo et al., 1989, 520)

The bureaucrats at the April 9 meeting included James Cirona, president of the Federal Home Loan Bank of San Francisco, which had been investigating Lincoln Savings and Loan. With him were Michael Patriarca and Richard Sanchez from the FHLBB, who had been supervising the investigation, and William Black, general counsel for the San Francisco Home Loan Bank.

The senators' position at the meeting was that Keating's hard work and entrepreneurship had transformed Lincoln Savings into a huge success by. Now, Keating was complaining that he could not execute his business plan as he wanted, because of prolonged and hostile investigations from the FHLBB. The senators wanted to know why Keating was being investigated and why the investigation was going on so long.

After listening to the senators, Cirona began his response with a mild question about the propriety of having the meeting at all: "This meeting is very unusual. To discuss a particular company." Senator DeConcini responded, "It's very unusual for us to have a company that could be put out of business by its regulators" (Pizzo et al., 1989, 517). The senators were clearly determined to get an explanation on behalf of Keating, no matter how unorthodox the meeting was.

Cirona and his team then explained to the senators that the investigation was motivated by more than a difference of opinion about the evaluation of a few pieces of property. The FHLBB's examiners had documented that Lincoln was not doing the required underwriting of its loans, was getting bad appraisals of its projects, was recording false profits, and was extending too much credit to particular favorites. They had found that Lincoln had no credit reports for any of the 52 people in the 52 files they examined.

When Sen. DeConcini heard this, he said, "I have trouble with this discussion. Are you saying that their underwriting practices were illegal or just not the best practice?" (Pizzo et al., 1989, 518). At this point, the regulators reminded the senators that Keating was not merely exercising bad judgment with his own money – he was also misusing federally insured deposits. They made it clear that Lincoln Savings was in great danger of becoming another very large expense to the Federal Savings and Loan Insurance Corporation (FSLIC), and thus one that the increasingly unhappy American taxpayer would have to bear. When pressed, the regulators revealed that they were also referring the case to the Department of Justice for criminal prosecution.

During the meeting the senators were clearly struggling to readjust their view of Keating and Lincoln Savings. They had come to the meeting prepared to defend the property rights of a constituent who was evidently providing jobs and paying taxes in their respective states. Now they were being asked to see Keating as a crook and the bureaucrats as the defenders of property rights and sound business practice. The senators referred to a letter in support of Keating by noted economist Alan Greenspan, later chairman of the Federal Reserve System of the United States from 1987 to 2006. They also referred to a letter from the major accounting firm Arthur Young, which Keating had passed around the Senate, claiming that the FHLBB's examination was "inordinately long and bordered on harassment" (Pizzo et al., 1989, 519). In response, in an exchange that seems prescient in view of the Enron/Anderson accounting scandals a dozen years later, Patriarca pointed out cases of manipulation and deception in Lincoln's books, and said, "Now I don't care how many accountants they get to say that's right. It's wrong. The only thing we have as regulators is our credibility. We have to preserve it." (520).

In reply, DeConcini asked, "Why would Arthur Young say these things? They have to guard their credibility too. They put the firm's neck out with this letter."

PATRIARCA: "They have a client."
DECONCINI: "You believe they'd prostitute themselves for a client?"
PATRIARCA: "Absolutely. It happens all the time" (Pizzo et al., 1989, 520).

The meeting ended with the FHLBB bureaucrats reminding the U.S. senators that the criminal referral was confidential information and warning them that the Department of Justice would view leakage of this possibility with hostility. They made it clear that Lincoln would either have to change its practices or it would go bankrupt. The senators, except DeConcini, seemed to have a dawning awareness that they, not the bureaucrats, were the ones who had put themselves at risk by attending the meeting. The bureaucrats seemed to have more independence than the senators had thought. In a meeting between the political masters and the bureaucratic servants, it was the servants who were setting things straight.

WHEN BUREAUCRATS ACT INDEPENDENTLY

Bureaucracy is not an obstacle to democracy but an inevitable complement to it.
– Joseph Schumpeter (1950, 206)

Governments all around the world, democratic as well as dictatorial, naturally regard the control of bureaucrats as an important aspect of effective governance. This conception is mirrored in political science and public administration, where bureaucratic "accountability" is taken as the ultimate standard of democratic administration and "accountability" refers to bureaucratic responsiveness to political figures. Yet here was a case in which bureaucrats confronted five U.S. senators head-on and let them know that they were going to proceed in a way that was exactly the opposite of what the senators had in mind. Where did the bureaucrats from the FHLBB get the nerve to defy the senators?

The case of the FHLBB bureaucrats is especially dramatic, but it illustrates a much larger question – under what circumstances do bureaucrats act independently of their political masters? In what ways do bureaucrats seek to exercise independence, and what resources do they rely on to guard their independence? And perhaps most provocatively, why do elected officials sometimes tolerate or even encourage bureaucratic independence?

Clearly, one of the resources that bureaucrats have is expertise. Even in a Weberian bureaucracy, the political master appears as a "dilettante" before the expertise of the bureaucrat. This was especially true in the Keating case. The U.S. senators did not have their own staff with them at the Keating meeting, and their lack of knowledge about banking, accounting, the practices of the FHLBB, and the Keating case in particular was apparent.

When Cirona began his remarks, he asked, "How long do we have to speak to you? A half-hour? An hour?" (Pizzo et al., 1989, 517). By the way he asked the question, it is apparent that he knew that his team had the answers to the questions the senators had raised in their opening remarks and could give them, if the senators would allow them enough time to respond. And Cirona was correct. With each passing stage of the meeting, as the transcripts show, the senators had fewer and shorter remarks, whereas the bureaucrats provided longer and more detailed declamations on the shortcomings of Keating and Lincoln Savings. When challenged, the senators, who had been confident enough to appear without the support of committee staff, could not match the expertise of the bureaucrats.

Furthermore, the bureaucrats' professional standing reinforced their bureaucratic expertise. The bureaucrats did not just happen to know a great deal about the Keating case; they did not just happen to have strong opinions. The four bureaucrats at the meeting were trained as lawyers and accountants and acted with the assurance that any professional of good standing would see the facts largely as they did. They also knew that other professionals would offer them a degree of encouragement and protection, as long as they maintained appropriate standing as professionals – and that their standing would be at risk if they perverted professional standards in the face of political pressure.

This nexus of expertise and professionalism was supplemented by a second important combination of factors: the law itself supported bureaucratic independence at the FHLBB. The FHLBB was not acting outside of the law in investigating Charles Keating and Lincoln Savings. On the contrary, it was acting pursuant to a charge in the statutes that the senators had themselves voted on. Under the statutes, the FHLBB had the authority to pass rules with the power of law, and the direct investment rule being flaunted by Keating was one such rule. It was the FHLBB's expertise, in combination with the dawning recognition that their constituent might be on the wrong side of the law, that gave the senators pause.

The force of law worked together with public support for the agency. In general, the public views bureaucrats in a strongly negative light. References to "bureaucrats" in the media are largely critical and often hostile. Members of Congress and even presidents are able to win election based in part on denunciations of "Washington bureaucracy" and on their avowed intention to represent their constituents in battle with those bureaucrats. This was a major theme of the successful campaigns of Jimmy Carter, Ronald Reagan, and George W. Bush. It was also a theme that Keating himself expressed quite clearly in his own defense, claiming to be persecuted by "faceless bureaucrats" who demonstrated their typical antipathy toward true-blue American entrepreneurs. When the news media picked up on the meeting with the Keating Five, Cranston took aim at the bureaucrats as well; he said that his only message to the FHLBB officials had been, "Don't keep Keating twisting in the limbo of your bureaucrats' malicious indecision" (Adams, 1989, 254).

The public distaste for bureaucrats only goes so far, however. The public also holds politicians in some contempt – especially politicians who intervene on behalf of privileged constituents and at the expense of taxpayers. Bureaucrats who can claim that they are "above politics" – that is, uninfluenced by the partisan considerations that drive their political masters – can use that claim to gain leverage. Even bureaucrats who are quite politically savvy and strategic – such as Robert Moses of the Triborough Bridge Authority (Caro, 1974), J. Edgar Hoover of the FBI, and Admiral Rickover, the advocate of the nuclear submarine (E. Lewis, 1980), to name just a few – often make the claim of being "above politics," and the credibility of that claim is one of their most successful political stratagems. These bureaucrats were all quite aware of the advantages of claiming to be "above politics," and they knew that this claim of political neutrality was itself a foundation for their political influence (Safire, 2008, 4).

That is just what happened in the case of Lincoln Savings. One of the bureaucrats leaked news – and detailed notes – of the meeting to the press. Subsequent newspaper editorials focused on the link between Keating's campaign contributions and the senators' efforts on his behalf, casting the meeting as improper political interference with the actions of bureaucratic experts trying to protect the public interest. As the cost of the S&L bailout ballooned with each passing month, the public was sympathetic to the bureaucrats, seeing them as trying to protect taxpayer money. By 1995 almost 50% of the thrifts (1,645) had been closed, most with evidence of criminal wrongdoing. The assets lost in the thrift failures totaled $150–$175 billion (Black, 2005, 62). The single most expensive thrift failure was Keating's Lincoln Savings, which cost taxpayers $3.4 billion when it was finally taken over two years after the meeting with the Keating Five. Citizens increasingly realized that, even though their individual deposits were safe, they faced risks in the form of higher taxes or deficits – risks imposed in part by legislative unwillingness to confront the Keatings of the thrift industry.

The confrontation between five senators and four mid-level bureaucrats turned out quite differently than the senators ever could have imagined. The actions of the bureaucrats, in defying the senators and in leaking the transcript of the meeting, had real, negative effects on the reelection goals of the senators involved. All of them felt intense pressure. The senators were soundly pilloried, and their political careers threatened with a sudden end. Some of the senators apologized publicly. Senator Cranston chose to retire in 1990 after his approval rating plunged to a record low. DeConcini and Riegle did not run for reelection. Senator McCain felt that the publicity surrounding his participation was more painful than his years of torture in a North Vietnamese prison camp (M. Lewis, 1997), and he rebuilt his political career around campaign finance reform. The meeting with the FHLBB bureaucrats had changed all these senators' lives.

THE STRUCTURE OF BUREAUCRATIC INDEPENDENCE

In addition to these two factors – having expert professionals and public support for a legal obligation – the most surprising source of bureaucratic independence from elected politicians is a set of institutions for which elected politicians are themselves responsible. Like many other agencies created throughout the 20th century, the FHLBB was established in such a way as to protect the professional staff from immediate political pressure. It was an example of an "independent regulatory commission." Such multi-headed commissions are assumed to be more difficult to control than single-headed commissions (D. E. Lewis, 2003; Seidman, 1970). Furthermore, the Bank Board, by law, had to be bipartisan: the three board members could not all be from the same party. As a result of the decision in *Humphrey's Executor* v. *United States* (1935) 295 U.S. 602, commissioners such as Gray from the FHLBB could not be fired at the whim of the president or anyone else: they served for fixed five-year rotating terms.

In 1985 and 1986, because Gray could not be fired, both Keating and Treasury Secretary Regan applied pressure to get him to quit the Federal Home Loan

Bank Board. Keating disparaged his abilities and then offered him a job in his own bank at an exorbitant salary. Nevertheless, nothing could move Gray until his term ran out, shortly after the meeting with the Keating Five.

The FHLBB was also structurally independent, in that it reported to no administrative organization above the Bank Board. In fact, it was even more independent than other independent commissions because it supervised 12 regional Federal Home Loan Banks, themselves privately capitalized and acting as banks. Further, because it was an independent agency, only Bank Board chair Edwin Gray could fire its staff (including the four bureaucrats meeting with the Keating Five). Despite bitter denunciations from members of Congress, Gray refused to fire his regulators.

The point is that, when it created the FHLBB in 1934, Congress built structural features into the agency that ultimately enabled its bureaucratic defiance toward five powerful U.S. Senators. This case is multiplied many times over, because there are many independent agencies in the federal and state governments. The FHLBB is just one of numerous agencies created in the image of a reform model developed as part of a Progressive Era recipe for change.

Progressivism was a response to the hierarchical partisan politics at the turn of the 20th century, in which the abuses of state and local party "bosses" were apparent to any newspaper reader and were especially hated by professionals, the middle class, and small business operators. These groups avidly supported the crusades of such doughty Progressive leaders as Robert M. LaFollette of Wisconsin, George W. Norris of Nebraska, and especially Teddy Roosevelt. Whereas Progressive reforms such as primary elections and stricter registration requirements were directed at reducing the electoral influence of party machines, other reforms were designed to give a larger role to professional experts. Although the Progressive movement ended with World War I, bureaucracies maintained their structures of bipartisan commissions, fixed terms of office, professional staffs, and a charge to regulate "in the public interest," the vagueness of which served to establish an expectation of independence.

BAD BUREAUCRATS?

On the one hand, granting bureaucrats independence increases their capacity to make welfare-improving decisions. On the other hand, that independence gives them opportunities to act without regard to the public's preferences. Politicians could limit that independence by imposing tighter accountability standards. An alternative is that bureaucrats would be responsive to internal checks that would guide them like a lodestar away from narrow interests to the broader public good.

And this alternative is what we argue happened with the FHLBB's San Francisco bureaucrats. Bill Black and his fellow bureaucrats stood up to politicians in a way that limited political control but improved policy outcomes. In this case, the FHLBB's independence tied the politicians' hands. The bureaucrats had the opportunity to act in the public interest and against the misapplication of the law, but only if they defied the policy preferences of five senators.

In a sense, this was an equilibrium outcome that could have disintegrated if either side had deviated – if politicians had sought to damage the FHLBB's independence or if the bureaucrats had acted in ways that were in their own narrow interest (as opposed to politicians' narrow interests).

Both of these deviations happened shortly after the April 1987 meeting of the Keating Five. As mentioned earlier, Chairman Gray's term ended in June 1987, and M. Danny Wall, a former Senate staffer, replaced him. Wall's tenure as chairman was the beginning of the end for the FHLLB. The Financial Institutions Reform, Recovery and Enforcement Act of 1989 (FIRREA) killed it. This act transferred oversight responsibility of the individual Federal Home Loan Banks to the new Federal Housing Finance Board, and a new agency, the Office of Thrift Supervision (OTS) in the Department of the Treasury, took over FHLLB's regulatory responsibilities.

When nominated, Danny Wall was the staff director of the Senate Committee on Banking, Housing, and Urban Affairs. He had served under Senator Jake Garn from 1975 to 1979 and then as minority staff director of that Senate committee from 1979 to 1980. As Mason notes, "unlike Gray, he had no prior experience in finance and lacked an analytical knowledge of the thrift industry" (Mason, 2004, 234), graduating from North Dakota State University with a bachelor of architecture degree. But he represented the quintessential solution to the problem of control: a congressional staffer as the new agency head. He was a politician's "man in Havana."

Unfortunately Wall lost the confidence of Congress because he had no grasp of the magnitude of the thrift crisis or the prospects for its solution. During his tenure, his optimistic forecasts were so unrelated to reality that "some legislators and staffers on Capitol Hill began to refer to the Board chairman as M. Danny Isuzu (after the chronic liar on a television commercial) or as M. Danny Off-the-Wall" (Mason, 2004, 234).

More importantly, the bureaucrats in the San Francisco office were to learn that the change in agency leadership both removed a source of their protection and installed in the office a bureaucrat (albeit an appointed one), who had no commitment to the professional standards that had motivated their actions. Danny Wall chose not to push the case against Keating, and the agency and he paid for it in the long run. Under Wall's leadership, regulatory pressure was called off, and Wall resigned in December 1989 in part because of this failure to act (Mason, 2004, 238).

Wall defended his actions at that time:

We had the San Francisco folks saying one thing, Lincoln's Big Eight accounting firm in direct contravention and the institution itself all saying different things.... I did not feel skilled enough in the nuances, so I naturally turned to my senior staff. (Nash, 1989)

In 1998 Wall ordered Darrel Dochow, head of the Office of Regulatory Policy, Oversight, and Supervision, to review the San Francisco bureaucrats' case on Lincoln Financial. The proximate result was more delay. Wall and Roger F. Martin of the Bank Board then voted to remove the San Francisco office's jurisdiction over Lincoln and start a new investigation in Dochow's office, "a move that shocked top officials at other regulatory agencies" (Nash, 1989). But this delay only fueled the fire:

From mid-1987, when the San Francisco examiners first recommended action, until April 14, 1989, when the regulators actually moved in, Lincoln's assets grew by almost 40 percent, to nearly $5.46 billion, from $3.91 billion. According to Lincoln's financial statements, the growth was fueled by large increases in its portfolio of risky investments: a 77 percent jump in holdings of raw land, a 300 percent increase in construction loans, a 70 percent increase in non-residential real estate loans and a major increase in junk-bond holdings. (Nash, 1989)

In the end, Lincoln failed, Wall resigned, and the FHLBB was dismantled under FIRREA. The equilibrium of regulatory independence and professionalized bureaucrats was disrupted when politicians inserted a bureaucrat who would transmit their own preferences. The consequence was a larger-than-necessary bailout of a failed S&L.

The S&L crisis illustrates the idea of a tradeoff in institutional design. Clearly, in a democracy, some expectation of bureaucratic accountability is legitimate, but the tenure of Danny Wall reveals that hiring an unknowledgeable "man in Havana" is not a panacea.

A DILEMMA AND A TRADEOFF IN INSTITUTIONAL DESIGN

Governments are integral elements of discussions of the roots of economic growth. At a minimum, governments affect economic performance via Keynesian fiscal mechanisms such as taxing and spending decisions. Some of those spending decisions involve investments in goods and services that serve society broadly (via the provision of public goods), whereas others transfer income and wealth both vertically and horizontally. In addition, because of the presence of market failures, governments often intervene in problems associated with externalities, information problems, and thin market competition. Government also plays a fundamental role in managing the money supply. The performance of each of these functions depends on the particular institutions in place for the purpose of achieving higher levels of social welfare.

It is hard to define an "optimal institution" that allows markets to reach peak performance. Douglass North sees the state as "an organization with a comparative advantage in violence, extending over a geographic area" (North, 1979, 250). Each economy has a technical production frontier, determined by the stocks of knowledge and resources in society, that represents the best possible levels of productivity and output. Inside this technical production frontier lies a structural production frontier that represents all the forms of economic organization that minimize costs and maximize output, and there is a frontier for each structure of property rights in society. The nature of the state – with its ability to exclude as it determines property rights – determines how close this structural production frontier is to the economy's technical production frontier, and the closer the two frontiers are, the better. What makes organizational sense in the market depends on the structure of property rights, and that structure depends on the political system. Some systems are more capable of moving the structural frontier closer to the technical frontier because they have avoided "failures of organization" (Eggertsson, 1990, 321).

The problem with democracy is its frequent incoherence – its lack of clarity, consistency, or stability regarding the kinds of policies that governments make and that determine the fates of economies. Democracies are subject to "social losses of disorder": losses in the market that may be due to monopoly, externalities, a failure to provide public goods, markets for "lemons," violence, squatter takings, and other losses that provide a prima facie case for governmental intervention. At the same time, there are "social losses of dictatorship" that come from the unrestrained actions of government, such as extortion and corruption, excessive taxation, and bribery.

This is the dilemma that gives birth to a tradeoff. "A government capable of protecting property against private infringement can itself become the violator and thief" (Djankov, Glaeser, La Porta, Lopez-de-Silanes, & Shleifer, 2003, 596). Think of it as an optimization problem in two dimensions. If on the vertical axis we have social losses from dictatorship and there are social losses from disorder on the horizontal one, a society would like to be located as close to the origin as possible. But no society achieves zero costs due to disorder or dictatorship, and what is feasible varies across societies. For instance, a society ruled by warlords could experience high costs of both types. A society could identify better institutional arrangements by considering the tradeoffs between the costs of disorder and dictatorship.

Alternative institutional arrangements are possible, and we can compare these feasible arrangements in terms of their tradeoffs; moving from one to another will reduce the social losses due to dictatorship, but increase the losses due to disorder, and vice versa. This "institutional possibilities frontier" divides the feasible from the infeasible, shows the tradeoffs between the types of losses, and is convex because with reduction it is increasingly costly to eliminate the last of the losses from either dictatorship or disorder.

Different societies will find different institutional forms to be most efficient (Djankov et al., 2003). In the 12th and 13th centuries, France faced steeper disorder costs and had to invest in a more coercive system of civil law than did Great Britain in the same period. Similarly, to control the disorder of the Gilded Age and the social losses of tainted drugs, labor strife, financial panics, and increasingly powerful party bosses, the United States in the Progressive Era found that "marginal regulation was relatively productive" (607).

For many agencies tasked with regulating the economy, given their relative independence, the Progressive Era was marked by the choice of a institutional arrangement that leaned toward reducing the costs of disorder, although at the cost of increasing social losses due to dictatorship. Although such an arrangement made government less accountable, it gave added responsibility to bureaucrats and less to politicians. Consider the S&L crisis. An accountable amateur like Wall enhances the chaos caused by public policy being sold to the highest bidder (like Keating). Compared with that amateur, the regulator can minimize the social costs of disorder with minimal risk of costs of dictatorship – as long as the bureaucrat is professionally constrained.

In the aftermath of the Great Recession, the American public is reevaluating the discretionary powers held by a system of regulatory agencies. We see the structural arrangements of these agencies as a particular choice – one that can be explained with reference to emerging theories of human action and choice – that has had significant consequences for the performance of the American economy and polity. Bureaucracies that are "above politics" and practice discretionary authority to oversee the state are created when politicians choose to make credible commitments to "bind their own hands." When, as in a theory of congressional dominance, those politicians damage those commitments, the tension over responsibility reemerges, with consequences for the kinds of social losses that society incurs.

The Tension between Political Accountability and Professional Responsibility

As the national bureaucracy expanded in the New Deal with the creation of these new institutional innovations we call independent commissions, the problem of reconciling hierarchy and expertise soon became more pressing and emerged at the center of what was to become a classic controversy in the field of public administration. Carl Friedrich of Harvard and Herman Finer of University College London each promoted a different feature of Weberian bureaucracy. Their debate formed the bounds of our common understanding of the tension between political accountability and professional responsibility in modern bureaucracies.

These scholars observed a lack of consistent political oversight of these new agencies, which were populated with expert bureaucrats. Friedrich saw this arrangement as inevitable:

At best, responsibility in a democracy will remain fragmentary because of the indistinct voice of the principal whose agents the officials are supposed to be – the vast heterogeneous masses composing the people. Even the greatest faith in the common man...cannot any longer justify a simple acceptance of the mythology of "the will of the people." (Friedrich, 1940, 409)

As a consequence, he worried about the performance of underscrutinized agencies: "under the best arrangements, a considerable margin of irresponsible conduct of administrative activities is inevitable" (Friedrich, 1940, 399).

Yet Friedrich believed that, because of the weakness of the links between principals and agents in modern government, we could – and ultimately, must – rely on (trust) the professional technical knowledge of the bureaucrat to constrain their practices. This "inner check" is part of John Gaus's description of the professional:

The responsibility of the civil servant to the standards of his profession, in so far as those standards make for the public interest, may be given official recognition.... Certainly, in the system of government which is now emerging, one important kind of responsibility will be that which the individual civil servant recognizes as due to the standards and ideals of his profession. This is "his inner check." (Gaus, 1936, 39–40)

In contrast, Finer focused on the institutions for the control of bureaucrats by democratic principals ("my insistence upon distinguishing responsibility as an arrangement of correction and punishment even up to dismissal both of politicians and officials"), disparaging Friedrich's belief "in reliance upon responsibility as a sense of responsibility, largely unsanctioned, except by deference or loyalty to professional standards" (Finer, 1941, 410). Instead, elected representatives "are to determine the course of action of public servants to the most minute degree that is technically feasible" (336), thus putting a premium on hiring legislatively responsive officials such as Danny Wall.

In modern parlance, Friedrich was concerned about solving the problem of "adverse selection" – the difficulty in finding the best person for the job – whereas Finer was addressing "moral hazard" – the tendency for bureaucrats to take opportunistic actions that fail to benefit society as a whole. For Finer, the "trust" mechanism, unsupported by sanctions and incentives, played no role: "political responsibility is the major concern of those who work for healthy relationships between the officials and the public, and moral responsibility, although a valuable conception and institutional form, is minor and subsidiary" (Finer, 1941, 350).

Observationally, Finer's view seems like wishful thinking. Far from maximizing the vulnerability of bureaucrats such as Black or Gray at the FHLBB, to a large extent we have insulated them – through civil service protection, formal constraints on political oversight, and, perhaps as importantly, an article of popular faith that officials must be allowed to use their expertise free from political interference. In fact, many formal and informal institutions allow bureaucrats to wield a degree of independence, contrary to Finer's notion of hierarchical control.

According to Friedrich, "all the permanent officials of the British government, as well as our own and other supposedly popular governments, are once and for all rendered irresponsible" (Friedrich, 1940, 404). He thus asked,

"If government and other officials are to be responsible, how can they be induced to respond?" (199). Friedrich dismissed some options as too coarse to be of much use (e.g., brute dismissal, double-edged financial measures of control and audit, the limited power of judicial measures). He argued that the most powerful method for holding bureaucrats accountable, one growing in importance rather than diminishing in power, was professionalism and its "modes of approval and disapproval," because bureaucrats are "more sensitive to and more concerned with the criticism made of their activities by their professional peers than by any superior in the organization they serve" (201). In contrast to Finer's accountability mechanisms, Friedrich saw a nuanced world with professional discretion, credible commitment, and trust.

This tension between political accountability and professional responsibility has been at the center of concerns expressed about the amazing transformation of the machinery of government during the New Deal and the Cold War, and it continues today. There is no doubt that Finer's voice is dominant in the current public debate. It reflects the fear that bureaucrats are "out of control" – making discretionary decisions in ways that are not just unresponsive, but also hostile to the public; "fear of bureaucracy" is a "raging pandemic" (H. Kaufman, 1981a). To gain votes and influence, politicians since George Wallace have promulgated a fear of Washington bureaucrats and "pointy-headed intellectuals," portraying them as a new power elite inimical to the interests of the ordinary citizen and out of the control of the people's elected representatives. Presidential candidates, including Carter and Reagan, gained office with versions of those indictments. Friedrich's trust in the professional expertise of bureaucrats seems merely quaint.

In academia as well, Finer is ascendant. In the 1970s, economists increasingly turned from the price mechanism to focus on more complex incentives operating in firms and other organizations. "Today, for many economists, economics is to a large extent a matter of incentives: incentives to work hard to produce good quality products, to study, to invest, to save, etc." (Laffont & Martimort, 2002, 1). The emphasis on externally imposed incentives has transformed the study of public bureaucracy. Elected officials, especially the legislature, are seen as the principal, shaping the incentives of bureaucratic agents. The answer to the question, "Why does this bureaucrat behave in this way?" is often "because of the incentives imposed by Congress" (Weingast, 1984) or the president.

The generalized prescription offered by principal-agency theory to overcome the opportunism of bureaucrats is to provide copious incentives and burdensome sanctions – an orientation that would have pleased Finer. Congressional grants of discretion must be grudging, closely watched, and capable of being called back. In academia, as well as politics, bureaucrats are regarded as inevitable bearers of moral hazard and therefore as requiring hierarchical control through incentives.

Two Sides

The tension between accountability and professionalism is also a debate about two versions of responsibility, *one focusing on principals and the other on agents*. Largely as a consequence of the Friedrich-Finer debate, research has focused on bureaucrats, their motives and incentives, and how politicians and bureaucrats together form and deliver policy solutions to public problems.

Recently, political scientists like Daniel Carpenter in his *The Forging of Bureaucratic Autonomy* have demonstrated how bureaucrats can carve out a degree of autonomy by earning a reputation for high-quality work, thus causing politicians to give them room to deliver policy (Carpenter, 2001). Another fine example is Sean Gailmard and John Patty's *Learning while Governing*, in which bureaucrats develop policy-making expertise after politicians grant them autonomy to do so (Gailmard & Patty, 2013). Those political science approaches and others in public administration have sought to provide analytic traction on the pro-social actions of bureaucrats.

Our view in this book is not that we should focus on *either* bureaucrats *or* politicians, but instead that we should focus on *both* bureaucrats and politicians. Even in the broader principal-agent game, superiors and subordinates are engaged in a kind of negotiation – a clamoring for a point of agreement that helps the two jointly deliver some outcome that principals want. The politician negotiates with the bureaucrat, and the bureaucrat negotiates with the politician. In this negotiation, as in any negotiation, the politician may have to engage the bureaucrat not as a production function but instead as an actor with her own interests and abilities.

The end result is a kind of agreement – a negotiated solution to a problem that might be described as "the principal's problem" or, alternatively, "the bureaucrat's burden." This agreement is a fragile outcome: a grant of independence to an agency of experts is reciprocated by a felt obligation to act prudently.

The tension is thus between responsibility to expertise and knowledge, and accountability to democratically elected public officials. Political scientists and public administration scholars have come to see the tension in institutional terms: should bureaucrats respond to politicians, or should they be protected from politicians so they can make decisions on the "merits of the case"?

As is usually the case with long-standing, unresolved conflicts, common sense and more formal analysis both suggest that the best possible solution may involve a tradeoff between extremes. Although we believe that the case of the FHLBB bureaucrats illustrates a professionalized and independent role for bureaucrats that Friedrich would have supported, we want to make clear that the independence of bureaucrats is conditional, not absolute, and is subject to tradeoffs. That is, we do not see bureaucratic autonomy as an invariant institutional mandate. It is not a deterministic solution.

This choice to commit to a policy, expressed via a grant of independence to an agency staffed by experts, can balance the interests of even very different constituencies such as consumers and producers (Estache & Wren-Lewis, 2009, 747). How government navigates the problems that inevitably arise when implementing that policy – of having sufficient capacity, of efficiency, of credibility – depends on what we mean by independence (757). One unique contribution this book makes is to push the boundaries of such definitions by helping fill a recognized gap in the literature on independent regulators:

This multitude of different ways that regulatory independence may reduce commitment problems emphasizes the need to examine the concept of independence more thoroughly. In particular, there is a need to break down the various aspects of "independence" and consider which are likely to be more important and which are likely to have the greatest risks. (Estache & Wren-Lewis, 2009, 757)

Moreover, although we focus on examples drawn from the economic functions of government in both developed and developing political economies, we believe that the conditional value of bureaucratic independence (and the professionalism of bureaucrats that may enable it) is important well beyond the regulatory agencies and central banks mentioned throughout this book. The Friedrich-Finer debate shows how important the responsibility-accountability construct has become for our prevailing understanding of agencies as agents of policy change in systems of political representation. Regulation and macroeconomic performance are valuable venues for observing the tension between responsibility and accountability, primarily because of the continuing tradeoff between disorder and dictatorship in the long-term evolution of economies. But our emphasis in this book is relevant for understanding other types of bureaucratic performance as well.

The "Capture" Leitmotif

Regulation and macroeconomic management present important cases for considering the limits of delegation to experts. For at least 60 years, political scientists, economists, and lawyers have sought to understand the prospects of "regulatory capture" – the possibility that bureaucrats (or the politicians who direct them) will pursue the interests of narrowly affected interests over the public interest. "Captured" regulators might seek to protect the regulated, or macroeconomic managers might choose to serve the interests of only a small sector of the economy. In the 1950s, political scientists such as Samuel Huntington and Marver Bernstein warned of this prospect (M. H. Bernstein, 1955; Huntington, 1952); later, in the 1960s and 1970s, economists such as George Stigler and Sam Peltzman formalized such intuitions (Peltzman, 1976; Stigler, 1971). The capture leitmotif continues to be alive and well in political science, economics, the law, and practical politics (Novak, 2014).

The policy domain of financial services raises special issues in considering the prospects for regulatory capture, which may present in various ways (Levinton, 2014). One problem is that prudential regulators are often called on to ensure the stability of the system – with the consequence that they may focus on preventing the failure of banks or other institutions. A second problem is that often regulators, especially in banking, carry out their duties using "soft law" rather than formal mechanisms with roots in administrative law; this practice brings the regulated and regulator together frequently. Both of these special types of capture focus on the bureaucrat and the need for bureaucrats to maintain proper motivation when called on to oversee complex financial systems. The more common example of capture, however, is when there is a destructive relationship between an interest group and bureaucracy that results in the captive bureaucrat. The solution to the problem of the captive bureaucrat is seen as bringing *more democratic control* over the bureaucracy.

A separate and distinct problem, in Levitin's view, is when interest groups lobby legislators and when those pressures are transmitted through the oversight process onto the agency. Just as in the case of Keating and his relationships with elected officials, politicians remain important targets of the financial services industry. In this second case, a destructive relationship emerges between the interest group and legislator. The problem is seen as resulting from the captive politician. The formula for reform is *less democratic control* and more bureaucratic autonomy.

In developed and developing economics, there is a real possibility of pressure from the regulated in the form of bribes, campaign contributions, future employment in the industry, or even direct physical punishment (Dal Bó, 2008). Levitin (2014) does not hold out much hope for "democratically-responsive financial regulation" as a solution in the long term.

Many have settled on regulatory independence as a barrier to politicians representing the narrow interests of the financial services industry over the broader public interest. As with Friedrich, we look to bureaucratic responsibility – on the nexus of expertise and professionalism – as a focal mechanism for mitigating capture. Others also see its importance for helping address possibilities like capture.[1] We maintain this focus throughout the book – on the moral hazard of politicians, on the credible commitment value of institutional independence, and on the power of professionalism as social control – to move forward the debate about regulatory capture.

Tradeoffs and Dilemmas in Institutional Design

In their important recent book on the organizational structure of governance, Gailmard and Patty (2013, 19) claim that, rather than articulating a positive

---

[1] Dal Bó (2008, 221) sees professionalism as an important avenue of future research in helping address the capture question. Addressing the relative value of specialization and expertise in

theory of design, their goal was to "help interpret the effects of organizational structure" and to "analyze the trade-offs that organizational structures create for political principals." Likewise, in his *Managerial Dilemmas*, Gary Miller emphasizes the tradeoffs and dilemmas individuals and groups face when navigating the incentives shaped by organizational choices – and how those choices are part of the broader game of institutional design (Miller, 1992).

Our intent is similar in this book. We also see the normative claims that are inherent in our observations about the roles of politicians and bureaucrats in a game of credible commitment. We recognize that no one model definitively explains the "supergame" of political and economic development in regulatory states such as the United States. Although we question the emphasis often accorded the principal-agency paradigm in stories about bureaucratic accountability, the narrative we develop still benefits from insights from that theoretical tradition.

We focus on what some might consider the peculiar institutional development of specific working arrangements among politicians and bureaucrats in a democratic society – arrangements supporting credible commitments. Born in conflict, these arrangements, once established, performed admirably for many years, but once damaged, may be very difficult to resuscitate. The negotiated agreement that defines that working arrangement – a grant of discretionary authority accompanied by an obligation to uphold the law – is itself both a tradeoff and a dilemma.

THE STRUCTURE OF OUR ARGUMENT

The story of the Keating Five and the S&L crisis raises questions about just how effective political direction of bureaucratic activity really is. It calls for a reexamination of principal-agency theory – the family of theories that have been used to study hierarchical control. In Chapter 2 we review this theory, noting its remarkable contribution to the study of public bureaucracy and its applicability to numerous bureaucratic agencies. We focus on the principal's problem, as conceived by agency theory – shaping incentives to induce constituency-serving behavior by potentially reluctant or recalcitrant bureaucrats. Members of Congress are indeed powerful, and Chapter 2 examines several policy areas in which elected legislators were much more successful in shaping bureaucratic behavior in line with their reelection goals than were those in the case of the Keating Five.

In Chapter 3 we discuss what we call the paradox of the principal's *other* problem. If the principal's first problem is shaping subordinate behavior, the other problem is constraining his or her own behavior. We argue that politicians have an array of goals, some of which are *time-inconsistent* goals.

financial regulation, Levitin (2014, 2059 fn. 338) quotes the film *300* to illustrate why it is good to have the right tool for the right job ("Spartans, what is your profession?").

For example, legislators would like in the long run to gain electoral benefits from strongly supporting a balanced budget, but in the short run, they are going to demand their share of pork-barrel benefits – especially if other legislators are demanding theirs. Likewise, presidents would like to have the benefit of controlling inflation, but in the year before the election, they would like the electoral benefits of a loose monetary policy. Both legislators and presidents would like to implement the best possible advice regarding energy independence and conservation to prevent global warming, but when gasoline prices increase rapidly (as they did in the middle of the 2008 campaign), they end up supporting a gas tax holiday, even in the knowledge that such a possibility is potentially tremendously damaging in the long run.

These are not cases of individual – or cognitive – time inconsistency, but instead are interpersonal – or strategic – time-inconsistency problems that flow from the interaction of multiple parties seeking advantage in a dynamic setting. In these and other cases, the principal may be best served in the long run by a trustee, who can only be useful if her preferences are *not* aligned with those of the principal. The foremost examples of these strategic problems are the maintenance of the rule of law, stable property rights, and effective contract enforcement. These attributes are fundamental to economic development, but as economic historian Douglass North revealed in his Nobel prize-winning economic history, political elites typically have short-term incentives to take governmental actions that undermine these fundamentals.

Although Chapter 3 discusses the possibility of a time-inconsistency problem, Chapter 4 presents its inevitability. Drawing on an impossibility result from economics (Holmström, 1982), we argue that collective action inevitably creates moral hazard that plagues the efficient allocation of benefits. The agent's moral hazard can be controlled, but only by creating a moral hazard for the principal – so the problem of credible commitments outlined by North is not an historical accident, but a political inevitability. This leads us to conclude that the more fundamental role for bureaucracy is not to be tamed by politicians, but to constrain them. Bureaucracies can play their most important role as part of a system of checks and balances.

Chapter 5 looks at the motivations for ambitious politicians to create autonomous bureaucracies – bureaucracies that are by definition unresponsive to politicians' short-term reelection needs. If the problem is political moral hazard, how might that shape the design of bureaucratic agencies? If politicians cannot be trusted with monetary policy, for example, how can they be entrusted with the creation of an agency that will shape monetary policy? Can we rely on the integrity of political actors in the design of regulatory agencies designed to remove power from the hands of those same politicians? David Lewis's definitive research (D. E. Lewis, 2003) establishes that autonomous bureaucracies are not just leftovers from the Progressive Era; since World War II Congress and the president continue to create a sizable number of new agencies with the structural characteristics that promote independence, and these agencies are more likely in periods of divided government when the president and Congress are of opposite parties.

The question is why do they continue to create those agencies. Self-interested politicians are not known for their willingness to give away power and influence, especially when power can be used to influence reelection opportunities. Why do presumably self-interested, ambitious politicians house bureaucrats in structures that give them the possibility of defying their political masters?

The thesis of Chapter 5 is that bureaucratic autonomy emerges as a compromise. Politicians are not in the main motivated by an admirable understanding of time-inconsistency issues or the possible efficiency advantages of independent bureaucracies. Rather, bureaucratic autonomy is a compromise position on which political interests with sharply different preferences for bureaucratic policy, personnel, and structure can agree (Moe, 1989). Each group finds its most preferred position blocked by some other constituency with countervailing interests. Once each constituency finds that its first choice is not an option, then the question becomes, "What kind of bureaucracy would I want if my enemies got control of Congress and the White House?" In response to this question, the advantages of bureaucratic autonomy – the capacity to resist your enemies in office – look a lot more attractive.

Given that no interest group is able to guarantee its first-best solution – a bureaucracy that is designed to serve its own interests – each interest group becomes more interested in designing an agency that will *not* be responsive to its worst enemies. When this is done, the credibility of the bureaucracy is guaranteed by the separation-of-powers system. Investors believe that inflation is not a problem in the near future because monetary policy is in the hands of the Fed, and they believe the Fed will be able to maintain its independence because of the difficulty of constructing a coalition of lawmakers to rein it in. It is because of the difficulties in assembling a cross-institutional coalition, inclusive of all necessary veto points, that they believe the central bank can be effective. We argue that the separation of powers in the U.S. Constitution has served to establish and protect bureaucratic discretion.

Given that independent bureaucracies are systematically created in response to conflict in a separation-of-powers system, Chapters 6 and 7 discuss the forces that shape the decisions of autonomous bureaucrats. As Kaufman's classic *The Forest Ranger* (H. Kaufman, 1960) reveals, an autonomous bureaucracy cannot allow subordinates within the bureaucracy to engage in anarchic behavior. Kaufman discusses two possibilities: one is programming, monitoring, and enforcement; the other is inculcation with professional norms. Chapter 6 discusses the "control paradox" – the possibility that increasing the level of monitoring and enforcement can actually cause deterioration in subordinate performance. We explain this through a model of repeated game theory. The conclusion is that political control over bureaucracy is once again less straightforward than it would seem and that the most dysfunctional bureaucracies are often those that are most under the rigid control of politicians.

If Chapter 6 may be thought of as aligning with Finer's motivations of bureaucrats, Chapter 7 may be thought of as Friedrich's alternative. Friedrich argued that professionalism is both a motivator of effort by bureaucrats and a system of social control that mitigates the worst forms of bureaucratic misconduct. We argue in Chapter 7 that professionalism acts as an alternative incentive system for bureaucrats that constrains them to a particular vision of service. As such, it can constrain bureaucrats who are beyond the reach of political actors. The power of professionalism stands in contrast to other possible mechanisms, such as structures like merit protection systems or restrictions on bureaucratic preferences as in the case of public service motivation. Professionalism helps define the culture of the organization that we describe in Chapter 6 (Kreps, 1996; Miller, 1992).

Chapters 8 and 9 focus on the record of financial regulation in the United States in guaranteeing stable, predictable property rights and contract enforcement. We document how the early effectiveness of the SEC and other financial regulators was undermined by the politicization of the agencies by political pressure from interest groups, legislators, and political appointees in the executive branch. We also document the catastrophic effect of this politicization on the ability of the government to react effectively to the financial chaos of the banking crisis of 2008 – a politicization that even the business community sometimes sees as antithetical to stability in markets (Garten, 2005).

In Chapter 10, we return to our central concern: the value of bureaucratic independence in a system of policy making by politicians. The meeting between the Keating Five and the FHLBB bureaucrats can be thought of as a kind of metaphor for the complicated relationship between elected officials and bureaucrats. Elected officials *do* have the opportunity to impose rewards and sanctions. However, these incentives may be a blunt instrument that cannot be wielded with much effect in a separation-of-powers system. It may require major negotiations to put together a coalition capable of (say) changing the legislative charter for an agency, and politicians may find that other forces may trump congressionally imposed incentives. For many bureaucrats, their ability to apply professional expertise is relatively unhindered and is reinforced by professional norms and the desire to remain in good standing with their peers. In a Madisonian sense, bureaucracies are often more correctly thought of as another source of checks and balances in a separation-of-power system than as "agents" of either Congress or the "unitary" executive.

2

The Moral Hazard of Bureaucrats and Politicians

The "political master" finds himself in the position of the "dilettante" who stands opposite the "expert."

– Max Weber (Weber, Gerth, & Mills, 1958, 232)

The fact that when there are asymmetries of information, markets are not, in general, constrained Pareto efficient implies there is a potentially important role for government.

– Joseph Stiglitz (Stiglitz, 2002, 516)

PICKING WINNERS AND LOSERS

In 2008, Andimuthu Raja, then Indian Minister for Communication and Information Technology and Member of Parliament, was charged with the task of allocating licenses for companies to use those parts of the electromagnetic spectrum that are capable of carrying radio frequencies – specifically, the spectrum that could support 2G mobile telecommunications services. The stakes were enormous. Consumers would benefit through text messaging, and digital encryption of calls meant that more people could be served (Qi, Zysman, & Menkes, 2001). The growing demand for data services and an expanding market base meant that providers would also gain. Many expected India to be the world's second largest mobile broadband market by 2016 (ASA & Associates, 2012).

In such situations economists and politicos may have different goals. Granting access to the spectrum can be financially rewarding for politicos. For economists, in contrast, the goal is to allocate access to the spectrum in a way that reveals its true price when there is no natural market. Usually, they suggest that auctions be held to set the price and, as a consequence, maximize the revenue the government receives from sharing access to that scarce resource. Most of the robust debate about designing and implementing auctions focuses on ensuring that the public benefits from the private use of a public good (Klemperer, 2002).

Economists know a lot about designing efficient institutions for granting access to the spectrum, largely from the experiences of the United States and other countries. For instance, economists such as Ronald Coase argued for radio spectrum auctions as early as 1959. The Federal Communications Commission has held auctions since 1994, and many other countries auctioned access to the electromagnetic spectrum throughout the early 2000s. Economists have come to believe that most problems can be solved through good market designs – that "good auction design is mostly good elementary economics" (Klemperer, 2002, 170).

Any allocation yields winners and losers. Just like drawing from a hat, an auction results in winners and losers. Ideally the rules of the game pick winners based on a criterion that serves a higher good and maximizes the social benefit. Bids in government auctions reveal valuations; when paid, those bids move revenue from the private sector to the state's coffers.

By 2000 cell phone and text messaging service remained limited for a number of reasons. One of these was the failure of regulatory agencies; "specification of common standards by a regulatory agency could facilitate growth" (Jain 2001, 683), but these standards were not always forthcoming from political elites.

The stakes were higher in India than in developed nations. And although one could point to ways to improve the allocation process, the real problems seemed to be deeper, at an institutional level. As one observer noted at that time, "it appears that while the instruments for managing public service regulation and defaults were 'right', the supporting institutional mechanisms and the political will for implementing them were not adequate" (683). The social surplus was in danger of being less than it could be, because of the self-serving actions of politicos who had been directing the process since India began using auctions in the early 1990s.

In 2003, under a new Unified Access Services (UAS) policy, the Department of Telecommunications (DOT) within the Ministry of Communication and Information Technology continued to allocate access based on an entry price set in 2001, rather than via a bidding system. The DOT then sought to allocate a large number of licenses to service providers, but still based on that 2001 price; in 2008, the DOT issued 122 licenses to providers paying 2001 prices. By forgoing the benefits of an auction and issuing licenses at old (lower) prices, the politicians were giving those lucky providers a windfall.

Yet, our focus is on the aftermath of this license-granting process. In 2010, the comptroller and auditor general (CAG) of India estimated the loss to the state, due to choices made in implementing the law, to be Rs. 1,766.5 billion (Comptroller and Auditor General of India, 2010). In 2011, the Central Bureau of Investigation alleged that Minister A. Raja pocketed Rs. 30 billion in bribes for his part in this process. In 2012, the Supreme Court of India scrapped all

122 licenses, arguing that the ministry had allocated them in a "totally arbitrary and unconstitutional" manner.

What did the Ministry of Communication and Information Technology do that shifted so much money from the public coffers to the pockets of politicians and service providers? First, according to the CAG report, it ignored a directive in the United Access Services policy to set a new, higher fee for spectrum access, but instead charged the 2001 price. Second, A. Raja rejected the prime minister's suggestions in 2007 to hold an auction to revise the entry price. These decisions determined the price of entry.

Next, the ministry determined the winners and losers. The Department of Telecommunications (DOT) within the ministry issued a press release on September 14, 2007, that it would only accept applications until October 1, 2007, effectively violating a "no cap" policy on the number of bidders. On January 10, 2008, it made two announcements. First, only those who applied for licenses up to September 25, 2007 (and not those applying between September 26 and October 1) would be eligible for licenses. Second, there would be a new first-come, first-served decision rule for determining allocations: those who complied first with the new conditions documented in the Letters of Intent would receive licenses. It announced the new rule via press release at 2:45 p.m., noting that providers would need to meet at headquarters at 3:30 p.m. to prove their compliance and receive approval. The actions of the DOT thus guaranteed significant gains to those in a position to make this arbitrary deadline.

The CAG report paints a stark picture: even though the process took between 100 and 550 days to handle applications (not the 30 days prescribed by policy), the DOT "gave not even an hour to the applicants to assemble…and less than half a day to comply" with the new rule (Comptroller and Auditor General of India, 2010, 29). Moreover, when proving their financial compliance, 13 applicants offered bank drafts drawn before January 10, indicating advanced knowledge of the compliance process (28). Perhaps the most striking aspect of the process was that two agency employees, the Permanent Secretary and Raja's private secretary, had been charged with following orders from A. Raja and altering the application dates to block other telecom companies from proving compliance (Press Trust of India, 2011).

The contrast between this account and the earlier case of the Keating Five is clear. With the Keating Five, defiance on the part of bureaucrats put limits on the illicit gains of politicos trying to use their political power to earn the support of Keating and others. In the case of Indian telecommunications, there was no bureaucratic defiance – just compliance. The politicians/principals were able to buy off bureaucratic subordinates to make sure they were no impediment to the politicians' preferences. In Weber's phrase, the "political masters" (a member of Parliament) directed an agency to shape the regulatory process and pick winners and losers, for his gain and that of his allies (Weber et al., 1958). This is a case of what may be thought of as "normal" relationships between politicians and bureaucrats – in which incentives and sanctions have the expected effect on bureaucratic accountability.

In this chapter, we examine the growing interest in incentives and bureaucratic oversight and provide other examples that fit expectations. We also point out that bureaucratic accountability, from a normative perspective, is inescapably connected to the normative standing of the politicians' goals. Bureaucratic responsiveness to harmful political goals is no formula for advancing public welfare. Indeed, when legislative goals are themselves destructive, then bureaucratic defiance (as in the case of the Keating Five) may actually prove to be a useful version of a Madisonian "check."

INCENTIVES AND THE INVISIBLE HAND

In referring to the "political masters," Weber identified a relationship that is common to business organizations and politics alike – an asymmetrical relationship in which hierarchical authority is located on one side and informational advantage on the other. The example in the previous chapter – U.S. senators versus FHLBB bureaucrats – is a case in point. Other examples include NASA political appointees attempting to pressure a NASA scientist to hedge on the implications of global warming (Bowen, 2008). Clashes between the elected school board and the high school biology teacher on the subject of evolution or birth control occur in many local school districts.

Such asymmetrical relationships are fraught with difficulty and even conflict. If the political master defers to the expert, then what happens to the constitutional rule that places the official in a position of authority? But if the expert defers to the political master, of what good is the expert's knowledge, either to the politician or the majority that elected him or her? Is there a way in which the "political master" can gain the advantage of the expert's knowledge without giving up authority?

Runaway Bureaucracy?

To their constituents, elected politicians often characterize bureaucracies as "runaway" or "out of control" – claims voiced by several of the Keating Five senators to justify their intervention. More recently, elected officials have openly chastised the EPA for pursuing attempts to regulate the climate-changing aspects of air pollutants, while expressing skepticism about the existence of climate change. Republican presidential candidates have denounced the chairman of the Fed, with a leading presidential candidate suggesting that the chairman would be treated "pretty rough" if he were to come to his state. In all these cases and many more, politicians claim that control over the bureaucracy and its accountability are at risk because of the inadequate tools and resources for congressional and presidential oversight. The weakness of overt legislative oversight is frequently held up as evidence to support a concern for runaway bureaucracy (Dodd & Schott, 1979). However, the systematic study of the tools available to political overseers suggests that overt monitoring and punishment of bureaucrats are only some of the ways to pursue accountability. Control can take place in more subtle ways.

Principal-agency theory is the term for the literature that has transformed our understanding of the relationship between rulers and experts. Hierarchical authority, held by the principal, is manifest as the authority to *define incentives* for subordinates – expert and otherwise. Principal-agency theory suggests that the use of incentives *can* effectively shape the behavior of expert subordinates – indeed, in a limiting case, the superior can induce from a more informed subordinate exactly the behaviors that she would pick if she had the information available to the subordinate! The study of principal-agent relationships suggests that the "political master" need not be a weak dilettante in relationships with expert subordinates. Here we review the development and contemporary status of principal-agent models in economics and other disciplines and the usefulness of these models to the field of political science.

Beyond Prices: Incentives outside Markets

Starting in the 1960s and 1970s, economists focused on the mechanics and efficiency of the marketplace. For this research, the concept of "incentives" was peripheral; instead, the dominant concept used was "price." Indeed, the word "incentives" did not appear in such fundamental economics volumes as Debreu's *Theory of Value* (1959), Walras's *Elements of Pure Economics* (1954), or Schumpeter's *History of Economic Analysis* (Schumpeter & Schumpeter, 1954). According to Laffont and Martimort (2002), only one major economist (Marschak, 1955) was doing research on incentives in organizations in the 1950s.

In the market, the price mechanism, not artificially fixed incentives, shaped individual behavior. Individuals, as price-taking atoms in a competitive market, could only buy when the price was low enough and sell when it was high enough; prices were the "incentives" that drove market behavior and outcomes.

Since 1776 with the publication of Smith's *Wealth of Nations*, the most tantalizing motivation for studying the price mechanism was the conjecture that market prices could guide self-interested market participants to efficient outcomes. The market participant is *"led by an invisible hand to promote an end which was no part of his intention"* (Smith, 1776, Book 4, Chapter 2).

Faith in this idea was borne out with the Arrow proof of the fundamental theorem of welfare economics. According to Arrow (1963) the price mechanism was in fact the "invisible hand" that guided self-interested market behavior to efficient market outcomes (Arrow & Debreu, 1954). Arrow showed that, with a few basic assumptions, a market would achieve a Pareto optimal distribution of goods and services – an outcome such that there was no way to make one market participant better off without hurting another. With this distribution, all opportunities for mutually beneficial gain had been exploited, and no value was left to discover. Government interference could only make one participant better off at another's expense. Laissez-faire as a political philosophy seemed suddenly a result of reason, science, and mathematics, not ideological preference.

Beyond the Market: The Invisible Hand versus Coercion

As mentioned, in the study of markets leading up to the work of Arrow, discussion of categories of incentives was superfluous because the price mechanism was the unique, efficient motivator for behavior in the market. However, Arrow's very success elicited work on *nonmarket* decisions in hierarchical firms, nonprofits, and government agencies. These institutions operate without a price mechanism – but why? Why do hierarchical institutions exist when a market is available (Coase, 1937)? Decision making in hierarchies, as illustrated by Dagwood Bumstead and his boss, Mr. Dithers, in the classic comic strip *Blondie*, was epitomized by close monitoring, required conformity to established rules, responsiveness to authoritative pronouncements, and unpleasant sanctions for those found in violation.

Especially in light of the Arrow-Debreu theorem, hierarchical control seemed especially coercive, unappealing, and, indeed, unnecessary. Why not give Mr. Dithers the boot and work out a market system inside (or replacing) the corporation? The same question applied to government agencies. The Arrow theorem seemed to render much of government (and corporate) activity ripe for reform brought about by instituting more extensive laissez-faire policies over a wider range of activities.

In short, the typical hierarchy seemed to be in gross violation of the invisible hand. People – as employees, as taxpayers, as the objects of regulation – were coerced into following orders, paying taxes, and obeying regulations. But was this reliance on coercion inevitable in politics?

The answer seemed to have something to do with Arrow, in particular with the assumptions necessary to guarantee the efficiency of self-interested choice. These assumptions became the subject of a literature on "market failure" that not only provided an explanation of the existence of hierarchy as islands in an ocean of free-market activity but also offered the hope that the harsh reality of hierarchy could be ameliorated – with the right incentives. If incentives could shape efficient behavior outside of a market, then perhaps Adam Smith's invisible hand could be imported inside corporations, regulatory agencies, or street-level bureaucracies – and the broader the scope of incentives, the narrower the need for hierarchy and coercion.

MARKET FAILURES AND INCENTIVES

The beneficial results attributable to price-mediated market competition were not, in fact, guaranteed if the assumptions of the Arrow theorem were not met.

At least three literatures developed – one for each of three sources of market failure: public goods, monopolies, and information asymmetries. In each case, one of the objectives was to see whether the informed use of incentives could ameliorate the effects of market failure and better align self-interested choice with Pareto optimality. As Marschak wrote in 1955,

Organization rules can be devised in such a way that, if every member pursues his own goal, the goal of the organization is served. This is exemplified in practice by bonuses to executives and the promises of loot to besieging soldiers; and in theory, by the (idealized) model of the laissez-faire economy. (Marschak, 1955, 128)

Marschak was interested in importing the invisible hand of incentives into hierarchical organizations.

Incentives and Public Goods

National defense is the classic example of a natural public good. A public good (by definition) must be provided to everyone if it is supplied to anyone at all, so self-interest will guide free-riders to a deficient outcome. Everyone would be better off with a national defense, but no one has any reason to buy (or contribute to) such a goal.

The literature on incentives started to develop around the provision of public goods. Are there ways to induce self-interested citizens to contribute appropriately to public goods? That is, could the government impose a tax law or voting mechanism that would provide incentives that would encourage efficient (or nearly efficient) contributions for public goods?

Vickrey noted that the problem was that mechanisms that tried to induce citizens to provide an honest evaluation of public goods would be "vulnerable to strategy. This means that individuals may be able to gain by reporting a preference differing from that which they actually hold" (Vickrey, 1960, 517). If a citizen's tax bill depended on how much she valued national defense, then if she opposed defense spending, she could minimize her tax (but not her benefits from effective national defense) by claiming a zero valuation. If her tax bill did *not* depend on her evaluation, then she could of course claim that public goods on offer were worth millions to her, in hopes of convincing politicians to provide them.

Gibbard showed that the problems of gathering essential information regarding public goods were very real: in particular, "nondictatorial collective decision methods cannot be found where truthful behavior [about public goods] is a dominant strategy" (Laffont & Martimort, 2002, 17). This result seemed a strong obstacle to an invisible hand system of incentives for public good provision. Perhaps states were ineluctably the domain of coercion after all.

Or was coercion really necessary? Instead of coercion, could incentives be "tweaked" in such a way as to realign individual interest and Pareto optimality? The literature emerging in the 1970s on "demand-revealing mechanisms" sought ways in which individuals would confront "incentives" that led them to efficient outcomes, even in the presence of externalities (Tideman & Tullock, 1976). Even pollution control need not invoke the heavy hand of the state; "regulation lite" could achieve efficiency gains by creating an artificial "market" for rights to pollute (Tietenberg, 1990).

Although there are no possible incentive-compatible mechanisms that *always* induce truth telling, one could find some that induce equilibria-supporting efficient outcomes, discovered through self-interested revelation of private valuations of public goods. E. H. Clarke (1971) and Groves and Loeb (1975) imposed strict restrictions on the assumptions about citizens' preferences, and then, based on those assumptions, found that individuals would consult their self-interest and find a reason to reveal the information necessary to supply efficient levels of public goods. To a limited extent, at least, this process made feasible Marschak's goal of bringing the invisible hand into the hierarchy.

Monopoly and Incentives

In a competitive market, no single seller has the power of monopoly. When there are competitive markets, everything turns out fine, but the classical monopoly result is patently suboptimal – too high a price, too little consumption. In addition, monopolists gain less than consumers lose, compared to the competitive equilibrium.

One unpleasant alternative is a classic coercive outcome, in which the government sets the price for the monopolist in a way, one hopes, that allows for recovery of some monopoly rents. A more pleasant alternative is to manipulate outcomes with incentives.

In some ways, the mechanism design problem for monopolists is like the mechanism design for public goods in reverse. Instead of getting public good consumers to tell the truth about their valuation of public goods, a key problem in regulating monopoly is to get the monopolist to reveal her true costs, so that an efficient outcome can be devised. In both cases, incentives are shaped to elicit the essential information. More recent approaches abandon the normal efficiency requirement (marginal cost pricing) to induce information revelation in order to obtain a second-best outcome (Laffont & Martimort, 2002, 18).

In both the public goods and monopoly literatures in the 1970s, there was growing interest in overcoming informational distortions through the sophisticated use of incentives. Both approached the ideal invisible hand argument through second-best alternatives. Nor did these literatures only have theoretical value: the academic literature on regulating natural monopolies had an impact on the actions of both the Federal Trade Commission and the Department of Justice. The literature on public goods and externalities has had an impact as well, leading to a growing use of market-like mechanisms in the market for pollution rights (Hahn & Hester, 1989).

Analysis of efficiency gains from market-like incentives addressing external-
ity and monopoly problems seemed promising. However, both literatures ran
into a third, more encompassing problem: information asymmetry. Efficiency
gains were limited as long as free-riders could hide information about their
valuation of externalities and monopolists could hide information about costs.
Even a market without public goods or monopoly is disrupted – seriously disrupted – when one party in a transaction knows something the other does not.
During the 1970s, the nature of these information problems came to be under-
stood, and much of this understanding was codified in principal-agency theory.

Incentives and Imperfect Information

Ultimately, the most devastating form of market failure is caused by imperfect information (Stiglitz, 2002). Stiglitz and other scholars in this field have
demonstrated that the optimistic results of competitive market efficiency fail to
be achieved in the face of imperfect information – and imperfect information
is inescapable.

Akerlof (1970) showed that the effects of incomplete information could be
dramatic: for example, because used car buyers cannot distinguish between
good used cars and lemons, the result is a failure of the market for good used
cars. There are buyers who are willing to pay for a good used car and sellers
willing to part with them for a price. But the claims of the sellers are cheap
talk and all sound the same. As a result, the buyers have to assume that used
cars are lemons. The market for good used cars dries up, even though there are
owners and sellers who could jointly benefit from trading.

Even worse, Grossman and Stiglitz showed that there is a logical inconsistency in the efficient market argument. A competitive equilibrium "is defined
as a situation in which prices are such that all arbitrage profits are eliminated"
(Grossman & Stiglitz, 1982, 393). But this means that arbitrageurs have no
reason to undertake the costly efforts that are necessary for the efficient market. The two assumptions that "all markets including that for information, are
[both] always in equilibrium and always perfectly arbitraged" are inconsistent.
Grossman and Stiglitz argue that there must be an "equilibrium degree of disequilibrium."

Given the need for costly action to gather information, Greenwald and
Stiglitz extended the argument on information asymmetry (Greenwald &
Stiglitz, 1986). Obtaining perfect information requires exerting effort to gather
and process information – a costly undertaking that free-riders avoid. Furthermore, free-riders typically benefit from the efforts of others to identify market-
relevant information. When free-riders free-ride, the result is typically an under-
supply of information, Greenwald and Stiglitz argued. They then showed that
this claim leads to the conclusion that there is a knife's-edge result as regards
markets. Markets with perfect information will supply efficient outcomes, but
any deviation from perfect information guarantees Pareto inefficiency. There is

always some government intervention possible that would make at least one person better off while hurting no one else.

The study of information asymmetry changes how we evaluate perfect competitive markets and government: in Stiglitz's world, perfectly competitive markets not only are not efficient but also are not possible. And there is always room for the state to increase efficiency, although it is not automatic, easy, or inevitable to find and implement those Pareto improvements. This dramatic form of market failure has become the most compelling justification for government regulation – governments need only require accurate information disclosure to generate large economic gains in pharmaceuticals, housing, and financial securities.

As shown in the next section, over time, the drive to understand the effects of information asymmetry in insurance and in sharecropping proved to be crucial in formulating the general problem of overcoming information-advantaged behavior with incentives.

INCENTIVES IN PRINCIPAL-AGENCY THEORY: MORAL HAZARD

One of the first areas in which the effects of incentives were studied was automobile insurance. The driver is risk averse, and the insurance company clearly is more risk acceptant: the company can offer an insurance premium that would cover the driver's risk and make both better off. The problem emerges if the car owner drives more recklessly when he is off the hook for auto damages – an opportunistic change in behavior called "moral hazard."

Moral hazard would not be a problem if recklessness were observable to the insurance company: it could punish recklessness by threatening to withdraw coverage. But if the actions of the owner are *hidden*, then the insurance company might choose to cancel the insurance even if the driver does not drive recklessly, because it cannot afford to insure reckless drivers. The driver knows that the company cannot distinguish good drivers from bad drivers, so the driver faces incentives to drive too fast, run red lights, or drink alcohol, which the insurance company cannot economically monitor. If the insurance company must cancel coverage, both the insurance company and car owner would be worse off: the information asymmetry results in a severe Pareto suboptimality.

The (partial) solution involves incentives. Rather than trying to monitor driver behavior, the insurance company can simply demand a deductible payment. That is, the driver must pay the first $1,000 of damages. This amount is presumably big enough to induce the driver to obey the speed limit, observe red lights, and limit alcohol consumption. In other words, the deductible payment gets the driver to act as though his hidden behavior were observable to the insurance company, even though it is not. The deductible aligns the driver's incentives with those of the insurance company.

Because the driver behavior is not itself monitorable, the incentive is contingent on what is observable – the damage done to the car. And certainly, some accidents occur that are *not* caused by the driver's recklessness, for which the driver still has to pay the deductible. The driver has to take part of the risk; that is why the deductible works. Still, forcing the driver to accept risk that would be more efficiently held by the insurance company is evidence of efficiency loss. The reason that the incentive solution is only a partial solution is because risk coverage, although efficient, is not complete. There is a tradeoff between efficiency in risk aversion and efficiency in incentives. The lower the deductible, the greater the incentive for dangerous driving; the higher the deductible, the lower the efficiency gains from assigning risk efficiently.

So this analysis of insurance has an ambiguous message: incentives *can* provide partial correction for a market failure caused by imperfect information. Yet, the solution is only second best, because the incentivization of the driver implies a failure to realize the efficient assignment of risk that is the basis for the insurance market in the first place. There must be a *tradeoff between efficiency in risk bearing and efficiency in incentives*. The driver is forced to carry risk she would prefer to avoid, or else she is fully insured and open to moral hazard.

The insurance problem led not only to the concept of moral hazard but also to the problem of *adverse selection*. This notion is based on the existence of variation in driver types – intrinsic driver qualities that are not obvious to the insurance company and not easily conveyed by the drivers themselves. For instance, there are some drivers who are quite content to drive safely and would not take advantage of insurance by changing their behavior once they are insured. If these drivers could be identified, they could be completely insured for a smaller premium rather than forced to carry a deductible. The adverse selection problem is that every driver would like to claim to be such a safe driver, and identifying the truly safe drivers from their claims is impossible.

Incentives can *partially* solve both the adverse selection and the moral hazard problems. The insurance company can offer different contracts that appeal to different types of drivers – a strategy that Rothschild and Stiglitz call *screening* (Rothschild & Stiglitz, 1975). For example, the deductible charge helps sort out types of drivers. The better drivers are more willing to carry a high deductible because they are confident that they will not drive unwisely, whereas the riskier drivers are more daunted by a high deductible (Stiglitz, 2002, 496). However, the use of incentives helps reduce market inefficiencies – but does not eliminate them. The contracts offered to screen drivers may not be the ones that also allocate risk efficiently.

Tenant Farming

Around the time economists began exploring insurance transactions, Joseph Stiglitz was examining incentives in the hierarchical relationship between a landowner and a tenant farmer. Here again the agent (the tenant farmer) is risk averse (because the compensation for producing the year's crop is all that supports his family). The landowner is more risk acceptant, perhaps because she has a scattered portfolio of properties that limit her overall risk due to cɾ damage. The tenant would like to be provided with insurance against a baɾ outcome – in the form of compensation that does not drop drastically in the case of a bad crop year. Because of their differences in risk preferences, the owner and the tenant can agree that both would be better off with a smaller fixed payment, rather than a larger but riskier payment.

But the efficient allocation of risk clashes with the possibility of moral hazard. Under a risk-free compensation scheme, the tenant farmer can work harder or shirk, raising or lowering the likelihood of a good crop, without affecting his own compensation. Yet the landowner cannot easily monitor the farmer's efforts. Hiring a foreman to monitor the farmer would be expensive for the landowner and offensive to the farmer. In addition, a bad crop may be the result of the weather, not shirking by the farmer. As a result, the preferred risk-free compensation for the tenant farmer would provide no incentive for the farmer to do the best that he can (Stiglitz, 1974).

The appropriate contract between the tenant farmer (agent) and landowner may include a share of the crop as at least one component of the compensation package. As an owner of part of the crop, the tenant will have a strong incentive to bring in a good crop – as the owner wishes. However, imposition of unwelcome risk on the farmer is also inefficient: money is left on the table when the risk-acceptant landowner must force a risky compensation package on the unwilling tenant farmer. The final outcome trades efficiency in incentives against efficiency in risk assignment.

The problem of adverse selection also appears in the tenancy case. Some potential tenants are just smarter or more energetic than others. Some would provide the best farming effort possible, even if they received a flat wage contract. The adverse selection problem, once again, is to sort those productive farmers from the lazy and incompetent farmers. The principal can implement screening by offering a sharecropping contract that discourages tenants who are not good farmers.

Whereas in a screening model, the owner takes the initiative by offering revealing alternative contracts, a *signaling* model is one in which the tenant (who may be presumed to know his own type) makes the first move. The high-quality farmer does this by taking an action that would be prohibitively expensive or impossible for the unqualified farmer. An example of such an action is planting and maintaining a hugely successful home garden, of the sort that could not be equaled by the mediocre farmer.

For economists, the big discovery was that it is not necessary to monitor the *hidden actions* (effort levels) of the agents; the use of incentives based on the *observed outcome* can reduce the problem of moral hazard in many cases – mainly those in which the agent is not very risk averse. When the driver knows she must pay a deductible in the event of an accident, the insurance company does not have to monitor her driving behavior or enforce rules about speeding or where to park the car. When the tenant farmer is being paid with a share of

ıer does not have to go to the trouble and expense of hiring an
ɛ sure that the farmer is in the fields early in the morning and
t care he can for the crops. The incentives are largely sufficient
ıct in ways that are consistent with the *preferences of the princi-*
ɣes serve to *align* the preferences of the agent with the principal.

The problem of information asymmetry matches neatly with the information asymmetry between superior and subordinate in a bureaucracy. Informational economics came to have many applications in understanding bureaucracy – from the "efficiency wage" to the use of information disclosure as a means to regulate market failure. But the aspect of information economics that came to have the most application is principal-agency theory.

PRINCIPAL-AGENCY THEORY

Theorists have generalized the information asymmetry problem to the principal-agency problem, which was perhaps the first truly new way to look at bureaucracy since Weber. The applications have been many and have included the political oversight of bureaucracy.

The exploration of sharecropping and insurance led to a codification of principal-agency theory, influenced largely by three 1979 articles (Harris & Raviv, 1979; Holmström, 1979; Shavell, 1979). These articles claimed that the lesson learned from insurance and sharecropping was that close monitoring and hierarchical coercion could be largely dispensed with if the appropriate incentives were in place. In effect, the correct incentives could import the "invisible hand" from the world of competitive markets to the inside of the hierarchical organization; the appropriate incentive contract allowed the agent to make self-interested choices that nevertheless aligned with the interests of the principal.

The Canonical Principal-Agent Model

These three articles presented a shared, coherent picture of the five elements of principal-agency theory:

1) *Agent impact*. Together with chance outcomes such as weather (for the sharecropper) or other drivers (for car insurance), the agent's hidden action is seen to determine some outcome that is critical to the principal. For instance, an auto salesman's monthly sales are determined not only by factors beyond his control but also by his energy, personality, and effort.
2) *Information asymmetry*. The principal can readily observe the outcome of the agent's actions, but not the actions themselves. Monitoring of agent actions may be theoretically possible, but gathering complete information is regarded as prohibitively expensive. The owner of the car lot may not be able to tell whether the salesman's poor sales in a given month are due to the economy, bad luck, or the agent's own inadequate

effort. So, the employer's problem is the same as that of the insurance company: given the information asymmetry, should the employer substitute incentives for monitoring?

3) *Asymmetry in preferences.* The agent is assumed to have different preferences than the principal. For example, the actions that affect the principal's well-being may be costly to the agent, resulting in a preference for shirking. Another key difference is that the agent is assumed to be more risk averse than the principal.

4) *Backward induction based on common knowledge.* The principal and the agent both know everything that is important about their interaction, such as who moves in which order, the costs of effort, and the probability distribution of outcomes. Just as important, they share common knowledge of the agent's rationality; both know that the agent will prefer any incentive package with an expected utility that is slightly more than her opportunity cost. This means the principal can guess the agent's best response function from the known parameters and can identify the best possible outcome ("backward induction"). In effect, the principal-agent interaction allocates "all bargaining power to one of the parties" (to the principal and away from the agent) (Salanie, 2005, 5).

5) *Ultimatum bargaining.* Once the principal knows the agent's best response function, the principal is able to impose the best solution for herself. Or as Sappington says, "The principal is endowed with all of the bargaining power in this simple setting, and thus can make a 'take-it-or-leave-it' offer to the agent" (Sappington, 1991, 47).

These five core assumptions lead to two primary results:

Outcome-based incentives. When the principal cannot contract on the agent's hidden effort, the principal will prefer compensation in the form of a bonus based on the final outcome. This bonus will serve to align the agent's payoff with that of the principal. And because in general the agent's effort is only one of the determinants of the final outcome, this compensation approach necessarily transfers risk to the risk-averse agent.

Efficiency tradeoffs. The risk-averse agent will want compensation for the extra risk that comes with outcome-based bonuses. The more risk-acceptant principal and the risk-averse agent could be made better off by insuring the agent with a smaller, flat wage. However, the smaller, flat wage leaves no incentive for agent effort. Just as with insurance, there is a tradeoff between efficiency in incentives and efficiency in risk bearing. The best tradeoff involves paying the risk-averse agent a risky, outcome-based bonus.

Incentives versus Hidden Action

Consider a simple illustration, from Dixit and Nalebuff (1991) and Watson (2002), that shows the substantively important contributions of principal-agency theory. In this example, a politician controls a school system that will produce $100,000 of benefits if it is a success and nothing if it is a failure. The politician needs a teacher to help produce those benefits. The teacher can either supply a HI effort or a LO effort. A HI effort results in an 80% chance of success (p), whereas a LO effort results in a 60% chance of success (q). The HI effort requires an effort cost of $40,000, and the LO effort requires an effort of $30,000.

If the politician could measure the effort level of the teacher, there would be no problem. The agent could be paid $40,000 for a HI effort or $30,000 for a LO effort, depending on which would be more advantageous to the politician. A HI effort creates expected benefits of $80,000, less the necessary wage of $40,000. The social surplus generated by a HI effort equals $40,000. Similarly, the benefits of a LO effort yield an expected gain of $60,000 – $30,000 = $30,000. The social surplus is greater with a HI effort. Furthermore, with monitoring and a first-mover's advantage, the politician could clear virtually all of the expected social gain for herself.

The problems arise (as they do in insurance or sharecropping) when there is information asymmetry. We presume that the politician *cannot monitor* the teacher effectively and so cannot pay based on effort. The question is whether the information asymmetry reduces the politician to powerlessness. In effect, the problem is exactly that stated by Weber. Does asymmetric information render the superior powerless in the face of the more expert subordinate?

The politician can offer a fixed wage that does not vary with the outcome to help keep an agent from exiting the relationship. Yet, this fixed wage does not motivate HI effort, because (by definition) a flat wage is paid out regardless of the outcome.

An outcome is Pareto suboptimal if we can imagine a different outcome that makes everyone better off. A Pareto suboptimal outcome is one, then, that leaves money on the table. The outcome under a fixed wage is suboptimal, because it does not motivate the HI effort that is more likely to lead to success.

The politician wants the expected value of the HI effort to be higher than the expected value of LO effort. This happens when the politician pays a bonus that is contingent on a successful outcome occurring instead of a failure: S versus F. If HI effort makes S more likely, the bonus helps motivate a HI effort.

The effective bonus B^* changes the agent's expected net benefit with a HI effort so that it is greater than that with a LO effort:

$$pB^* + W - C_{HI} \geq qB^* + W - C_{LO}. \tag{1}$$

This can be written as

$$B^* \geq \frac{C_{HI} - C_{LO}}{p - q}. \tag{2}$$

The right side of the equation tells us how the marginal cost of a HI effort compares to the agent's efficacy. A high efficacy ($p - q$) implies that the agent's choice of HI or LO has a greater impact on the principal's well-being and on his own chances of a bonus. Lower efficacy means the bonus must be higher to offset the lower gains that happen, given the probability of S that comes with a HI effort. This is the *incentive constraint*. The bonus has to be high enough to keep the agent from exiting. The *participation constraint* is satisfied where either $pB^* + W - C_{HI} \geq 0$ *or* $qB^* + W - C_{LO} \geq 0$. The former ensures participation with *HI* effort; the latter ensures minimal participation.

In traditional principal-agency theory, incentives are perfectly effective with risk-neutral agents.

In our example, B^* must be at least equal to $\$10,000/20\% = \$50,000$, to give the risk-neutral agent a self-interested reason to supply a HI effort. No other inducement or hierarchical monitoring is needed. This bonus makes the principal better off because it induces high effort. With this bonus, the principal-agent relationship is one in which the principal is able to use incentives (the bonus) to achieve a favorable outcome *without* costly monitoring of agent effort levels, sanctions, and coercion.[1]

This is the standard conclusion from principal-agency theory: an outcome-contingent bonus causes an efficient level of effort by risk-neutral agents and is Pareto optimal. Investments in monitoring and oversight are costly, inefficient, and unnecessary. The incentive solves the principal's problem of having no information about the agent's actions.[2] As Harris and Raviv (1979, 223) conclude, "There are *no* gains to be derived from monitoring the agent's action when the agent is risk neutral."

Inevitable Inefficiency? The Risk/Incentives Tradeoff

In expected utility terms, a correctly designed bonus system gets the principal everything that monitoring actions garners. Of course, one problem is that the agent may be risk averse. She might not regard an 80% chance of a bonus of $\$50,000$ as justifying effort costs of $\$40,000$. She might demand a risk premium with a bonus of $\$55,000$ or more.

---

[1] In fact, in some cases the principal can offer a fixed wage lower than zero and still (with the inducement of the bonus) count on the agent accepting the contract. This idea has limits in bureaucracies where an employee paying for a patronage appointment is a sign of corruption, and where employees are not expected to pay entrance fees to participate in outcome-based gambles.

The negative wage also illustrates the bias in the literature toward the principal's point of view. The solution to the principal's problem is to find the best (for the principal!) contract that will both induce agent effort and distribute essentially none of the surplus to the agent, beyond the minimum to keep the agent from leaving for another contract. The solution could be defined as the contract that divides revenue equitably enough to leave both parties satisfied with the outcome, or willing to establish a pattern of cooperation for the long-run.

[2] A related problem is when the agent's efficacy is low. See the Technical Appendix for a discussion of this situation.

Risk aversion undermines the efficiency result of principal-agency theory. A risk-averse agent would prefer a flatter wage to a larger, risky bonus – and the principal would agree. When both sides prefer a transfer of risk from the agent to the principal, the use of a bonus leaves both sides worse off. The efficient use of incentives comes with the *inefficient allocation of risks*. In canonical theory, risk aversion on the part of the agent is more troubling for designers of optimal incentives, because risk aversion induces an "insurance/incentives" tradeoff for which the design must account (Laffont and Martimort 2002). The risk-averse auto owner must bear the risk of a deductible, and the farmer must bear the risk of a "share" contract. The agent in our example must bear the risk of missing a bonus. *Both the principal and the agent* would prefer a contract featuring a smaller fixed wage to a larger, riskier bonus. This tradeoff has been empirically investigated through the use of experiments (e.g., Bottom, Holloway, Miller, Mislin, & Whitford, 2006; Fehr & Falk, 1999; Miller & Whitford, 2002; Whitford, Bottom, & Miller, 2013).

If the agent is risk averse, a probabilistic chance at a bonus does not sound as good as a fixed wage. The risk-neutral principal would like to offer the agent a smaller fixed wage as well. However, the efficient division of risk is not possible, because using a wage instead of a bonus eliminates the incentive effect.

The tradeoff between efficiency in risk allocation and in incentives results in a two-part principle of principal-agency theory: incentives can be used to correct for information asymmetry, as long as the agent's risk aversion is at a reasonable level. The standard conclusion from principal-agency theory is that an outcome-contingent bonus causes an efficient level of effort by risk-neutral agents and is Pareto optimal. Investments in monitoring and oversight are costly, inefficient, and unnecessary. The incentive solves the principal's problem of having no information about the agent's actions.

But if we assume that risk neutrality is a special case and that risk aversion of various sorts is the more general case, then the result is one of a tradeoff of inefficiencies: either risk-averse agents are paid by a flat wage and have no incentive to provide optimal effort, or they are paid with a bonus that misses the opportunity for Pareto-efficient risk bearing.

AGENCY THEORY COMES TO POLITICS: CONGRESSIONAL OVERSIGHT

Importantly, principal-agency theory is also a convincing explanation for the behavior of a range of bureaucratic agencies in the executive branch. With a research agenda that straddled economic theory and legislative politics, Barry Weingast (1984) was in a position to see the immediate applicability of agency theory to congressional oversight of bureaucracies. Students of public administration had argued that the absence of vigilant oversight by congressional committees implied a lack of control (Dodd & Schott, 1979; Rourke, 1984; Wilson, 1989). They assumed that bureaucratic autonomy *must* be rampant because, apparently, no one was watching what bureaucrats were actually doing. Bureaucratic appropriations kept flowing with little interruption in the form of congressional sanctions.

However, as Weingast (1984) correctly observed, principal-agency theory demonstrated that the absence of massive monitoring and frequent punishments could nevertheless be quite consistent with congressional control *through incentives*. If agency incentives are designed correctly, then congressional monitoring is no more necessary than an insurance company hiring a detective to check on the driving habits of its clients; agency officials simply consult their own self-interest within the bounds of the congressionally mandated incentives and then do the "right thing" – they provide benefits to those interest groups that can help members of Congress get reelected.

To all external appearances, the bureaucrats are unwatched and unsanctioned, just as a tenant farmer operating on a share crop contract may be left alone to make decisions that will maximize the crop that will determine his welfare for the next year. In fact, if asked, agency officials may honestly deny that they are under the control of the legislature, because they believe they control their own actions under what may be a subtle incentive system. They will not be sanctioned, as a rule, because their self-interest guides them to actions that will make sanctions unnecessary – not because they are "out of control." Discretion in the implementation of legislation is not a problem if agency officials can be convinced to use their expertise in the interests of the elected officials who created the bureaucratic incentives.

For Weingast, effective congressional control extended far beyond legislation to the details of implementation. Members of Congress sought appointment to key oversight committees precisely so they could affect the discretionary actions that legislative delegation of authority allowed agency officials.

Evidence for this control came from studies of the Federal Trade Commission (FTC) (Weingast & Moran, 1983) and the Securities and Exchange Commission (SEC) (Weingast, 1984). In both agencies, legislation gave agency officials significant discretionary authority to make decisions. The evidence suggested that many decisions by officials tracked the ideology of key congressional oversight committees and committee chairs. It appeared that agency officials made decisions consistent with the preferences of their congressional overseers, so it was unnecessary for Congress to undertake costly actions: Congress did not have to inflict punishments for agency defiance that did not happen. Weingast observed this relationship even in the case of independent regulatory commissions – agencies that had long been thought to act in a functionally independent manner (M. H. Bernstein, 1955).

This reconceptualization of the role of bureaucracy as an agent of elected officials has been enormously important to the study of bureaucracy. There is no doubt that it has advanced the scientific study of public administration (McCubbins, Noll, & Weingast, 1987; McCubbins & Schwartz, 1984). It made it impossible to sustain conventional and accepted assumptions about bureaucracy – that congressional oversight is completely ineffectual, for instance. It generated new interest in the Administrative Procedures Act, in the appointment process, in mechanisms of congressional control, and in the role of incentives – topics that had previously received little attention. It gave rise to elegant models of congressional delegation (e.g., Bawn, 1995; Bendor, Glazer, & Hammond, 2001; Epstein & O'Halloran, 1999) and created rigorous new standards for what constitutes a theory and for the relationship between theory and empirical testing.[3]

What is most striking about this literature is how different authors reconceived the control relationship between the political principal and the bureaucratic agent. Each layer of analysis added new possibilities for understanding the structure and effects of the control relationship. For instance, McCubbins and Schwartz answered the complaint of a perceived lack of congressional control by pointing to politicians offloading the oversight problem onto interest groups; they claimed that politicians would intervene in the discretion wielded by bureaucrats using their delegated powers only when the groups pulled "fire alarms" that notified politicians of egregious errors. The complaint that politicians were not actively overseeing bureaus was wrongheaded because politicians were smart enough not to incur the costs of constant oversight. The interest groups carried out those tasks so that politicians did not have to operate "police patrols" of bureaucratic discretion.

The importance of McCubbins and Schwartz's argument is that it implies there is a solution to a fundamental tradeoff: politicians do not have to incur greater control costs when they delegate to agencies in order to obtain valuable technical expertise. It also means that politicians do not have to reduce the quality of their bureaucrats' technical advice when they pursue a control strategy. But this tradeoff is usually real.

Bawn (1995) provides an elegant representation of this tradeoff in her study that claims that politicians would like to design agencies so that their policy decisions are politically accountable and technically correct. Yet, a tradeoff between control and expertise is usually apparent, and Congress's challenge is

---

[3] A related question is why rewards are used so infrequently for compensation in the public sector. Rather than offering bonus-based compensation, the modal compensation scheme is mostly composed of rewards that do not depend on agent performance (a "flat wage"). Interestingly, although such rewards seem rare in public-sector organizations, they are less present in the private sector than often assumed. The problems of connecting rewards and measureable performance have long been recognized (Kerr, 1975). The private sector increasingly uses ownership to help align rewards and performance (e.g., Knez & Simester, 2001), with findings of moderate performance differences (Blasi, Conte, & Kruse, 1996). In the case of bonus-based plans for executives, the factors behind decision to adopt and plan effectiveness are complicated and likely unrelated (in many situations) to the concerns of principal-agency theory (Murphy, 2012). One fundamental barrier to applying traditional bonus-based compensation schemes to the public sector is that the necessary bonus becomes much higher as the agent's individual efficacy falls (a common problem in improving social outcomes) (Miller & Whitford, 2007). Ownership-based schemes are restricted by constitution.

to design a control technology that takes this tradeoff into account. Congress worries about both technical and political uncertainty, but those exogenous factors shape the procedural choice that defines the control technology. Although a "sweet spot" of high control and technical quality is possible, it is not automatic; in fact, "optimal agency procedures can maximize technical competence, maximize political control, or achieve a combination of the two" (Bawn, 1995, 62).

By portraying this tradeoff, Kathleen Bawn's approach makes visible the problem for politicians. Yet, few political science papers that center on the principal-agency paradigm recognize or, more importantly, accept this tradeoff. Most see the problem almost as one of optimal control: the principal chooses a contract that reduces agent volition to the point that the agent returns the principal's ideal policy, even if the agent does not realize she is doing so.

A good example of framing the problem in terms of control is the so-called McNollgast hypothesis. The impact of the work of McCubbins, Noll, and Weingast in shaping our understanding of certain procedures (and especially so, the Administrative Procedures Act; APA) cannot be overstated. The basic point they made was that politicians could construct defenses against bureaucratic drift through the procedures that govern delegated implementation in practice (McCubbins et al., 1987). The APA is just one example of such procedures, but the McNollgast hypothesis is significant if only because we now see clearly that procedures shape the practice of discretion for bureaucrats who do not see their actions as being influenced.

For Bawn, however, the concept of procedures is less clear than it has been portrayed in papers that followed McNollgast. Procedures for Bawn are broad concepts (almost enveloping concepts) that give Congress means for limiting discretion. However, the term "control technology" is more descriptive because procedures are not just the rules that shape the game between agencies, politicians, and affected interests. Instead, the selection of procedures encompasses "such structural issues as which agency makes the decision, how the agency is organized, what qualifications are required for key personnel, and how the agency relates to the rest of the bureaucracy" (Bawn 1995, 62). These control technologies are ways to reduce bureaucratic drift – they are ways to "stack the deck."

Bawn tells us that Congress chooses procedures to dictate the groups to whom the agency must respond, to pick the agency's effective preferences, and to reduce (or expand) congressional uncertainty about agency preferences. Essentially, Congress picks the level and quality of agency independence, and that choice depends on technical uncertainty about policy and uncertainty about the general political environment. There is no "silver bullet": no single prediction about the type or level of delegated discretion. Bawn's model predicts heterogeneous delegations of power to agencies in different policy arenas: "agency procedures and agency independence will vary according to the technical and political features of the policy area" (Bawn, 1995, 71).

In contrast, Weingast and Moran earlier portrayed an agency under tighter control – a relationship not that different from the models of canonical principal-agency theory. The McNollgast hypothesis also envisioned limited agency for the bureaucrat, perhaps regardless of the intentions of the authors of the original papers. Bawn's view is more conditional and, along with models such as those advanced by Epstein and O'Halloran (1999), sets the stage for seeing tradeoffs and attained independence as the result of political choices in uncertain environments. For Epstein and O'Halloran, congressional abilities to intervene after the fact and with access to information increase the zone of discretion and decision making that Congress hands over to the agency. Agencies are handed discretion because of policy uncertainty, but ex post procedures for control sweeten the deal: they give politicians a measure of control for pulling the agency back if independence is abused.

Like Bawn, Epstein and O'Halloran see a tradeoff, although they view actual discretion as sometimes illusory. Regardless, like Bawn, they attribute more discretion to the agency than do Weingast and Moran and more control than does the canonical view of a disengaged Congress. Epstein and O'Halloran, as well as Bawn, make claims about the likelihood of seeing one type of arrangement or another in government agencies at the federal level in the United States. It is difficult to see a direct representation of the canonical principal-agency model in any of these approaches.

None of the studies documented in this section makes much use of "incentives" like those seen in traditional principal-agency theory. One way to reconstruct incentives is to broadly interpret procedures – perhaps even more broadly than intended in any of these models. Another way is to admit that the models do not discuss incentives in the canonical sense because incentives "undersocialize" agencies; in most of these types of models the control relationship exists between a single principal (or coalition) and a single agent. A third route is to admit that the politicians who control agencies are not an "it" but a "they" and that this diffusion of control responsibility in a separated powers system can affect the practice of control.

Consider the difficulty of developing a typology of models of bureaucrat-politician relations. One set of models might center on the multiple principals ("common agency") problem (e.g., Bernheim & Whinston, 1986). A second set might emphasize the time-inconsistency problem, as seen in models of organizational trust (e.g., Miller, 2001) or "relational contracting" (e.g., Halac, 2012). A third could focus on chains of principal-agent relationships (e.g., Tirole, 1986). We can also conceive of other types, such as those in which there are multiple tasks (e.g., Holmström & Milgrom, 1991). The problem is that there are almost as many classifications as there are models – because each model emphasizes a set of institutional features of a specific sort of relationship. Although, as Bertelli (2012) ably shows, there are ways to generalize across some groups of models, George Box's famous adage that "essentially, all models are wrong, but some are useful" resonates (Box & Draper, 1987, 424).

Instead, in the rest of this chapter, we consider the argument that politicians can engage in their own form of moral hazard – of shirking from pursuing improvements in social welfare. We then introduce claims that, considered together, form the basis for a new understanding of the empirical regularity of politicians not exercising control over agencies whose employees tend to do things that are in the public interest. We see this understanding as providing a basis for broadened consideration of institutional innovations that support credible commitments in Chapter 3 and of the motives of principals when producing with teams examined in Chapter 4.

DO PRINCIPALS EVER PREFER INEFFICIENT CONTRACTS?

Defense contracts, agricultural subsidies, and pork-barrel projects: all of these policy outcomes result from agency officials responding to the interests of congressional masters. This responsiveness is consistent with principal-agency theory. But we also notice a pattern: these are three of the policy arenas most frequently cited as examples of "government failure." As with farm subsidies and pork-barrel projects, weapons procurement is periodically castigated for its waste and inefficiency. Yet in the case of weapons procurement, devotion to the interests of key weapons contractors (and their legislative allies) may result in sending forces into battle with deficient weapons systems (Mayer, 1995).

"Pork-barrel politics" has become a popular synonym for the misuse of tax dollars. If legislators are duly elected representatives of the public, and if bureaucrats are responsive to the wishes of legislators, what can go wrong? By "wrong," we are using a simple and standard normative principle – Pareto optimality. Our question boils down to this. Can a principal-agency equilibrium be Pareto suboptimal? A simple change in the principal-agent model we offered earlier demonstrates that Pareto suboptimal outcomes can occur, not because of the agent's moral hazard but because of temptations facing the principal (Miller & Whitford, 2007).

The Principal's Calculus

Very slight changes in parameters can induce a self-interested principal to choose a Pareto suboptimal incentive scheme. Consider a situation with the same possible outcomes ($S = \$100,000$, $F = \$0$), cost parameters ($\$40,000$ for a HI and $\$30,000$ for a LO effort), and probability of success with a HI effort of $p = 0.8$. Now modify the probability of success with a LO effort to be $q = 0.65$, instead of 0.6.

It is still efficient to use a bonus to induce high effort. High effort will cost an extra $\$10,000$, but because it generates an extra $0.8 - 0.65 = 0.15$ probability of a success worth $\$100,000$, the expected gain is $\$15,000$. Because the expected gain is more than the effort cost, it is socially efficient to induce a high effort.

The necessary bonus of $\$10,000/15\% = \$66,667$ can induce the agent to supply the high effort. This yields the principal an expected gain of $0.8*(\$100,000 - \$66,667) = \$26,666$ in net expected benefits. Once again, incentives induce the higher, efficient level of effort from the agent.

The problem is that the principal no longer wants to pay more for the higher level of effort, given the bonus that would be necessary to induce it. Suppose the principal decides not to offer a bonus, knowing full well that the agent will simply supply a LO effort. With a LO effort, the expected value of the outcome is $\$65,000$; subtracting C_{LO} yields a net expected benefit of $\$35,000$. The principal's use of a fixed wage induces an inefficient LO effort and produces lower social surplus, but it generates greater net expected benefits for the principal!

The principal faces a form of moral hazard because she expects more benefit by inducing a low effort than a high effort, even though a high effort produces greater net social benefits. The principal has every incentive to sabotage the efficient outcome because she wishes to minimize the payment to the agent. The obstacle to efficiency, in other words, is no longer agent shirking. In principal-agent terms, it is the principal's profit maximization.

This is a significant point. Much of principal-agency theory takes the principal's point of view and treats the maximization of the principal's profits as being the same thing as efficiency. However, efficiency (maximizing the size of the pie to be divided between principal and agent) is not the same thing as maximizing the principal's share of the pie. As long as the choice is restricted to a positive fixed wage or a positive bonus, there is no incentive scheme that can in general reconcile the requirements of organizational efficiency and the principal's self-interest. There is no bonus less than $\$66,667$ that will induce a HI effort, but a bonus greater than $\$66,667$ diminishes the principal's share of the benefits. Because the principal cannot keep enough of the extra expected benefits, she will not motivate the agent to take a high effort because the revenue must flow toward the agent's bonus in order to gain the agent's effort. In general, the principal may prefer not to take the action that generates the extra social surplus gained by inducing the efficient level of effort. This drives a sharp wedge between social efficiency and principal rationality. A self-interested solution to the "principal's problem" often entails ignoring efficiency. See the Technical Appendix at the end of the chapter for details on the profitability constraint.

The situation we outline here can become even worse, yielding less social surplus and less efficiency, if the principal also engages in unobservable effort that affects the outcome that follows the agent's effort. The teacher takes actions that affect performance, but the principal might also take unobservable actions, such as choosing among education policies. In that case, the contracts that would work for the principal and agent depend explicitly on how their unobservable actions interact in determining the product's success (Cooper & Ross, 1985).

This "double moral hazard" problem is endemic. It shows up in product warranties (Cooper & Ross, 1985; Dybvig & Lutz, 1993), marketing arrangements (Golosinski & West, 1995; Mann & Wissink, 1988), buyout agreements (Demski & Sappington, 1991), occupational safety and health (Lanoie, 1991) and venture capital financing. It happens because principals are not passive. They can take actions that affect project success just as agents can. Our stylized example shows how principals might reject actions that maximize social welfare, but damage their own prospects. The double moral hazard problem, as documented in the economics literature, shows their range of action to be even wider: a principal can ask the agent to "do the right thing," but as long as the principal's unobservable actions continue to affect success, then her own incentives to shirk can produce socially suboptimal outcomes.

One solution in the double moral hazard situation is fairly simple: having the outcome depend jointly on the unobservable efforts of two actors, so that limiting the impact of one actor simplifies the situation. Literally, an institution that minimizes the marginal impact of the principal will also make the agent's contribution clearer. This approach makes it easier to guide the agent through the use of a contract. It also makes it easier for the agent to act in ways that improve the overall outcomes. Literally, one solution is to remove the principal from the equation.

In the case of the Indian 2G spectrum allocations, the bureaucrats played a strikingly important role: they alone could end the allocation prematurely and decide who would receive the licenses. The politicians on trial for subverting the public process (to allegedly obtain very real personal profits) needed compliant bureaucrats to carry out their plans. Yet, the CAG report specified that it was the bureaucrats – not politicians – who actually certified ineligible bidders. It clearly documented the economic effects of misallocation in such bidding system. The political mechanisms in place to allow misallocations were a result of the strict incentivization of bureaucrats to respond to the politicians they serve – not a lack of political control or of too much independence.

Political Moral Hazard

We believe that principal-agent relations in bureaucratic oversight may illustrate the same problem: the limitations on efficiency may come from temptations facing the legislative overseers as readily as from those facing the bureaucrats. For instance, legislative interests in agricultural price supports, highway bill benefits, or favorable weapons contracts may have efficiency implications for the actions of bureaucrats. When legislators' preferences are perverse, bureaucratic accountability can only magnify those preferences. Bureaucratic responsiveness is not sufficient to guarantee efficient outcomes, because it only empowers political moral hazard if congressional actions and impulses are misconceived. To put it more positively, bureaucratic autonomy may be the means of controlling political moral hazard.

Notable examples of these "perverse" preferences are often found in distributive politics, in which the beneficiaries of policy are narrow, organized, and powerful and the potential opponents are numerous, diffuse, and unorganized. In such situations, members of Congress follow a clear best strategy regarding reelection: serve the narrow, organized interests and ignore the rest. This clarity of goals can be transferred via incentives to bureaucrats. National interests are least involved, and national party leaders and presidents least present, in the arena of distributive politics. Presidents may be silent on the subject of distributive politics, or they may side with organized interest groups for the marginal benefit doing so brings to them. But they are unlikely to choose distributive politics as their core campaign message.

In other situations, interests on both sides may be more equally informed and mobilized. For instance, by serving the interests of labor unions, politicians may make an enemy of the business community, and vice versa. As Fenno (1973) notes, such conflict wells up in congressional committees. When this is the case, what kinds of incentives are likely to flow from the legislative committee to the bureaucracy? When a bureaucrat consults her self-interest, does that end up promoting the interests of Congress? The preferences of Congress can be "perverse" in the sense that they are conflicted or inconsistent.

In this book, we are most interested in a third way in which congressional preferences may be "perverse." Suppose that what the principal would like to do at a later stage in the game is different from what the principal would want to do at an earlier stage. In this view, the principal's preferences are "dynamically inconsistent."

For instance, a monetary policy maker may want to create inflation as a way of fueling economic expansion and reducing the real value of sovereign debt. Outsiders can anticipate this motive so in the end the policy maker's actions may not have the intended effect; unfortunately, however, the outcome can still be higher-than-expected rates of inflation. The policy maker's commitment to a rule can make this prospect less likely (Barro & Gordon, 1983b). Although policy makers may still want to cheat, the commitment device "binds their hands," almost like a long-term agreement between the government and the private sector (Barro & Gordon, 1983a).

More broadly, in the delegation game, the preferences of congressional committees interact with the actions of other economic and political actors. In such situations, the principal-agency problem becomes much more complex. What is missing in the traditional principal-agent account, as it has developed as a theory of political control in political science, is a way of understanding how the principal can align the interests of the agent with her shifting interests.

CONCLUSION: WHY INSULATION?

Prescriptions drawn from principal-agent models are elegant solutions to the problem of gaining bureaucratic compliance when agents cannot be monitored. Yet, even in the canonical principal-agent context, principals may prefer that agents not pursue socially beneficial outcomes; Pareto-efficient outcomes are not guaranteed if politicians benefit more from low levels of agent performance. The principal's moral hazard changes the traditional model to one that is now defined by double moral hazard: both principals and agents face incentives to shirk. Narrow prescriptions to "get the agents' incentives right" will not solve this problem.

In the study of electoral politics, we understand that general approaches like the Downsian approach to electoral competition are different from specific models, such as a Downsian model that assumes that candidates are completely informed about voters' preferences. Traditional models of delegation fail to account for the parallel development of three foundations in modeling principal-agent relations that are particularly important for understanding public bureaus. By and large, these parallel developments have had little impact on the literature on delegation.

Canonical delegation models do well at explaining tight control relationships, such as those we see in agricultural subsidies and other types of distributive politics; their explanations of these types of accountability are useful, but anomalies remain. For instance, why did the Progressives go out of their way to insulate bureaucrats? And why are policy arenas where bureaucrats are most accountable also often the arenas most complained about on grounds of disservice to the public interest? If bureaucrats are accountable to political masters, is principal-agency theory – as an explanation for political and policy behavior – only useful for explaining low-quality political outcomes? How can we reconcile such outcomes with the views of Djankov and his coauthors that institutional quality supports long-term economic growth and development?

Accounting for these developments requires a significant shift in how we understand observable institutional arrangements that are present in real agencies. To understand the range of lessons to be learned from principal-agency theory in its entirety, we have to examine three foundations for a more informed model of delegation. Starting in the next chapter we introduce three claims that, considered together, form the basis for a new understanding of the empirical regularity of politicians not controlling agencies, whose employees tend to do things that are in the public interest.

In Chapter 3, we show that dynamic inconsistency can lead politicians to make credible delegations of power and authority to bureaucrats. When the principal's preferences are time inconsistent, the delegation of policy discretion to unaccountable bureaucrats helps tie the state's hands in a commitment that "levels the playing field." We introduce credible commitment models from North and Weingast (1989), Barro and Gordon (1983b), Kydland and Prescott (1977), and Spulber and Besanko (1992) in which dynamic inconsistency plays a pivotal role. We offer evidence from the Federal Reserve Bank as a primary example of these kinds of delegation. The central message is that *lack* of political control is an important solution to an acute political problem.

In Chapter 4, we argue that every distributional problem is a peculiar type of credible commitment problem. Generally, credible commitment models show that there are occasions for tying the state's hands. But as noted earlier, politics and policy making are often defined by motives to distribute – the eternal problem of "dividing the pie." We rely in this chapter on a result, due to Holmström, that shows that every efficient distribution scheme leaves very real incentives for the principal to engage in a self-serving sacrifice of efficiency. Knowing this, the principal may seek to remove himself from the equation – to build a firewall against this move – and delegation to an unresponsive agent is one important solution. This delegation can help alleviate efficiency problems caused by distributional politics.

In Chapter 5, we present a meta-model to explain when self-interested politicians empower compliant, responsive bureaucrats and when the same self-interested politicians create (as did the Progressives) insulated structures in which bureaucrats may exercise discretion. Issues characterized by consensus and unanimity lead politicians to exercise maximal control over vulnerable bureaucrats. Issues characterized by partisan debate, interest group conflict, and institutional stalemate more likely lead to bureaucratic autonomy and discretion. Delegation is a solution to a proximate problem of political compromise, but this delegation has long-lasting consequences for policy and administration. In fact, this delegation can be "unintentionally efficient."

Together, these three claims provide a foundation for the second part of this book. In the language of our model of the politician as principal and the teacher as agent, these claims are foundations for understanding why most governments do not use the primary tool of principal-agency – monetary incentives – to motivate bureaucrats. Instead, we show that, for practical purposes, even an organization staffed with risk-neutral employees may nevertheless end up employing monitoring, rule-making, directives, and coercive sanctions – either because of an efficiency constraint or the moral hazard of the principal. But we also show that in many cases politicians intentionally build barriers to the use of such tools – and in many of those cases bureaucrats still carry out public missions and do not shirk.

TECHNICAL APPENDIX

Efficiency Constraints on the Agent's Efficacy

As agent efficacy decreases to a certain point, it is no longer efficient to try to induce HI. This point occurs when the extra social surplus generated by the extra effort is larger than the marginal effort cost of HI. The basic measure of the benefits of the principal-agent interaction is the expected revenue less the agent's effort costs. The expected social surplus depends on whether the agent supplies a HI or LO effort. In the former case, the expected social surplus is equal to $pS + (1 - p)F - C_{HI}$. If the agent supplies a LO effort, the expected social surplus is equal to $qS + (1 - q)F - C_{LO}$.

The expected social surplus resulting from a HI effort is greater than that from a LO effort if and only if

$$(p - q)(S - F) \geq C_{HI} - C_{LO} \tag{3}$$

This efficiency constraint can be rewritten as a constraint on agent efficacy $(p - q)$:

$$p - q \geq \frac{C_{HI} - C_{LO}}{S - F} \tag{4}$$

This means that, for given asset values and effort costs, there is a critical level of efficacy $(p - q)$ below which *incentives are inefficient*. That is, the use of an incentive bonus does nothing but generate an inefficiently high level of effort. With $S = \$100,000$, $F = \$0$, and the cost parameters from the original example, then $(p - q)$ must be at least equal to 0.1 to justify the use of the minimal incentive bonus B^*. Whenever $(p - q) < 0.1$, then the extra $\$10,000$ in effort costs associated with a HI effort cannot result in the extra expected value.

This possibility clearly has real-world significance. That is, most jobs are ones in which it is simply inefficient to provide outcome-contingent incentives for success. If the teacher's effect on learning is largely determined by economic, social, and political factors beyond her control, then $p - q$ would be low, and the bonus necessary to motivate high effort would be prohibitively expensive. The alternative, once again, is to hire a supervisor (e.g., a principal) who tries to detect whether the agent is in fact providing full effort and to sanction the agent (e.g., a teacher) who is found shirking. Incentive bonuses are efficient for only a special category of jobs.

Profitability Constraint on the Agent's Efficacy

The profitability constraint, like the efficiency constraint, can be written as a constraint on the agent's efficacy. The agent's efficacy must be *higher* than a certain level to make it worth the principal's while to pay the bonus necessary to induce HI effort. Further, the profitability constraint is higher than the efficiency constraint, which implies that there is a mid-range of efficacy levels in which the principal's self-interest is the obstacle to the use of efficient incentives.

The principal's expected cost of inducing high effort with a bonus B^* is pB^*, the expected cost of inducing a flat wage is C_{LO}, and the expected marginal revenue is $(p - q)(S - F)$. The principal's individual rationality constraint for the use of the bonus B^* is

$$pB^* - C_{LO} < (p - q)(S - F) \tag{5}$$

or

$$B^* < \frac{(p-q)(S-F) + C_{LO}}{p}. \tag{6}$$

The upper bound for the region in which the principal will select a Pareto-inefficient contract can be found by substituting from (2) into (6), stated as an equality and then solving for $(p-q)$ with the quadratic equation. The minimum level of $(p-q)$ for a given p at which feasible contracts can be written is

$$(p-q) = \frac{C_{LO} + \sqrt{4p(S-F)(C_{HI} - C_{LO}) + C_{LO}^2}}{-2(S-F)}. \tag{7}$$

Empirically, this means that we should see efficient incentives chosen by principals only when the agent's efficacy is especially high.

3

Political Moral Hazard and Credible Commitment

If control of my decision is in the hands of an agent whose preferences are different from my own, I may nevertheless prefer the results to those that would come about if I took my own decisions.

– Vickers (1985, 138)

Bernanke, like Greenspan and Volcker before, subscribed to the view that the best way to protect a democratic society from undesirable rates of inflation was to keep control of interest rates and the supply of money away from elected politicians.

– Wessel (2009, 271)

BUILDING IN AUTONOMY

Innovation in the creation of new organizations is often associated with FDR and his "alphabet soup" of New Deal agencies. But the Federal Home Loan Bank Board (FHLBB) was an accomplishment of the previous Hoover administration, desperate to find a solution to the collapse of the housing bubble that accompanied the Great Depression.

Housing starts had boomed in the 1920s, increasing from around 100,000 new starts in 1918 to a high of more than 550,000 new starts in 1926 (Wheelock, 2008, 135). The upshot was a bubble to rival the recent housing crisis – complete with land and construction booms in Florida (Allen, 1931) and speculation that the bubble came from lax lending standards and the growing use of securitization of debt for new construction (Gordon, 1974).

In a 2009 article, economists Steven Gjerstad and Vernon L. Smith argued that this early housing bubble precipitated the Great Depression: "The standard explanation of the precipitating factor in the crash of 1929 has been excessive speculation on Wall Street. Speculation does appear to have been a factor, but then, as now, we believe that mortgage and consumer finance growth were also at the core of the problem" (Gjerstad & Smith, 2009, 287). And as

Ernest M. Fisher pointed out in 1950, "The general economic expansion of that period found no more dramatic expression in any area than in that of mortgage lending. The expansion of mortgage lending was, in turn, a manifestation of a rapid expansion of our urban real estate inventory" (Fisher, 1950, 307). Construction surged, home ownership rapidly increased, indebtedness jumped by 174%, and mortgage bond issues rose from $300 million in 1920 to between $5 billion and $10 billion in 1935 (309).

Just as the economic collapse, which occurred between 1929 and 1932, bore an eerie resemblance to recent events, so did the 1920s bubble stem from a cause similar to that of the recent crisis: "Arguably, this factor was, in both cases, excessive debt among borrowers with especially limited assets and income – hence with an especially constrained ability to repay. The mortgages made to these borrowers turned on poor credit assessment" (Gjerstad & Smith, 2009, 293).

Hoover's political problem was to find a way out of the housing mess that would clearly address the real-life consequences of the bubble. Although thrifts initially failed at a much lower rate than banks, depositors continued to withdraw funds, new deposits slackened with rising unemployment, and commercial bank failures began to put pressure on the thrifts. Thrifts that had deposits with those commercial banks first lost their funds and then were asked to pay back the lines of credit they had outstanding. Thrifts without sufficient funds to pay those calls went into bankruptcy. By 1932 banks were failing at a 20% rate in a single year, and the rate of thrift failures had doubled (Mason, 2004, 78). Mortgage holders were themselves affected by rising unemployment, and foreclosures soared in part because bank failures made it difficult to refinance (Bernanke, 1983). Mortgage delinquency data for 22 cities showed that 43.8% of urban, owner-occupied homes with first mortgages were in default in 1934, as were 54.4% of those with second or third mortgages; half of all urban houses with mortgages were in default (Bridewell, 1938, 172). Extensive foreclosure moratoria implemented at the state level stemmed the tide for some time (Wheelock, 2008, 569).

Hoover's solution was to convene a conference, the White House Conference on Home Building and Home Ownership, to help plan a route to making home ownership realistic in an America in the midst of substantial economic troubles. Hoover had promoted home ownership since his days as Secretary of Commerce, holding such conferences regularly as a primary way of encouraging business interests to come together to attain quality social outcomes (Mason, 2004, 79). Before the 1931 conference, Hoover met extensively with a range of housing and financial interests to discuss ideas. Discussions centered on the liquidity problem. One central player in these discussions, the U.S. League of Local Building and Loan Associations, argued that thrifts should be eligible to become part of the Fed. Thrifts were regulated at that time by the patchwork laws of the states, and membership in the Federal Reserve would have added significant credibility.

Hoover's motivation in proposing the creation of the FHLBB in 1932 was to find a way to solidify expert knowledge about lending for mortgages in an agency with limited exposure to the whims of Congress. He did not want political influence to undermine the efforts of those with professional expertise.

He achieved that goal by making the FHLBB in the Fed's image: Hoover proposed the creation of a central mortgage reserve bank, and the League of Local Building and Loan Associations decided to support the position. "The new system provided for a bi-partisan board (the Federal Home Loan Bank Board) of five citizens appointed by the President to supervise and coordinate the functions of the twelve Federal Home Loan Banks, one such bank located in each of the twelve districts comprising the country" (McDonough, 1934, 670). Not only was the FHLBB bipartisan and independent of the president but also the 12 federal banks were owned and governed by member institutions, operating as a cooperative. After a series of legislative maneuvers by a number of parties to shape the final bill, Hoover signed the Federal Home Loan Bank Act into law on July 22, 1932. Intense opposition to the plan, which was expected from banks, never materialized. Thrifts were given their own liquidity reserve system largely because of the efforts of the growing building and loan community.

The Federal Home Loan Bank system opened for business in October 1932, largely serving the thrifts' needs for liquidity. Its impact was marginal at first, although "the public had heightened expectations that the home loan bank would provide immediate assistance" (Mason, 2004, 88).

The thrifts' perceived lack of direct lending to homeowners became a campaign issue for Democrats in the 1932 elections. After his election, President Franklin Roosevelt was presented with an opportunity to get rid of what some called "Hoover's banks" when the terms of the first board members expired. Instead, the FHLBB became the centerpiece of a series of attempts to stabilize mortgage markets and lenders, including direct lending through the Homeowner's Loan Corporation (HOLC) and deposit insurance through the Federal Savings and Loan Insurance Corporation (FSLIC).

Indeed, by solidifying the presence of the federal government through a member-based independent agency whose oversight was left to interested parties, Hoover had built another mechanism for intervening in the economy while leaving the decision making about the implementation of the intervention to those with supposedly greater expertise. The FHLBB's member banks, the HOLC, and the FSLIC all represented tools for the FHLBB to wield in bringing the housing market back to shape. In his 1934 *American Economic Review* article, McDonough foresaw the degree to which these types of tools could lend lasting stability to the system, writing, "But none of the agencies here described, even at the moment, can be dismissed as inconsequential. All will undoubtedly exert considerable influence on the financial system of the future" (McDonough, 1934, 685).

The FHLBB, like the Federal Reserve System, was created so as not to guarantee control by political principals – Congress and the executive. This poses a puzzle. For canonical principal-agency theory, responsiveness of the agent to the preferences of the principal is the goal, and manipulation of incentives is the means to achieve that goal. Why would a principal or political master seek to create an agency that would not give it guaranteed control of the bureaucratic agent? A full answer to this question takes us out of principal-agency theory.

MORAL HAZARD AND CREDIBLE COMMITMENT

To illustrate this idea, we rely on an old idea by Thomas Schelling (1960): credible commitment. It is our contention that the problem identified by Schelling is distinct from the problem identified by principal-agency theory and that much of what we observe in public administration is more understandable in terms of Schelling's ideas than of the principal-agency perspective.

To illustrate Schelling's idea, consider a wealthy mother who is concerned about news reports of kidnapping. She realizes that, because of her wealth, her child is at risk. A kidnapper knows that, once the child is kidnapped, the mother's preferences are such that her only choice is to pay a ransom. Given that the kidnapper can safely predict that the parent will pay the ransom, the kidnapper can expect to receive a payoff of 10, as opposed to -5 if the ransom were not paid. So the kidnapper finds it in his interest to kidnap the child, whereas of course the mother has every reason to pay the ransom once the kidnapping has occurred. Neither the kidnapper nor the mother can do any better than pursue these choices – and the (pay ransom) outcome is an equilibrium.

The parent would like to be able to commit publicly to not paying the ransom. If the parent were not to pay the ransom, the kidnapper would actually be made worse off by kidnapping the child. The kidnapper's best choice is a function of the anticipated action of the parent. If the kidnapper knew that the ransom would not be paid, then his self-interest would lead him not to kidnap.

The problem is that a public statement from the parent – "I will refuse to pay a ransom in the event that my child is kidnapped" – is not believable. The kidnapper knows that the parent loves her child and believes that her public statement is exactly what it is: cheap talk.

The parent has a *time-inconsistency* problem. Before the game is played, the parent would like to commit to an action that would not serve her self-interest once the kidnapping has occurred. If she could commit to withholding the ransom, she could deter the kidnapper. But a pre-kidnapping promise not to pay the ransom is a bluff, and not credible. Therefore, *credible commitment* is the key to the mother's problem.

We can define a *credible commitment* problem as a strategic interaction between first-mover A and second-mover B in which A (the kidnapper) will condition his choice on B's (the mother's) expected behavior. The source of the threat to the mother is her own freedom of action. Constraining her own actions can actually make her better off.

But now suppose the mother could hire a trustee to control her wealth and thus control whether or not to pay a ransom in the event of kidnapping. This

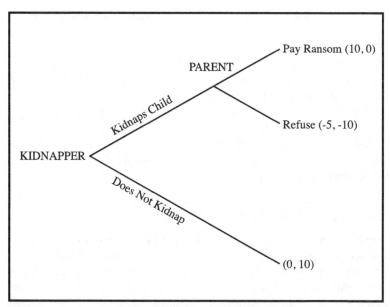

FIGURE 3.1. A Credible Commitment Game. Inspired by Schelling (1960).

level of autonomy differentiates the trustee from the typical agent. Figure 3.1 shows this situation graphically.

A publicly known commitment to the trustee's autonomy changes the strategic interaction. The trustee (unlike the typical agent) could articulate a commitment *not* to pay the ransom. This statement, apparently inconsistent with the parent's preferences, would lead the kidnapper to decide against kidnapping. The kidnapper would recognize that the trustee's threat not to pay the ransom in the event of kidnapping is believable – but only if the trustee has preferences different from those of the parent. To deter a kidnapping, the trustee must have quite different preferences at the "ransom" decision node. If the trustee (perhaps an uncle or family friend) loves the child as much as the mother does, then the trustee is worthless at deterring the kidnapping.

The trustee can only serve to deter the kidnapping if he acts in defiance of the mother's concern for the child. The trustee is only useful to the mother insofar as he is committed to denying a kidnapper's request for ransom and to resisting the mother's urgent demands to pay the ransom if the kidnapper actually chooses to proceed with a kidnapping. That is, at the ransom node, the trustee must *not* act on the parent's most compelling and overriding preference to protect her child from a kidnapper. For instance, he should be contractually required to forfeit a sizable bond if he ever agrees to pay a ransom to a kidnapper.

Clearly, the trustee is like an agent in that the trustee receives a delegation of authority in the interest of the principal. It is the requirement that the trustee resolve a time-inconsistency problem that clearly distinguishes between the trustee (as formulated here) and the agent in principal-agency theory. The trustee can only serve to avert the possibility of kidnapping by *denying* the parent's problematic interests.

Furthermore, the delegation of authority to the trustee must be inviolable. The mother must not be able to come to the trustee, in the event of a kidnapping, and change the terms of the trust arrangement so that he is required to pay a ransom, rather than being prohibited from doing so. Although principal-agency theory affirms that the structure of the relationship must be elastic to the principal's wishes, Schelling's trustee theory stipulates quite the opposite: any suspicion that the mother can redefine the relationship in response to changing conditions is counterproductive.

Time Inconsistency and Tying the Principal's Hands

A single individual can also face a time-inconsistency problem. Consider Elster (1983), in which an individual constrains himself (for instance, Odysseus tying himself to the mast) out of an awareness that his future preferences will change (e.g., the Sirens will cause Odysseus to want to jump into the sea). The difference is that our credible commitment problem of the kidnapping arises from strategic interaction between two players, not a change in preferences for one player. The parent wants to commit to not paying a ransom simply because of the effect that this commitment will have on the other player – the kidnapper.

Principal-agency theory commonly prescribes that selection of a like-minded agent reduces agency costs and minimizes problems in the principal-agency relationship. The trustee (unlike an agent) is useful only to the extent that he acts on *different preferences* from those of the principal (parent) and only to the extent that authority over the parent's wealth has been visibly, credibly, and irrevocably handed to the trustee. In other words, the delegation process must tie the parent's hands.

As we saw in the previous chapter, the principal's first problem is to shape the agent's preference, so that she can guarantee a degree of accountability over the agent. The principal's other problem is to design a trustee relationship, where appropriate, that will secure for the principal the benefits of credible commitment and agency autonomy.

To the extent that similar problems can be identified in political oversight of the bureaucracy, then the solution is the same: bureaucratic delegation and defiance.

Credible Commitment and Military Strategy: The Agent with the Bloodshot Eyes

Schelling was quite aware that the credible commitment problem took him into unorthodox territory when he wrote about the defense bureaucracy. Writing two years before the Cuban missile crisis, Schelling (1960) was concerned about making nuclear deterrence believable. In a simple game-tree version of the problem, the Soviet Union can either invade Europe or not. In response to a Soviet invasion, the United States can either use its nuclear weapons or not. The problem is that the latter course of action would result in the worst case for both the United States and the Soviet Union. For that reason, the Soviet Union can use backward induction to conclude that self-interest would prevent the United States from using its nuclear deterrent. The subgame perfect equilibrium of the game is for the Soviet Union to invade and for the United States to acquiesce. Nuclear deterrence, in the hands of any reasonable individual, is a hollow threat – and an invasion of Europe is to be expected.

Although this presentation is vastly oversimplified, it portrays the heart of a very troubling problem that concerned not only Schelling but also key members of the armed forces and the Kennedy administration: the self-interest of a rational U.S. political leader (unwilling to unleash Armageddon on himself, his family, and the entire population) can only discourage the actual use of a deterrent and thereby actually *encourage* a Soviet invasion of Europe.

Schelling (1960, 29) noted that, paradoxically, self-interested actors often find themselves in situations in which they would do well to constrain their own self-interested behavior. This conclusion came from his extended analysis of the strategy of mutually assured destruction. Initiating a nuclear war is not in anyone's self-interest; recognizing this, one's enemy may make threats that induce concession after concession. Reasoned self-interest in such a case is a certain path to exploitation and ruin.

Conversely, an "irrational" commitment to initiate a nuclear war when a given line is crossed may deter the enemy from seeking those concessions. However, deterrence is only possible when the enemy believes in the commitment – that is, the enemy must believe in his adversary's willingness to make that irrational choice when the line is crossed.

What is the solution to this problem? How can a rational, self-interested individual convince the enemy of his willingness to make that final irrational, self-destroying act? Schelling offers an answer: by delegating the decision to someone whose preferences are *known to be different from your own*. Schelling's agent must have *entirely different preferences from those of the principal* – in this situation, a willingness to use nuclear weapons and thereby engender nuclear holocaust. But finding such a person is only half the solution. The *agent must be insulated from pressure from the principal*, so that the principal's last-minute (post-invasion) attempts to prevent the agent from wreaking global havoc are powerless. The useful agent must be out of the principal's control and must prefer mutual annihilation to acquiescence.

The point of Schelling's analysis is that the usefulness of the agent depends on the agent having preferences and pursuing goals that are quite different from those of the principal. This view of agency contrasts sharply with principal-agency theory, which insists that the "principal's problem" is to *align* the preferences of agent with principal by the appropriate incentive system.

The person with preferences appropriate for deterrence was in fact the chair- ·man of the Joint Chiefs of Staff at that time: Curtis ("Boom-boom") LeMay, who was a fan – or a fanatic – on the subject of nuclear weapons. (Later, when George Wallace made LeMay his vice-presidential candidate during the 1968 presidential campaign, LeMay embarrassed Wallace with his cheerful enthusiasm for nuclear war [Carter, 1995]. Wallace had to send LeMay on information-gathering trips to Vietnam to get him out of the public's eye.)

During the Cuban missile crisis, LeMay's counsel was the most insistent on an air attack, presumably ending in a nuclear exchange. After the crisis ended, when Khrushchev had backed down and the missiles were on their way back to the Soviet Union, LeMay argued for an air strike against Cuba anyway. While Kennedy was experiencing enormous relief at the termination of the immediate threat of nuclear annihilation, LeMay was demanding exactly the nuclear exchange that Kennedy had been working so hard to avoid. From the standpoint of principal-agency theory, it was insanity for Kennedy to keep an agent with such strikingly different preferences and with possibly enough autonomy to bring on the crisis that Kennedy was trying to avoid. But that view merely shows the theoretical limitations of canonical principal-agency theory.

From Schelling's standpoint, LeMay was useful precisely because he had preferences that were perverse enough and with authority sufficient to make the United States' use of nuclear weapons a credible threat. The Soviet Union had enough intelligence to know that LeMay and other hardliners were arguing for the use of nuclear weapons during the crisis. They also knew that civilian control of the military was a question, not a certainty.

This knowledge made Kennedy's bargaining posture (blockade followed by the threat of attack) more effective with Khrushchev and induced the Soviet leader to withdraw the missiles. As Schelling (1960, 22) wrote, "The sophisticated negotiator [Kennedy] may find it difficult to seem as obstinate as a truly obstinate man [LeMay]. If a man knocks at a door and says that he will stab himself on the porch unless given $10, he is more likely to get the $10 if his eyes are bloodshot."

The point is that this problem is not comprehensible in terms of conventional principal-agency theory, which has the sole avowed purpose of finding incentives that align the agent's actions with the principal's preferences, and thereby eliminate shirking. For Schelling, the problem is finding someone with the appropriate nonaligned preferences, but having perverse incentives is not enough: the principal must convincingly give up some of his control to the agent with the bloodshot eyes. To be credible, the use of such an agent must involve "some voluntary but irreversible sacrifice of freedom of choice" by the principal (Schelling, 1960, 22). In this view of military bureaucracy, the agent's responsiveness to the principal would paradoxically destroy the agent's value to the principal.

In the case of nuclear deterrence, credible commitment through delegation plays a role even when the principal has laudable and reasonable preferences. It becomes even more desirable when the principal is plagued by moral hazard – preferences that, when acted on, diminish social efficiency.

In principal-agency theory, only the agent can exhibit "moral hazard" because the formal responsibility is strictly unidirectional – from the agent to the principal. The phrase "principal's moral hazard" makes no sense in the original formulation, because the principal's proclivity to follow her own interests is presumed to be natural and legitimate. However, from the perspective of the overall efficiency of the relationship between principal and agent, it is possible for the principal's pursuit of her own self-interest to be inefficient, and therefore ultimately self-destructive.

Schelling used the notion of credible commitment to understand the problem in nuclear deterrence, and that problem might be unique to a particular time and place: the Cold War in the 1960s. Writing several decades later, North and Weingast, in contrast, have used credible commitment to understand fundamental dilemmas facing every state.

NORTH AND WEINGAST ON THE GLORIOUS REVOLUTION

North and Weingast (1989) use the example of the predatory behavior of the Stuart kings to illustrate how, due to the problematic preferences of rulers, economic development requires credible commitment of the state. All governments face this dilemma when using the powers of *confiscation*. Likewise, economic actors worry about how rulers will constrain the state's use of confiscatory power.

The Ruler's Moral Hazard

In their seminal paper, North and Weingast analyzed the political economy of the Stuart kings to reveal something basic about states, rulers, and economic development. The Stuarts, like most kings, had an endless appetite for the resources needed to conduct wars. When they identified a source of wealth, they went after it. They required the wealthy to loan them money and then were lax about paying interest or returning the principal. They used their control over judges to sell justice. They granted monopolies in exchange for cash. And they manipulated the taxation system to their benefit.

In all these ways, their search for wealth undermined the property rights of asset owners and created uncertainties for entrepreneurs. The sale of monopolies distorted economies and harmed potential competitors. Investors were deterred from loaning money to individuals who might have sufficient political connections to refuse to repay the loan and not be held accountable in court. The knowledge that the king would come after wealth discouraged entrepreneurs from following through on ideas that might generate riches.

Clearly, a similar analysis could have been undertaken in any authoritarian regime. At its heart, the problem is once again one of credible commitment,

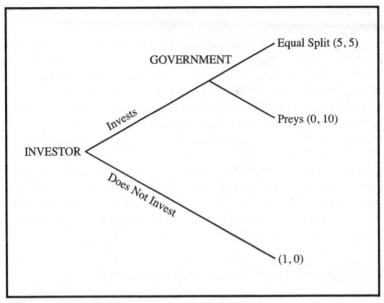

FIGURE 3.2. The Investor Game. Inspired by North and Weingast (1989).

as shown by the following simple game described in Miller (2000) (see also Gilardi, 2008, for an elaboration).

The Investor-Ruler Game

Consider the game between an investor and a ruler shown in Figure 3.2. The investor has $1 worth of gold hidden in her mattress, and the ruler has nothing. She, the investor, can either take her gold from her mattress to invest it in the ruler's economy or keep it. If she does invest it, the investment generates $10 worth of benefit. The ruler can either steal the $10, leaving the investor with nothing, or tax the investor $5, leaving the investor with $5. In the backward induction equilibrium of the game, the investor, anticipating that the ruler will choose $10 over $5, leaves her gold in her mattress. The problem is that the equilibrium of the game is Pareto suboptimal: both investor and ruler are worse off than if the ruler could be counted on to constrain his self-interest.

In this example moral hazard resides with the ruler; the ruler's self-interest is itself the problem. The fact that the ruler has the power and the motive to exploit the investor deters investment, and this ultimately harms the ruler as well as the investor.

Both players prefer the outcome in which the investor invests and the government chooses an "equal split" to the one-shot Nash equilibrium. Because it is Pareto-preferred, the problem could be resolved by cooperation arising from repeated plays of the game. In an infinitely repeated game, the long-term promise of cooperative gains (\$5 for each, in each period), together with the threat by each side of retaliation against noncooperation, could sustain the cooperative outcome. In such a case, delegation would not be necessary.

However, repeated play has its own problems. The first problem is that one side (say the government) may be too oriented toward short-term payoffs. This would be especially true in the case of instability in the ruling elites. If this were the case or even if the investor simply suspected that the government was impatient, then the cooperative equilibrium would collapse. More generally, the folk theorem demonstrates that there are many possible equilibria to the repeated game – including mutual noncooperation (Miller, 1992, 199–205). Settling on one beneficial equilibrium requires perfect coordination: each player has to know that the other player knows that both know they are playing strategies consistent with a chosen equilibrium, and no other. Any imperfection in their shared common knowledge could again lead to collapse.

Delegation

The problems limiting repeated play as a solution to the investor-ruler game do not affect a solution in which the ruler "ties his hands" (Root, 1989) by delegating authority to others. If the government delegates the "equal split" or "prey" decision to an appropriately rewarded, autonomous trustee, then there are no coordination problems due to multiple equilibria and no problems due to short-term time horizons. The appropriate incentive for the trustee is, of course, that the trustee must *not* have preferences aligned with those of the government; the trustee must prefer an equal split outcome to the "prey" outcome. And like the parent in the kidnapping problem, the ruler must not be able to call back the authority of the trustee when times are bad and a one-shot \$10 reward for preying seems particularly attractive. In other words, the ruler must be credibly constrained by the authority of the disinterested trustee – and constrained so visibly that investors and entrepreneurs know that, if they enter into a contract, an independent judiciary, supported by an independent parliament, will enforce their contractual rights.

North and Weingast argue that it was only by visibly constraining the ruler– through the institutional change that accompanied the Glorious Revolution – that economic development was encouraged. These reforms curtailed the king's ability to appoint judges. The common law was allowed to rule commercial transactions. Parliament gained the exclusive authority to raise taxes; it also procured the right to audit government expenditures and to veto them. The process of government borrowing was transformed, and the Bank of England was created to administer the loan accounts. Tax money was earmarked to pay interest. These institutional changes provided certainty where previously there was risk of exploitation. All of these changes also divorced the king from management of the affairs of state, credibly committing the state to property rights and contract enforcement. The supply of money increased as lenders' confidence improved, interest rates dropped, and entrepreneurs had cheap money available to finance their mills and other projects.

North and Weingast correctly place a great deal of emphasis on the role of Parliament in constraining the ruler. As they note in their paper, with the Glorious Revolution of 1688, Parliament was able to gain control of taxation, sale of the king's lands, an independent judiciary, and government borrowing. But this degree of parliamentary control raises several other questions. First, given the same powers as the king, would not Parliament succumb to the same predatory temptations?

In fact, Parliament did give in to the same temptations, at least to some extent. For example, the Stuart kings had been able to sell monopolistic licenses; in effect, the kings were able to stake an ownership claim to monopolistic rents by charging a fee approaching the expected monopoly profits for the opportunity to become a monopolist. Eighteenth-century England saw similar kinds of behavior of monopoly profit-maximizing behavior from Parliament.

Adam Smith's *Wealth of Nations* can be seen as an indictment of the predatory practices of mercantilist 18th-century England. The most glaring examples were those pursued by the sugar lords of the British West Indies. Having sufficient wealth, many of them purchased seats in Parliament, either by getting a title in the House of Lords or by purchasing election to one of the "rotten boroughs," electoral districts that contained few voters. These districts were available for purchase, often by sugar lords who had disproportionate wealth and legislative influence. Once in Parliament, they used their influence to restrict the importation of sugar from other colonial powers, thereby maintaining their monopoly profits. Collectively, the sugar lords used their ruling power in much the same way that a Stuart king would have – and in a way that was contrary to long-term economic growth.

Stasavage (2002) claims that, as long as Parliament was governed by a Tory coalition, it was (like the Stuart kings) not credibly committed to protection of the property rights of economic actors; in addition to the actions of the sugar lords, this lack of credible commitment was observable in the interest rate. Only when a Whig coalition was in power, and able to serve as a blocking coalition protecting the sanctity of the government's commitment to bond repayment, did the interest rates decrease. In other words, Stasavage argues that the existence of a majority-rule parliament is insufficient to control moral hazard in the political system; credible commitment requires the existence of mutually blocking veto players.

North and Weingast show ways to credibly constrain the state's powers of confiscation so that economic development occurs. Credible commitments reduce the chance that leaders will operate in *time-inconsistent* ways, using the power of the state to transfer wealth and thus reducing economic incentives that govern markets.

Bureaucratic Trustees and Credible Commitment

The problem of politicians acting in time-inconsistent ways is fundamental for how we understand the institutional arrangements that emerged in 20th-century America. For North and Weingast, the solution is to put up a wall around the trustee – a wall made more credible when there are separated powers.

Economists have observed this same time-inconsistency problem in the actions of elected officials who have found electoral advantage in supporting and creating policies that generate unexpected expansionary boosts to the economy. Although these boosts also generate inflationary tendencies, investors and other economic agents adjust their actions accordingly, and eventually such governmental actions generate inflation with little impact on unemployment. A government that campaigned on promises not to provide such inflationary shocks would not be believed. Time inconsistency leads to inflation, and by reducing the value of future dollars, inflation acts like a tax – a confiscation.

The credible commitment model corresponds in several ways to our best understanding of the political economy of central banking and the control of monetary policy (H. Jensen, 1997). In 1977, Kydland and Prescott pointed out that countries could find themselves with self-generated inflation. Even when they announced they would try to control inflation, politicians could not credibly commit to a stable policy path (Kydland & Prescott, 1977). One solution, which worked better than discretionary policy, is prior commitment to a rule that stabilized policy (Barro & Gordon, 1983b). The path and the rule would help policymakers establish a reputation for combating inflation, which would affect market expectations about the future.

This commitment device allows politicians to escape a trap created by their own potential for time-inconsistent behavior. Just like the Stuart kings, politicians often use the levers of monetary policy to benefit the present time at the expense of the future. The way out of the trap is to bind their hands – to constrain policy making. This intuition underlies the creation of the Federal Reserve as the agency tasked with managing monetary policy. It is also why politicians built the FHLBB to solve the housing problems of the Great Depression. The creation of both the Fed and the FHLBB show us how politicians will bind their own hands when creating agencies for managing the market.

In the case of monetary policy, rules needed to be simple. The solution was to delegate the choice of rule and its implementation to an expert, with known views that would favor the long-term solution, in an agency separated from politics: an independent central bank. In making this observation, economists built an extended defense, entirely in the language of economics, for the independence of agencies to keep politicians from acting on dynamically inconsistent preferences (Rogoff, 1985).

More generally, the need for credible commitment to property rights and contract enforcement is generally recognized as a prerequisite of economic development in a given society (North & Weingast, 1989). The essential feature of credible commitment is delegation of substantial decision-making authority to public agencies. Governments are credibly committed to property rights and the rule of law *only when* investors believe that a group of professional officials (making and enforcing rules) are insulated from political control and given the authority to make key decisions affecting property rights and contract enforcement.

Regulators can fulfill the same purpose: independent agencies can serve to commit the government to a course of action that balances the interests of consumers and producers (Estache & Wren-Lewis, 2009, 747). For instance, a monopolist facing a regulator knows that the regulator's enforcement action will determine its profitability, so it may act to influence that regulator (Laffont & Tirole, 1993). There are problems of having enough regulatory capacity, of keeping regulators and politicians accountable, and fiscal efficiency, but the government also faces commitment problems. Can it commit not to change the rules of the game later? Can it commit not to underenforce the rules?

Independent regulators can sustain commitments that reduce the likelihood of either over- or underenforcing regulatory policy. The problem is that what we really need is a better understanding of the concept of independence (Estache & Wren-Lewis, 2009, 757). As noted in Chapter 1, regulatory independence can reduce commitment problems in a "multitude of different ways," so Estache and Wren-Lewis see the need for research to "examine the concept of independence more thoroughly ... to break down the various aspects of 'independence' and consider which are likely to be more important and which are likely to have the greatest risks" (757).

Protections are often granted even to bureaucrats inside cabinet departments. For instance, civil service protection guarantees that most bureaucrats (below the top political appointees) are selected for merit rather than political connections. Civil service tenure means that they cannot be fired as long as they are doing their jobs competently. In particular, the Hatch Act, passed in 1939, prohibits federal bureaucrats from engaging in partisan political activity and so protects them from pressures from their political masters.

We are not the first to recognize the importance of the institutional design of mechanisms of independence in bureaus. In 1955, Marver Bernstein pointed out that independent commissions dotted the landscape of American regulatory policy and that this independence created unique design and management issues for the regulatory policy pathway – that regulatory agencies had a "life cycle" that could eventually lead to regulatory capture (M. H. Bernstein, 1955). This alternative view is particularly important because it shows how differently we conceive of credible commitment.

Commitment also plays an important role for Horn's (1995) transactions-cost–flavored theory of the institutions of public administration. Specifically, the principal is able to select an institutional form from a grab bag of bundled attributes, choosing a level of delegation, a governance structure (levels of independence), a monitoring technology (as participation rights), and the possibility of direct intervention. The important part of Horn's theory is that the politician selects this bundle by minimizing four kinds of costs. Three are familiar – the costs of making decisions, the potential policy losses from delegation, and uncertainty. The fourth kind is commitment costs.

We want to be very clear that commitment in Horn's model is different from the credible commitments that concern us. The question for Horn's legislature is how to commit to a particular policy outcome right now when politics may change the future players who will have power to alter the institutional arrangements in place. This view is akin to Moe's "political uncertainty" concept (Moe, 1989). For Horn, the problem of commitment is posed by people other than the current institutional designer. For North and Weingast, for Kydland and Prescott, and for Barro and Gordon, the problem is the current institution designer in the future. In our theory, commitments are needed not just because the politician fears that future politicians might change the rule. Our politician also fears himself – that he might not abide by the agreement, that his preferences will be different in the future. Even the current politician, designing the current institution, faces incentives to cheat against the socially beneficial outcome. In our model, commitment is not designed to be credible against another political opponent; it is designed to be credible against a future state of one's current self. The politician is not tying another political actor's hands; he is tying his own hands because he does not trust himself or because those outside the circle, who may differently benefit from the policy at different points in time, do not trust the politician to restrain his own "animal spirits."

One way to see these "mechanisms of independence" is through three narratives that traverse the history of economic policy making: the evolution and practice of central banking, the commitment to regulatory independence as a way of sustaining investor confidence in the system, and the emergence of professionalized bureaucracies as a response to problems associated with the spoils systems. The next section develops these three narratives.

DELEGATION CONSTRAINS POLITICAL ACTORS

Delegation, Separation of Powers, and Central Banking

Credible constraint of the government is the key to controlling inflation. The most effective and well-studied constraint is delegation to a known anti-inflationary banking central official – a delegation that can resolve the time-inconsistency problem (Rogoff, 1985). Multiple researchers have found that central bank independence is associated with effective inflation control and with economic development (Franzese, 1999). Governments are constrained because their hands are tied.

The central bank's credibility is enhanced when private economic actors perceive that its decisions are irrevocable. In contrast, if private actors perceive that partisan administrations influence the decisions of the central bank, then the credibility of a nominally independent bank is undermined. However, even if the government creates a central bank and grants it independence, could it not take back the authority it handed over at a later point; for example, before an election in which it wanted to gain favor by inflationary policies? The answer is that of course it could; the credibility of the bank's independence depends on the obstacles placed in the path of politicians hoping to reclaim that authority. This leads to the conclusion that central bank independence in a democracy is *contingent*, rather than unconditional. In particular, it is contingent on having divided political power and stalemate among those who share divided power.

Like Lohmann (1992), Keefer and Stasavage (2003) argue that a delegation of autonomy to central banks is one of the necessary conditions for effective constraint of interest rates. However, central bank autonomy interacts with the existence of *multiple political actors with conflicting preferences*; it is only when both factors combine that banks are able to maintain low interest rates effectively. Investors do not believe that autonomous bureaucrats, in a unified political system, are stable; it is the existence of stalemate among political actors in conflict that makes the bank's independence believable.

Assuming that Keefer and Stasavage are correct about the relationship between multiple blocking powers and credible commitment, what is the connection between both of those concepts and bureaucratic autonomy? The existence of multiple blocking powers, as in a government with separated powers, creates the bureaucratic autonomy that guarantees credible commitment. That is, the extent to which investors believe that politicians will block each other's attempts to influence the Fed forms the basis for the Fed's bureaucratic autonomy. To be precise, long-term interest rates can be low (an indicator of confidence in inflation control) *because* investors feel that the separation of powers prevents opponents of the Fed from effectively undermining its autonomy.

The picture that emerges is not one of absolute, but of contingent bureaucratic autonomy. Clearly, Congress and the president have the authority to change the Fed's policy, impose requirements (as in the case of the monetary guidelines required in the 1970s), or even eliminate the Fed altogether, as happened with Andrew Jackson. Just as clearly, however, all of these possibilities are unlikely, precisely because of the virtual inevitability of stalemate among political actors in conflict. Ultimately, the constitutional separation of powers must play a significant role. To pass legislation that impinged on bureaucratic autonomy would require the usual coalition of the president and a majority of both chambers, key substantive committees, and procedural committees in both chambers, and party leadership in both chambers. The self-interest of a variety of ambitious politicians is put to work guaranteeing what none of them intends: bureaucratic autonomy.

Alan Greenspan

Alan Greenspan had a strong reputation as chairman of the Fed, primarily because of the importance that he placed on maintaining his autonomy from politicians. His approach is illustrated by an episode reported in Woodward (2000). During the George Bush administration, in August 1989, the Office of Management and Budget director Richard Darman appeared on *Meet the Press*, expressing (for President Bush) the same kind of concern about the economy that Nixon had expressed just before his reelection in 1972. Darman said that he feared the Fed "may have been a little bit too tight. If we do have a recession, I think it will be because they erred on the side of caution." Greenspan was furious. As Woodward summarizes Greenspan's concern:

Public bashing by the president's top economic advisers would only encourage the opposite of what they wanted, forcing the Fed to assert its independence and delay lowering interest rates.... The Fed's interest rate policy had to be credible. A particular fed funds rate had to be seen by the markets as the best rate for the economy, not as an artificially low rate influenced by political pressure. (Woodward, 2000, 30)

This is an extreme form of the Schelling trustee argument; not only are the preferences of principal/politicians the threat to the bank/trustee's effectiveness but also the very *expression of the principal's interests* is a danger that must be met by a *visible demonstration of noncompliance*. After enduring a short, mild recession, the economy was positioned for what became a record expansion in the 1990s; President Bush was of course not reelected.

None of the presidents whom Greenspan served under would have called him their "agent" or an "ally." They all chafed at the handcuffs that an independent Fed chairman can keep on a president.

Greenspan relied on obstacles to political interference that had been available to previous Fed chairmen if they had wanted to use them. The primary such obstacle is the existence of multiple "veto points" within the government, preferably in the hands of opposing political interests, all of which must act in concert to reclaim the delegated authority of the central bank. Investors perceive the Fed as independent of the political ambitions of politicians precisely because it takes the joint action of *both* chambers of Congress and the president to reverse its decisions – and joint action is not likely, given their different goals and the likelihood of strategic behavior by the Fed chairman (Keefer & Stasavage, 2003). From the perspective of credible commitment, the loss of control implied by its multiplicity of principals is not an efficiency loss, as argued by the original advocates of congressional control. On the contrary, *the loss of political control is the prerequisite for effective performance* of the Fed's function.

That is, if the relationship between Congress and the Federal Reserve Board were like a principal-agency relationship, then we would want the Federal Reserve Board to be responsive to the electoral interests of members of Congress; anything that can align the interests of the Fed with those of Congress would then be a good thing. But if the Fed acts as a Schelling-style "trustee" of Congress's interests, then anything that causes the Fed to make decisions in a way that is responsive to the electoral interests of Congress is in fact subversive of the true role of the trustee. A Fed chairman who promises to serve the reelection interests of her political masters in Congress and the White House would, of course, be a disaster on Wall Street. One of the Fed chairman's primary jobs is to convince the public that the appearance of insulation is matched by reality. The Fed chairman has to be ready to control inflation with stringent measures, even (and especially) when those actions endanger the reelection aspirations of her political masters (Knott, 1986).

Bureaucratic Independence and Economic Investment

Central banking is not the only arena in which credible commitment plays a role in economic development; we see a similar dynamic in balancing the potential costs of under- and overenforcing regulation. A range of regulatory functions help determine the rights and responsibilities of investors, labor, and utilities, for example. In nations where investor rights are secure, economic investment leading to economic development is much more likely.

For instance, Globerman and Shapiro (2003) show that foreign direct investment responds to the perceived quality of state regulatory regimes. However, what features of a regulatory regime are viewed as generating a high-quality regulatory regime? Bertelli and Whitford (2009) look behind the measure of perceived regulatory quality to examine the impact of regulatory independence on those perceptions. For example, in the telecommunications arena, conditional on the effects of various political variables on regulatory independence, investors value the existence of a structurally independent telecommunications agency, viewing the regulatory regime more positively if it has such an agency. "Independent regulators help to stabilize [business elite] expectations if they are institutionally buffered from political influence" (518).

Likewise, the model of regulatory independence reveals that a measure of democratic (versus authoritarian) regimes is positively associated with the probability of structural independence for telecommunications regulators, at least up to a moderate degree of democracy. The expected probability of such an agency is 0.1 in the most autocratic regimes and 0.7 in the most democratic governments. This presents us with a paradox. Democratic regimes apparently *constrain the impact of democratic politics* by creating agencies that are insulated from democratic politics. Evidently, democratic regimes carry their own constraints within themselves.

Spoils and Progressive Reform

Economic development is often dependent on fulfillment of the most basic of governmental functions – paved streets, lighting, clean water, and basic public health. For much of the late 19th and early 20th centuries, in a number of states and cities, these public goods were largely under the control of political party bosses, who dispensed these services as leverage for political gain. Of even greater concern, the same politicians were committed to dispensing justice in the same way, through the electoral and political control of police, district attorneys, and judges. Central to this electoral strategy was "spoils," the allocation of public employment to private (political) purposes.

At the beginning of the 20th century, the use of spoils in the United States was comparable to that in Latin America and other nations that were not destined to have the same level of economic growth as the United States. The difference in economic paths undoubtedly was related to a reform movement that took hold in the United States (but not in Latin America). The limitation of the spoils system allowed businesses to expect paved streets, clean water, and public hygiene as a matter of course. The neutral enforcement of contracts and the protection of property rights against political manipulation were visible results of the Progressive reform movement.

Boss Politics as Confiscation

Although the U.S. Constitution had mandated a separation of powers as a protection against political abuse of governmental power, there were obvious political advantages for the political entrepreneur who could overcome that separation of powers with a political organization that extended to all the branches. The politicians who succeeded in influencing the legislature, executive, and judiciary could use governmental jobs, contracts, and extortion to enrich themselves while controlling key positions in government.

The common element for positions in the executive, legislative, and judiciary in state and local government was that they were elective. Between 1815 and 1840, a set of new state constitutions and municipal charters simultaneously democratized state and local politics and allowed for the election of long lists of state and local officials under partisan banners.

With all these positions available for the taking, the political party then became the mechanism for harnessing majority-rule democracy to private ends. Party organizations rapidly became sophisticated mechanisms for capturing and using government power. They developed labor-intensive technologies for the new mass electorates created by expansion of the suffrage and by immigration. These technologies required large numbers of party workers who "got out the party vote," and obtaining those workers required strong incentives. The strongest such incentives were government jobs, which were made available at the effective discretion of party leaders as a result of electoral victory. Postal workers, land office bureaucrats, teachers, police, street cleaners, and customs officials were all at stake in each local election. The widespread use of patronage was legitimized by the ideology of majority rule – the argument that any new majority capable of winning the election had the right to guarantee that its policies would be carried out enthusiastically by supporters of that policy.

At the same time, patronage jobs became the means of creating a disciplined hierarchy of party loyalists.

At the top of the hierarchy in each election district or ward was the ward boss, and coalitions of ward bosses determined citywide and statewide bosses. The party machines, as they were called, nominated slates of legislative, executive, and judicial candidates, all of whom were beholden to the party organization and the boss. Because district attorneys and judges were themselves party nominees, legal limitations on the boss's exercise of state and local power were minimized. And because the state and local government controlled transportation, regulation, taxation, and police power, the possibilities for economic exploitation of political power were immense.

Examples of Confiscation

The most common form of exploitation was simply a bribe, demanded by the party organization to pass legislation necessary for the successful operation of a business. Needless to say, acceptance of a bribe hardly constituted a long-term credible commitment to the property rights of the business. In the short run, the political boss could renege on one commitment in favor of a competitor with a larger bribe. In the long run, the boss's commitment was at best only as sustained as his current political prospects. Businesses in boss regimes had to factor in enormous amounts of political uncertainty – something that inevitably discouraged the kind of investment needed for long-term economic development.

Public construction projects were excellent for short-term gain, but did little for economic development. The construction of the New York County Courthouse at that time should have cost $250,000, but ultimately cost the taxpayers $13 million over 13 years; the famous Boss Tweed and his four principal henchmen claimed 65% of each contractor's payment (Callow, 1966, 198–206). This high proportion is a primary indicator of the degree of centralization of power created by the political party.

Big Business and Small

Some accounts have emphasized the "functionality" of urban political machines, arguing that corruptible machines provided a means by which industrialists and other economic actors could obtain needed infrastructure improvements and other politics from government, of course for a price (Merton, 1957). Indeed, the largest national corporations may well have been in an advantageous bargaining position vis-à-vis party machines. Because they operated on a national level, they were less dependent on any single local party boss. Further, their scale of operations was such that they could much more easily afford the expense associated with transacting political bribes. Their close relationship with party bosses also made it possible to use the machinery of government to erect entry barriers against competitors. These advantages served the large businesses and government well, although in the long run everyone was harmed by the diversion of economic activity into short-term consumption and under-invested small business activity.

The mutual benefits of such a cooperative relationship between big business and party machines at the turn of the 20th century in the United States are illustrated by several classic examples. The state government of California was at times virtually an extension of the Southern Pacific Railway – the Southern Pacific lobbyist openly bought and sold votes on the floor of the legislature like a stockbroker (Mowry, 1951). The New York State legislature was dominated by a coalition of party politicians known as the "Black Horse Cavalry" and the major life insurance companies (Callow, 1966). In Wisconsin, the railroads and lumber industry were in open alliance (Maxwell, 1956). The Pennsylvania machine had a close relationship with Standard Oil (Tarbell, 1904).

However cozy the relationship between big business and party bosses, smaller and local businesses were greatly threatened and inhibited by the uncertainties and transaction costs imposed by the party system. Uncertainty existed in part because of the rapid and unstable coalition formation within and between parties. Shifting coalitions among ward bosses could result in a new administration, with the subsequent wholesale replacement of governmental officials by supporters of the new coalition. A business firm's agreement with one administration would inevitably need to be renegotiated with the incoming officials.

Furthermore, even within a given administration, bribed politicians did not always "stay bought": ex post opportunism was a severe problem. There was a tendency for political actors to renege on bargains if a higher bidder came along (Steffens, 1904, 78–80). Because the two-party system was highly competitive (hence the need for patronage-paid precinct workers), politicians had no long-term incentive to develop a reputation for "trustworthiness" that would then keep them from opportunistic reneging on corrupt agreements. In contrast, politically stable autocrats sometimes tied their own hands by creating merit-based, long-term civil services (Lapuente, 2010).

Small business paid the greatest costs in resources, uncertainty, and threat to property rights. State and local governments had the authority to pass strict building and health codes – perhaps so strict that no profitable business could operate legally. This made payoff to the party organization a mandatory cost of doing business (Steffens, 1904).

Another favorite and commonly used method to wield the political power of the party machine was the threat of a "strike bill." This bill would be so detrimental to a corporation or business that it would be induced to pay large sums to "put the strike bill to sleep." The strike bill was also known as "macing," as in the Philadelphia case in which a group of politicians formed a new streetcar line with sufficient franchises to drive existing lines out of business. The politicians either required the existing lines to buy a franchise or to bribe them to stop the competing franchise legislation (Steffens, 1904, 156). Macing increased uncertainty to local business and diminished the payoff to long-term investments.

Progressive Reform
The close relationship between big business and party bosses became the primary target first of the Populist revolt and then Progressive reformers. The Populist revolt of 1896 had little impact on government, but the Progressive movement sponsored a series of reforms that changed the nature of the relationship between big business and the government and ultimately created a set of institutions that guaranteed property rights and contract enforcement and boosted the long-term benefits of investment and entrepreneurship.

The Progressives promised to weaken the power of the party bosses. Instituting primary elections eliminated the nominating power of the bosses, greatly reducing the obligations of elected officials to the bosses. Some positions were shifted from elective to appointive, and some of the elective positions were made nonpartisan. At-large elections bypassed the neighborhood power of ward bosses (Schiesl, 1977).

Civil service reform deprived party bosses of their army of precinct workers and thus of their ability to leverage control over bureaucratic behavior. A police officer protected by civil service tenure could not be required to protect party supporters and hassle party opponents with the same expectation of success. The Progressive Era was fully established when police (Fogelson, 1977), social work (Scott, 1965), and teaching (Tyack, 1974) started the transition to professionalization, which created a wholly new set of incentives for expert bureaucrats, putting them at odds with hierarchical control in general and party bosses in particular. Reformers in city after city put in place elaborate systems of financial accountability and neutral procedures for making key economic regulatory decisions (Dahlberg, 1966). These reforms were obvious signals of credible commitment from government to economic actors – but not every municipality succeeded in committing to reform in the same way.

Victor LaPuente has provided evidence showing that at least two institutional reforms could signal an irreversible commitment. One was an independent civil service commission, which had the effect of protecting civil service workers from arbitrary or politicized pressures coming from politicians in the council or the mayor's office. The other effective institutional technique was the city manager form of government. The city manager charter reduced city council members to amateurs, weakened the mayor to the position of council chair, and placed most day-to-day business in the hands of the technical manager, operating (often for very long periods) with an ideology of service to the city's residents (Lapuente, 2010).

LaPuente's data indicate that, although both city manager governments and civil service commissions are effective in creating a sense of bureaucratic protection from the demands and attacks of political figures, they are in fact substitutes for each other, rather than complements. That is, cities with city manager institutions have a sufficiently strong enough reputation for political neutrality that they do not need to bind the city manager's hands with the machinery of independent civil service commissions. A case in point is the first city manager of Austin, Texas, who knew that employees were expecting wholesale firings to accompany imposition of the new city council structure and the new form of government. "Realizing their fear, the manager immediately started to build up an atmosphere of stability that would permit employees to put their energies into work instead of into worry" (Stone, Price, & Stone, 1940, 109). Frant (1993) also argues that the purpose of the civil service commission is not only to insulate city bureaucrats from political influence but also to limit the efforts of mayors and key politicians to entrench themselves in power.

The impacts of Progressive reform were not intended to be political only, nor were they. Rauch offers evidence that reformed cities were more likely to make long-term investments in infrastructure. Rauch interprets this conclusion as "showing that professionalization of the state bureaucracy lengthens the period that public decision makers are willing to wait to realize the benefits of expenditures" (1995, 977–978).

CONCLUSION: COMMITMENT AND MORAL HAZARD

The evidence from central banking, comparative regulation, and Progressive municipal reform suggests that delegation to bureaucracies can solve time-inconsistent credible commitment problems. Such delegation insulates critical decisions from the vagaries of political forces. In the North and Weingast version of the credible commitment problem, it was the "ruler" (e.g., the autocratic Stuart kings) who faced a time-inconsistency problem – after all, in an autocracy, one person's will is sufficient to undermine contract enforcement or undermine the rule of law. However, analogous problems exist in a democracy. It is politicians who are tempted to intervene in monetary policy or regulatory policy for short-term electoral gain. The implications for democratic theory of this potential for intervention are substantial. The point is certainly not antidemocratic. As noted by Bertelli and Whitford, independent bureaucracies are *more likely* in a democracy. Ironically, perhaps, there is a complementarity between democracy and the creation of agencies that are credibly constrained from democratic decision making. As Majone points out,

The commitment problem is further aggravated by the fact that in collective decision making there are many possible majorities, whose respective preferences need not be consistent. Again, since "political property rights" are attenuated – a legislature cannot bind a subsequent legislature and a government cannot commit another government – public policies are always vulnerable to reneging and thus credibility. (Majone, 1997, 153)

In nations with a higher degree of politicization, as measured by democratization, the political system complements its majority-rule institutions with institutions that are insulated from the majority. "Thus, delegation – a non-majoritarian strategy ...– attempts to restrain majority rule by placing public authority in the hands of officials who have limited or no direct accountability to either political majorities or minorities" (Majone, 1997, 160).

The three vignettes in the preceding section all characterize "the principal's moral hazard" – that the principal could make herself better off by convincing another player that she cannot choose her preferred alternative. Another example is the FHLBB, discussed in the opening pages of this chapter. As became apparent by the 1970s, the FHLBB was the target of political pressure that undermined its ability to perform the functions for which it was created under the Hoover administration.

The question asked in the next chapter is how systematic are these efforts to undermine the bureaucracy. Is there any reason to believe that members of Congress, for example, find themselves consistently in situations in which pursuit of their goals leads to inferior outcomes? How widespread is the need for delegation to bureaucracies to reduce the range of inefficient political action?

4

Political Moral Hazard and Bureaucratic Autonomy

From the redistributive societies of ancient Egyptian dynasties through the slavery system of the Greek and Roman world to the medieval manor, there was persistent tension between the ownership structure which maximized the rents to the ruler (and his group) and an efficient system that reduced transaction costs and encouraged growth.

– Douglass North (1981, 25)

BRACKED

May 13, 2005, was known as "BRAC Friday" around the country, as the Pentagon revealed the selection of 33 major military installations to be closed. These closings, together with significant reductions at 29 other bases, would result in a net loss of more than 10,000 military positions and 18,000 civilian positions. Many of the bases had a Cold War mission; others were just outdated or had missions that could be accomplished more effectively elsewhere. The Department of Defense (DoD) regarded these closures as a boon to operational efficiency and essential to its goal of shifting resources in such a way as to get the most national security benefits for the buck. With the security challenges posed by 9/11, wars being waged in Iraq and Afghanistan, and threats from Iran, North Korea, and other hot spots, providing an adequate level of national security required the efficient use of every dollar.

Legislators saw these base closings differently from the DoD. One base scheduled for closing was Portsmouth Naval Shipyard in Maine. Senator Olympia Snowe of Maine, not someone known for purple prose, called the recommendation a "travesty and a strategic blunder of epic proportions on the part of the Defense Department" (CNN, 2005). Other bases scheduled to be shut down were Ellsworth Air Force Base in South Dakota and Pascagoula

Naval Station in Mississippi; legislators from these locations were equally vehement in their opposition to the plan.

Base closings are an example of political moral hazard: the incentives for political actors to take actions that aggregate to inefficient outcomes. National security is the classic example of a public good. Effective protection against external and terrorist threats is non-exclusionary – everyone gets the benefits of an effective national security apparatus if anyone does. Although the benefits of national security go to all, the costs of closing useless military bases are local. The loss of jobs and contracts hurts the pocketbooks of everyone in the vicinity of a base closing. As a result, the political pressure to protect those jobs and contracts is overwhelming. No Maine legislator could afford to support a base closing in Maine, even of bases that diverted millions of dollars from the effective provision of national security. The same was true for legislators in other areas where bases were to be closed.

One might think that these legislators, all of whom professed a profound patriotism, could make a pitch like the following to their constituents: "We all want a strong defense against threats from abroad; we all need to do the patriotic thing and support our Defense Department when it can more effectively protect our communities by spending money on missions outside our state and congressional district." But the political pressure to represent the parochial interests of constituents evidently trumps a patriotic concern with effective national defense. This form of moral hazard is built into the structure of Congress. From the standpoint of a local legislator, federal dollars wasted on useless bases are more important than dollars wisely allocated on programs that the DoD deems essential for the fight against terror.

Base closing can be seen as a classic n-person prisoners' dilemma game (Hardin, 1971). Each legislative district would prefer to have an effective national security system and in particular would like to close useless bases in *other* parts of the country. However, each district has a dominant strategy to protect its own bases, however useless. If other useless bases are protected, then cutting one naval shipyard is hardly going to guarantee an effective defense. And if other useless bases are protected, then a high level of national security is guaranteed, and the country could surely absorb the costs of the naval shipyard, which local residents (alone) rationalize as being essential. No matter what happens in the rest of the country, the marginal political cost of closing a base is greater than the marginal benefit from enhanced provision of the public good.

Here, clearly, is an example of political moral hazard. The problem is not (or not just) due to the perverse preferences of bureaucratic subordinates. The Department of Defense had repeatedly asked Congress to close bases that impeded its ability to provide national security for the nation as a whole. But the logic behind normal legislative logrolling was too compelling: the parochial incentives to keep inefficient bases open were too strong. A military budget that allocates money to military bases is one in which a legislator's vote can easily be obtained by trading with other legislators who are equally dependent on support for their own military bases. The morally hazardous preferences of legislators are thus institutionalized in the logrolled, parochialized military budget.

So if the incentive to protect one's own was so strong, how did these base closings ever take place? As we discuss later in this chapter, the closing of military bases required extraordinary legislative procedures – procedures that aimed at credible commitment through delegation. The theme of this chapter is that the domain of credible commitment problems – problems with solutions that require bureaucratic delegation and some degree of autonomy – go well beyond central banking and the other issues discussed in the previous chapter. Instead, there are numerous well-understood reasons to expect *normal* legislative processes to be costly to the Republic – and bureaucratic autonomy to be part of the solution – in other important government decisions such as fiscal choices like military spending.

This chapter reviews three of these reasons for political moral hazard – the condition in which political actors face incentives that are inconsistent with social efficiency. They are the biased representation of group interests discussed by Olson (1965), majority-rule "chaos" (McKelvey, 1976), and the logical problems associated with allocating jointly produced benefits analyzed by Holmström (1982). Each of these sources of political moral hazard provides reason to suspect that the pursuit of normal electoral incentives results in clear inefficiencies such as those portrayed by politicians protecting useless military bases. The point of this chapter is that the problem of credible commitment is general and systemic, rather than rare or unusual.

These systemic failings of normal majority politics offer good reasons to reexamine the role of bureaucrats. Clearly, to the extent that political interests promote inefficiency, then aligning bureaucratic interests with those of their political masters does nothing to solve the underlying source of inefficiency. Making Defense Department planners responsive to the electoral incentives of legislators does not help close inefficient bases. On the contrary, having Defense Department planners who can accurately assess the contribution of military bases – independently of political pressures from legislators – is essential, especially given tight budgets. The argument generalizes broadly: to the extent that politicians have incentives that are misaligned with social efficiency, then bureaucratic experts can contribute the most by checking, rather than implementing, those perverse incentives.

SYSTEMATIC BIAS IN REPRESENTATION: THE OLSON ARGUMENT

Not every group of citizens with a shared interest in public policy is equally effective in advancing its cause. Even in a small, local governmental unit such as a school district, it is costly for citizens with shared interests to identify each other, to organize themselves as a political force, and to have an impact on the school board or other governmental decision makers. The reason is that any benefits from collective action, achieved by costly and dedicated efforts by activists, are equally available to free-riders – citizens who may share the same public education preferences, but contribute nothing to the shared effort of guaranteeing that those preferences are heard. The costs of attending meetings, stuffing envelopes, and even just identifying and voting for preferred candidates can be substantial. On the one hand, an individual may realize that, if other citizens do enough work, then success will probably come even if he or she stays at home. On the other hand, if few others are putting in the effort, then the individual's effort may be pointless. The incentives for free-riding on collective action are powerful.

It is on distributional questions that biased representation of interests is most likely to be the rule. A classic example is milk price supports (Frohlich & Oppenheimer, 1978). An increase in milk price supports takes money from milk consumers and puts it in the hands of milk producers. But milk consumers are much more numerous than milk producers, and each consumer has only a low-level stake in understanding milk price supports or lobbying legislators to reduce those supports. Milk producers, in contrast, tend to regard the provision of milk price supports as a make-or-break issue and are very knowledgeable on the subject. What is more, a selective incentive motivates producers to contribute to the political groups that lobby: producers have to pay marketing organizations in order to get their milk to market, and some of these payments to marketing cooperatives are directed, ultimately, to the lobbying effort in Washington. The net result is that legislators hear the voice of milk producers loud and clear, and that voice is the more compelling because of the echoing silence coming from milk consumers.

Biased representation often affects regulatory issues as well. The typical regulatory issue pits concentrated industry influences against a diffuse consumer interest. Although "watchdog" groups may attempt, with limited resources, to take on industrial lobbyists, "client politics" emerges when industry's benefits are concentrated and costs dispersed: "client politics produces *regulatory legislation*" characterized by producer dominance (Wilson, 1980, 369; emphasis added). Wilson's quote shifts responsibility to "legislation" with good reason: the blandishments of clients are most compelling to legislators, not bureaucrats.

A similar bias extends to base closings. Those interested in keeping a base open are passionate and geographically concentrated – the best possible configuration for leveraging a member of Congress. The general public's interest in the efficient use of resources for national defense is diffuse, low key, and mostly uninformed about the issue – a configuration that members of Congress can safely disregard.

Representative Bureaucracy

Bureaucracy has long been recognized as a potential corrective for biased legislative representation. Because bureaucrats do not have to be reelected, they do not necessarily have to cater to the interest groups that are most likely to have an impact on the politician's fate. Because bureaucrats aspire to a career in the bureaucracy, they can take a more long-run perspective, "representing" future generations' interest in (for example) controlling global warming (Bowen, 2008). And because bureaucracies are part of a national bureaucracy, they may be more responsive to national (rather than local) constituencies.

The idea of representative bureaucracy has been explored in schools. Meier, Polinard, and Wrinkle (2000) show that representation of Latinos by Latino teachers in Texas schools has a great impact on the number of Latino students taking and passing Advanced Placement exams and in scores on SAT and ACT exams. Similarly, Meier, Stewart, and England (1991, 169) show that representation by black teachers has a negative impact on the assignment of black students to special needs programs and a positive impact on black student admission to gifted programs. They conclude, "The key to finding service distributions that *reflect underclass* or electoral influences is bureaucratic discretion" (172; emphasis added).

Not only can bureaucracies represent unrepresented groups but they can also directly address a bias in representation by helping constituencies organize themselves to serve as the Olsonian political entrepreneur. Carpenter describes how the U.S. Postal Service coordinated the efforts of farm populations to demand heavily subsidized postal service via Rural Free Delivery (Carpenter, 2001, 132). In the 1960s, the Office of Equal Opportunity felt that its mission was to facilitate the organization of low-income constituencies that had been ignored by elective officials (R. M. Kramer, 1969). In these and other cases, bureaucracies may be thought of as representing a constituency different from the electoral body, potentially correcting for Olsonian biases in the electoral system.

MAJORITY-RULE STABILITY AND INSTABILITY

The desirable characteristics of majority rule, as a preference aggregation rule, are rendered suspect in multidimensional settings, because majority rule is unstable, unpredictable, and arbitrary. This instability means that normal electoral incentives lead to inefficiencies – and that the credible commitment problem is systemic, not unusual.

The fundamental problem caused by majority rule's instability is the lack of a core in multiple dimensions. Whereas one coalition may prefer I to II and a different majority may prefer II to III, a third majority may prefer III to I. Any of the three possible choices would be a violation of majority rule. Majority rule suffers from incoherence generated by intransitive choices.

The base-closing example, like similar examples in trade policy, tax policy, and agricultural subsidies, is a form of a "divide the dollar" game. In each case, there is no logical stopping place for majority-rule coalition formation, nor is there any uniquely legitimized "majority-rule winner": there is no core. Every

TABLE 4.1: *Allocative Politics Is Unstable Politics*

	A	B	C	D	E
PROPOSAL I (SQ)	$100	$100	$100	$100	$100
PROPOSAL II (DoD)	$120	$120	$120	$0	$0
PROPOSAL III	$140	$40	$60	$50	$50

possible distribution of the benefits can lose by majority vote to an alternative division of the benefits.

For example, assume there are five equal-sized legislative districts (or clusters of legislators), given by A through E; each contains a military base that currently receives $100 million. This is the status quo (SQ) distribution. The Defense Department would like to close the bases in Districts D and E (because they are out of date and nonproductive), while moderately increasing DoD funding to bases in Districts A, B, and C. This is given as the DoD proposal, Proposal II in Table 4.1.

What would the will of the majority be?

With the DoD proposal as the motion on the floor, groups A, B, and C could propose a successful bill that saved the military bases in their three districts, providing funding of $40 million for each of the three bases. To keep the proposal revenue neutral, the costs could be spread to a losing minority. As long as each legislator votes her district's economic interests, then the DoD proposal beats the status quo by a 3–2 vote.

One might argue that Proposal II represents the majority will, but that is not the case. Consider Proposal III. Proposal III restores half the money for D and E and gives extra money to A, at the expense of B and C. It would presumably get the votes of A, D, and E against Proposal II.

However, at this point, all the legislators but A would prefer the status quo to Proposal III. The DoD proposal beats the SQ, Proposal III beats the DoD proposal, and the SQ beats Proposal III – each proposed distribution losing by majority rule to the next in the cycle.

Although this example may not be particularly realistic, it illustrates that every divide-the-dollar proposal is vulnerable to another proposal preferred by a majority coalition; at the same time, every proposal could be reached by majority rule given the appropriate agenda of alternatives to be voted on – including inefficient proposals. Majority-rule intransitivity (or majority-rule cycling) is the source of political moral hazard that calls for a special role for delegated bureaucracies.

"Disequilibrium, or the potential that the status quo be upset, is the characteristic feature of politics" (Riker, 1980, 443). This is not a desirable feature; majority rule must be mistrusted and suspected of illegitimacy when any policy chosen can only be viewed as an arbitrary choice from among equally illegitimate alternatives. "The possibility that social choice by voting produces inconsistent results raises deep questions about democracy. Can the democratic ideal be attained if the method used to attain it produces confusion?" (Riker, 1982, 18).

Stability can be achieved through institutional modifications such as agenda control, but it is not clear whether the outcomes produced by this means are more legitimate merely because they are favored by the new institutional rule. As Riker points out, rules themselves can be altered by majority rule, so presumably the rules are themselves "not in equilibrium.... Thus the only difference between values [preferences] and institutions is probably a longer process [of instability]" (Riker, 1980, 445).

Distributional fiscal policies, like trade policy or military base protection, have as many dimensions as there are districts. These issues invite logrolling or vote trading, in which support for others' distributional benefits is traded for support for one's own benefits. Further, logrolling has been shown to imply majority-rule intransitivity. That is, the presence of vote trading in a legislature is indicative of the absence of a core (Oppenheimer, 1975; Schwartz, 1981).

In the game of musical chairs that constitutes trade, tax, or appropriations politics, the distribution of benefits at the end of the game has little more to command respect than those other distributions that fail. The implication, of course, is that the legislation that is produced in multidimensional cases and sent to the bureaucracy for implementation is the more or less arbitrary result of an incoherent process. In these cases, bureaucratic care in implementing legislative mandates cannot be more legitimate than the chaotic process that produced the mandate.

Credible Commitment and Tariff Policy

Majority-rule instability is of course a major concern as regards credible commitment to property rights and contract enforcement. Tax policy, regulatory policy, and trade policy are examples of issues that investors and entrepreneurs would like to have set so they can engage in long-term planning. If a new majority coalition could theoretically pass confiscatory taxes or impose tariffs that undo entire industries, then unconstrained majority rule could be a major threat to economic development. The tension is that making regulatory and distributional judgments by majority rule is inconsistent with the kind of stability in the regulatory playing field that seems to be essential to economic growth. One possible answer is insulating policy making from the chaos of majority rule.

Consider the important example of trade policy. For many years, the trade bills that periodically worked their way through Congress were debilitating exercises in the arbitrariness and instability of majority rule. For any given distribution of trade benefits, there was always another distribution of benefits that some majority coalition would prefer and could enact. In one of his first books, a young E. E. Schattschneider portrayed the frantic and chaotic logrolling in

Congress leading up to passage of the Smoot-Hawley Tariff (Schattschneider, 1935).

The means by which the Smoot-Hawley Tariff of 1929 became law were especially disturbing: the outcome was widely judged to be as incoherent as the process that generated it. Retaliation against the tariff drastically reduced U.S. exports, and the onset of the Great Depression in the wake of its passage left many politicians and voters convinced that the tariff was a major contributor to the poor state of the economy. The widespread public disgust with Congress's tariff policies resulted in a movement toward bureaucratic delegation.

Created in 1916, the United States Tariff Commission was meant to augment the vagaries of an unstable coalition process in which narrow legislative reelection interests could be injected into trade negotiations. The 1934 Reciprocal Trade Agreements Act, however, resulted in "an unprecedented transfer of power" to the executive (Goldstein, 1989, 64). The evaluation of most experts is that bureaucratic decision making exercised through the Tariff Commission was a marked improvement over legislative tariff making; with the initiative in the hands of the Tariff Commission, a postwar regime of low tariffs encouraged economic expansion. Goldstein (1989, 59) writes unequivocably, "If Congress had not relinquished tariff-making authority, trade liberalization would never have succeeded. And of course, *the key to bureaucratic success is insulation of the trade commission from the political pressures coming from Congress*" (emphasis added; see also Milner and Rosendorff, 1997). Here clearly, the success of post–World War II trade liberalization was dependent on a bureaucracy that did not act as the agent of congressional reelection strategies. Even a supporter of congressional authority like Senator Arthur Vandenberg later agreed that legislating tariffs had been a failure, lacking "any element of economic science or validity" (Goldstein, 1989, 65).

But is there any systematic empirical evidence that demonstrates the effect of bureaucratic independence? Indeed, De Groot, Linders, Rietveld, and Subramanian (2004) show that regulatory regimes help explain the expansion of trade benefits. Commercial interests evidently (and wisely) worry that political actors might succumb to the temptation to raise tariff barriers, the better to advance their political interests. A stronger regulatory regime is evidently seen as a source of protection against that behavior. In fact, De Groot and colleagues' paper shows that a one standard deviation improvement in perception of regulatory quality increases trade by between 16% to 26%. Perceived regulatory quality has been similarly linked to increased foreign direct investment (Globerman & Shapiro, 2003), productivity (R. E. Hall & Jones, 1999), and per capita income (Kaufman, Kraay, & Zoido-Lobatón, 2002).

Regulatory Politics: Clean Air, Dirty Coal

Regulatory politics, like distributional politics, is typically multidimensional by nature. It is normally the case that multiple differences among producer groups or consumer groups allow coalitions to shift in surprising (and often debilitating) ways. A case in point is the 1970s debate over air pollution. Congress set out to revise the New Source Performance Standards (NSPS) in 1979. "Rather than consign the regulation of new power plants to an independent expert agency of the kind idealized by New Deal theory, Congress tried to play a more aggressive role in policymaking" (Ackerman, 1981, 3).

For example, one might think that all coal producers shared an interest in avoiding strict regulation. However, there existed a basic division between high-pollution eastern coal interests and cleaner western coal, which introduced a dimension of conflict *within* the coal producers. Western coal interests preferred regulation that would allow coal consumers to reduce production costs simply by buying cheaper western coal.

Another way to reduce pollution that Congress discussed, in addition to buying western coal, was the requirement to use "scrubber" technology. Through the use of chemical scrubbers, utilities could greatly reduce overall levels of sulfur. However, the process of scrubbing was expensive, and the utilities could reach the same standard just by using low-sulfur coal from the west. Parochial interests broke out in Congress, with western legislators supporting a policy of achieving emissions standards by whatever means the utilities found cheapest, while eastern coal legislators wanted to insist on the use of scrubbers because their universal use deprived clean western coal of its competitive edge.

Environmentalists felt that encouraging western coal development would lead to more development in environmentally sensitive areas. They also felt that the combined use of scrubbers and low-sulfur coal would be better than having one policy or the other. The coalition succeeded in part because of a low level of understanding of the interaction between low-sulfur coals and scrubbers (Ackerman, 1981, 118).

Environmentalists also might have felt that just imposing a numerical standard for the amount of pollutants in the coal was not sufficient, because this number could and would be lowered by new politicians after the next election: future politicians might not be as committed to clean air as the current Congress. In contrast, requiring the purchase of scrubbers, expensive as they were, constituted a better credible commitment to long-term emissions reductions, which is what the environmentalists sought. For these reasons, environmentalists joined the eastern coal interests in what became known as the "clean coal/dirty air" coalition. The result was both a higher cost and smaller emissions reductions.

Ostensibly, the key to the clean air legislation was pollution reduction – not cost reduction. But the votes from producers and utility companies were just as determinative as environmentalists' votes. And once again, the coalitional result was negative. The extra profits from the dirty coal producers were lower than the costs due to pollution and the losses from the more expansive use of clean, western air.

As Ackerman points out, if this process had taken place in an institution other than Congress, the clean-coal/dirty-air coalition would never have resulted. If the cost-reduction policy had been fought out before an expert and cost-conscious agency *insulated from direct congressional intervention*, eastern coal would have left its coalition with the environmentalists to rejoin its friends in the utility industry (Ackerman, 1981, 118–119).

POLITICAL MORAL HAZARD AND DISTRIBUTION

The previous two sections have analyzed well-known reasons for the presence of political moral hazard. Because of the biased articulation of interests before legislatures and the instability and illegitimacy of majority-rule logrolling, democratic politicians are perversely incentivized, resulting in outcomes that all can agree are suboptimal – trade wars, agricultural subsidies, politically protected military bases and weapons contracts. The evidence suggests that political moral hazard is of special concern in multidimensional policy settings where interest groups are disproportionately influential and majority rule is unstable.

This part of this chapter investigates an even more sweeping reason for political moral hazard. This is an impossibility result by Holmström (1982) that shows that the distributive benefits generated by teams of bureaucrats cannot be distributed to meet minimal expectations of stability, efficiency, and full allocation. We argue that this result implies that moral hazard is more sweeping than previously expected; indeed, it is *inevitable* when distributing the benefits of team production.

Team Production and Distribution

For example, many government benefits are the product of interactive teams of agents – fire departments produce benefits from fire safety, teachers transfer knowledge, the military produces national security. These team production settings have been the object of study by the economist Bengt Holmström. He has famously produced an impossibility theorem that is disturbing in its simplicity and in its implications for political moral hazard.

Imagine a group of N workers whose activities are mutually *interdependent*. That is, the marginal productivity of each member of the group is dependent on how hard each of the other members is working. As an example, the amount of benefits generated by the team may be a simple multiplicative function of each person's effort level a_i. Thus, Q (for example, the benefits generated by military bases in a three-base case) would be

$$Q = a_A * a_B * a_C$$

For concreteness, we can think of the three actors as Amy, Bill, and Celeste.

In this case, the output is zero if any one of the three actors shirks (i.e., contributes a zero effort level). If Amy shirks, the marginal productivity of the other team members drops to zero – *no matter how hard they work*! Furthermore, a low level of output cannot be attributed to any single team member; the multiplicative production function obscures the responsibility for low output.

Although Holmström conceived of this theorem as a basic picture of activity within the firm, it generalizes, of course, to any interdependent form of social production, including fighting for military bases. The multiplicative production function captures externalities that are characteristic in the production processes of many public agencies, as well as private firms. On a firefighting team, every person has a task, and if any team member fails to do that task, it will drastically limit the effectiveness of every other member of the team.

Furthermore, as we do with our second assumption of information asymmetry in Chapter 2, Holmström assumes that only aggregate production level Q, not the individual effort levels, is readily observable to an outside monitor. Thus, the production process is characterized both by *information asymmetries* and interdependence. If the crime rate goes up in a police precinct or if the response time of a firefighting team is unacceptably high, there might be a lot of recriminations among the members of the team, but it may not be easy to determine whose actions are responsible for the failure.

The members of the team must be compensated, or presumably they will shirk.[1] The benefits produced by the actions of the three agents have to be allocated among them, so that they will have a self-interested reason to continue working effectively, despite the fact that their costly individual effort levels cannot be observed. The question then becomes the following. Is it possible to distribute Q (the product of their effort or a monetized version of it) in such a way that it creates incentives for each member of the team to take the actions in equilibrium that result in the Pareto-optimal output for the team as a whole?

In other words, Holmström proposes that an allocation system should have three simple characteristics:

1. Nash equilibrium. That is, there is at least one stable outcome in which each person finds that her own self-interest is maximized, given the actions of the other two participants.

---

[1] One question about the applicability of Holmstrom's theorem is whether it applies to public agencies. Perhaps applicability is decided by whether the policy issue is relatively more distributive than ideological. The Civil Rights Act of 1964 or the Marshall Plan might be considered ideological questions; on these issues, vote decisions are driven not by the amount of taxes avoided or the amount of benefits received but by underlying beliefs. The Civil Rights Act is passed for all if it passes for one; in contrast, the Model Cities Plan could be negotiated by marginal increases and decreases in distributive benefits. Denomination in dollars for benefits means we can discuss the divisible "output" the group will divide. We note, though, that the division of "spoils" is akin to the division of costs, although the game then is to minimize the loss instead of maximize the residual.

2. Pareto optimality. The three participants should not find that there is some outcome other than the Nash equilibrium in which they would all be better off.
3. Budget balancing. The Q produced at the Nash equilibrium is exactly divided among the participants, with no excess thrown away and no deficit created from thin air.

What Holmström then demonstrates is that these three simple requirements are mutually inconsistent. Every budget-balancing Nash equilibrium will be inefficient. Put another way, every budget-balancing Pareto-optimal distribution scheme is unstable due to the self-interest of one of the participants. The implication is that there is no incentive system that can reconcile self-interest and social efficiency, as long as the team benefits are exactly divided among the team members. Moral hazard within the team will undermine efficiency as long as budget balancing is satisfied.

Assume each agent gets exactly one-third of the revenue generated by the team's efforts. When she receives only one-third of the fruits of her efforts, each agent then finds it worthwhile to work less than efficiently. Assume that staying an extra hour in the evening would cost Amy an additional $15 in effort costs. She may be able to bring an extra $30 of revenue for the team, so it would be efficient to stay late, but because she would only get one-third of the extra revenue, or $10, it would not be worth her while. In every budget-balancing distribution scheme, there is a similar tension between what is good for the individual agent and what is efficient for the team. The team is a prisoners' dilemma game.

The only way that Pareto optimality and Nash equilibrium are simultaneously satisfied is if Amy were to get *all* of the marginal revenue generated by her last unit of effort. But this is true for all the players, so each of the players must get all of the marginal revenue generated by his last effort levels. Yet, as long as their efforts jointly contribute to the production of the last unit, they cannot *each* get the last dollar generated by their joint efforts, because there is only $1 to go around. Thus, Holmström shows that efficiency cannot be guaranteed by a budget-balancing distribution of the team's product among self-interested actors:

As long as we insist on budget-balancing...we cannot achieve efficiency. Agents can cover improper actions behind the uncertainty concerning who was at fault. Since all agents cannot be penalized sufficiently for a deviation in the outcome, some agent always has an incentive to capitalize on this control deficiency. (Holmström, 1982, 327)

Budget Breaking Allows Stable, Efficient Outcomes

Holmström argues that the solution to moral hazard has to be breaking the budget-balancing criterion. Imagine that someone (the Budget Breaker, or Residual Claimant) who is *not involved* in the production of Q, obtains the rights to the residual that is generated when productive team members are (minimally) compensated from the pool of benefits Q. As long as there is such a passive repository for the residual, then it is possible to create an efficient incentive scheme.

The Budget Breaker, or Residual Claimant, knows exactly each team member's effort cost function, so she knows exactly the efficient level of Q. However, she is not able to monitor the agents to see which ones are working at an efficient level and which are not. In the absence of individual effort data, she can offer the following *group punishment incentive scheme*:

Group Punishment Incentive Scheme: each employee of the firm will be paid enough to cover his effort costs if the efficient level of production, Q, is observed. If the efficient level of production is not observed, then *no one* gets paid.

This incentive scheme, a type of joint-forcing contract, breaks budget balancing in order to reconcile stability and efficiency. It creates a Pareto-optimal Nash equilibrium for the employees – with a surplus for the Owner. It works because, with joint production, if *anyone shirks, no one gets paid*. As long as each employee's pay is greater than his effort costs, no one has an incentive to shirk. The Owner does not need to identify the shirker, as long she is willing to punish everyone alike if the Pareto suboptimal outcome (less than Q) is observed. The group punishment scheme, although draconian, eliminates the incentive for individual shirking; each individual knows that her own shirking is sufficient to eliminate the possibility of payment. The group incentive scheme supports a Nash equilibrium that is socially efficient for the team members.

As long as the value of Q is greater than the effort costs of the productive team agents, then there will be a surplus, or residual, for the Owner. The group punishment incentive scheme is designed to generate efficient effort and a residual left over for the Residual Claimant.

Separation of Ownership and Control: The Moral Hazard of Ownership

The Budget Breaker need not contribute to the productive efforts of the team members. Quite the contrary: in the interest of efficiency, she cannot! The reason is that, as a fourth team member, she and the three original team members would constitute a *budget-balanced* incentive team; there is no money coming or going outside the four of them together. What do we know about budget-balanced schemes? They cannot be stably efficient. If the Budget Breaker is interested in stable efficiency (we soon show that typically she is not), then she must remain hands off – and she must not be incorporated into the team. The role of a Budget Breaker must be to absorb nonzero residuals – *but not try to increase them*. If she succeeds in increasing her profit residuals, then it must come at a greater loss to the social product for the team.

Holmström regarded his impossibility result as explaining the existence of passive shareholders in a corporation: they absorb the profits and losses of the managers and employees of the corporation. As long as the shareholders are powerless to do anything other than to accept profits or losses, they have served the purpose of stable efficiency. But given the chance to intervene in the management of the firm, the shareholders will always trade efficiency away for greater residual profits.

For example, assume the group punishment scheme is offered and accepted by the team members. Let us say the group scheme promises to pay each team member $10 if the efficient Q, worth $50, is produced. To have a stable, efficient outcome, the Budget Breaker must receive compensation of $20.

But that is not a stable stopping point. The Owner could undermine the group compensation plan by offering one team member a larger compensation (a $15 bribe) that will be paid only if he shirks just enough to produce a team product Q that falls short of the efficient level. Then the Budget Breaker does not have to pay the other two team members anything under the terms of the group punishment incentive scheme. Her profits are $50, less the $15 bribe, or $35. As Budget Breaker, she faces her own form of moral hazard: she can increase her own profits by sabotaging Holmström's efficient incentive scheme!

We do not have to examine every possible efficient, residual-generating distribution scheme to see if there is a similar contradiction. As Eswaran and Kotwal (1984) point out in their criticism of Holmström's argument, this tension between efficiency and budget balancing is systemic. The Owner's interest in maximizing the residual will inevitably cause her to seek out ways to undermine the efficiency of the firm. The proof of this is just another application of Holmström's theorem. The three agents and the Budget Breaker are a closed system; their actions generate a level of benefits Q, and those benefits are distributed among the four of them. We know that the group punishment incentive scheme is efficient and stable – but overall those characteristics are inconsistent with budget balancing. Therefore it is the Budget Breaker, not the agents, who has an incentive to undermine stable efficiency (Eswaran & Kotwal, 1984).

The point of this example is not that the group punishment scheme is a particularly plausible scheme; the point is that the *self-interest of the Budget Breaker is necessarily at odds with the efficiency of the organization*. For every efficient incentive scheme, there must necessarily be another incentive scheme that creates a larger residual for the Budget Breaker – but an overall lower level of production. Maximization of a Budget Breaker's profits is inconsistent with efficiency.

Team Production as a Credible Commitment Problem

The problem gets worse. Even if the Owner decides for some altruistic reason *not* to undermine an efficient incentive scheme, how will the employees know that is her intention? Employees have every reason to mistrust any efficient incentive scheme offered to them, precisely because of the Owner's incentives to subvert the residual. Employees who are offered Holmström's efficient group punishment scheme may well think, "I would be willing to take this job with its group punishment scheme, because I know that it is a Nash equilibrium for each of us three team members to work as long as everyone else does so. But how can I know that the contract would be honesty administered? Why should the Budget Breaker not seek to enhance her own profits by bribing a co-worker to shirk? I must expect that a bribe – and no payment to the rest of the employees – will be the ultimate outcome; therefore, it would be stupid of me to accept the contract."

Thus, Holmström's efficient group incentive scheme does not *eliminate* moral hazard – it merely relocates it. The budget-breaking residual Owner (shareholders or the public) makes possible the elimination of moral hazard in team members by focusing the moral hazard in the person of the residual Owner herself.

Budget Breaking, Moral Hazard, and Credible Commitment

The problem of incentivizing a three-person team has become a problem in credible commitment. The Owner knows that the employees' suspicions about Owner sabotage are realistic. But her ownership of the residual is worthless if she cannot commit *not* to bribe one of the three employees, because none of them will accept the contract unless convinced that the Owner has her hands tied. The Owner would like to be able to commit to a group punishment incentive scheme (with no bribes!), because without a commitment, the default Nash equilibrium is for no worker to work at all.

The Owner may well wish to be publicly constrained from making the bribe that could potentially increase her profits; otherwise, she knows the employees will anticipate that she will make the bribe and then will converge on the zero-effort Nash equilibrium. Constraining herself ahead of time is the *only positive action* she can take to encourage efficiency in the firm. Paradoxically, the only action the Owner can take to enhance her profits is to deny herself any authority to act on her profit-maximizing motives. As in the classic credible commitment problem, the Owner can make herself better off by denying herself the authority to pursue her self-interest in setting incentives. Thus, the Eswaran and Kotwal problem is exactly the opposite of principal-agency theory – the Owner cannot be allowed to use incentives to align employee actions with her own self-interest – because her own self-interest is inevitably morally hazardous.

Our claim is that the real message of Holmström's impossibility result relates to credible commitment. To be effective, the separation of ownership from control must solve a fundamental constitutional problem of credible commitment: it must deny the residual Owner any opportunity to pursue his or her own self-interest in the politics of the team. The Budget Breaker must not only be distinct from the firm but must also be made impotent. And one of the most effective ways to make an actor impotent is to delegate her authority to someone who is known to have motivations other than profit maximization.

Separation of Budget-Breaking Ownership from Managerial Control

As usual, the simplest means of credible commitment is delegation. Consider Vickers (1985), who argues that there are widespread, systemic advantages of delegating decisions to agents with distinctly different preferences from those of the principal. Specifically, profit-maximizing shareholders benefit when they hire sales-maximizing managers to handle the firm because those managers can credibly commit to waging price wars that profit-maximizing managers would not wage. As a result, sales-maximizing managers can deter actions harmful to the profit-maximizing shareholders. Most importantly, Vickers, through yet another impossibility result, points out that such advantages for delegation *must* be present.

Consider also Gibbard (1973) and Satterthwaite (1975), who demonstrate that truth telling can virtually never be a dominant strategy in otherwise well-ordered social choice situations. In some situations, a participant has an incentive to misrepresent preferences – that is, to put into the social choice mechanism a set of preferences different from his own. Hiring a delegate to act is simply the most convincing way for that person to misrepresent his preferences. The occasions to misrepresent one's preferences are endemic and systemic, and in all such occasions the incentive to lie can be implemented by delegating to someone with different preferences.

In a third example, Falaschetti points out that prospective bondholders, suppliers, and shareholders must view with suspicion any firm in which active shareholders take a role in management of the firm – their interest in maximizing profits makes assurances as to their fair treatment of other stockholders dubious. For example, evidence from corporate bond markets indicates that the increased moral hazard of active shareholders, exercised via systems for representing shareholder rights, increases corporate financing costs in order to compensate prospective bondholders (Falaschetti, 2009, 109; Klock, Mansi, & Maxwell, 2005). Likewise, active shareholders are under more pressure to offer golden parachutes to management because parachutes are a commitment from active shareholders to managerial independence on the part of managers, who otherwise would be damaged in their negotiations with employees, suppliers, and credit-holders (Falaschetti, 2002).

In light of these insights, Besanko and Spulber, North and Weingast, and Holmström have all described one small part of a more general phenomenon: advancing one's interests by delegating authority to someone who promises not to act on her own interests. The delegation from shareholders to corporate managers makes sense of otherwise problematic empirical evidence. The next question is how well concern about the moral hazard of budget breaking transfers to the state.

Moral Hazard and the Distributive State

As North notes in the chapter epigraph, rulers and their coalitions have from the earliest times faced a moral hazard problem: "there was persistent tension between the ownership structure which maximized the rents to the ruler (and his group) and an efficient system that reduced transaction costs and encouraged growth" (North, 1981, 25). But why should that be the case? Why should the ruler always be tempted by actions that "maximize his rents" at a cost to the efficiency of the system? Why is there no invisible hand aligning the interests of the ruler with those of his subjects?

Holmström, together with Eswaran and Kotwal, provides a way to understand the inevitable divergence between efficiency and the ruler's interests. Consider the primitive state, sometimes called the "hydraulic state" because of the critical role that irrigation systems often played. These states came into existence with the development of shelters to defend and store a year's crop. The ruler delegated control of the distribution of the crop to his military, his bureaucrats, and his productive workers; disloyalty (on the part of soldiers, bureaucrats, or peasants) would result in starvation.

Consider that the ruler may rule over a number of villages. In each village, the subjects, in a team production system, produce a crop of a certain size. The ruler has a good idea about how many bushels each village should be able to produce. Perhaps tradition provides an expectation of a 50:50 sharecropping system, which motivates effort without expensive monitoring or coercion. The ruler may transform part of his share into luxury trade goods.

Now consider the last bushel of grain to be allocated between the ruler and the village. Perhaps an extra bushel to the village could improve the health and vitality of the peasants in the village and increase the size of next year's crop by a bushel and a half. However, the ruler would only get 50% of that increased production. He prefers a bushel now to 50% of a bushel and a half next year because he is better off with a larger share of a smaller pie.

The problem, as Eswaran and Kotwal note, is that, for any sharecropping scheme that induces efficient effort from the workers, there must logically exist incentive schemes that result in a larger ruler surplus, while diminishing efficiency. Whatever efficient incentive system is offered to the peasants, they are also aware that the ruler has incentives to "cheat" at the margins, to extract more than promised.

Because the perverse incentives facing the ruler are clear, the peasants may not be motivated to work at efficient levels: the myth of the "lazy peasant" results. As Eswaran and Kotwal explain, Budget Breakers may resort to direct monitoring, no matter how inefficient and costly compared to a sharecropping scheme. Monitoring leads to inefficient gamesmanship and needless coercion. It is chosen as a second-best solution to a problem of credible commitment. Because of the lack of credible commitment and the inevitable resort to costly direct monitoring and coercion, the ruler's incentives diverge from the requirements of social efficiency.

The same logic holds in other autocratic states. Many ancient rulers exhibited moral hazard by coopting peasants for the construction of their tomb. In historical China, the maintenance of ownership rights discouraged technological growth. Typically, among Stuart kings, forms of moral hazard were expropriation of wealth, creation of monopolies, and the selling of justice that served the king's interests while discouraging economic entrepreneurship and investment. In all of these settings, Holmström's impossibility result applies: rulers with ownership rights to residuals have an incentive to undermine the efficiency of the state to achieve greater short-term profits. North's observation from history tracks Holmström's theorem.

Distribution in Democratic States

Pools of benefits supplied by the state offer the same temptations to democratic politicians as to autocrats. However, democratic institutions have an advantage, compared to autocracies, to the extent that they serve to block political moral hazard, we argue, with a crucial role played by bureaucrats. The best indicator of political development is when the bureaucracy serves to enhance credible commitment instead of serving the autocrat and his needs.

Yet democratic institutions, at their best, do only a partial job of controlling political moral hazard. To the extent that democratic coalitions can dominate the flow of benefits from the provision of certain public goods, the same coalitions (factions, in Madisonian parlance) have a stake in inefficiency. That is, they may protect a resource stream coming from an out-of-date military base at the cost of an efficient national security system. Fundamentally, firms, autocracies, and democracies are the same in the light of the Holmström theorem: a plausible stake in the residual inevitably sabotages a commitment to efficiency. Bureaucrats work in teams and inevitably confront the temptation to free-ride. But their political masters confront the temptation to respond to narrow interests, to join logrolling coalitions, and to seek distributional benefits at the expense of the well-being of the republic.

MORAL HAZARD, CREDIBLE COMMITMENT, AND DELEGATION

If Chapter 3 established that credible commitment problems could be addressed by delegation (in particular, delegation to a trustee who does not share the principal's problematic preferences), Chapter 4 shows that problematic preferences systematically generate credible commitment problems and that trustee delegation may well mitigate those problems.

Credible Commitment and Base Closing

The case of base closings illustrates all three of the reasons why we might expect bureaucracy to play a role in limiting inefficiencies by credible commitment.

Clientelistic politics serve to encourage the immediate beneficiaries of military bases, while discouraging the broad public's involvement. Majority rule decision making undermines the stability and significance of legislative decisions, while affording those with agenda control favored positions to protect bases arbitrarily. And the bases create a reservoir of benefits that motivate morally hazardous actions by those who can stake a claim to them.

Congressional inability to deal with base closings shows the importance of delegation. The problem in any social organization is not finding an efficient incentive system; the problem is finding an efficient incentive system that members believe will not be subverted by those with a stake in the residual. For example, members of the Armed Services Committee try to determine the bases the Pentagon should close. Arnold argues that this committee is driven by the interests of those representing military districts and is unrepresentative of societal interests. Seeing military employment as a political asset, committee members diminish the probability of base closings in their districts without regard to the effect on the budget and overall military capacity. Because of the decentralized decision-making process in Congress, the Armed Services Committee can block the full House or Senate from deciding on base closings (Arnold, 1979, 113–127).

But the case of base closings also illustrates the possibilities of tying the hands of politicians through delegation. During the first Bush administration, pressure from the White House forced Congress to recognize its own inability to mandate the base closings necessary for an effective military. The problem was analogous to that presented by congressional tariff legislation, and the solution was analogous: creating a special commission insulated from congressional reelection. "The conventional wisdom holds that base closures end congressional careers, and few legislators are willing to sacrifice themselves" (Mayer, 1995, 396). This was a case in which Congress itself recognized that its reelection desires were at war with its institutional responsibilities. Its members realized that Congress would look irresponsible, during a period of record-breaking and destructive deficits, if it allowed the reelection goals of its members to waste defense resources.

Despite these very good reasons for closing outmoded bases, the parochial interests of politicians prevented closings until a new procedure was created – one that, once initiated, deprived legislators of an effective way to protect their districts. The solution was for members of Congress to delegate away their ability to protect their parochial interests in outdated military bases. They created a commission composed of nine independent members that had the power to modify a list of base closings initially proposed by the Secretary of Defense. The commission's modified proposal went to the president, who approved it on the condition that it could be voted up or down as a whole. Congress had 45 days to vote the whole list down; if it did not do so in that time, the closings went into effect.

Congress's options at this point were severely limited. The legislation would not allow them to subtract bases from the secretary's list. This prohibition was crucial, because the normal process would be one of logrolling – trading support with other district legislators to save a subset of the bases. "[T]he base-closing process would have failed if legislators could easily overturn the list of closure or subtract individual bases from the list. To insure success, members had to give up their review power" (Mayer, 1995, 295). Congress as a whole could overturn the entire list, but the list was carefully constructed to guarantee that majority support was there for the list as a whole.

The military base closing commission was an attempt to delegate responsibility to an agency beyond the reach of Congress's strongest and most authentic parochial impulses. As Mayer described the process,

Legislators agreed to restrict their own parochial tendencies by delegating authority to the Independent Commission and granting it the power to make and effectively enforce decisions on the group (saying, in effect, 'stop us before we vote again'....The most important element of the process is that Congress retained no effective means of stopping the secretary of defense from shutting down any base the commission wanted to close. (Mayer, 1995, 394–395)

From the congressional perspective, this delegation was a success. Individual members had adequate opportunity to mount a symbolic attempt to save bases in their districts – an electorally essential but losing battle – and Congress as a whole was able to contribute to the more effective use of military appropriations. No member of Congress lost his or her seat because of the closing of the military bases. This outcome was accomplished not by creating the kind of ideal agent visualized by the "congressional dominance" approach – one that is demonstrably responsive to Congress's every reelection-motivated demand – but rather by creating a kind of perverse agent that was designed to be insulated from Congress and to deny the particular reelection demands of its members.

The Budget Supercommittee

The fate of the Supercommittee in the fall of 2011 further illustrates the burdensome incentives carried by members of Congress. The Supercommittee, like the base closing commission, was an attempt to delegate authority in such a way that the problematic incentives would be rendered powerless by means of delegation.

Created by the Budget Control Act of 2011, the Supercommittee was charged with cutting $1.2 trillion of discretionary spending cuts over 10 years; if this goal was not met, deep and unpleasant cuts, including $600 billion in defense cuts, would automatically go into effect. The automatic sequestration was not designed to be good policy – in fact, it was designed to be so unpleasant that it would motivate the Supercommittee to reach a better solution. It was intended to commit the Supercommittee to serious budget cutting, while eliminating the distributive budgetary negotiations that had brought about the budgetary crisis in the first place.

Was it really credible, however, that Congress would allow its hands to be tied by the legal requirement of sequestration, in the event of a Supercommittee failure? A group of pro-defense advocates undermined the Supercommittee's motivation by reminding everyone that what Congress could do, it could undo. As Sen. John McCain said, "We'll do everything we can to prevent [the trigger] from being implemented. You can't bind future Congresses" (Rogin, 2011).

Sovereign power engenders a form of powerlessness in an inability to credibly commit. Sen. McCain was correct: Congress in the summer of 2011 could not bind Congress in 2012, if the latter wanted to pass legislation to get around the sequestration of Defense Department funds.

The failure of the Supercommittee to do serious budget cutting, thereby allowing the sequestration to take effect, did not cause much of a reaction in the investment community. The reason is probably that, looking down the game tree in the fall of 2011, the investment community anticipated the outcome that in fact occurred – the sequestration trigger was not credible enough to induce a superior budgetary outcome. Investors expected the Supercommittee to fail to respond to the sequestration trigger, and they were correct.

More Independence for the Food and Drug Administration – or Less?

The failure to address credible commitment has efficiency consequences – no matter how perfectly political masters reproduce their own incentives in their bureaucratic agents. As an example, consider political scientist Dan Carpenter's appeal for greater independence of the Food and Drug Administration (FDA). The occasion was the decision by the Obama administration to block the FDA's decision to permit pharmacists to sell Plan B One-Step contraceptives to minors. This was the first time in the history of the FDA that the administration had overruled any FDA drug approval decision.

No matter what you may think of the contraceptive issue, the danger of this precedent is apparent. The decision had electoral consequences for President Obama, and one can hardly imagine that his decision was not motivated by those expected consequences. For the first time, electoral consequences replaced scientific and professional considerations for a major FDA decision. As Carpenter notes, "A radical pro-business secretary could now, in principle, bypass the clinical trial system and the FDA approval process and decide to approve a drug. A different secretary, one distrustful of the pharmaceutical industry, could stop a drug despite strong scientific support behind it" (Carpenter, 2011).

Investors, drug companies, and consumers would all be harmed by the increased uncertainty and risk posed by injecting the vagaries of electoral politics into the regulation of drugs. And if a new president could unilaterally change drug approvals, then why would shifting legislative coalitions refrain from using the power of the purse to prod the FDA and advance their electoral prospects? Drug regulation as distributive politics – it is a prospect that is surprisingly easy to imagine in the contemporary political landscape, in which regulators are not to be trusted and accountability to elected officials is the primary desideratum.

To protect against this prospect, Carpenter proposes a Fed-style insulation from political considerations – with a longer term of office for the FDA Commissioner and removal only for cause. The FDA would be moved out of Department of Health and Human Services (HHS) and become an independent agency, thereby removing the secretary of HHS from the picture. Perhaps ironically, the opposite is more likely to occur: the Fed is more likely to lose some of its autonomy than the FDA is to gain it.

CONCLUSION: MORAL HAZARD IN POLITICS

This chapter has examined a series of reasons why democratic politicians in unconstrained pursuit of political agendas can impose costs on everyone. Majority-rule instability in tax, tariff, and regulatory policy can undermine the confidence of investors and the boldness of entrepreneurs. Concern that competitors have special access to legislators can discourage any firm. The claims of interest groups and their political sponsors to streams of benefits coming from government can diminish efficiency.

What role do bureaucrats play in this process? Much of the time, as predicted by principal-agency theory, bureaucrats are incentivized to facilitate the pursuit of the political strategies of their political masters. Department of Agriculture scientists accede to the demands of members of Congress as to the allocation of research funds, with few questions or challenges (Law & Tonon, 2006; Law, Tonon, & Miller, 2008). The Department of Education's unusually politicized higher ranks decide the distribution of educational benefits (D. E. Lewis, 2008b). The Iraqi occupation in 2003 replaced professionals with young Republican election staffers, who were tasked with regulating financial markets, administering electric utilities, and contracting for rebuilding – and did an inadequate, politicized job of it (Chandrasekaran, 2006; Ricks, 2006). These examples are not random errors; they are the systematic manifestations of politicians responding to moral hazard and using their control over bureaucratic incentives to enlist agency actions in that morally hazardous behavior.

If some agencies are shaped as the means of obtaining advantage for politicians, other agencies are insulated from the political pressures that constrain their peers. The International Trade Commission has maintained a basically free-trade policy of the sort that would not last a year on the floor of the Senate. The National Aeronautics and Space Administration has an unusually nonpolitical elite cadre and (with exceptions) protects its scientists in the objectivity of their research. The FDA has turned a strong reputation for scientific integrity into a position of authority in pharmaceutical regulation (Carpenter, 2010).

If bureaucrats can either be subject to the constraints imposed by politicians or may establish a position of autonomy, it is important to understand why we see sometimes one and sometimes the other. Where does discretion come from? If politicians are ambitious, why would they give up valuable policy discretion to bureaucrats? We cannot assume that politicians turn suddenly altruistic – giving up authority to bureaucrats because of a desire to do the right thing. If politicians were committed to doing the right thing, then improvements in a variety of fronts could be expected, with or without bureaucratic discretion. This question is addressed in Chapter 5, in which we offer an explanation for bureaucratic delegation.

5

"Above Politics"

The Separation of Powers and Bureaucratic Autonomy

What is government itself but the greatest of all reflections on human nature? If men were angels, no government would be necessary. If angels were to govern men, neither external nor internal controls on government would be necessary. In framing a government which is to be administered by men over men, the great difficulty lies in this: you must first enable the government to control the governed; and in the next place oblige it to control itself.

– James Madison in Federalist No. 51 (Madison, 1788)

DELEGATION AND STALEMATE

The possibilities for credible commitment, especially in response to morally hazardous incentives for politicians, were discussed in Chapter 3. Chapter 4 discussed the inevitability of moral hazard. We concluded that bureaucratic autonomy may play a constructive role in the creation of credible commitment in a range of policy areas. However, we did not explain why self-interested politicians, infused with moral hazard, would cooperate in the creation of autonomous bureaucracies. After all, it is through their control over bureaucracies that politicians hope to satisfy their electoral and other preferences. Must we then assume that, at the moment of creation, legislators stand down from their selfish interests and make a public-regarding sacrifice of political control to bureaucratic agencies?

The typical explanation for delegation argues that legislators make a calculation about the benefits of gaining expertise in exchange for a loss of authority (Bawn, 1995). There is no doubt that professionalized bureaucracies frequently can bring to bear a degree of expertise that legislators themselves lack. However, Bawn assumes that the delegator is a unitary political actor with no perverse preferences that may distort the tradeoffs chosen by him. This is an unrealistic assumption because, clearly, the separation-of-powers system means that multiple interests are involved in the delegation decision and that the degree of political stalemate in that system may be the determining factor about how much delegation actually takes place. In particular, when conflict is high, there may be more delegation taking place than would be implied by an optimal tradeoff made by a unitary actor between the availability of expertise and the loss of control.

As Moe (1989) argues, the legislative process is much more messy and parochial than the standard model of delegation suggests. Instead of deliberating about the eventual and general benefits of delegation to experts, legislators often take the most parochial, wary, and short-sighted positions with regard to bureaucratic decision making, process, structure, and personnel. Further, the standard story of delegation does not explain why politicians intervene, when possible, to undermine the authority of bureaucratic experts – by pressuring for certain contracts to go to certain constituents, by shaping the administrative process in such a way as to bias the probable outcome, or by moving a bureaucratic agency from one location to another one that is more amenable to the legislator's preferences.

The challenge is to show how such power-seeking and ambitious politicians, laden with moral hazard, end up following their self-interest to a point that results in autonomous bureaucratic decision making – even when none sought that outcome. In this chapter, we show that legislative delegation is the unintended byproduct of a short-sighted, parochial, power-protecting political process.

Delegation as an Unintended Consequence of Political Stalemate

The key is to remember that different politicians often want different things from a bureaucracy. If they all wanted the same thing, they would have the authority to impose that result on the bureaucracy – *regardless of the expertise available through that bureaucracy*. In setting agricultural policy, for example, politicians may receive all sorts of benefits from allowing bureaucrats to allocate agricultural research funds according to a peer-review process that puts a premium on expertise. However, legislators with strong preferences regarding agricultural research have basically compatible preferences and are willing to impose them on the Department of Agriculture – and that is the end of bureaucratic autonomy.

Yet, delegation may occur as a compromise solution even when there is little expertise available. The delegation of authority to the Occupational Safety and Health Administration (OSHA), soon after it was created in 1971, was a response to intense political pressure, even though the agency had (at least initially) very little to offer in the way of expertise (Moe, 1989). So we argue that expertise is a less reliable predictor of delegation than separation-of-powers conflict. Politicians typically delegate authority when it resolves separation-of-powers conflict, whether or not the degree of expertise justifies the loss of control.

When politicians represent a large number of mutually incompatible preferences, conflict is inevitable. This conflict, especially in the context of a complex separation-of-powers system, means that *no one* will get his first choice; there are too many conflicting interests controlling different veto points.

Delegation to a (relatively neutral) professionalized bureaucracy serves as a natural conflict-resolution mechanism – one that has been used over and over again in American politics. From the standpoint of the individual politician, each legislator may start to think about her second choice, given that she will not obtain her first choice (complete control over some aspect of policy). Her second choice may be "if I can't have control over policy, I want the kind of agency that will deprive my worst enemy of control as well." Delegation to a neutral bureaucracy is the natural form of compromise between competing political perspectives.

An analogous process is fair division (Brams & Taylor, 1996). Imagine two children, each of whom would love to eat the same entire pie. It is a zero-sum game, characterized by complete conflict and laden with the potential for destructive conflict – the pie might be damaged or taken away by the mother in each child's rush to consume as much as possible. But even in a game of conflict, the children could agree on a "you cut, I choose" rule. As Brams points out, this rule harnesses self-interest to implement a solution with which everyone can live.

We envision political conflict in a similar way to Moe (1989). Given the opportunity, a politician may have strong preferences about policy, structure, and personnel. If she finds that others agree (or at least all the others who control some vital veto point), then she would be happy to coerce a certain policy, shape a biased structure, and impose personnel decisions that render the bureaucracy open and responsive to her own wishes. This happens a high proportion of the time – regardless of any technical expertise that may promise public good benefits through an alternative policy, structure, or decision.

But it does not happen all of the time. Bureaucratic autonomy results when control of the bureaucracy is available to none of any number of political interests – due to high levels of conflict. The result, we argue, is that bureaucratic expertise *is* empowered in the context of this conflict of political interests; a structure emerges that is a fair semblance of even-handedness and facilitative of the development and wielding of such expertise, and even political appointments take on the nature of a search for an independent expert rather than a politicized "ally."

In short, bureaucrats have no discretion when politicians are united. It is only when politicians are divided into conflicting factions that bureaucrats find a zone of independent authority. We argue that political compromise among veto groups in different institutional locations serves to support bureaucratic autonomy at three different levels: policy, personnel, and structure. At each level, politicians are limited by their own internal conflicts from impinging on bureaucratic autonomy.

This offers the most satisfying answer to the question – why do self-interested, ambitious politicians, who have quite overt electoral reasons to control the operations of bureaucratic agencies, cede the kind of independent authority that will deprive them of much of their influence with those agencies? To answer this question *we need not assume temporarily altruistic politicians.* Individual legislators would be more than happy to dominate the policy, personnel, and structure of bureaucracies, given the chance, but are generally prohibited from doing so by other politicians at key decision points. So, politicians fall back on the second-best option – preventing their enemies from exercising the same kind of influence. What kind of agency would a politician want if her worst enemy earned a majority in Congress or control of the White House? Politicians in conflict can agree on a compromise that mutually denies influence to all of them.

POLICY AND BUREAUCRATIC AUTONOMY

Of particular importance to bureaucratic autonomy is what we refer to as the "policy connection": policy decisions are more likely to be determined by bureaucratic experts when political stalemate occurs in one or more dimensions of policy. First we consider independence in one policy dimension.

Ferejohn and Shipan (1990) were among the first to recognize that oversight of bureaucracy in a democracy with separated powers did not bear much resemblance to principal-agency theory. In contrast to Weingast (1984), who argued that congressional committees were responsible for effective oversight of the bureaucracy, Ferejohn and Shipan showed that this conclusion did not necessarily follow from even the simplest recognition of multiplicity in the institutions of government. They examined a model in which the oversight committee was embedded in a (unicameral) legislature with its own policy preferences.

For example, consider a single policy dimension and three actors – the agency (A), the oversight committee (C), and the median voter on the floor of the legislative chamber (F) – each with single-peaked, symmetric preferences. The agency prefers $A = 0$, the committee prefers $C = 0.5$, and the floor prefers $F = 0.75$. C(F) is the policy that is just as far from the committee's ideal policy as the floor's preferred point.

Ferejohn and Shipan assume that the agency makes the first move: it picks a policy that the committee can approve or disapprove. If the committee prefers the agency's policy to that of the floor, it can protect the agency's action by introducing no legislation to change the agency's choice. If the committee does introduce any policy, then the floor immediately enacts its first choice: f.

With this simple game, the agency does not necessarily implement its first choice, but implements the closest policy to the one that the committee will protect by gatekeeping. That is the point $C(F) = 0.25$. The committee selects that point because it would prefer the agency proposal to the floor median at F, and the floor would be powerless to overturn the outcome.

Yes, the agency is constrained in this model, but to what degree? One way to analyze the outcome is to imagine that the preferences of the other two actors are fixed and then to determine the outcome for every possible ideal point for the agency. If the outcome exactly matches the agency's ideal point, then the outcome function would be a perfect diagonal line: the agency would be a dictator. If the outcome is a horizontal line, then the agency's preferences have no impact on the final outcome.

With the rules as given, the agency can enforce its own ideal point as long as that ideal point is between $C(F)$ and F. In this range, the agency could offer the committee an outcome that the committee just prefers to the floor's ideal point. The agency would get its own way as long as its ideal point is centrist: between $C(F)$ and F.

Although the agency is powerful over centrist proposals, the best it can do for more liberal proposals is put a limit on them – to the left of $C(F) = 0.25$ and to the right of F. The outcome line is a flat line for these intervals. When its ideal point is above 0.75, the agency is unable to impose any outcome more than 0.75.

Overall, the final outcome is quite responsive to the agency's preference. The range over which it can pick its preferred outcome narrows when the preferences of the two legislative actors are more similar; it widens when the preferences of the two legislative actors diverge. This finding reinforces the point of this chapter: bureaucratic discretion is enhanced by disagreements among other political actors and constrained by political consensus.

Furthermore, each additional actor with some kind of veto power can only increase the agency's discretion. For example, imagine that there is another chamber, S. If S is located between $C = 0.5$ and $F = 0.75$, then it has no impact on the agency's discretion. However, if S is located at $S = 0.82$, for example, then the bureaucrat can choose any outcome in the range of $C(F) = 0.25$ to $S = 0.82$. The existence of an additional veto player allows the agency to impose its ideal point for a wide range of agency ideal points.

The Fed's Policy Impact

I. L. Morris (2002) created a similar model (one-dimensional with veto points but no committee gatekeeping) to analyze the behavior of the Fed. In time periods in which the president has basically similar preferences to those of Congress, the Fed finds itself more tightly constrained. Morris's model uses the example of the Fed's actions during the early Carter years, when Carter, the House, and the Senate were all more expansionary in their preferences than the Fed; "the Fed had no choice but to institute a significantly more expansionary policy in 1977" (49).

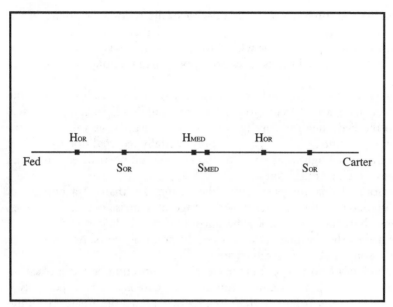

FIGURE 5.1. A Single Policy Dimension.

However, although the political constraints are sufficiently binding to keep the Fed from its ideal point, that does not mean that the Fed had no say in the final outcome. Even among the Democratic institutions of the early Carter administration, there were differences of opinion, creating a zone of discretion for the Fed. The Fed could consistently choose the least constraining of the feasible outcomes.

For example, I. L. Morris (2002) used Americans for Democratic Action (ADA) scores of political liberalism to calculate the 1977 House and Senate medians, and the House and Senate veto override preferences on both sides of the median. They are shown in Figure 5.1. The House median is measured as 40; the Senate median is measured as 47.5. The House veto override on the left-hand side is 15; the Senate override on that side is 25. On the right-hand side, the House veto override is 55; for the Senate, it is 65.

Although Morris does not use this terminology, the core is the set of points that cannot be overturned by any decisive coalition; in other words, it is the stable, undominated outcome. In Morris's model, the decisive coalitions include the president and a simple majority of both chambers, or an override majority of both chambers. In the example shown in Figure 5.1, the core of this game is the interval [40,65]. Any point less than 40 can be defeated by a decisive coalition of the president and a simple majority of both chambers. On the other side, even if Carter wanted a monetary policy more liberal than 65, he could not get it. Any point to the right of 65 can be defeated by an override coalition of both chambers.

And so, the Fed still has a significant degree of discretion – 25 points, in this metric. Assuming the Fed is more anti-inflationary than any of the legislative leaders, it can select 40, which is what Morris calls the "pivot." The pivot can be thought of as the Fed's most preferred policy from among the core alternatives.

Both the core and the pivot shift substantially with a conservative president. If we assume that Carter had lost to Ford in 1976 and that Ford had preferences similar to the Fed, then the core (assuming all the legislative values stay the same) is now the interval [15, 47.5]. A presidentially led coalition can defeat any outcome to the right of the Senate median, and an override coalition can prevent any outcome to the left of 15.

The lessons of this analysis, in one dimension, are that (1) a bureaucrat can impose her preferences over a wide range of centrist outcomes and (2) an extremist bureaucrat can choose her most preferred policy from the centrist range defined by the clashing preferences of the political actors. As it turns out, the same lessons apply in two dimensions.

Hammond and Knott (1996) make clear the connection between constitutional stalemate and bureaucratic autonomy. The core is the set of points that is impervious to upset from *any coalition*. As they argue, the greater the number of constitutional veto actors and the greater the conflict between them, the larger the core – and the more autonomy available to the bureaucracy.

As Hammond and Miller (1987) have argued, differences in preferences between different elements of our separation-of-powers system inevitably increase the probability that there will be a core, as well as the size of that *core* – the set of policy outcomes that cannot be changed due to the opposition of a vital blocking coalition. In other words, core outcomes are undominated: there is no separation-of-powers coalition that can agree to upset any core outcomes. The set of core outcomes is a minimum level of bureaucratic autonomy; an agency head can select any outcome in the core without fear of being reversed by politicians. The presence of more veto players only enlarges the core.

Hammond and Knott analyze the implications for the core in a more realistic two-dimensional policy space. The outcome is basically the same as that posited by Morris: with more veto points (chamber medians, oversight committees, party leadership, president) the agency's discretion can only increase.

As constitutional complexity increases, so does the degree of bureaucratic autonomy. With two chambers, rather than one, the core becomes the union of the cores as calculated within each chamber – so bureaucratic discretion necessarily increases with bicameralism. If additional veto points exist, as in a House Rules Committee controlled by party leadership, they can only add to the potential for stalemate, as captured by the concept of the core.

Thus, the implications of the core analysis are that the more veto points among the politicians and the more conflict among those veto points, the larger is the core and the greater is bureaucratic discretion. However, bureaucratic discretion is just that – discretion. Discretion means that the final outcome is in part due to the preferences of the bureaucrat herself.

SEPARATION OF POWERS AND BUREAUCRATIC STRUCTURE

Democratic institutions make not only policy but also *institutional* decisions about how to make policy. Since the Progressive Era especially, the U.S. political system has been a subtly creative inventor of new institutions, many of which make policy in ways that are more or less independent of congressional and presidential politics. The Federal Reserve Board, the Securities and Exchange Commission, the base-closing commissions, the machinery of tariff reform – all of these result from democratic *institutional choice*. The logic here is much like that described in the previous section on policy: politicians united leave little room for bureaucratic autonomy, but divided and conflicted politicians tend to create insulated bureaucracies.

Structural Politics and Systematic Autonomy

As Hammond (1986) and Moe (1989) have argued, structural decisions go a long way in determining policy outcomes. That is why different interest groups and their political allies fight so hard for particular structures that they deem supportive of their position. If they oppose a particular structure, they may well succeed in incorporating structural forces that make it difficult or impossible for a new agency to do its job. This is seen in David Lewis's empirical work on the Moe hypothesis.

Drawing on the insights of Seidman (1970), Lewis (2003) identifies five structural features that promote bureaucratic autonomy in new agencies: (1) the location of the new agency outside of a cabinet department, (2) organization as a multiheaded commission, (3) specific qualifications for appointees such as partisan balance, (4) chain-of-command independence, and (5) fixed terms for administrators. These structural features all produce an institutional palette that is virtually infinite in scope and capable of producing subtle variations in bureaucratic independence, professionalism, and accountability. He examines 182 administrative agencies created in the United States between 1946 and 1997, many of which had such features. Why would legislators vote for such structural independence in a postwar period that saw nothing but an increase in anti-bureaucratic rhetoric and feeling?

One of the strongest results of Lewis's remarkable analysis is that strong congressional majorities have different impacts on the probability of insulating new agencies, depending on whether or not they are of the same party as the president. When the majority is large and the president is of the same party, then the majority party coalition "clearly get[s] what they want: uninsulated agencies" (D. E. Lewis, 2003, 60). However, when the majority party is in opposition to the White House, the degree of insulation goes up; apparently, institutional competition and jealousy encourage a strong majority coalition to insulate the new agency from presidential influence.

This is consistent with Lewis's dictum that "[p]oliticians who insulate want to decrease presidential influence and the impact of changing administrations on agency policies" (D. E. Lewis, 2003, 44). Consider how the impact of the president's approval rating on the likelihood of insulating itself depends on whether there is divided or unified government. With a unified government, presidential popularity decreases the likelihood of insulation, as might be expected. However, in the case of divided government, presidential popularity *increases* legislative wariness of presidential dominance; in such cases, presidential popularity increases the probability of independence, specific qualifications, commission governance, and fixed terms.

The case of the birth of the Fed illustrates the role of a variety of types of conflict – interest group, partisan, and institutional conflict – in the creation of agencies capable of autonomous action.

Autonomy out of Compromise

The Panic of 1907 convinced banking interests of the need for a central bank. Many of the major New York banking houses could see the benefits of having a state agency with control over credit and money supply. In particular, New York bankers wanted a central bank relatively free of intervention by the federal government.

Politically, the city banks had strong connections to the Republican Party, which had dominated government and presidential elections since Reconstruction. But in 1912, the Republican Party lost control of the White House. The Republican incumbent, William Howard Taft, placed third behind the Democratic candidate, Woodrow Wilson, and Teddy Roosevelt, the Progressive defector from the Republican Party. The Republican Party was split between the conservative and Progressive factions. Combined with their loss of the House in 1910 and of the Senate in 1912, the results of the 1912 elections injected uncertainty into Republican views on their future electoral prospects.

Country bankers, farmers, and populists feared a central bank dominated by the large city banks. They opposed the tight monetary discipline favored by the eastern bankers who saw such discipline as a necessary condition for elevating the dollar to international currency status. They also preferred decentralized control of local funds (Broz, 1997, 178). Consequently, they sought to limit the influence of the large city banks by advocating a central bank that was controlled by their political representatives. As a Wisconsin country banker testified in a Senate hearing, they were "more willing to take our [their] chances with the government than with big bankers."[1] The congressional "Money Trust"

---

[1] U.S. Congress, Senate, Committee on Banking and Currency, Hearings on H.R. 7837, 63rd Congress, 1st session, 1913.

investigations during the summer of 1912 further inflamed farmers and populists and elevated the visibility and potency of populists' concerns over the
concentration of wealth and influence in large banks in general and on Wall
Street in particular. During eight months of hearings, this congressional investigation "frightened the nation with its awesome, if inconclusive, statistics on the
power of Wall Street over the nation's economy...five banking firms held 341
directorships in 112 corporations with an aggregate capitalization of over $22
billion...the nation was suitably frightened into realizing that reform of the
banking system was urgent – presumably to bring Wall Street under control"
(Kolko, 1963, 220). For farmers, the federal government was the only power
that could counter the influence of the powerful city banks, so if a central bank
were created, they wanted to make sure that it was strongly controlled by the
political system (Greider, 1989, 253). A central bank for them was valuable if it
tamed the influence of "the money trust" in favor of the interests of the farmers
and merchants of the land west and south of the Hudson River.

The conflict was clear: some legislators wanted a strong bank independent of
political control, whereas others wanted a strong, governmentally dominated
bank that would control the eastern bank interests.

From Compromise to Autonomy

The compromise prevented any single interest group or branch from exercising
dominance over Fed policy and operations. The big banks got what they most
wanted out of their initial proposal – a bank centralized and strong enough
to mitigate the devastating effects of monetary instability – but they conceded
to farmers and populists on the issue of public control. The Fed was to be a
governmental body and not a private central bank, despite the wishes of large
city bankers.

Populists also got some of what they wanted. There was a certain amount of
decentralization in the form of a dozen regional banks. They also received the
guarantee of one-third public representation on the regional bank boards, with
another third being appointed by the Federal Reserve Board, which was itself
appointed by the president with the advice and consent of the Senate. Bankers
were excluded from the central board. Still, bankers were guaranteed a seat at
the table by means of guaranteed banking representation on the regional bank
boards, and they could anticipate that this presence, magnified by their own
expertise in banking matters, would allow them to block harmful actions by
the other interests represented.

The balance between centralization and decentralization accommodated the
interests of city bankers seeking to promote an environment conducive to their
expanding international economic activities while still assuaging Main Street's
fears of Wall Street. This political compromise created a bureaucratic agency
with quasi-private ownership, employment protections, and budgetary autonomy, which make it relatively independent from political interference.

The Fed's decentralized structure and private ownership of the reserve banks protect against political control and promote insulation from political influence. The Federal Reserve Board is located in Washington, DC, but the 12 regional reserve banks, which do much of the work in the system, basically operate as autonomous units. Banks in each district subscribe to the reserve bank, meaning the reserve banks are basically privately owned. Local businesspeople and bankers select the bulk of the directors of each reserve bank. This mix of a public-private ownership and appointment structure diffuses political influence and embeds these countervailing interests in the structure of the Federal Reserve System.

The provisions for tenure of the members of the Federal Reserve Board also promote bureaucratic insulation by limiting the fear of possible termination as reprisal for adopting policies contrary to the interests of Congress or the executive. The Federal Reserve Act of 1913 (12 U.S. Code §226) dictates that the president appoints governors, with Senate confirmation, to serve 14-year terms.[2] The president also designates a chairman and vice chairman from the Board to serve four-year terms. Congress limited presidential influence by staggering the tenure of appointees beyond the president's term of office (one term expires each even-numbered year). This feature was not particularly painful to majority Democrats in light of the anticipated return to Republican rule. The Banking Act of 1935 prohibits the reappointment of members to further limit the possible influence of the president.

The Federal Reserve Act of 1913 also provides for budgetary autonomy, stating that "[t]he Federal Reserve Board shall have power to levy, semiannually upon the Federal Reserve banks and in proportion to their capital stock and surplus, an assessment sufficient to pay its estimated expenses and the salaries of its members and employees for the half year" (Federal Reserve Act, Section 10). Thus the Fed raises funds for its operation from open market operations and fees from the reserve banks, and this budgetary autonomy frees it from the congressional appropriation process. Congress cannot use the power of purse to pressure the Fed or sanction Fed activity when it goes against the wishes of Congress. This provision, however, appears problematic regarding the dimension of democratic responsiveness and accountability, a fundamental concern of the principal-agency literature.

Clearly, the new structure was not what either side most wanted. The banking interests, in particular, complained about it, and their Republican representatives voted against it. However, Paul Warburg, a New York banker with influential input in these deliberations, concluded that these compromises "demonstrated progress of great significance for freedom from politics and governmental control" (Warburg, 1930, 127). In private correspondence before the passage of the bill, Frank Vanderlip of the National City Bank wrote,

---

[2] Originally, the term of the governors was set to be 10 years by the Federal Reserve Act of 1913. Later, the Banking Act of 1935 increased the term to 14 years.

"It is workable and I think bankers should recognize the difficulties of getting an ideal measure....Perhaps if bankers would show opposition to it there would be more chance of passage....I think the measure is vastly better than the present law under which we are operating."[3]

Both sides decided they could live with the Fed, even though (or because!) neither one was clearly in the driver's seat.

Accord

> *"[T]here is going to have to be a determination, probably by the Congress, as to whether we are to have a central banking system, such as we thought we had, or whether it is to become, in essence, a bureau of the Treasury."*
>
> – Allan Sproul, president of the New York Federal Bank, in 1951, quoted in Lucia (1983, 119)

Although for decades the Fed has had a reputation for being a paragon of central bank independence, that was not always the case. The independence of the Fed was more of an aspiration than a reality during the decade of the 1940s. The unity created in American politics from the need to support the war effort extended to the Fed, as it became de facto an agent of the Treasury Department, dutifully performing that department's assigned functions.

Independence Day for the Fed has been dated as March 4, 1951. Its declaration appeared in a bland-looking document that came to be known as the Treasury/Fed Accord, which was the result of multi-institutional negotiation by interested parties located in different branches of government. The Accord illustrates the theme of this chapter – unity and consensus limit bureaucratic autonomy, whereas conflict leads to more bureaucratic independence.

During World War II, the Fed had agreed to support the government's need to finance the war. In particular, the U.S. government needed to sell a lot of treasury bonds at a low interest rate. The Fed was charged with the responsibility of keeping interest rates low – pegged at 3/8ths of a percent on Treasury bills – so that the government could afford to make interest payments on its massive debt. However, keeping the interest rate low deprived the Fed of control over its portfolio and the money supply. It felt that its particular role was to fight inflation, and the continued low interest rates were placing significant inflationary pressures on the economy. Further, the Treasury mandate frustrated the Fed's efforts to respond to a recession in 1949.

The dispute became a crisis by the summer of 1950, when the members of the Federal Open Market Committee (FOMC) – a committee composed of seven members of the Federal Reserve Board and five presidents of the Federal Reserve Banks – reached agreement that they were going to have to defy

---

[3] Frank Vanderlip to J. M. Smith, 19 June 1913, Frank A. Vanderlip Papers. Recited from Broz (1997, 201).

the Treasury. It is perhaps suggestive that the leader of the revolt was not a member of the Federal Reserve Board of Governors, but Allen Sproul, who had not been appointed by the sitting president. As the New York Federal Reserve president, he had a permanent seat on the FOMC. Sproul complained that the Fed's monetary policy had been handcuffed by its obligation to follow Treasury directives: "we are not the masters in our own house" (Timberlake, 1978, 309). At an FOMC meeting held in August 1950, Sproul declared that the Fed had been compliant long enough: "we should act on the basis of our unwillingness to continue to supply reserve to the market by supporting the existing rate structure and should advise Treasury that this is what we intend to do – not seek instructions" (Hetzel & Leach, 2001, 36).

The Treasury position was bolstered from the top – President Harry Truman, who had a populist's distrust of the banks and a commander-in-chief's concern with financing the hot war with Korea. But the Fed had two masters – *and was able to play Congress off against the White House*. Congress, as usual, housed supporters of a variety of positions. House Banking Committee chair Wright Patman was a well-known populist, who supported Truman's efforts to pay for the war and keep monetary policy loose. But in hearings held by Patman's committee, it became obvious that the Fed had its congressional advocates.

At the hearings, former Fed chairman Mariner Eccles said, "As long as the Federal Reserve is required to buy government securities at the will of the market for the purpose of defending a fixed pattern of interest rates established by the Treasury, it must stand ready to create new bank reserves in unlimited amount. This policy makes the entire banking system, through the action of the Federal Reserve System, an engine of inflation" (Hetzel & Leach, 2001, 43). Patman responded flatly, "You are sabotaging the Treasury. I think it ought to be stopped" (44). Eccles replied, "[E]ither the Federal Reserve should be recognized as having some independent status, or it should be considered as simply an agency or a bureau of the Treasury" (44).

On the Senate side was Paul Douglas (D-IL), a renowned economist, who held hearings and issued a report that strongly supported greater freedom for the Fed to use monetary policy "both ways" – to expand the economy in a recession and contract money supply in the face of inflation. He had held hearings in December 1949 that had the effect of demonstrating that "any attempt to bring the Federal Reserve forcibly to heel would encounter considerable resistance in the Congress" (H. Stein, 1984, 258).

The outbreak of the Korean War in June 1950 increased the administration's urgency to keep the interest rate low. When the newspapers carried leaks about the Fed's growing concern about inflation, Truman called Fed chairman McCabe at home to express his priorities.

In late January 1951, Truman called an unprecedented meeting of the entire FOMC at the White House and then took it on himself to reinterpret the Fed's expressions of concern about inflation as expressions of support for keeping interest rates low. He released to the news media a letter to McCabe that thanked the FMOC members for their "full cooperation" and left the impression that the Fed had deferred completely to Truman.

To maintain a degree of independence for the Fed, one member of the Fed Board, Mariner Eccles, then challenged Truman and the Treasury's interpretation of the January meeting. Eccles retaliated by releasing the official Fed version of the meeting, which made it clear that the Fed had not committed itself to the president's position – in effect calling the president a liar. Eccles had been Fed chairman until 1948 and had stayed on the Board as vice chairman after Truman failed to reappoint him to finish his 14-year term as governor. A report indicated that Truman had failed to reappoint the respected Eccles to show him "who's boss" (Hetzel & Leach, 2001, 46). Eccles' release of the meeting notes confirmed that the Treasury had not been consulted (as Treasury implied) and that the Fed had never agreed to the policies that Treasury claimed. This amounted to a slap in the face to the president and brought the obscure debate to the front page.

On February 19, 1951, the Fed sent the Treasury a letter declaring that it "was no longer willing to maintain the existing situation in the Government security market" (Hetzel & Leach, 2001, 49). Negotiations were then initiated that resembled difficult peace talks between warring nations. The negotiations got nowhere until lower level staff from the Treasury and the Fed began to work out an agreement. Significantly, the assistant secretary of the Treasury Wiliam McChesney Martin represented the department at these meetings.

Perhaps unsurprisingly, the banking community did not rally around the Fed. At a meeting with the representatives of large New York banks, Eccles accused them of needing more "courage and realistic leadership" (Hetzel & Leach, 2001, 49).

The Fed did rely, however, on support in the Senate. The Senate was barely Democratic at this time (49–47), but many Democratic senators, including the widely respected economist Douglas, made it clear that they sided with the Fed. Sproul, of the New York Fed, made strategic use of the distance between the Democratic Senate and the Democratic president. As noted earlier, Sproul said, "[T]here is going to have to be a determination, probably by the Congress as to whether we are to have a central banking system, such as we thought we had, or whether it is to become, in essence, a bureau of the Treasury" (Lucia, 1983, 119).

Calling for a congressional "determination" was, of course, a smart strategy for Sproul and the Fed backers. Senators are always in a state of institutional competition with the president – that is, they have nothing to gain by helping the president assert domination over an agency. In the case of the Fed, asserting presidential control would be bad policy for some senators, but giving the president free rein over an independent agency was a dangerous precedent that might lead to the freezing out of Congress on monetary policy. Furthermore, Truman, by 1951, had very little political capital left. He had made enemies in the years since his surprise 1948 victory. In particular, the confrontation between

Truman and MacArthur had ended with the firing of the popular general, which resulted in calls for Truman's impeachment.

Legally, the administration had no authority to demand compliance from the Fed. The legislation creating the Fed had guaranteed it an independence that could only be undone by additional legislation. In 1950, the probability that Truman could build a successful legislative coalition to undo the Fed's independence was nil. "For Truman to triumph over the Fed, he would have had to prevail in Congress" (Hetzel & Leach, 2001, 52).

The stalemate meant that Truman had to acquiesce to a public "Accord" that was announced as separate news releases from the Treasury and the Fed on March 4, 1951. The document was presented as a compromise, in which the Fed would keep the discount rate at 1¾% for the rest of the year. However, the substance of the Accord represented a full acquiescence to the Fed's demand for an end to Treasury pressures. The modern independent Fed can be traced to that date.

Despite the Accord, Truman made one more attempt to influence the Fed – through the appointment process. He could not touch Allan Sproul, who as head of the New York Fed, was not appointed by him. Nor could he fire the Fed chairman, McCabe, who was in the middle of a four-year term. However, he could undermine McCabe's position so that he had no choice but to resign. Consequently, within a few days of the Accord, Treasury Secretary Snyder let Truman know that he could no longer maintain a working relationship with Chairman McCabe – a development that showed the vitriol behind the bland words of the Accord. In turn Truman informed McCabe of the Treasury secretary's comments, with the clear understanding by both parties that a Fed chairman could not do his job without such a relationship. McCabe sent in a bitter letter of resignation, whose tone was subsequently softened at the request of the administration. His resignation, however, was contingent on his successor's acceptability to the rest of the Fed Board.

The compromise replacement for McCabe was William McChesney Martin, who had until that time worked for the Treasury Department and had been the central figure in the negotiations resulting in the Accord. He was a compromise figure because he had been representing Treasury, but at the same time wrote the document that became the Fed's charter of independence. Truman believed Martin to be, like himself, an inflation dove.

Because of Martin's reputation, the Board staff and Wall Street figures both believed that Truman had lost the battle over the Fed's operating independence, but had won the war by placing his ally as Fed chairman (Hetzel & Leach, 2001, 52). However, as chairman, Martin supported not only Fed independence but also a strong anti-inflationary program for the Fed. In fact, years later, after Truman was out of the White House, he met Martin on the street and uttered one word to him: "Traitor!" (52).

The common element between the 1913 Federal Reserve Act and the 1951 Treasury/Fed Accord was that negotiations between strongly conflicting interests eventually resulted in a compromise in the form of enhanced bureaucratic insulation. The 1913 Act provides the characteristics that Lewis identifies as the building blocks of an independent commission. The 1951 Accord, which resulted from Fed officials playing Congress against the presidency, reasserts the independent and autonomous role of the Fed as a central bank.

SEPARATION OF POWERS AND THE APPOINTMENT PROCESS

William McChesney Martin famously said that the job of the Fed was to take away the punch bowl just as the party got good. This philosophy supported 20 years of postwar expansion with little inflation. Martin served five terms as Fed chairman, a year into Nixon's first term of office.

The first renowned departure from Martin's philosophy occurred as a result of Richard Nixon's reelection compulsion and the actions of a conveniently compliant economist, Arthur Burns, the Fed chairman. Nixon's plan for reelection was to boost the economy in the reelection year of 1972 (the year of Watergate) and keep inflation down with wage and price controls (Greider, 1989, 342). Burns was happy to comply, despite warnings from a minority coalition in the FOMC of inflation in 1973. "Their warnings...proved to be an accurate forecast of what did occur after Nixon's electoral victory" (343): inflation hit double digits in 1973.

When Carter became president, it was time to appoint a new Fed chair. Burns wanted Carter to go across party lines and appoint him as a bipartisan Fed chair, like Martin. His White House allies reassured him that "Carter can be seduced" (Greider, 1989, 346). Instead, Carter appointed G. William Miller as the new Fed chairman in March 1978. Miller's dovish position on inflation created fuel for further inflation. Miller became "without question the most partisan and least respected chairman in the Fed's history" (Beckner, 1996).

Anxiety about inflation was just one of the several debilitating factors that caused a crisis in the Carter administration. Carter gave his famous "malaise" speech on July 15, 1979. At the same time, he needed to send a signal to Wall Street – a credible signal – that his administration was going to take a strong position to get inflation under control. The appointment of someone acceptable as Fed chairman would be the most effective way to give such a signal, but Miller, the inflation dove, had two more years in his term. For Carter to satisfy Wall Street, he would have to find a way to promote Miller out of his position as the Fed, because he obviously could not fire him. Then Carter could appoint someone to the Fed who could provide the reassurance of Fed independence.

The way to get Miller out of the Fed chairmanship was to promote him to Secretary of the Treasury – a move Miller was pleased to make because it gave him a broader scope of authority and made him the only person in U.S. history to serve as both Fed chairman and Treasury Secretary. To make the Treasury position available, Carter had to fire the incumbent, W. Michael Blumenthal.

Blumenthal did not want to resign, but the cover for the resignation was a wholesale redesign of Carter's cabinet.

The question then became who would replace Miller at the Fed. Administration officials wanted to satisfy Wall Street on the inflation issue, but also wanted a "team player" – a euphemism for someone who would be responsive to the administration's reelection needs the next year.

After the Bank of America president declined, an obvious candidate was New York Fed president Paul Volcker. Volker was a creature of the Fed. As head of the New York Fed he was the most important regional Fed president, the only one guaranteed a permanent seat on the FOMC, and the person overseeing implementation of the FOMC's decisions via market transactions.

Thus Volker was a natural choice for Fed chairman – but some of Carter's friends saw danger in his appointment. Burt Lance spelled out the electoral implications to Carter: he would be "mortgaging his re-election to the Federal Reserve" if he appointed Volcker (Greider, 1989, 47). But the president had few degrees of freedom by this point. He appointed Volcker, but not because he was an "ally" with the same preferences and reelection constraints. As Stuart Eizenstadt, Carter's domestic policy advisor, said, "Volcker was selected because he was the candidate of Wall Street. This was their price, in effect. What was known about him? That he was able and bright and it was also known that he was conservative. What wasn't known was that he was going to impose some very dramatic changes" (47). The importance of the Volcker appointment was that it was *not* the unconstrained choice of the president: Carter was constrained by other political and economic forces and the need to appear credibly committed to an independent Fed – no matter how much he may have wanted a malleable Fed chairman.

The appointment caused the bond market to rally, it stopped the month-long slide in the dollar, and it caused the price of gold to fall – all in anticipation that Volcker would get inflation under control. But thoughtful observers knew how he would accomplish this task – by raising interest rates, cutting monetary growth, and causing a recession.

Indeed, within a year of Volcker's appointment, the Fed had engineered an attack on inflation that included higher interest rates, with one big increase coming in September of the turbulent 1980 presidential campaign. A week after the interest rate increase, Carter criticized the decision as "ill-advised" (Greider, 1989, 217). This was the opening shot in a recurring campaign theme. Reagan was able to turn Carter's criticism into an advantage: "The Carter-dominated Federal Reserve Board has now become Jimmy Carter's whipping boy for at least trying … to remedy the damage to the economy caused by the highest budget deficit in the history of the country" (217). Reagan managed to claim that Carter both dominated the Fed and was punishing the Fed for its independence.

Reagan found himself in Carter's position by the 1982 mid-term election, when the economic consequences of Volcker's anti-inflation policies had worsened. One Treasury Department official revealed the costs that the Fed's single-handed fight against inflation was imposing on its political masters: "Everybody was just frantic. They saw the 1982 elections coming up and they were desperate for a recovery. It was miserable at Treasury; it was frantic. We could see all these House seats going down the drain" (Greider, 1989, 491).

Fed Appointments

Generally speaking, presidents can influence the Fed's interest rate policy through their appointments to the Board of Governors (Chang, 2003). The evidence is clear; we accept this. Yet, the interesting point is that this influence must remain marginal for a variety of reasons.

One reason is the influence of the five regional bank presidents serving at any one time on the FOMC. As Chang notes, the administration has "no control" over these votes on the FOMC, because the presidents are selected by the boards of the regional banks, subject to veto power by the Fed's centralized Board of Governors. Because the regional banks tend to be more hawkish on inflation, those five votes tend to be more hawkish. During the 1960s and 1970s, Wooley (1986) found that 90% of the dissents of regional presidents were in a conservative direction, in contrast to 40% of the Board of Governors' dissents (Greider, 1989, 313). These regional bank presidents can have a real impact on the FOMC.

Chang shows that the U.S. president can move the position of the median member of the FOMC when there is an appropriate opening. The median voter does not change when a liberal president replaces a liberal governor with another liberal governor. The median voter only changes at the margin when a conservative president replaces a liberal governor (or vice versa).

Yet, although the Senate has a record of strong support for presidential nominations to the Fed, senators, too, have an influence on the median governor's preferences: "For example, when the president and Senate are far left of the status quo, a vacancy in the last five seats produces the largest policy change toward their ideal points. Timing matters because if the vacancy occurs when the president is closer to the status quo, his ideal point may be the outcome, whereas if the Senate is closer, the outcome will be more favorable toward the Senate" (Chang, 2003, 140). There is a built-in reward for moderation in the Fed's appointment process.

CONCLUSION: CHECKS AND BALANCES

We normally presume that politicians are rational, self-interested, ambitious, and therefore power hungry. In particular, members of Congress seek their own reelection, and presidents seek reelection and enough of a record to go down in history favorably.

As the Federalist papers argued, in a separation-of-powers system "ambition must be made to counteract ambition." Blocked ambition among multiple political principals gives a degree of bureaucratic discretion in policy, process, structure, and personnel.

Yet this is clearly not an unconditional grant of authority. When united, Congress, the president, and the courts can impose outcomes, process, structure, and personnel on the bureaucracy. It is the increase in conflict among principals that provides options for bureaucrats, as predicted by Ferejohn and Shipan and by Hammond and Knott. Lewis finds autonomous bureaucratic structures more likely in the presence of conflict, and Chang finds compromise choices to be more likely in similar circumstances.

With this Madisonian explanation, we do not have to make the heroic assumptions that politicians are noble, risk acceptant and public-minded. Bureaucratic autonomy is not the result of conscious planning or self-denial by politicians. Instead, bureaucratic autonomy, of the sort we see at the Federal Reserve Board, occurs as a result of self-interested negotiation and compromise in the context of a separation-of-powers system with heightened uncertainty over electoral horizons. The professionals at the Fed are themselves checked by transparency and accountability constraints, to be sure, but the existence of the Fed serves to counteract the most harmful ambitions of politicians themselves. In such a setting, the creation of a new bureaucracy results from various blocking coalitions attempting to deny their competitors unconstrained power over the new agency today and in the future. The tendency toward bureaucratic delegation (and insulation) increases when those in power anticipate that other political actors may soon be in power.

In the creation and operations of the Fed, compromise turned out to be essential. Widespread dissatisfaction with the status quo and uncertain political horizons over who would control the levers of government in the future underpinned the efforts that led to political compromise. This compromise satisfied a broad coalition of interests, constrained the exercise of political influence over monetary policy by those on the other side of the aisle, and created a high degree of bureaucratic autonomy for the new central bank. No group got its first choice, but each group walked away from the compromise with some assurance that its competitors would not control the new agency. In short, the Fed was the result of compromise in a Madisonian constitutional system. The compromise was one that guaranteed effective autonomy for the new agency, merely because all of the simple levers of power are obscured by shared power and compromise.

As D. E. Lewis (2003, 161) notes, "Delegating control over interest rates and monetary policy to the Federal Reserve, for example, is probably a case where the losses of efficiency in coordination are outweighed by the potential policy losses from flip-flopping presidential economic policy." More generally, politicians who disagree sharply about policy may agree that an insulated bureaucracy, staffed with experts, is preferable to a more responsive agency that would oscillate in and out of the hands of one's political enemies.

If bureaucratic autonomy is a result of conflict among political forces, then it may serve a role when needed most. On all those matters for which members of Congress, the president and top appointees, and the court are in agreement, then their positions are very likely to be the right ones, and additional information from the experts in a bureaucracy is unlikely to add anything to the process. On the other hand, bureaucracy can be a way of guaranteeing coherence and minimizing conflict when political principals work at cross-purposes.

6

The Control Paradox, Trust, and Leadership

Any fool can make a rule. And every fool will mind it.
— Henry David Thoreau (Thoreau and Shepard, 1927, 327)

RULES FOR FOOLS

On July 10, 2014, the U.S. House Committee on Financial Services held hearings on H.R. 5018, the Federal Reserve Accountability and Transparency Act of 2014, a bill sponsored by Representative Bill Huizenga (R-MI)

to amend the Federal Reserve Act to establish requirements for policy rules and blackout periods of the Federal Open Market Committee, to establish requirements for certain activities of the Board of Governors of the Federal Reserve System, and for other purposes.[1]

Dr. John B. Taylor, noted Stanford economist, was the first witness – and for good reason. Taylor was famous for his advocacy of the so-called Taylor rule, which holds that central banks should tune the nominal interest rate according to a reaction function (a rule expressed as an equation) that depends on important economic conditions such as inflation. In a series of papers starting in 1993, Taylor had argued that a policy rule could be devised that allowed the federal funds rate to move as inflation increased above its target or real GDP increased above its trend. He noted, "Although there is not consensus about the size of the coefficients of policy rules, it is useful to see what a representative policy rule might look like" (J. B. Taylor, 1993, 202). He went on to show that a simple rule was a nice approximation of actual policy performance.

---

[1] "Federal Reserve Accountability and Transparency Act of 2014." H.R 5018. 113th Congress, 2d Session (2013–2014). https://beta.congress.gov/bill/113th-congress/house-bill/5018/text. Last accessed on September 9, 2014.

Since then, economists have done more than treat this rule as an academic exercise, writing hundreds of papers that have sought to elaborate what should go into such a rule, the coefficients or weights for those items, the general value of such a rule, and other important matters. Of course, some economists viewed divining such a descriptive model of the Fed's actions as a way to predict its actions in the future, and so to take market positions that account for that foresight. But for many, taking market positions was not the end-all of the research agenda Taylor started when he tried to describe this "representative rule." For a number of academic economists and many political interests, the goal was a normative model of Fed behavior – a policy rule that would determine the actions the Fed should take (given the data) that would optimize national economic performance.

The proposed bill from Representative Huizenga would require the Fed to first adopt a policy rule and then to adopt a second policy rule against which the first policy rule would be referenced. The second rule would be Taylor's rule. The Fed would set the first rule, with deviations from Taylor's rule (and later from the Fed's own policy rule) allowed only after the Fed chair testified before Congress.

Much has been written about the Taylor rule and Congress's intent in pushing legislation to restrain the Fed's discretion (including effectively outlawing unconventional behaviors such as those taken during the Bernanke years amid the Great Recession) (e.g., Davies, 2014; Nikolsko-Rzhevskyy, Papell, and Prodan, 2014; O'Brien, 2014). Practically speaking, the push behind this effort has been "that some members of Congress are seeking to shackle the Fed, not because policy has been too tight, but because they think it has been too accommodative" (Davies, 2014). Although the legislation would allow for the Fed to change, as it sees fit, the way in which data enter its decisions about monetary policy, its real consequence would be that the FOMC "would need to report to Congress after every meeting, allowing for much greater political interference in monetary policy"; one commentator at least viewed this change as a "high price to pay for any advantages the Rule might bring" (Davies, 2014).

Rules do have advantages: they offer predictability and transparency. But using rules to control the discretion of experienced, professionalized bureaucrats can have a dark side as well. Whether managing monetary policy or the care of an aging population, greater congressional control of policy may, surprisingly, lead to inferior outcomes. To further explore what we refer to as this "control paradox," we next turn to the care of the aging in nursing homes as a regulatory problem.

SOMETIMES, MORE CONTROL LEADS TO POORER PERFORMANCE

We are interested in the efficacy of rules because we established in Chapters 3 and 4 that there are theoretical reasons to establish regulatory clarity, contractual clarity, and property rights clarity. Further, delegation to bureaucracies is often an efficient and effective way to establish a credible commitment to North's institutional transparency and stability. Delegation for that purpose does not mean that political officials who are in a hierarchical relationship with bureaucrats will forbear from using whatever influence they have in order to control bureaucratic behavior. Very often control consists of rule regimes monitored by hierarchical supervisors, and leading to punishment if mandated behavior is in fact in violation of the rules.

We note that if hierarchical superiors are successful in using rules, monitoring, and punishment to control bureaucratic behavior, then the use of bureaucrats in providing credible commitment will be in the realm of theory only. We are looking for a means by which bureaucratic autonomy can be real – not hypothetical, random, or meaningless. In this chapter, we establish that bureaucratic autonomy, rather than being an obstacle to policy success, can be the means by which policy success is guaranteed.

In this section we analyze the contrasting actions taken by two directors of the Illinois Department of Aging in the late 1980s and early 1990s. Jan Otwell closely watched and punished subordinates in the interest of democratic control over the agency, but in the process, undermined bureaucratic autonomy. Her successor, Victor Wirth, figured out a way to signal a commitment to bureaucratic autonomy without releasing dark and random forces from the apparently unguided and liberated social workers at the department. Otwell spent much more of her time than her successor attempting to maintain strict control over subordinates, but she got less effort from them in return. The comparison between the two directors guides us in the rest of the chapter as we explore the topic of the control paradox.

Writing and enforcing more rules are a way to enforce democratic control over the bureaucracy. During her tenure Otwell wrote several manuals specifying the required actions of the evaluators of nursing homes. These manuals were enormously thick. Wirth, who had worked as a professional in the department before leaving years earlier, did not approve of the proliferation of rules. When he returned as director, he said, "I'd been gone from the department six and a half years. I came back and looked at the paperwork in that program and I called my staff in and said, 'My God! How did we get here?' Just unreal!" (Koremenos, 2005, 68).

Wirth believed that the amount of paperwork that resulted from this fixation on monitoring was a distraction from the real job of the organization – which could not be specified by elaborate rules and procedures. Instead, Wirth tried to place emphasis on "providing quality services" (Koremenos, 2005, 42). He believed that the best service would only be accomplished if the knowledge and motivation of the professionals were unleashed:

These nonprofits, these social workers, these providers: they're in it for the right reasons. It's a small minority that isn't. But the whole measuring system was aimed at that minority rather than giving everyone the benefit of the doubt, involving them more. The system that was built had one basic assumption: people were basically dishonest and they would try to falsify paperwork. This is not the case – 99%. If you've ever spent time in the field, in nonprofits in the state, you'll find very, very dedicated people, very client-oriented people. (quoted in Koremenos, 2005, 49)

Wirth was convinced that too much effort was placed on monitoring and enforcement. He said, "[T]he only thing the Department was interested in was formal compliance. Employees viewed this as an infringement on their professional autonomy" (Koremenos, 2005, 40). On his first day he announced, "[W]e're going to do business a new way. That our purpose for being in the Department was only one and that was to see that older people received the best service they could" (59).

Wirth was effectively offering a trade of autonomy for effort. In exchange for ensuring "that older people received the best service they could," lower level employees were granted a level of autonomy and involvement. One way to give this autonomy was to hear and respect the opinions of lower level employees. As Wirth stated, "Any issue that folks in the field feel should be discussed – it's going to be on that agenda: it's going to be discussed in the meeting" (Koremenos, 2005, 61).

To implement this proposed outcome, Wirth chose to use informal communication patterns. Wirth spent much more time than his predecessor in communicating with subordinates up and down the hierarchy. This effort included an unusual open door policy and "management by walking around." He saw these actions as necessary both to communicate the goals of the organization and to decrease the emphasis on monitoring and sanctions. Wirth wanted to create the expectation on the part of employees that someone who made a mistake while honestly trying to serve organizational goals was protected from sanctions – in other words, he wanted to build trust. The new approach was quickly communicated within the organization. One bureau chief said,

(We've) relaxed somewhat on specifics. There's more flexibility on what can be accepted; this gives the case management level more discretion and autonomy. For social services, we were too rigid in the past. (quoted in Koremenos, 2005, 49)

A lower level employee recognized that an emphasis on close monitoring could only do so much in any event. This subordinate recognized the ability of employees to strategize over rules:

Audits only catch those who don't know how to play the game, get around the rules. You all know how to do that; you could write a book on it! ***You won't need to do that anymore.*** (quoted in Koremenos, 2005, 49, emphasis added)

By Koremenos's account, the less control-oriented style had the desired impact of improving organizational performance. Not only did service quality improve but it also did so while saving money. The department was able to cut the budget by $5.4 million in Wirth's first year and $10 million in his second year (Koremenos, 2005, 36). Much of this savings could be attributed to decreased monitoring and paperwork costs, which were themselves indicators of expanded bureaucratic autonomy.

MONITORING ACTIONS VERSUS REWARDING OUTCOMES

The case of the Illinois Department of Aging illustrates the control paradox: more control may result in less success, and decreased supervisorial control may result in better outcomes. To the extent that these results are understandable and even predictable, we may need to alter our expectations about the impact of bureaucratic autonomy. Instead of viewing bureaucratic autonomy (with Finer) as the antecedent for government corruption, waste, and despair, we may instead look for ways that bureaucrats may be encouraged to do a better job, even with lower monitoring costs.

Intellectually, this argument is related to that in the preceding chapter: more incentives do not always yield the hoped-for consequences because of nearly inevitable information asymmetries in measuring performance. As Holmström and Milgrom pointed out in two papers (Holmström & Milgrom, 1991, 1994), incentivizing the visible aspects of performance is often a mistake; it is better to deemphasize tangible incentives in favor of other forms of motivation.

Sometimes, replacing an incentive system with rules and monitoring is a viable alternative. But many tasks are like those facing the professionals at the Illinois Department of Aging – lots of indicators of *activity* can be monitored, but there is little way to tell from the outside whether the ultimate goals of the organization are being met. In such situations, the temptation, both for the supervisor and many subordinates, is to rely on monitoring the indicators that are easy to measure. Subordinates can justify their salaries that way, and supervisors can tally aggregate indicators to show political overseers just how productive their staff has been. But this is often a mistake.

Control with Constrained Observability

As an alternate to incentives contingent on outcomes, the principal can always invest in supervisors who resolve the information asymmetry directly – by monitoring the agent's actions, rather than the outcomes. This was accomplished most famously at Henry Ford's assembly plants (Halberstam, 1986; Nelson, 1975). The assembly line required very specific activities from each employee on the line. The tasks were broken down to such a degree of specificity that it was easy (relatively costless) to hire supervisors to monitor employee actions. But for jobs that are more complex than tightening a bolt on an assembly line, exerting control by monitoring actions may be limited. The limitations are graphically illustrated by the strategy of "working to rule."

Working to Rule, and Contractual Incompleteness

In 2008, teachers in Stafford County, Virginia, started a "work to rule" campaign (Gonzalez, 2008). "Work to rule" is a tactic in which employees follow the rules in their contract exactly, doing nothing that is not specifically required.

While the strike proceeded, the teachers in Stafford County, one of the wealthiest districts in the country, did not arrive early or stay late. They did no voluntary tutoring. One can imagine that, carried to an extreme, the teachers would not prepare elaborate lessons, decorate the classroom, or encourage students with a word or a smile. A teaching "contract" proves to be more of a minimum acceptable effort than an inspiration to good teaching.

"Work to rule" is a paradoxical labor tactic – why should it be destructive to follow rules? The answer is interesting and telling. For teachers it is impossible to write a contract with sufficient detail that would make the administrators or parents happy if the teachers did only what was required of them. The same could be said for nurses, police, or virtually any public employee who is hired for the tacit knowledge in his or her head. This is just the organizational manifestation of the phenomenon known as "contractual incompleteness" in economics (Coase, 1937). Many of the activities that the principal would like agents to undertake cannot be documented or contracted. Sales staff must watch customer body language for signals that indicate what sales arguments will be most persuasive. Teachers learn to be alert for "teaching moments" when students are especially receptive to particular lessons. Effective police officers learn to watch for subtle cues that indicate suspicious behavior. These are behaviors that cannot be routinized, explicitly specified ex ante, or rewarded ex post.

In short, efficient behaviors for most public employees' jobs generally cannot be mechanically elicited from officials. Unmotivated teachers can learn how to get through the school year with a minimum of fuss – and a minimum of impact on their students. Police officers can easily figure out strategies consistent with any set of standard operating procedures that keep them safely out of danger – and render them useless to the community. As a result, virtually any public organization would grind to a halt if its members did nothing more than provide minimal compliance with rules and orders. Hence, as a way of applying pressure on management, "working to rule" may be as effective a strategy as going on strike without the legal implications.

A MODEL OF MONITORING AND CONTROL

There are paradoxes that come with constrained opportunities for direct monitoring of employees. The most striking is the control paradox, which, as already mentioned, occurs when increased control by employers results in inferior performance by employees.

Consider a model involving an employee (call him Steven) whose employment contract, like most employment contracts, specifies that he will work for a flat wage (W). Steven will receive W in exchange for accepting the direction of the organization, in the form of supervisory commands and fixed operating rules. If he fails to follow the directives, he will receive a sanction in the form of a penalty that is subtracted from his wage. We can operationalize the penalty

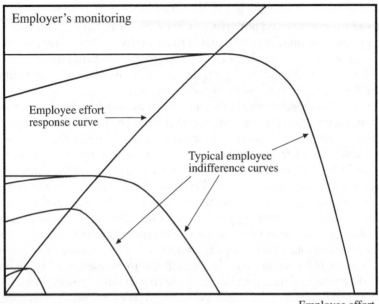

FIGURE 6.1. More Monitoring Results in More Effort in a One-Shot Game.

as a parameter K. In the event that Steven is caught shirking, Steven is paid only (W-K).

Steven has to decide how much effort to supply. The more effort Steven supplies, the smaller the probability that he will be discovered breaking the rules, and the larger the probability that he keeps his flat wage intact, without losing K.

The other actor in this model is Steven's employer. The employer moves first and selects a monitoring level, which appears as a horizontal line. That is, for every possible monitoring level, the boss's selection is constant. As K increases, the y-coordinate increases as well.

The set of Steven's optimal effort responses to every possible level of monitoring is the employee effort response curve, shown as the upwardly sloping line in Figure 6.1. The upward slope of the response curve indicates that, consistent with conventional wisdom, a higher level of monitoring leads to higher levels of effort by Steven. But if the employers' monitoring can induce higher levels of effort, how can this be turned upside down to arrive at the control paradox? Part of the answer comes when we analyze the equilibrium of the monitoring/effort game.

We assume that Steven's indifference curves are like the four sample indifference curves shown in Figure 6.1. Each indifference curve is open toward the lower part of the graph and is convex and single-peaked. These assumptions guarantee that for every level of monitoring by the employer, there will be one

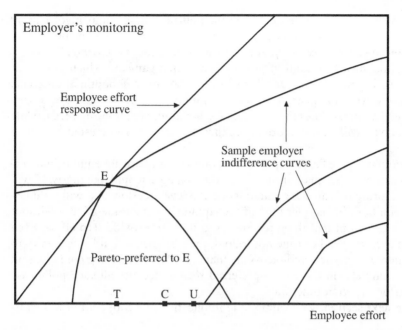

FIGURE 6.2. Cooperation in a Repeated Game Results in a Trade of Effort for Leniency.

best choice of effort level by Steven and, by extension, one best monitoring level by the employer.

The Employer's Effort and Pareto Optimality

The employer's most preferred outcome is for Steven to supply 100% effort with no rule monitoring (because rule monitoring is costly). The employer has indifference curves that are convex around that point. The employer's indifference curves will be positively sloped, as shown in Figure 6.2.

What else do we know for sure about the equilibrium outcome E? As shown in Figure 6.2, E must be Pareto suboptimal. Both the employer and Steven could agree that there is some outcome that is better for both of them.

The reason why we know that equilibrium E is suboptimal is that, at the point E, Steven has an indifference curve with zero slope. Steven's indifference curve is tangent to a horizontal line (the monitoring level selected as the first move of the game) and therefore is flat. The employer's indifference curve is tangent to an upwardly sloping effort response curve. The indifference curves are not tangent at E; they cross at E.

When two indifference curves are not tangent to each other, there is a region that is internal to both indifference curves. This means that there is a region (shown in Figure 6.2 as a cone from Point E to the points T, C, and U) that is internal to both players' indifference curves at E. The entire Pareto-preferred region involves *less monitoring* than at the point E. These points involve *more effort by Steven* than the point E. In other words, a trade should be possible in which Steven supplies *extra effort* in return for *reduced monitoring*.

The game must be a kind of prisoner's dilemma game, in which pursuit of self-interest by both Steven and his employer creates a suboptimal outcome. Cooperation would appear as a trade of employee effort for employer laxity, where "laxity" means the employer reduces her ability to monitor Steven, while hoping Steven will supply more effort than he has a self-interested reason to supply.

Unfortunately, the Pareto-optimal outcomes (like E) are not equilibrium outcomes – in a one-shot play of the game. The manager would like to say, "I will stop monitoring if I can trust you to work at a level of effort that will yield C – and we will both be happier than at the equilibrium outcome E." But without monitoring, the optimal thing for Steven to do is to provide zero effort. Even if Steven agreed ahead of time not to loaf, the statement would be contrary to his self-interest and not credible to the manager. The same thing could be said for everything else in the Pareto-preferred region, because all such points are off the effort reaction function.

In the next section, we examine the implications of cooperation in hierarchies.

"GIFT EXCHANGE": AUTONOMY FOR EFFORT

Sociologist George Homans in his paper, "The Cash Posters," illustrates the possibility of an equilibrium that is Pareto preferred to the subgame perfect equilibrium (Homans, 1954). He examined employees of a public utility who registered cash payments against the accounts of utility company customers. The company had supervisors who had the capacity to monitor the employees' behavior closely and to enforce work rules, including one prohibiting conversation among cash posters. The output standard was 300 postings per hour, with a high degree of accuracy. The cash posters were paid a flat wage, with no bonus for exceeding the standard. Punishments included rebukes or even the possibility of firing any employee who consistently could not meet the standard.

Economist George Akerlof, in his analysis of the cash posters, notes that, because there was no bonus, "the standard economic model of contract would predict that workers set their work habits to meet the company's minimum standards of performance" (Akerlof, 1982, 547). However, as Homans observed, cash posters exceeded the minimum productivity by an average of 17.7%, with increases ranging from 2% to 46%. Akerlof interprets this extra effort as a "gift" to the firm.

The firm reciprocated the extra effort with what Akerlof calls "leniency." Employees consistently expressed a preference for leniency, which they valued as freedom or autonomy. Instrumentally, they valued leniency because it meant a reduction in the possibility of punishment. Employees experience a utility loss from "having someone breathe down their neck." In the eyes of the employees, a "good" employer is one who will allow employees the flexibility to arrive late occasionally when the children are slow to get ready for school, will allow changes in work rates to correspond to varying energy levels during the day, and will turn a blind eye to minor rule violations, such as conversing on the job, that relieve tedium.

An exchange of leniency for unrewarded effort was observed among both management and the cash posters. Indeed, Homans documented that this was to some extent a conscious strategy among the managers at the utility company:

The fact is that cash posting looked to an outsider like a hard and dull job. A number of girls who were offered it had turned it down. The supervisors wisely felt that they would have a still harder time getting recruits and getting out production if they tried to bear down on a group of young girls like this one. (Homans, 1954, 726)

The management realized that "a group of young girls like this one" would have resented a managerial style of "bearing down" on them. As a result, they did not enforce a variety of work "rules" – notably the work rule forbidding conversation among the employees:

They were convinced they could do their work without concentrating on it – they could work and talk at the same time. In theory, talking was discouraged. In practice, the supervisors made little effort to stop it. (Homans, 1954, 727)

Different cash posters worked at different rates, and those who worked less hard tended to regard the hard workers as foolish for working as hard as they did. The lowest producer among the cash posters was critical of the high producers: "They try to get four or five hundred and walk their legs off. I tell them they don't know how we had to fight to get things the way they are now" (Homans, 1954, 732). Those who worked less hard feared that management would simply increase the expected effort level. But this concern did not manifest itself in work restriction group norms:

*The attitudes characteristic of restriction of output were present in the group; the thing itself was not, certainly not as an organized group practice. But neither did the girls feel under any pressure to work particularly fast. Indeed, **the lack of pressure may have been the very thing that helped some of them to work, in fact, very fast indeed.*** (Homans, 1954, 728, emphasis added)

In fact, the voluntary "gift exchange" that Homans saw among the cash posters had not always been present. The women who were there longer remembered when work restriction norms (working to rule) were standard. For most of the women in the room, there seemed to be a delicate balance, in which extra effort rewarded and *sustained* the leniency of the managers, just as the leniency of the managers rewarded and sustained the extra effort by the cash posters.

However, although the cash posters are a provocative illustration, they still do not provide a compelling explanation for cooperation as an equilibrium.

COOPERATION THROUGH REPEATED GAMES

Public bureaucracies, especially those protected by merit systems, have a longer "time horizon" than firms in the market. In most public organizations, both sides recognize they are in it for the long haul, and this time horizon is the basis for the cooperative equilibrium. The future casts a long "shadow" in public bureaucracies, justifying more cooperative efforts.

Suppose the game described in Figures 6.1 and 6.2 is repeated a number of times. In each period of this game, the superior sets a monitoring level, the subordinate picks an effort level, and both sides receive a payoff. If this game were repeated exactly k times, Steven would have no incentive to provide any effort level deviating from the effort response curve. With the knowledge that the final outcome will be E, there is no reason to cooperate in the penultimate period. By backward induction, the outcome will consistently be E for any finitely repeated game.

Suppose, however, that the game does not terminate at a particular time. Like an ongoing organization, there is in any time period a probability d that the game will be repeated another time. This is the familiar scenario in which cooperation is sustainable.

Suppose the supervisor were to play the following trigger strategy: "I will supply zero monitoring as long as I find that you supply effort levels equal to e_C or greater. If I ever discover that you have supplied less effort than that, then I will revert to monitoring levels of m_E." To this repeated game strategy, it is rational for Steven to respond with the following trigger strategy of his own: "I will supply effort equal to e_C as long as you, in fact, provide zero monitoring. But if I ever find you supplying more monitoring than that, then I will respond with a point on my effort response curve forever after that." Each of these strategies is a best response to the other's strategy, as long as the probability of repeated play is sufficiently high. In other words, rational, self-interested individuals can agree to cooperate (play the given trigger strategy) as long as the other does (Miller, 2004, 111).

Each player has a threat that can "enforce" the other's cooperation. The employer's threat is to increase monitoring if Steven does not provide high levels of effort; Steven's threat is minimal compliance – working to rule – if the supervisor increases monitoring.

Thus the "gift exchange" observed by Homans among the cash posters could simply be the rational response of supervisor and employee to the other's implicit threats and promises.

Explaining the Control Paradox

To implement the cooperative solution to the control/monitoring game, the cooperative solution C involves *less* control but *more* effort, compared with the one-shot equilibrium E. To put it another way, *more* hierarchical control can destroy the multiperiod cooperative equilibrium C and result in a collapse of tit-for-tat exchange – and less effort. This possible outcome is the control paradox. The idea that more monitoring and supervision can result in less control seems paradoxical, especially in light of the effort response function in Figure 6.2. The control paradox occurs when a cooperative equilibrium, at C, collapses to E. Outcome E results in more monitoring and less effort, if it can be maintained.

Note that this result does not mean that monitoring and control are irrelevant – even when they are not used. In the cooperative equilibrium of the repeated game, it is the credible threat of tightened monitoring that encourages the employee to provide high levels of effort "voluntarily."

The Fragility of Cooperation: The Rigidity Cycle

Gouldner's classic study in the early 1950s analyzed effort and supervision in a gypsum mine and plant in Indiana (Gouldner, 1954). The local owners had a comfortable relationship with their employees. They were lax about enforcing rules against tardiness or socializing on the job. Employees could take some time during the workday to take care of personal errands. They could even "borrow" equipment or materials from the plant's supplies – for example, the largely rural employees would occasionally borrow a stick of dynamite for fishing. Furthermore, the employers and managers were not sticklers for enforcing status distinctions between themselves and the employees. The men wore overalls, and so did the managers. The employees called the managers by their first names. When they were hiring, managers would encourage close relatives of current employees to apply for the open positions. They felt that this helped lead to a close-knit community of employees who would be able to cooperate with each other in the mine and on the surface. In return, the employees would respond by working overtime when needed to fill an important order and thus contribute effort to improve both product quality and safety.

The owner and manager regarded the plant as basically a profitable enterprise and did not push too hard to try to increase productivity and revenue. Employees gave a greater effort than the level of monitoring or consequences for shirking really warranted. The outcome was apparently a C for cooperative equilibrium.

This all changed when a strict new management team took over. The new managers announced their intention to increase productivity. They attempted to achieve this goal by cracking down on following the rules and adding more rules. They put in a time clock so that they could monitor and sanction tardiness and absenteeism. The managers reinforced status distinctions by wearing different clothes (trousers with a crease; button-down shirts) at the plant.

Not only was hierarchy emphasized but monitoring and sanctions also increased awareness of the rules. Consequences for violating them were made very clear: "Failure to arrive on time will result in firing." One effect of these rules was to clarify how to get by without getting fired – in particular, employees became acutely aware of the *minimum* effort they could offer without getting fired. The clarity of rules interacted with the clarity of hierarchy to reduce the willingness of employees to work hard: the status distinctions led employees to be less willing to undertake voluntary compliance with the goals of the organization.

Less voluntary compliance in turn resulted in a further tightening of the rules and increased monitoring by hierarchical superiors, which in turn resulted in even less willing compliance. The pattern was a vicious cycle in which hierarchy and rules led to less voluntary compliance, which led to more hierarchical monitoring, sanctions, and further elaboration of the rules. Gouldner calls this "the rigidity cycle." It is understandable as the collapse of the C equilibrium and the reversion to the suboptimal E equilibrium

The net result, Gouldner suggests, was decreased performance. The case is a compelling example of the control paradox – when *stricter* attempts to control subordinates result in *less* effort by subordinates.

AN EXPERIMENT WITH CONTROL IN AN EMPLOYMENT AGENCY

The tasks of the street-level bureaucrat (teaching, police work, social service) are often those for which monitoring by supervisors is difficult. That does not stop supervisors from trying to monitor bureaucrats' performance.

Sociologist Peter Blau analyzed two sections of a state employment agency that were similar enough to provide the basis for a natural experiment. The two divisions, Section A and Section B, performed nearly identical tasks: trying to connect out-of-work clients with employment opportunities (Blau, 1963). Employees in both sections were closely monitored. In his study, Blau even gathered data that the employee agency did not. One key variable was the number of interviews resulting in referrals. Another piece of data was "hoarding" of good leads. Blau (but not the agency) gathered data on the proportion of job leads received by a bureaucrat that were eventually filled by that bureaucrat's clients; a disproportionately high figure indicated that the employee had found ways to "hoard" those job openings and was labeled by Blau as reflecting "competitive" behavior.

Section A had more competitive employees, along with a strict supervisor who based performance evaluations on the statistics available. The supervisor felt that "here, in the production figures, is the answer to the question, How good are you?" (Blau, 1963, 65). This supervisor's attitude induced (intentionally or not) a high level of competitiveness among many of the Section A interviewers. Within Section A, there was a strong correlation between competitiveness and productivity – and positive performance evaluations. The most competitive employment counselors (those who hoarded information most often) got the highest productivity figures and the most positive performance evaluations.

The Section B supervisor was perceived as being much less reliant on the productivity statistics. By monitoring the placement statistics less closely, the supervisor rewarded less such competitive behaviors as "hoarding." "Since their ratings were not primarily based on performance records, members of Section B were less anxious about productivity, and this encouraged the development and persistence of co-operative norms" (Blau, 1963, 65). In particular, the cooperative norms included much more sharing of employment opportunity information among employment counselors. As a result, there was no correlation between competitiveness and productivity.

The agency experienced an aggregation paradox: "the group much concerned with productivity [Section A] was less productive than the group unconcerned with it [Section B]" (Blau, 1963, 69). By sharing employment opportunities more widely, Section B was able to fill 67% of job openings compared to 59% for Section A. Section A supervisor's use of hierarchical monitoring and performance evaluations apparently triggered a manifestation of the control paradox – more monitoring led to less productive behavior. The comparative success of Section B was due to its supervisor's deemphasis on the overt use of control mechanisms, which was reciprocated by more non-monitored cooperation in the behaviors that really counted – the sharing of placement opportunities (Miller, 2004, 115).

The behavior of the section employees was certainly rational *given the behavior of their bosses*. It was rational for the supervisor of Section A to provide close monitoring and to link performance evaluation with performance, when that managerial style was so obviously efficacious in motivating strong performance figures; yet it was also rational for the supervisor in Section B to provide more lax monitoring and flexible performance evaluations when that managerial style was reciprocated by stronger section performance as a whole. Each actor's style was a "best response" to the respective partner, as is definitionally true of equilibrium behavior.

IMPLICATIONS: CONGRESSIONAL OVERSIGHT AND THE
CONTROL PARADOX

In the mid-1960s, William Crockett was the director of the State Department's Area O. Area O is responsible for all the housekeeping functions of the department (including personnel, office space, and supplies). Like many bureaucrats of the 1960s, Crockett found insight in Douglas McGregor's distinction between Theory X and Theory Y (McGregor, 1960). Theory X held that subordinates were basically unmotivated and needed to be forced by hierarchy and rules to accomplish their assigned tasks. Theory Y held that subordinates could be motivated by the satisfaction of a challenging assignment. Crockett felt Area O was ripe for reform rooted in Theory Y. He decided to grant more bureaucratic autonomy by decreasing the levels of hierarchy and red tape.

According to Warwick's account of the State Department Area O reforms, the changes yielded the inversion of the control paradox, at least initially: in

Area O, loosened control led to more efficiency (Warwick, 1975). Crockett eliminated many of the procedural rules that restricted individual behavior and many of the levels of hierarchy in the chain of command beneath him. With a flatter hierarchy, every subordinate found it difficult to turn to a superior for directions – they then had to take initiative and make decisions for themselves more often. The elimination of rules requiring higher level clearances of lower level decisions had the same effect. The net effect was to reduce drastically the level of monitoring experienced by each subordinate in Area O. One of the positive results was technical efficiency: more work was being done by a smaller staff. The section director's information level about Area O and thus his ability to make effective decisions also improved.

Despite signs of success, the changes were not greeted with a great deal of enthusiasm from either the managers or the employees. The officials at the State Department knew that they were in a hostile political environment; they had few interest group supporters working for them in Congress. At the time of the Area O reforms, Congressman Rooney of the House Appropriations Committee was known for his close scrutiny of State Department programs, searching for both waste and signs of un-Americanism.

Because of this hostile congressional environment, State Department managers felt a strong need for close control of their subordinates. Supervisors regarded both hierarchy and rules favorably, because they would help assure that no subordinate was taking some action that would threaten their careers. Similarly, subordinates at Area O knew that the reduction of monitoring by their own superiors did not mean that they were free from punishment. Warwick recounts stories of individuals brought from the depths of the State Department to account for decisions that Congressman Rooney did not like (Warwick, 1975, 74–75).

The surest way to be "selected out" of the Foreign Service was to stand out from the crowd. This built-in risk caused Foreign Service officers to feel the need to be able to justify each of their actions. Justification came through two routes: hierarchy and rules. Each officer wanted to be able to say, in justification of her behavior, either "My behavior was authorized by my immediate superior," or "My behavior resulted from a simple application of standard operating procedure" (Miller, 2004, 117).

Both superiors and subordinates, therefore, could agree on the need for hierarchy and rules, which meant opposing the Area O reforms. The opposition was strong enough to undo the reforms. Warwick reports that essentially all of the eliminated levels of hierarchy and rules were reestablished within a few short years. In the presence of a hostile environment and vague performance criteria, a high level of hierarchy and rules becomes an equilibrium in the bureaucratic game (e.g., Carpenter, 1996; Whitford, 2002).

The undoing of the Crockett reforms was also an example of the control paradox: increasing hierarchy and rules generated more control by superiors over subordinates, but the increased control led to a reversion to the inefficient levels of performance that the State Department was known for before the reforms. The net effect is that congressional attempts to increase control of the State Department were instrumental in the creation of the bureaucratic characteristics that Congress disliked – hierarchy, rule following, and red tape. The irony is that Congress's felt need for control was crucial to the process that resulted in the State Department that Congress loved to hate.

CONTROL OF PUBLIC VERSUS PRIVATE SCHOOLS

Other public bureaucracies have experienced a decrease in performance resulting from tightened control. One might think that the goal of a public school is a great deal clearer than that of the State Department. That is evidently not the case. Outstanding research by Chubb and Moe (1988) has found that democratic political processes impose multiple conflicting goals on our school districts. In some places prayer in schools is a contentious issue; in others, it is creationism. Schools are simultaneously asked to teach patriotic values, reduce teenage pregnancy, and fight the "war on drugs." Teachers, students, and parents in public schools are much more confused about their schools' goals than are the same constituencies of private schools. Chubb and Moe (1988) find that the presence of a clear vision for the school, parents, students, and educators in private schools makes it easier to generate satisfactory results, without a great deal of hierarchy or rule monitoring.

In public schools, goals are more ambiguous, and monitoring by principals is more threatening. "Politicians have the authority to shape the schools through public policy, and precisely because they have this authority, they are consistently under pressure from interest groups to exercise it...while principals and teachers may praise the virtues of autonomy, the 'one best system' is organized against it" (Chubb & Moe, 1988, 1069–1070). Private schools are much less likely to be monitored by outside administrators than public schools, and their boards are significantly less intrusive in matters of disciplinary and personnel policy (1073). In public schools, principals are less likely to have teaching experience, more likely to be motivated by a preference for administration, and less successful in demonstrating leadership in the eyes of the teachers (1078). Public school teachers experience more monitoring and less autonomy in curriculum, text selection, techniques, discipline, and the like. As a result, teachers in private schools are more likely to agree that "success is not beyond their personal control," and their job satisfaction is higher (1083).

Public school boards have evidently succeeded in exerting the control that they have sought to wield. Public school teachers are more rule bound and monitored and feel less in control and less satisfied. In the least effective schools, rules and hierarchy (as in the State Department) become the means for protecting teachers and school administrators from political flak. To some degree at least, politicians get what they want (reelection) and so do school officials (security): the only losers are the students, their parents, and teachers.

"The key difference between public and private environments – and thus between public and private schools – derive[s] from their characteristic methods of social control: the public schools are subordinates in a hierarchic system of democratic politics, whereas private schools are largely autonomous actors 'controlled' by the market" (Chubb & Moe, 1988, 1064). Public charter schools combine elements of both private and public boards. The control that parents exercise in private schools is through the market mechanism of choice, not through the hierarchical lines of principal-agency theory. The more school boards try to "control" teachers – by creating ever-elongated monitoring hierarchies, by proliferating rules that limit teacher autonomy – the more clearly they create the conditions for rigid, uninspired teaching (and decrease the overall effectiveness of their own schools). "The school is thus in the best position to know how to enhance its own organizational well-being. Hierarchical control...tends to be inefficient and counterproductive" (1068). Where does the external pressure come from in public schools? "The raison d'etre of democratic control is to impose higher-order value on schools and thus limit their autonomy" (1069).

Chubb and Moe attribute responsibility for the failure of public schools to democratic governance and hierarchical accountability. "It is no accident that public schools are lacking in autonomy, that principals have difficulty leading, and that school goals are heterogeneous, unclear, and undemanding. Nor is it an accident that weak principals and tenured unionized teachers struggle for power. These sorts of characteristics constitute an organizational syndrome whose roots are deeply anchored in democratic control as we have come to know it" (Chubb & Moe, 1988, 1084). This is a remarkable position to take in a society that values democratic governance and bureaucratic control above all. Stability is the first victim of democratic governance as described by Chubb and Moe.

Once again, Chubb and Moe offer the prospect of an inevitable tradeoff: "public schools cannot be anything we might want them to be....It may well be, then, that the key to school improvement is not school reform but institutional reform – a shift away from direct democratic control" (Chubb & Moe, 1988, 1085).

FROM COORDINATION TO COOPERATION

In a monitoring relationship, both sides may gain from a "gift exchange" of autonomy (more lenient monitoring) for voluntary effort. This exchange is sustainable as one of the cooperative equilibria to the repeated game. This implies that the "shadow of the future" – the shared knowledge of the benefits to be received from a long-term, committed relationship – is crucial to establishing and maintaining this cooperative equilibrium (Axelrod, 1984).

But what else is necessary to sustain this exchange? The folk theorem tells us that there are a number of equilibria in a repeated game (Friedman, 1971). Consider a repeated game in which Steven displays different levels of effort. The point T, on the horizontal axis, is sustainable as an equilibrium of a slightly different repeated game than that which sustains point C. The same is true for U. One player might prefer T, while another prefers the point U. They would be likely to have sharp differences in opinion about T versus U, even though both are cooperative equilibria. And, of course, the point C is also an equilibrium to the repeated game. The ambiguity of multiple cooperative equilibria is itself a threat to cooperation. What is needed is not just cooperation, but coordination.

The implication is that both a long "shadow of the future" and a shared desire to cooperate away from E are not sufficient to guarantee a cooperative outcome. What is also needed is a solution to the coordination problem created by the multiplicity of viable outcomes from cooperation. What would it take to coordinate on a single, Pareto-optimal equilibrium such as T, U, or C?

Solving the coordination problem requires a leader capable of generating a high level of confidence on the part of the players that everyone is converging on a particular cooperative outcome and that everyone (especially the leader) can be trusted to implement the cooperative strategies that support that equilibrium.

Moreover, "trust" clearly plays a role in "switching" equilibria – from E to C. The problem is one of coordination: creating common knowledge by all relevant players that each person can expect the appropriate behaviors for C from all other relevant players. The employees, notably, have to trust that the supervisor is in fact *not* going to monitor employees closely in order to affix blame in the case of external hostility. It is reasonable to believe that the supervisor is going to take this course only if she is a particular kind of bureaucratic leader – one who is committed to succeeding by making the organization work well, not by using the organization as a stepping-stone to higher office in a different organization. In the cases described earlier, the bureaucratic leaders who inspired the most loyalty and confidence in their subordinates were careful both to create a shared commitment to a set of organizational goals and to find ways to convince employees that they were protected from external threats as long as they took risks in furtherance of those organizational goals. As one official at the Illinois Department of Aging said of Wirth, "It's a whole different thing of trust ... They knew if Vic said he was going to do something he would. And if he said he wasn't going to do something, he wasn't" (Koremenos, 2005, 61).

But supervisors also need to have some trust in their employees. In offering outcome C instead of E as the coordinated equilibrium, supervisors are offering a deal: autonomy for voluntary effort. They have to believe that their employees value autonomy and are willing to make and honor the proposed "deal."

Choosing among various motivational and control techniques is therefore a major decision for a leader in a bureaucracy. For those leaders in technological settings in which it is difficult and costly to monitor effort or reward outcomes, creating an "autonomy for effort" trade may be the best of several imperfect options.

We have supplied numerous examples of the control paradox here. In public schools, democratic governance exacerbates the obstacles to effective teaching. In two sections of an employment agency, the section with the more control-oriented supervisor underperforms compared to the one with the laxer supervisor. In the State Department, an effective reform is undermined by demand for more control, up and down the hierarchy. In the Illinois Department of Aging, undoing hierarchical control allows for equilibrium with less control but more professionalism.

These examples, as wide ranging as they are, do not prove that it is never wise to seek control. As long as the employer is satisfied with work to rule, then cooperation is not an issue. But in cases in which work-to-rule–inspired minimal effort is insufficient, then avoiding hierarchical control offers the prospect of gains from cooperation in the form of leniency for effort trades.

Congress and the Taylor Rule

Consider again the use of the Taylor rule as a way for Congress to enforce its will with an independent Federal Reserve. On one hand, through its use politicians could achieve a proximate goal – such as reducing the chance that monetary policy might be too accommodative (or too restrictive). There is political advantage here: a compliant Fed is more likely to follow a policy path that interested parties in the market can take advantage of in their own market operations. On the other hand, a compliant Fed, or at least one that can be predicted because it follows a rule, will face internal and external pressure to avoid actions that require ex post explanation (or ex ante permissions for deviations from the rule).

One important point here is that such interventions – either directly via traditional mechanisms of control or through novel control strategies like the Taylor rule – damage the abilities of an organization's leaders to shape the fabric of its decisions. Leaders often achieve their goals not through strict hierarchical arrangements, but by shaping (over time and in numerous ways) the organization's culture. We briefly turn to organizational culture.

CULTURE, REPETITION, AND PRINCIPAL-AGENCY THEORY

Reciprocity-based trust is not equally available in every principal-agent relationship. It is no doubt hard to generate in distant, impersonal relationships among people who have no ongoing relationships or, worse, are in relationships already characterized by mistrust and suspicion. It is easiest to generate in face-to-face relationships among people who already have a basis of understanding and perhaps an ongoing relationship of trust. Building trust generates its own costs, perhaps in the form of establishing face-to-face relationships of shared expectations that facilitate coordination on a more, rather than less, cooperative equilibrium (Chwe, 1998).

Consider a hierarchical relationship occurring over a long period of time. Rather than a classic two-move game (offer and response), the principal and agent have a history of observing each other (Radner, 1985). In this "supergame," the principal could punish the agent statistically, based on the history of the interaction; while the agent might discount the future, the principal could use the history optimally as long as the interaction goes on basically forever. However, because the interaction is unlikely to go on forever (Prendergast, 1999), the principal instead might punish the agent for poor performance (or the agent might punish the principal for reneging on an earlier agreement) over something longer than a two-move game but shorter than forever. Most of the time, however, such organizations are made up of both explicit and implicit contracts – and when the relationship is repeated, policing the explicit contract might instead just damage the implicit contract (Baker, Gibbons, & Murphy, 1994).

Repeated games lead to a role for leadership that goes beyond many conventional views. Leadership is probably not best embodied in a charismatic, forceful person who inspires employees to do what they would otherwise not want to do. "Charisma" is probably less useful than clarity – in particular, clarity about the nature of the equilibrium that employers and employees are striving to maintain. This is an important point about organizations made up of both implicit and explicit contracts: the organization's ability to rely at all on explicit contracts turns largely on the presence of widely applicable, simple-to-understand principles that complete the gaps in the contracts. Principles and the way they are communicated form the organization's culture (Kreps 1990; Miller 1992).

Effective leadership involves the creation or at least maintenance of rituals that create common knowledge about organizational culture (Chwe, 2001). Because cooperation can unwind easily, it is important that everyone is fully aware of the long-term consequences of that unwinding.

CONCLUSION: A FRAGILE EQUILIBRIUM

A repeated game equilibrium can generate a Pareto-preferred exchange of employee effort for the employer's grant of autonomy. However, a repeated game equilibrium cannot persist if the shadow of the future shrinks.

In the State Department, the possibility of being forced out of the Foreign Service for nonconformity keeps the time horizon brief. Constant threats and pressure from interest groups and Congress instill in bureaucrats the rigid red-tape response that the political overseers had hoped to avoid. In the politics of schools, public school boards can only bow to the pressures of politics; private schools offer the prospect of an institutional regime that encourages bureaucratic autonomy. Blau's Section B supervisor decreased demand for control (compared to Section A) and reaped the benefits of cooperation in the form of more effort for increased leniency. In general, bureaucratic autonomy is not just laxity or laziness – it is the basis for a political inducement for bureaucrats to supply more effort. As in Gouldner's accounting of a rigidity cycle, employers' use of more monitoring through rule enforcement and hierarchy could cause a collapse of the efficient equilibrium. This would be perceived as a control paradox. Employers' views of hierarchy, monitoring, and rules would serve to clarify for employees the minimal efforts that would keep themselves from being fired. In response to employees "working to rule," employers would feel that cracking down on employees and their autonomy was the only rational response.

But does an autonomous bureaucracy imply an unhealthy dictatorship of bureaucracy or a weakened role for democratic institutions? What motivates autonomous bureaucrats? Are they completely lacking in constraint – engaging in random, feckless behaviors?

This chapter offers the possibility that bureaucrats can engage in systematic political negotiation that leaves both bureaucrats and their political overseers mutually constrained – and mutually better off. Bureaucratic autonomy as acknowledged by their superiors serves as the inducement for high-effort/high-quality outcomes. Bureaucratic autonomy can be consistent with bureaucratic responsibility.

In repeated games with a sufficiently long time horizon, bureaucratic autonomy is less an obstacle to bureaucratic success and more a means to negotiate greater success. Bureaucratic autonomy could advance the cause of credible commitment to a stable rights and contract enforcement regime. Although the vignettes in this chapter may seem one-off and unsystematic, they illustrate the kind of negotiation and contractual benefits generated by one type of central institution of society and government – the professions.

7

Professionalism and Credible Commitment

Professionals are difficult to control, but their behavior is fairly easy to predict. And that, of course, is at the heart of all this. A professional, if given total autonomy and insulated from external pressures, can be counted upon to behave in a manner characteristic of his type. That is what true professionalism is all about. This very predictability ensures business and labor that their mutual interests in stability, clarity, and expertise will be protected.

— Moe (1987, 259)

LAWYERS VERSUS ECONOMISTS

In 1969, the United States initiated a lawsuit against IBM, charging that its dominance of the mainframe computer industry made it a monopoly. The government wanted IBM to break itself into several smaller companies. IBM hired 200 lawyers to defend against the lawsuit, which lasted for 13 years (Konrad, 2000).

The Antitrust Division of the Department of Justice (DOJ), which had historically taken a strong position against monopoly, brought the government's suit. Part of the reason for the division's animosity toward monopoly was that it was an agency that was then dominated by lawyers, and their strong professional ties defined its priorities (Weaver, 1977, 1980). Acting as lawyers, they read the Clayton Antitrust Act (1913) as demanding action of this sort. But the position of the Antitrust Division regarding appropriate and inappropriate behavior began to change shortly after the suit was filed. The change was linked to a new infusion of economists into the division, who brought with them a different interpretation of the antitrust activities of government (Katzmann, 1980). They argued that monopoly as such was not necessarily a harmful structure for some industries.

Economists were very critical of the case against IBM. IBM continued to make innovations in the industry; it only began to lose its edge as the industry itself changed during the 13 long years of the government lawsuit. The shift was from mainframe to personal computers, and the suit against IBM may well have contributed to its increasing inability to compete in the new world of PCs.

Many economists argued (in effect) that the social control costs (e.g., IBM's legal expenses and loss of marketing edge) greatly exceeded the reduction in social disorder costs (the possible extraction of monopoly prices in the computer industry) (Djankov et al., 2003). Economists promoted a new bottom-line test – the Antitrust Division should only proceed with suits that could actually bring greater efficiency to the market. A more appropriate target for the division, the economists argued, would be actual price-fixing arrangements between competitors.

A transformation of the Antitrust Division was eagerly sought by a variety of sources, including members of Congress and eventually the Reagan administration. But how could change be initiated – what was the best lever available?

One early advocate for change was Assistant Attorney General Thomas Kauper, the head of the Antittrust Division. In 1972, he started to channel economists into the division by hiring them to staff its recently created Economic Policy Office (Eisner & Meier, 1990, 276). He hoped that there would be enough economists to conduct analyses, independent of legal staff, on case selection.

When he came to office in 1981, Ronald Reagan supported the Antitrust Division's narrowing of goals and its emphasis on improving market processes. In 1982, the government dropped the IBM case, and Reagan was given credit for the "revolution" occurring in antitrust litigation.

Eisner and Meier (1990) conducted empirical tests of the determinants of change in antitrust policy. They found that none of the indicators of political control (Reagan's presidency, congressional ideology) had any impact on the number of monopoly lawsuits or of price-fixing lawsuits. Instead, what did predict the activities of the division was an internal revolution: the changing staff makeup of the Antitrust Division. In the short run, the growing number of economists, who were involved in case selection, sharply increased the number of price-fixing cases and decreased the number of monopoly cases. In the price-fixing cases, the internal cause could be narrowed down further: the creation of the Office of Economic Policy in 1972 had increased the previously marginal impact of economists. Thus DOJ did manage to change direction not by hierarchical heavy-handedness, not by infringing on professional expertise, but by enlisting a different profession – economists – with a different worldview and a different set of expectations.

So the "revolution" in antitrust activity is best thought of as the result of an infusion of new ideas from the economics profession. This case raises several questions. What is the role of professionals in governmental bureaucracies? What demands do professionals make with regard to their employment relationship, and how successful are they in reaching these goals? Where does the loyalty of professionals lie? How effective are incentives or rule monitoring in controlling the behavior of professionals?

We argue that professionals play a unique role in government. "Professional" signifies more than an individual demographic, such as "homeowner" or "college graduate." A professional is a member of a *social code* that imposes its own expectations and norms on its members; the professional feels pressure to abide by these sanctions in order to stay in good standing as a professional (e.g., Levinthal & March, 1993, 108). A profession's demands for professional autonomy are strong and sustained. Because of this, the lines of authority in a bureaucratic hierarchy become tenuous; tensions are especially strong between a professional subordinate and a manager without professional credentials. The control mechanisms imposed by elected officials may be weakened or interrupted.

The weak political control over professionalized agencies may have its disadvantages, but it also has an important advantage: it makes professionals – and professionally dominated agencies – ideal vehicles for credible commitment (Knott & Miller, 2008; Miller, 2000). Investors, entrepreneurs, and other economic actors have to worry less about political instability and/or favoritism when the lines of control from politicians to professionals are weak. The same actors can take comfort that professionals are, in the long run, more stable and more even-handed than politicians with electoral motivations, interest group clients, and a strong taste for logrolling. Yet professionals – though minimally accountable to politicians – are *not* so many loose cannons in the ship of state. In addition to seeking autonomy, the essence of professionalism is predictability and constraint – as Moe reminds us in this chapter's epigraph. So, to the extent that professionals are following the professional model – the social code – then professions can help provide autonomy without arbitrariness.

We want to be very clear about our position here. We are not claiming that professionalism is a universal good – we know that professions are not perfect mechanisms that dictate the behaviors of bureaucrats. Instead, our view is that some fields, such as political science, have long neglected to acknowledge professions as an important, if not fundamental, source of social control over agency employees. Political principals hand over discretionary authority in many agencies (and in economic agencies in particular) in a process of socialized delegation, with the response to that delegation made more predictable when bureaucrats act as members of specific professions. Of course, bureaucrats may choose to act against the norms and socialized control of those professions, but doing so would violate the negotiated agreement we believe is the centerpiece of the credible commitment process.

In sum, we argue that professions such as law, economics, medicine, or the biological sciences have been overlooked as a source of bureaucratic motivation. Professions institutionalize a set of incentives that are at least as powerful, and more appropriate, than financial incentives. A professional orientation can serve to commit governments to a fixed set of rules governing property rights and contract enforcement – and at the same time constrain professionals from exercising their autonomy in an opportunistic way. Political control is minimized and economic actors reassured when monetary policy, securities regulation or the resolution of labor conflict is not in the hands of politicians.

WHAT MAKES PROFESSIONALISM DIFFERENT?

Students of professionalism are largely in agreement about the important characteristics of professions (Freidson, 2001; R. H. Hall, 1968; Scott, 1969; Wilensky, 1964). In this section we review these characteristics and note that (in the aggregate) they define a powerful alternative incentive system operating outside of that imposed by organizational hierarchy. We characterize this system as a social code – specifically, as a nexus of contracts. Professions inevitably seek a distinct status of "separateness" that transforms a professionalized bureaucracy into an obstacle to hierarchical control.

Expertise

At the heart of a profession is a body of knowledge. Training in this knowledge is the minimal requirement for membership in the profession. The training is extensive and costly to the trainee; it has high asset specificity (Williamson, 1983). One implication is that the training constitutes a barrier to entry; it is presumed that most people will not and could not successfully undergo the training necessary for professional status. The training process screens out (deters entry of) candidates for professional status whose abilities may be insufficient to the challenge (Kreps & Wilson, 1982). The high standards help develop and maintain a public reputation that is the ultimate resource of professionals in their dealings with the state.

Why should anyone undertake this costly training? The fact that the training constitutes a barrier to entry means that it is possible for the members of the profession to extract monopoly profits for the professional services they provide.

Expertise is an important element of most accounts of the delegation of policy by politicians to bureaus. But it is sometimes difficult to measure expertise when viewed from outside the policy process. For instance, Gailmard and Patty (2013, 79) define expertise as "whatever measures Congress, the executive, agency heads, or their contemporaries declared to be policy relevant at the time in question. In most situations, the measures were education based: technical training, advanced study, and professional certifications." For their purposes, subjectivity is appropriate because the principal is selecting what type of expertise to require of the staff it places in the organization.

Of course, psychologists have long sought to understand the cognitive bases for expertise (e.g., Chase & Simon, 1973; A. D. de Groot, 1965). Consider an expert chess player. An expert player brings knowledge to the game; she accesses that knowledge and uses it while discovering information (the other player's moves) during the game's course. The degree of endogenous learning (expertise development) that can occur during the game depends on the stock of held knowledge and how the expert player accesses that knowledge (psychologists often see this as access to knowledge "chunks") as the game develops – as she is exposed to different configurations of chess pieces.

Expertise is rooted in what Polanyi (1958) called "tacit knowledge": "we can know more than we can tell" (Polanyi, 1966, 4). Moreover, humans share this tacit knowledge as members of social groups or often within communities of practice (J. S. Brown & Duguid, 1991). The professional, as a member of the professional community, practices the highest level of specialist expertise: contributory expertise. Going beyond the kind of knowledge that comes from exposure to primary source material, contributory knowledge is not just the ability to do something – say, in Polanyi's terms, to balance on a bicycle. Reaching the level of contributory expertise also requires a social understanding of how to pass along and acquire tacit knowledge ("interactional expertise") (Collins & Evans, 2007). To become a chess master, the player must learn how to learn inside the group of players.

For professionals in agencies, their knowledge base that allows them to practice (and further increase) their expertise was usually developed before they came to the agency, within a practice community. When practicing that expertise – within an agency, in the context of new problems and issues – professionals build on that reservoir of tacit knowledge; they also continue to reference how they exercise that expertise against the larger practice community (or profession). Experience within the agency enhances tacit knowledge and interactional expertise by adding "procedural expertise" (Gailmard, 2010; Gailmard & Patty, 2007).

One might consider this investment in expertise as a kind of restriction on how bureaucrats act. Perhaps negotiations over decisions in agencies are like voting in multidimensional spaces, and professionalism acts as a domain restriction on the preferences people bring to the decision. Perhaps decisions are made in hierarchies, and professionalism acts as a type restriction on an agent's behavior – a limit on her preferences for certain actions. Domain and type restrictions would enable "normative isomorphism" (DiMaggio & Powell, 1983).

Perhaps, as is argued in the literature on public service motivation (Perry & Wise, 1990), this investment in expertise is a self-restriction on what goes into the bureaucrat's utility function – that the bureaucrat holds strong beliefs about the value of government service and work in the public interest. Indeed, Gazley provides evidence that a public service ethos among public employees is strongly connected to the professions they join (and even to the behavior of the associations representing those professions) (Gazley, 2014).

John DiIulio advocates for "principled agents" who engage in gift giving (DiIulio, 1994). For Brehm and Gates (1999), commitment to the job and peer expectations – along with professional standards – help explain why bureaucrats work hard. For Tonon (2008), professionalism imposes costs on bureaucrats that enhance their credibility; Miller and Whitford (2007) argue that this binding limits the power of oversight (in principal-agency terms). For Teodoro, professionalism helps define a career ladder that encourages administrators to consider views and values that reside outside the organization (Teodoro, 2011, 2014).

These are all plausible mechanisms for the role of professionalism in decision making, but our interest in these kinds of domain and type restrictions is limited to the ways an individual investment in a body of expertise, defined by held tacit knowledge, makes the professional unique among other professionals but at the same time the member of a group of similarly abled members.

Long-Term Career Perspective

Professional training not only serves as a barrier to entry in support of those monopoly profits but also provides the basis for a life-long career (Salop & Salop, 1976). It is not worthwhile to undertake years of training without expecting to benefit from the training for a lengthy period of time. For the professional, the cost of training is like paying a bond – a self-selection device that helps guarantee some measure of career longevity. This long-term time perspective creates a long "shadow of the future" (Axelrod, 1984). Thus professionals can expect a career that outlives partisan control over the White House or either chamber of Congress.

This orientation helps provide incentives for members of the profession to undertake costly cooperation in the maintenance of professional standards of training and service delivery. Because those without the training are deemed unable to perform professional tasks in the same way that the professional can, it is essential to the notion of "profession" that the expertise acquired in becoming a professional is valued by others in society.

Freidson claims that "monopoly is essential to professionalism, which directly opposes it to the logic of competition in a free market" (Freidson, 2001, 3). Self-selection into the profession via training changes the labor market for professionals – perhaps making it not an exact monopoly, but certainly introducing a layer of protection against replacement. A consequence of this process, of course, is that professions practice guild-like entry restrictions.

Professional Insularity

Because of the arduous training, the financial compensation, and the life-long career orientation, the professional normally experiences a psychological identification with the profession. A lawyer working for a company will normally think of herself first as a lawyer and only secondly as an employee of a particular company. She may change jobs, but her professional image of herself remains the same. "The training is likely to socialize the student into a distinct occupational culture that is shared with fellow-students, reinforced and elaborated first by the faculty and later by colleagues in practice. The course of training is also likely to foster a deep interest in the specialized knowledge and skill upon which it is focused" (Freidson, 2001, 102).

Of course, professionals could dissipate monopoly profits by acting individualistically. An orthopedic surgeon hopes that all his peers maintain the highest standards of patient concern and care, so as to prop up the profession's reputation; the dedicated efforts of others maintain the profession's reputation and allow her to do well financially. But each professional is aware that every *other* professional faces the same incentives to free-ride on the profession – with catastrophic results. If every orthopedic surgeon were to ignore patient needs and recommend unnecessary back surgery, then the demand for orthopedic surgeons would diminish and disappear, as doubts about the diagnoses of surgeons increased. Clearly, the success of the profession overall and of each professional individually depends on professional discipline in the interest of maintaining professional standards of patient care. If the profession fails to enforce the best standards of care, then the public's support for the discipline will erode.

Likewise, just as professionals within a given profession understand their mutual incentives, professionals across professions recognize the forces that reinforce insularity. Surgeons share a practice space with nurses, anesthesiologists, and even accountants. Each profession has its own unique forces shaping competition within the practice community; each has its own social code that shapes professional identification.

Professional Discipline

The solution to the professional collective action dilemma begins with training, and expertise becomes the basis for professional expectations of deference to professional authority. "A strong sense of competence is important because authority rests upon it. The professional in the last analysis has nothing else on which to base his authority. His authority is not charismatic, not based on tradition, nor on the occupancy of a formal position" (Gross, 1967, 45).

Professional authority is exercised to reinforce norms within a *professional association*. The association attempts to dictate the required training and testing required for membership in the profession, to safeguard the profession's boundaries, and to advance the profession's aspirations with the government.

As Wilensky notes in his excellent account of the development of professions, "eventually rules to eliminate the unqualified and unscrupulous, rules to reduce internal competition, and rules to protect clients and emphasize the service ideal will be embodied *in a formal code of ethics*" (emphasis in original) (Wilensky, 1964, 145). In a healthy profession, a code of ethics has aspirational, educational, and regulatory components, and enforcing the code of ethics disciplines free-riding by members (Frankel, 1989).

In addition to the lengthy training process, the professional's standing in the profession is determined in large part by the evaluation of other professionals, whose own self-interest requires them to punish norm violators. So discipline within professionals is by professional peers – indeed, no outside agent is likely to have the expertise necessary to discipline effectively. It is also effective in that disciplinary action within the profession impairs the good standing of the professional, her ability to have referrals and referees from other professionals, and ultimately her chance to have a life-long career in the profession.

The practice of seeking anonymous letters of evaluation for academics seeking tenure is an ideal case in point. The system of peer review for publications is another example of constraints; even after publication, questionable claims face critique and revision. Professionals know that their career success depends on their own compliance with norms as observed by nameless others who are largely capable of evaluating their own professional performance and who also have good reason to punish violators. This proves to be an imperfect but highly constraining system of incentives that operate on professionals as professionals, in whatever organizational setting they practice (Fournier, 1999).

Of course, there has always been vigorous debate about the practice of professional self-regulation. On one hand, some have called self-regulation by a profession "likely to be welfare reducing" (Shaked & Sutton, 1981) because the quality that professions would require of themselves is likely to be too high (Leland, 1979). Others have complained of lax regulation within such groups. For instance, behavioral economist Dan Ariely described the response to a speech he gave to a medical association in which he asked several thousand physicians whether their professional judgment was affected by any conflicts of interest; not a single person admitted any such influence on his own judgment, but all agreed that most physicians experienced such conflicts (Ariely, 2012). How then can we reconcile these concerns about self-regulation with our continuing reliance on professionals for helping solve technically complex tasks marked by uncertainty and incomplete information?

Some of the power of self-regulation derives from the professionalization process itself; specifically, the effects of training. Training (the process of specialization) is itself a form of commitment by the specialist over the generalist. Specialization is itself a commitment to provide more effort than the generalist can or will provide (Bar-Isaac & Hörner, 2014). The investment made in that specialization is itself a form of a bond – effectively a way of securitizing against the incentive for opportunistic behavior (Eggertsson, 1990, 42). In a nutshell, regardless of conflict of interests, is it better to choose a doctor over a barber for surgery? Having doctors is welfare improving, and of course, having better institutions for regulating doctors is also welfare improving, but the search for such institutions may not be efficient.

The training also justifies a significant exercise of discretion in the exercise of the profession. "Freedom of judgment or discretion in performing work is…intrinsic to professionalism, which directly contradicts the managerial notion that efficiency is gained by minimizing discretion" (Freidson, 2001, 3).

Professionals universally resist the inclusion of nonprofessionals in key professional decisions – even when the nonprofessional is a hierarchical superior in a firm or agency.

Profession versus Hierarchy

The other major threat to professional autonomy is organizational hierarchy. Some professionals operate within professionalized partnerships where there is no internal threat to professional autonomy. However, other professionals operate within business forms and public bureaucracies that operate with a strict Weberian hierarchy – and professionals do not reside at the top of the hierarchy.

The early reading of Weber's work on bureaucracy was that bureaucracy was a technically efficient machine, molding the actions of many toward a single coherent goal. However, Weber's own discussion of expertise opened the door for a view that emphasized the possibility of conflict. In particular, conflict is preordained between the hierarchy and the professional employee because of the latter's loyalty to the profession as an alternative incentive system versus the hierarchical insistence on authority due to place and position, rather than expertise. This professional loyalty runs against a defining characteristic of the classical ("monocratic") hierarchy: "[e]ach subordinate is guided (supervised or directed) in carrying out...instructions by his superior and no one else" (Thompson, 1961, 496).

Observers have long recognized the tension between hierarchy and group-based governance. How accommodation between these two occurs, in a given organization, varies. Many organizations become "professionalized bureaucracies," not because every employee is a professional, but because members of the profession occupy the *key* spots in the hierarchy and because the process of vetting for the professionals has been delegated to the profession itself (Litwak, 1961; Mosher, 1968). "The term *professional*...refers to a person who by virtue of long training is qualified to perform specialized activities autonomously – relatively free from external supervision or regulation The word *bureaucrat* refers to a person performing specialized but more routine activities under the supervision of officials organized in a hierarchical fashion...should a person trained to function as a *professional* find himself in the role of *bureaucrat*, there is at least the possibility of conflict" (Scott, 1969, 82–83).

Consider the social workers described in Chapter 6. In a foundational essay on the development of the professions, Scott (1969) offered a close and textured analysis of a county welfare office in the mid-20th century. In contrast to the traditional Weberian conception of bureaucracy as a finely tuned machine, Scott claimed that incorporating even a modest degree of professional expertise into a government bureaucracy inevitably built tensions and conflict into the bureaucracy. In the office setting he examined, only a handful of bureaucrats had earned advanced social work degrees, and 14 of 86 line social workers had completed some graduate training. This minority of social workers with additional training were noticeably different from the rest of their peers. They looked to external professional organizations for guidance. They were more likely to be critical of the county office they worked for and to feel that laws and policies "limit my performance of casework services" (92). They advocated a flexible interpretation of agency procedure when it conflicted with what they saw as their duty to their clients (11). Even those workers who had started but not completed a professional degree seemed to believe they were obligated to uphold a professional ethic and that a larger institution, the profession, demanded a degree of loyalty beyond that offered to the agency that paid their salaries.

Maintenance of professional autonomy becomes one of the explicit goals of every professional association. "Elaborate social arrangements, formal and informal, sustain this autonomy" (Wilensky, 1964, 146). Members of the profession are mobilized to help fight for this autonomy against the threat of hierarchy inside the agency and from political superiors outside the agency. Of course, some organizations are more dominated by professionals (especially so autonomous professional organizations) and even, to a degree, are heteronomous professional organizations (that have external legal standing) (R. H. Hall, 1968). Government agencies are at the most heteronomous end of the continuum, but most professionals are located as groups within departments in larger organizations.

What if a professional is the manager? As D. E. Lewis (2008a) shows, putting professionals, with their greater experience and longer tenure, in charge seems to lead to higher performing organizations. In contrast, political appointees of government agencies often find it difficult to recruit and keep career professionals (Gailmard & Patty, 2007).

Thus, in most agencies, professionalism runs directly counter to the ideology of managerialism, which "denies authority to expertise by claiming a form of general knowledge that is superior to specialization and because it can organize it rationally and efficiently" (Freidson, 2001, 117). Most managers pride themselves on their ability to manage across a number of specialties. Professionals, in contrast, regard oversight by managerial "generalists" as equivalent to forfeiture of their professional autonomy to amateurs – and fight it at every turn. Indeed, the use of nonprofessional criteria for judging performance has long been seen as a core source of conflict (R. H. Hall, 1967). Hammond and Miller (1985) demonstrate formally that the professions complicate the neat operation of hierarchy.

Professions and the State

The basic characteristics of professionalism put it on a course for conflict with the state. The profession demands autonomy, but the state seeks to maintain its policy authority. The state would prefer to manage its employees as responsive bureaucrats.

Governments are especially threatening to professionals, because professions need something from governments. Governments are typically necessary to enforce the profession's monopoly privileges – but this role of government carries with it the threat of interference in what the profession regards as its internal business: the standards for licensing, the examination of professional trainees, rules regarding internal competition, and so on. Governments, for example, can support or undermine rules regulating competitive advertising by professionals in good standing. Professional associations typically engage in ongoing lobbying strategies to obtain the most advantageous laws and regulations. Their ideal, of course, is for the government to create a professional licensing board, with rules that allow the profession to staff and dominate its decisions.

As a result of this tension, professions are endlessly in pursuit of autonomous authority over the key personnel decisions involving professions. "Professionalism may be said to exist when an organized occupation gains the power to determine who is qualified to perform a defined set of tasks, to prevent all others from performing that work, and to control the criteria by which to evaluate performance" (Freidson, 2001, 12). For example, an economist who goes to work for the Securities and Exchange Commission is hired on the basis of letters of recommendation from other economists, rather than a test administered by noneconomists.

The profession offers its ambitious members an alternative to hierarchical promotion. A doctor who is offered a position as president of a pharmaceutical company is, to some extent, being promoted outside the profession. "Colleagues who continue to work at their discipline often regard such movement as selling out" (Freidson, 2001, 77). In contrast, professional careers offer the prospect of "horizontal careers of achievement," as with a professor who never takes the position of dean, but stays with the same job title throughout a distinguished career. That a horizontal career is regarded as normal is evidence that the profession itself offers inducements and rewards that compete effectively with those offered by hierarchical organizations (R. H. Hall, 1967).

It is our contention that professions are self-created and self-enforcing institutions that emphatically attempt to create their own incentives for their members. Furthermore, professions specifically and consistently try to *diminish* the impact of hierarchical incentives on them. Professions seek autonomy within the hierarchy, and the more successful they are at creating professional autonomy, the more broadly recognized they are as true professions.

A profession's relationships with the government are key. The profession would like to use the mechanisms of government to enforce its own control – for example, making it illegal to practice medicine without a license. The profession is of course territorial about its prerogatives. It is essential that the profession set the requirements for the license, not the government; the professional association argues that it, not the government, must be allowed the right to evaluate the quality of work of members of the profession and (when necessary) deprive the unworthy professional of status. Law and Kim (2005) demonstrate that improving service quality – not erecting barriers to entry – was the main reason professionals formed licensing boards during the Progressive Era.

The exercise of professionalism is by itself, then, a challenge to the authoritarian state, simply because it defines a domain in which government officials are expected to have no authority. Professionalism "directs the economic and political institutions of practice independently of the state" (Freidson, 2001, 131). Freidson points out that totalitarian states seek to absorb the professions – the leaders of the totalitarian state realize that the existence of the profession constitutes a limit to the scope of state authority. To the extent that the state is successful in absorbing the profession, it is also responsible for the diminution of that profession's usefulness, as fear replaces the exercise of autonomous expertise. The very existence of professions implies limits on the role of the state.

In a pluralistic society, what the state gets by employing a professional is the unhindered exercise of her expertise. "Dependence on qualified members of a profession (or expertise) for the very exercise of state power stems from the fact that what is at issue is the institutionalization of a body of knowledge and skill – however tentative or flawed, but authoritative in its time – that has developed well beyond everyday knowledge and is mastered by a limited number of people" (Freidson, 2001, 139). Experts provide the means to distill the human experiences of an uncertain world (Collins & Evans, 2007).

THE PROFESSION AS A NEXUS OF CONTRACTS

A profession would like to be able to lobby government for recognition, licensing authority, and control over its internal process. At the same time, it would like to resist infringements on professional decisions from politicians seeking professional licensing for favored constituents or family members as a condition for political support for the profession. Politicians will on occasion perceive political gain from demanding that a professional be disciplined or expelled from the profession. For example, there are many politicians who would no doubt be pleased to be able to expel from the medical profession doctors who perform abortion. However, the professional association will fight this demand with great determination and to ensure that these core personnel functions, in the pure case, are insulated from political influence; to the extent that these functions are permeable to political influence, the profession will have lost its independence and standing as a profession.

Professionals might not only prefer that the profession as a whole be insulated from politics but also the individual professional who is hired by a corporation, public bureaucracy, or nonprofit be inevitably insulated to some extent from the hierarchical forces that operate on nonprofessionals in the same hierarchy. A case in point is Dr. James Hansen, the NASA meteorologist who reported pressure from hierarchical superiors to conform with the Bush administration's statements on global warming (Bowen, 2008). As Freidson notes, "Freedom of judgment or discretion in performing work is also intrinsic to professionalism, which directly contradicts the managerial notion that efficiency is gained by minimizing discretion" (Freidson, 2001, 3). The notion within the government that accountability requires control is inevitably mitigated to some extent when the target is a professional.

Earlier we described the social code that shapes the obligations, expectations, and behaviors of professionals working in a public bureau. This social code places the professional within a profession and makes the profession itself a nexus of contracts. M. C. Jensen and Meckling (1976, 310) famously claimed "that most organizations are simply legal fictions which serve as a nexus for a set of contracting relationships among individuals. . . . It makes little sense or no sense to try to distinguish those things which are 'inside' the firm (or any other organization) from those things that are 'outside' of it" (311). In this view, the organization is a "they" and not an "it."

The nexus of contracts approach shows us the error of assuming that influence on the work of bureaucrats comes only from the president or elected officials in Congress. As with any organization, the bureau "serves as a focus for a complex process in which the conflicting objectives of individuals (some of whom may 'represent' other organizations) are brought into equilibrium within a framework of contractual relations" (M. C. Jensen & Meckling, 1976, 311). Professions, and the associations that organize them, operate outside bureaus, but the social code they create and enforce operates within agencies.

Professionals and Credible Commitment

Professions have been criticized because they inevitably challenge the lines of accountability from the profession back to the elected politicians with nominal authority. It is true that professionals threaten political accountability. Indeed we have argued throughout this book that it is precisely this fact that allows professional agencies to enhance the credibility of the state's commitment to tie its hands with regard to property rights, contract enforcement, and a level playing field. If and only if professionals are in the driver's seat at the central bank will investors not have to worry about politicians manipulating monetary policy for their reelection purposes. The same can be said for professionalized agencies in other fields.

Professionals were among the most fervent supporters of the Progressive reform movement of the early 20th century, and it is easy to see why. Their demand for discretion in the exercise of their profession was in complete conflict with the centralization of power in the hands of party bosses – who needed to be able to keep public services contingent on support for the party machine, a requirement that was offensive to professional training and ethics. The spoils system put nonprofessionals in positions (e.g., public health director, school district superintendent) that professionals thought were rightfully theirs by dint of their training and expertise. For example, professional social services sought to distribute welfare benefits in a way that would deprive the party of the personalized, contingent gratitude on which the party depended.

Not only were professionals a prime source of political support for Progressives but the influence of the Progressive movement was also directly linked to the creation of new professions. School administration (Callahan, 1962; Haber, 1964; Tyack, 1974), law enforcement (Fogelson, 1977; Walker, 1977), and social work (Lubove, 1965) were reimagined on a professional basis at about the time of greatest Progressive influence.

Professionals and Motivation

When we consider that professionals are going to be to some degree resistant to hierarchical control and therefore introduce potential lines of conflict, what do governments gain by hiring professionals in state bureaus, by creating the tension that comes from this particular nexus of contracts? Clearly, they get professional expertise, but governments obtain more than that.

Classic treatments of bureaucratic delegation such as that by Bawn (1995) discuss the tradeoff between control and expertise. Such models of delegation are always of *individuals* who either receive or do not receive delegations of authority.

However, when professionals receive grants of authority, the tradeoff is a bit different. In granting authority to a professional, the government is delegating it in part *to the corporate profession – to collectivities that exist outside the agency – rather than to the individual professional*. That is, the individual professional is monitored and constrained by other professionals, who are enforcing professional norms and holding up professional standards. Delegation to a professional is *socialized* delegation, rather than anomic delegation.

Delegation to a professional is more predictable than delegation to a nonprofessional precisely because professional discipline is so binding on members. This is the point Moe (1987) makes about the professionals at the National Labor Relations Board (NLRB). Filling professional positions with nonprofessionals would be disruptive in the extreme and troubling to all constituencies who value predictability.

We next illustrate the significant impact of professions in bureaucratic commitment by turning to two cases drawn from the world of economic regulation: the NLRB and the Securities and Exchange Commission.

THE NATIONAL LABOR RELATIONS BOARD

The history of the NLRB illustrates that antagonistic interests represented in Congress, fighting over a contentious issue, may nevertheless be able to use a bureaucratic solution as a form of "fair division." That is, both sides can agree on a procedure, embedded in a bureaucracy, even in a setting where both sides view the policy area as a zero-sum game of perfect conflict. In the NLRB, the "labor law" profession played an essential role in implementing the bureaucratic conflict-resolving procedure.

Throughout the first four decades of the 20th century, labor relations were increasingly violent and disruptive. This violence came to a head in the Great Depression, and in response a strongly Democratic coalition in Congress passed the National Labor Relations Act and fully empowered the existing NLRB. But as Moe (1987) indicates in his excellent account of the NLRB, the efforts of the congressional labor movement coalition did not end the conflict. Instead, the Republicans in Congress did everything they could for some years to undo labor's gains.

By 1953, however, the vision of prolonged legislative stalemate discouraged both sides from seeking a breakthrough legislative success. Moe notes, "The political world of labor-management relations was nevertheless about to undergo a transformation. Peace would replace conflict. Political action would shift its focus from Congress to the presidency" (Moe, 1987, 244). It was only when each side recognized that the other could not be vanquished that they reached an accommodation. "Stalemate encouraged a reordering of priorities, and the groups were less disposed to petition their political allies in Congress for action" (244). The accommodation was to redesign the NLRB as a neutral agency, constrained by a Weberian legal-rational procedure that limited the self-interested actions of any of the bureaucrats involved.

Moe's work on the NLRB has served as an important foundation for the "politics of bureaucratic structure" approach to understanding agencies and their relationships with politicians. Perhaps less recognized is Moe's focus on the NLRB as a preeminent example of agency independence as a result of differences among politicians and on the way in which that independence made the agency's operations pivotal in the game of political oversight. In addition, his work remains the most important social science investigation of the nature of the NLRB as the balancer between labor and employers in the U.S. political economy.

In our view, these sharp disagreements – in society as a whole, and as represented by politicians – are vital for understanding professionalization at the NLRB. Our position, however, differs from Moe's attention to "inefficiencies" that flow from organizational design carried out in a world of conflict. As we discuss, professionalism at the agency was part of a tentative truce in this conflict – and although there may have been better designed policy making on these issues, the agency's embrace of professionalism served it well as long as politicians saw value in that truce.

The Institutionalization of the NLRB

Over time, the focus of labor and business politics shifted to presidential appointments, with each side determined to counterbalance the effect of the opposition. "What kinds of people do business and labor look for? The established pattern, rationally based on the realities of power politics, is that the groups largely restrict themselves to moderates acceptable (asymmetrically) to both sides" (Moe, 1987, 259). Democrats in the Senate vetoed extreme conservatives nominated by Republican presidents, and vice versa. The result was the institutionalization of moderation on the board itself, which furthered the protection of professionalism within the staff of the NLRB.

As Mosher (1968) has noted, one of the foremost goals of any profession is to obtain autonomy with regard to accreditation and personnel decisions. This meant ensuring that no one, including the U.S. president and the board, had a great deal of political leverage over the increasingly self-defined labor-law professionals within the NLRB. This limited the amount of traditional "responsiveness" of the agency's staff – but that was not entirely a bad thing. Each side – labor and business – could be assured that day-to-day decisions were not going to be influenced by the lobbyists of the other side, but would instead be made in accordance with increasingly well-defined legal-technical criteria. This allowed both sides to spend their time, energy, and resources on activities other than lobbying Congress, president, or staff.

From the perspective of the bureaucrats themselves, it was clear that partisanship was not a good career move. A partisan bureaucrat (and bureaucracy) would inevitably be the target of some future political coalition in Congress. It was far safer and more sensible for the NLRB to wrap itself enthusiastically in all the trappings and mythology of a court system, dispensing even-handed justice.

And that is what the NLRB did. It was aided by social norms in the White House and Congress that resulted in balanced and relatively moderate bipartisan appointments to the agency (Moe, 1987). Even more important was the molding of the staff in the image of a profession: the newly created profession of labor law. The body of NLRB decisions defined the corpus of a labor law that had not previously existed, but that came to absorb and neutralize the historic labor battles in Congress.

As Moe aptly points out, a professionalized bureaucracy, pursuing a constraining administrative procedure with strict neutrality and headed by a scrupulously bipartisan commission, was a compromise that both sides could live with. Professionalization allowed both sides to make economic decisions and engage in long-range planning with a high degree of certainty about the nature of the rules of the game. There was no reason for politicians outside the NLRB to pursue advantage outside the appointment process. "The agency's decisions have been made under conditions that place great emphasis on individual autonomy and professional judgment" (Moe, 1987, 257).

Indeed, it is hard to imagine that the postwar U.S. economy could have performed as successfully as it did if the economy had been wracked by labor strife of the magnitude that occurred during the Depression. By taking labor issues off the partisan agenda, the NLRB allowed both corporations and unions to plan for (and invest in) the future in the confidence that everyone's rights would be largely protected by the enhanced legal system that it embodied. The agency, in other words, became the vehicle for credible commitment to a stable set of rules regarding labor; the professionals who constituted the core of the NLRB became the (relatively) neutral enforcers of those rules.

Re-Politicization of the NLRB

As Moe (1987) shows, Reagan's appointments to the NLRB, which re-imposed a partisan agenda, threw into doubt that credible commitment to a stable set of labor institutions and property rights. The Reagan episode underlines the threat that temporary electoral and legislative coalitions play in the professional and bureaucratic support for credible commitment.

Reagan re-politicized the NLRB by appointing individuals to his cabinet and to the NLRB who were not invested in the institutionalized negotiations and compromises that had emerged over the 1950s, 1960s, and 1970s. The first such appointment was of Ray Donovan as Secretary of Labor, who was an unknown. "Worse, he [Reagan] had chosen someone who was an outsider to the labor-management community and not even minimally connected to important components of it. Donovan did not even know the issues, the program, or the people. He had simply been a loyal and extraordinarily successful fundraiser in the Reagan electoral campaign – apparently his only qualification for the job" (Moe, 1987, 267).

Two vacancies on the NLRB itself were filled in similar ways, as the Reagan administration ignored the usual negotiation dance between business, labor, and the NLRB. Reagan even ignored the recommendations of his own Labor Secretary, who was not listening "to business or labor either" (Moe, 1987, 267). The appointment process was very much like a spoils system. "The criteria for judging candidates gave heavy emphasis to ideology and involvement in the Reagan campaign. Professionalism was a distinctly secondary consideration" (267).

Reagan's nominee for chair of the NLRB was not supported enthusiastically by business interests. The nominee was an "abrasive" supporter of Jesse Helms named Donald Dotson, who "spelled trouble" for the professional regime. "But the Reagan White House was interested in destroying established traditions, not in following them, and they turned a deaf ear to business's suggestions for filling the slot" (Moe, 1987, 268).

After confirmation by an unenthusiastic voice vote, "Dotson aggressively sought to extend his control and disrupt agency routines. Decision making was purposely slowed down to the point where the board's processing of cases nearly ground to a halt" (Moe, 1987, 269). Decisions that were allowed to be made often reversed major precedents from previous administrations, which greatly increased the uncertainty facing both unions and firms.

The NLRB in Recent Years

Moe's observations about the NLRB were built around his empirical analysis of how the agency processed labor disputes in a system where politicians could intervene and outside interests could bring cases (Moe, 1985). The agency's staff operated in the midst of "equilibrating properties," of compensating adjustments that balanced a "bipolar constituency" (1114). Moe sought to understand the agency's place in this system of politicians and affected interests – if only because he saw other popular theories of regulation as imperfect and incomplete.

A host of studies have sought to complete our understanding of the NLRB's case selection and processing (Cooke & Gautschi, 1982; Cooke, Mishra, Spreitzer, & Tschirhart, 1995; Schmidt, 1994, 1995, 2002; Snyder & Weingast, 2000). Most have sought, as did Moe, to understand the agency's actions qua responsiveness in this system of political power exercised via appointees. As shown earlier, because of Reagan's re-politicization of the NLRB, there were good reasons for focusing on the board and appointees. Political interventions in the appointment process showed the fragility of the truce – of the credible commitment – not to intervene in the agency. The temptation (for either side) to intervene remains a constant threat to the regime.

Bill Clinton's election marked a new era for the NLRB, perhaps exemplified best by his naming of William B. Gould IV to chair the board. Gould had served with a union, later worked for management and for the NLRB, and was a Stanford law professor. Perhaps he was the best example of a "neutral professional" to lead the organization; if not that, he certainly did not overtly fit the mold of a partisan appointee.

Gould's achievements (and missteps) at the NLRB are well documented (Flynn, 2000a; Goldberg, 2002; Gould, 2000; M. A. Stein, 2001). Some accounts focused on the agency's processing of many more cases during Gould's time than during the previous administration (M. A. Stein, 2001, 511). Gould himself claimed that the tide reversed after he left in 1998 – that "[t]he Bush II Board has made the Bush I era look like one of aggressive law enforcement" (Gould, 2005, 317). Others argued that rather than focusing on coarse interventions, the Bush II administration took a "thoughtful and measured approach" (Kilberg, Schwartz, & Chadwick, 2009, 997).

This level of politicization of the board was much worse under Gould than during the first four decades of the NLRB, when the consensus was for moderate appointees – a truce broken first during the Eisenhower administration (Flynn, 2000b). Even after the "taboo on appointing management or union-side personnel" was broken, the voting records of partisan appointees prior to 1980 were more one-sided than those for appointees drawn from government (Flynn, 2000b, 1362). Yet, then differences between the sides meant that most votes were partisan. In the case of Gould, many believed his partisan actions brought significant congressional attention (including attempts to cut the NLRB's budget by 30%) as partisan bickering flared over the NLRB. As Flynn (2000b, 516) notes, "Thus, far from being 'unprecedented,' the Republicans' aggressive oversight of the Gould Board marked a continuation of an age-old pattern; oversight bordering on or spilling over into harassment has been a leitmotif of NLRB history."

For Moe (1985), the NLRB's staff served as a conduit between affected interests bringing complaints and the board that would decide their fate: along with responding to broader, macroeconomic trends, the staff "filtered" cases as it responded to partisan changes on the board. But the staff also controlled much of the NLRB's cases effectively without the oversight of the board. One simple reason is that most of the agency's actions took place in the field; only 2.5% of cases handled by the NLRB's regional offices were eventually referred to the General Counsel and on to the board itself (Schmidt, 2002). In the vast majority of actions, the field officers made judgments in a quasi-judicial process, sometimes involving an administrative law judge, without the board's direct involvement. Second, of those cases that reached the board, the best estimates were that 80% of the board's decisions were influenced by the recommendations of the administrative law judges and the regional officers (Cooke et al., 1995).

Of course, we can debate the importance of that small fraction of remaining cases, because the board's decisions in those cases did help set precedent for other decisions made both within the NLRB and outside in the practice community. Indeed the legal community, especially in academia, and those directly affected by labor law decisions do broadly debate those remaining cases (e.g., Fisk & Malamud, 2009). But this level of attention by the legal community – and the fact that events surrounding the NLRB's creation and its decisions through the years form the basis for modern labor law – point to our focus on professionalism as a primary mechanism for the long-term development of the regulatory state as a credible commitment device.

The main decision maker at the NLRB is the General Counsel; the Regional Attorney is the main decision maker in a field office. The NLRB is built on labor law – a field of professional expertise it largely created. Its proceedings are quasi-judicial and its work is court-like. Federal labor law is a "rights regime," which its attorneys use (almost entirely) in considering the protection of laborers – ignoring the standard economic approaches to assessing the costs, benefits, and impacts of interventions (Fisk & Malamud, 2009, 2054). This approach may not be optimal from either a regulatory or responsiveness standpoint, but it is certainly professionalized.

Over time, the re-politicization of the NLRB has resulted in increased uncertainty, as professionalism has been challenged by a partisan agenda. Resolution of problems of credible commitment require constraint on powerful political forces – forces that will often want to shift property rights and undermine contract enforcement and the rule of law. It is difficult to find individuals and groups that can stand up to the powerful hierarchical pressure of politicians.

Professionals play a role that is difficult for other players in modern society to play. They have a built-in source of authority – their social code, training, and expertise – that is independent of hierarchical authority. More importantly, the profession's insistence on minimizing constraints on professional self-rule and autonomy inevitably ends up putting them in a state of conflict – or at least tension – with politicians. Furthermore, their independence comes with a completely separate source of ethics – so that the independence that professionals claim may come with ethical constraints that limit professionals, even as professionals limit politicians.

Professional nonresponsiveness was the key to the government's credible commitment to a transparent set of property rights and the rule of law in the area of labor.

PROFESSIONALISM AT THE SEC: A FOUNDATION FOR FINANCIAL STABILITY

The Securities and Exchange Commission (SEC) resembles the NLRB in many key aspects. In both cases a strong, professionalized, independent bureaucracy was not the primary goal of the players present at the origins of the agency. In both cases, the agencies that were created resulted from the pushing and pulling of partisan, institutional, and interest group conflict (Moe, 1987). As the professional compromise took hold, an individual member of Congress could do less and less, at any reasonable political cost, to affect the decisions of both agencies. In both cases, this professional compromise resulted in agencies that for a half-century earned a remarkable degree of respect and independence from their political masters.

In the election year of 1932, the Pecora Commission's revelations of fraud and corruption, and the economic anguish that accompanied the resulting Depression, created a huge public demand to do something. The Securities Act of 1933, passed during the first rush of New Deal legislation, sought to require accurate information for investors and prohibit fraud in the sale of securities. It placed responsibility for this task with the Federal Trade Commission (FTC). The FTC had a reputation as an agency that was safely under the control of "our gang," as brain-truster James Landis cozily described the Roosevelt supporters (Seligman, 2003, 97).

Because the FTC seemed solidly in the Democratic camp, opponents of effective regulation fought to have it regulated by a new and more independent agency. A coalition including brokerage firms, regional stock exchanges, and Republican newspaper editors united behind Richard Whitney, head of the New York Stock Exchange. This opposition preferred a new agency to the business-hostile, New Deal-friendly FTC – preferably one that would be free of presidential control and very possibly open to the blandishments of the securities industry.

Some members of Congress, already leery of FDR's expansive definition of the administration's goals, supported a more independent agency as well – one that would not be automatically in FDR's camp. Carter Glass, the chair of the Senate Banking Committee, formed a working alliance with lobbyists from the NYSE. Glass succeeded in getting a 10–8 vote in committee in favor of a new agency. The Securities and Exchange Commission (SEC) was to have organizational features that insulated the agency from the president – and from other institutional forces as well. It was to be led by a new five-member bipartisan commission with long, rotating appointments and be housed outside a cabinet department – features that promised to insulate the agency from the president and other political actors. FDR preferred an independent agency to none at all; thus, the structural features of bureaucratic autonomy sprang from a jealous conflict for control (Moe, 1989). "Ultimately, as a consequence of New York Stock Exchange lobbying to weaken the Securities Exchange Act and Senator Glass's antipathy to the New Deal, the SEC would be born. . . . [At] the time, the SEC had not been sought by the New Deal. Its birth, in a sense, was an accident" (Seligman, 2003, 97).

The conflicting political forces blocked each other as well when defining the mandate for the new accidental agency. "On most controversial substantive issues, Congress had been stalemated. Rather than providing the new Commission with a clear mandate, the legislators had granted the agency authority to study the controversy or issue its own rules. In effect, Congress had broadly defined the Commission's areas of expertise and invited it to forge its own mandate. The political processes that produced the jerry-built statute were allowed to continue" (Seligman, 2003, 99). The result of political stalemate was both an independent structure and a vague (and expandable) mission to develop expertise and do the best it could. This was clearly *bureaucratic autonomy by default*, as per Moe (1987).

The new agency, insulated from the FDR administration and from Congress, had no guarantee of success. One could easily imagine that organizational failure was a natural next step (Moe, 1987, 267). The question was whether a lack of accountability could be transformed into the kind of credible commitment that would bring investors back into the stock market.

Professions and the Establishment of the SEC

James Landis became the leading strategist in the implementation of the new SEC. Landis had been a brilliant young law professor at Harvard before coming to Washington as part of FDR's brain trust. Appointed to the new SEC, Landis sought a way to link the self-interest of all the major constituencies to a regime of accurate information disclosure that would bring investors back to the stock market – and make everyone better off.

One obvious candidate for an ally in this effort was the all-important accounting profession. Its cooperation would be required in standardizing and enforcing disclosure requirements in a way that would produce meaningful, accurate, and helpful financial statements for the investing public. Accountants had long nursed a grudge against management, which tended to be high-handed and did not recognize the professional aspirations of accountants. (See Halberstam [1986, 80] for a dramatic example at the Ford Motor Company.) Relegated to the role of "bookkeeper," accountants desired the autonomy to which all professions aspired – the ability to license and control the standing of the members of their profession. "Because their profession had labored for years to escape the tight grip in which corporate management held it, most accountants ardently wanted to exercise, in fact, more of that 'independence' they claimed to be essential to good accounting practice. Corporate managers, lacking respect for such independence, often tried to dictate to the auditors, encouraging them to shade the truth or even to misrepresent the state of a company's financial health" (McCraw, 1984, 190).

With the new financial disclosure requirements in the 1933 and 1934 laws, the accountants feared that the SEC would simply take the place of corporate management as obstacles to professional independence, issuing dictates that would impinge on accounting expertise. Instead, Landis made numerous appearances at accounting professional meetings, demonstrating his respect for the profession and promising an institutional structure that would insulate accounting professionals and enhance the development of the profession as the arbiter of transparent financial disclosure. In fulfillment of this promise, Landis created the office of Chief Accountant, which began in 1937 to issue Accounting Series Releases (ASRs). These ASRs improved standardization of accounting practice so that financial statements from different firms could be expected to be more meaningful, and the position of Chief Accountant was symbolic of self-regulation and of professional respect.

Landis left most of the task of creating uniform and meaningful financial statements to the accountants themselves. The Committee on Accounting Procedure (CAP), a committee of the professional accounting institute, formed and operated independently of (although with oversight by) the SEC. The CAP was the precursor of the Financial Standards Accounting Board created in 1973. It was these agencies that had the primary responsibility for creating the Generally Accepted Accounting Principles (GAAPs); the SEC requires that business firms use these in issuing their financial statements to the public. In Arthur Levitt's words, "Generally Accepted Accounting Principles (GAAP) are the backbone of transparent financial reporting" (Securities and Exchange Commission, 1999).

In addition to recognizing accountants' status as professionals, Landis was able to point to the increase in demand for accountants generated by an effective SEC. Between 1930 and 1970, the number of accountants increased by 271%, compared to an increase of only 71% in the number of lawyers during the same time (McCraw, 1984, 191–192).

As accountants joined the political coalition in support of the SEC, others became supporters as well. Increasingly falling in line were investment bankers and investors. Industrialists who had nothing to hide in their financial statements were happy to have a legitimate public agency certify the accuracy of their statements and to have the charlatans' inadequate finances revealed through the required financial disclosure process.

Also in support of Landis were the commission brokers, who bought and sold stocks, for a fee, on behalf of investors. They felt not only that their commissions would increase with public confidence in financial disclosures but also that they had not gotten a fair deal from Richard Whitney, head of the New York Stock Exchange, who seemed to favor traders who operated on their own behalf on the exchange floor. "With the SEC's cooperation," the commission brokers and other dissidents in the NYSE "engineered an internal coup" (McCraw, 1984, 196) that ended Whitney's dominance of the institution. The dissidents forced through tough rule changes at the NYSE regarding financial disclosure by its members.

Shockingly, the new reporting requirements uncovered evidence that Whitney himself had been using his clients' property as collateral for his own trading. Whitney was convicted of embezzlement and sent to Sing Sing prison for three years. This dramatic evidence of the need for a strong regulatory regime based on transparency ended effective opposition in the financial industry to the new regulatory agency and supported the independence of the SEC and other regulators for the next half-century.

Landis and the SEC took advantage of the accountants' professional aspirations to autonomy. Professional autonomy manifested itself as independence from political and economic forces, thus encouraging the public's trust in the SEC as a guardian of the nation's commitment to a transparent, fair market. This arrangement worked well, as investor confidence in the stock market returned.

As with the NLRB, the president and Senate went through a stylized routine of posturing for constituencies that nevertheless selected moderate commissioners for the SEC. The politicians had little to do with the agency's policy decisions after the appointments were approved. And as with the NLRB, the transparent delegation of day-to-day decisions to a professional agency created faith in the stability and neutrality of the regulatory regime.

The Professional SEC: A Half-Century of Financial Stability

The SEC quickly earned a reputation as one of the most useful and independent regulatory agencies in the U.S. government. By 1952, moderate Republicans had lost any resentment toward the SEC, saying that the SEC "stands out as a very model of what an administrative agency should be" (Seligman, 2003, 265). When the Eisenhower administration underfunded the SEC, the regulated industry was willing to support openly the funding for a stronger regulatory regime; "members of the securities industry recognized the SEC's enforcement programs, in particular, as necessary to restore investor confidence in Wall Street" (Khademian, 1992, 59). In 1981, even the incoming Reagan administration's regulatory task force (which approved of very few regulatory agencies) found that the SEC had a "deserved reputation for integrity and efficiency" and was evidently a "model government agency" (McCraw, 1984, 154).

Overall, the SEC was associated with an image of independence, rather than political responsiveness or accountability. It was trusted with this autonomy because the agency was dominated by a new profession – securities law – that was committed to the rule of law and careful adherence to professional norms and procedures.

The practitioners of that profession seem to have succeeded in attaining the four characteristics that Mosher (1968) termed the defining characteristics of a "professionalized bureaucracy." The securities professionals "staked their territory" within the agency (119–20). Within the SEC, the securities lawyers constituted "an elite corps with substantial control over the operations of the agency, significant influence on agency policies, and high prestige within and outside the agency" (120). The personnel decisions regarding professionals were largely made within the profession. And the agency provided the assurances of a professional career, including opportunities in securities law outside the agency.

The SEC professionals agreed early on that a primary goal was enforcement, and the primary outcome of enforcement was "trust" – investor confidence hinges on the belief that the U.S. government is committed to finding and punishing those who would misrepresent their financial data, manipulate stock prices, misappropriate funds, or self-deal in matters small or large. The SEC seemed to be achieving its mission: a book on the SEC published in 1984 described an agency with highly developed intelligence systems, effective apprehension, and effective prosecution (Shapiro, 1984).

Rather than challenge the SEC, Congress had good reason to encourage its professionalization. Since at least the 1940s, Congress has regarded the SEC as having a well-trained and knowledgeable staff (Herring, 1938; Khademian, 1992). As Anne Khademian observed,

Congress defers to the expertise of the SEC because of the technical and uncertain nature of securities policy, the diversity of regulated interests, and Congress's dependence on the SEC to enforce the securities laws. The result is a balance between the respect for expertise, on the one hand, and the demand for accountability to elected officials, on the other, that gives the SEC and its political overseers mutual and reciprocal influence over the framework ...for regulating securities. (Khademian, 1992, 210)

In her book on the SEC, she quoted an SEC official who said that congressional intrusions on SEC's independence were "too risky. They know the expertise lies here and not with them. If they override the SEC course, they will have egg on their face if they fail" (Khademian, 1992, 113).

Congress also had reason to defer to the SEC because intervening on behalf of one interest for electoral benefit could just as easily result in the enmity and opposition of other interests. "Small investors may differ from large institutional investors, the stock exchanges may have different interests than over-the-counter market ...and a vast array of professional groups, from accountants to brokers, dealers, and investment advisers, may have vastly different interests" (Khademian, 2002, 518). In the face of such diverse and opposing interests, it was difficult for any coalition to form to intervene and countermand SEC rulings.

Like other New Deal agencies (such as the NLRB), the SEC provided a legalistic and highly proceduralized venue for disputes between interest groups to be resolved. Giving the accounting profession a degree of autonomy in the proliferation of accounting rules made a credible commitment to the profession's independence and autonomy – and ultimately to the clarity of property rights and sanctity of contracts for which the SEC stands as the guarantor. And everyone benefited from the resulting depoliticization, political stability, and transparency of the basic rules of the game. The SEC, like the NLRB, was one in which professional demands for autonomy led both to insulation and agency predictability.

Presidents have had very little involvement in the SEC. "The primary presidential influence over the SEC's work is through appointments of the agency's five commissioners," who serve for five years with staggered terms (Khademian, 2002, 519). Most presidents, most of the time, have been guided by institutionalized norms governing the appointment process. According to these norms, an appointee is expected to have experience as a securities lawyer, dealing with the SEC, or working with the agency as a staff member and to have no ties to the securities industry or the White House (519).

The prohibition against ties to the White House was made more salient by the Robert Vesco scandal in the early 1970s. Vesco, a high school dropout, had successfully staged a hostile takeover of Investors Overseas Services in 1970 and then immediately began to loot the firm's funds of hundreds of millions of dollars. He also secretly contributed $200,000 to Nixon's reelection campaign in 1972. In return, Vesco wanted the Nixon administration to intervene with William Casey of the SEC – a particularly blatant attempt to politicize a regulatory agency. When Casey left office, Vesco succeeded in persuading Nixon to appoint Bradford Cook. Cook had to resign within 10 weeks of his appointment when a grand jury found evidence that both he and Casey (later Reagan's CIA director) had directly interfered with SEC investigations. In particular, Cook had deferred to John Mitchell's order to remove any mention of Vesco's secret campaign contribution.

Important support for these norms also came from Congress, which had come to respect the work of the SEC and which saw little gain to upsetting the norms. In addition, representing investor interests in a level playing field could still be good politics. "Over the years, members of Congress have come to expect the appointment of a technical expert in securities law to lead the commission" (Khademian, 2002, 519). Republican and Democratic legislators vied over the appointments that were due them, but symbolic conflict was sufficient to convince each side's constituency that they had been represented in the process. Meanwhile, partisanship meant less and less as the professionalization of the agency advanced in the form of a corpus of legal rulings.

Additional support for the norms came from elements of the securities themselves in the steadily expanding economy after World War II. Thanks to the SEC's reputation for protecting investor rights and establishing a level playing field, investors slowly began to return to the stock market. The Dow Jones Industrial Average reached the 1929 high of 380 by the middle of the Eisenhower administration. From its formation in the New Deal until the late 1990s, investors believed that SEC oversight of the auditing profession guaranteed objective data on which to base their investment strategies. The SEC provided a venue for lobbyists to be heard, but it was in the context of a neutral, judicial process (Khademian, 2002, 519). The respect given to the SEC was largely correlated with its demonstrated responsiveness to professional norms and standards, rather than its responsiveness to Congress. Professionalism offered increasing clarity as to the rights of individual investors, institutional investors, and financial firms.

CONCLUSION: POLITICIZATION VERSUS PROFESSIONALISM

If professions did not already exist, we would have to invent them. They are the key institutions that create incentives for the effective deployment of expertise in society. Through the monopoly rents they negotiate, they motivate some of the most capable people in society to the practice of the profession. Through the discipline of professional peer review, they provide incentives for professionals to practice responsibly. Through the cultivation of a Weberian neutrality, they offer some protection from political favoritism. Through the insistence on professional autonomy, they constrain the impact of democratic instability.

Agencies staffed professionally manage to decrease both social control costs and social disorder costs. For example, the NLRB clearly helped U.S. society move from the enormous market disorder costs of strikes, lockouts, and labor strife; it accomplished this task without the imposition of burdensome social control. The minimization of political influence and the development of the labor law profession allowed a reduction in costs due to labor unrest *without a huge imposition of social control costs.*

The same is true for the SEC. The disorder costs of a market subject to information asymmetries were made manifest first in the stock market crash and then the banking crisis. The SEC could have addressed the problem by imposing a very intrusive regulatory regime – but instead it cultivated the accounting profession to set the standards and execute disclosure requirements for firms. This strategy provided an effective reduction of social disorder costs for a minimum of social control costs. Without the deployment of expert professionals, regulation would have had to be implemented by a compliance hierarchy short on expertise and long on coercion.

Professionalism's predictability and its resistance to political interference are thus the mechanisms by which credible commitment is implemented – and so become a fundamental part of the story about independence in regulation

(Estache & Wren-Lewis, 2009, 757). In the traditional SEC, as in the traditional NLRB, corporations, investors, and financial institutions could rely on professional regulators to behave tomorrow roughly as they did yesterday.

This does not mean that professionalism is automatically or costlessly maintained – nor that professionals never yield to the temptation of capture. We recognize a tension in our argument: the possibility of a professional bureaucracy lives in tension with the possibility that the bureau might be responsive to powerful special interests. Some agencies systematically sort themselves out as professionals; others as readily politicized agents of corruption.

A Model of Professionalism and Politicization

The first element in this model, as shown by Hammond and Knott (1996), is that when institutions are in stalemate, bureaucrats and their agencies inherit the most discretionary autonomy. It is only when other governmental institutions have shared preferences that bureaucrats are constrained by those institutions. The results in the latter case will be an almost inevitable politicization of the bureau and, perhaps, cozy triangles.

Second, forces within the hierarchical setting may or may not facilitate the professionalization of the bureaucracy. Subordinates seek autonomy to exercise expertise; superiors seek control. A cooperative relationship will consist of more effort from the bureaucrat subordinate in exchange for more autonomy. This may be supported by a gift exchange (Akerlof, 1982) or a cooperative equilibrium over a long time horizon.

Last, professionalism affects the choices bureaucrats make (Brehm & Gates, 1999; Knott & Miller, 2008; Miller, 2000; Teodoro, 2011; Tonon, 2008). The more professionalized they are, the more they seek the autonomy necessary for exercising professional skills. More than other employees, the professional objects to governmental exercising of professional personnel functions.

Politicization emerges when agencies are facing unity in its institutional environment, have a competitive hierarchical culture, and there is government intervention in professional forces. In contrast, professionalism emerges when agencies are facing institutional disunity, when leaders are able to coordinate to a cooperative equilibrium, and professional forces dominate personnel and substantive decisions.

In the next two chapters, we explore whether these factors can help explain both interagency differences and intra-agency differences over time. The setting is financial regulatory agencies from the New Deal to the aftermath of the Great Recession.

8

The Politicization of Financial Regulation

But the truth is that the United States managed to avoid major financial crises for half a century after the Pecora hearings were held and Congress enacted major banking reforms. It was only after we forgot those lessons, and dismantled effective regulation, that our financial system went back to being dangerously unstable.
— Krugman (2010, 27)

PECORA'S CIRCUS

The stock market crash occurred in 1929, followed by several years of continuing economic deterioration. By 1933, the economy was in a tailspin, and the Senate Banking Committee was looking for someone to revive its lethargic investigation of the financial industry. Committee chair Peter Norbeck (R-SD) hired Ferdinand Pecora, the assistant district attorney of New York County. Michael Perino sets the scene for Pecora's activities in his excellent account, *The Hellhound of Wall Street: How Ferdinand Pecora's Investigation of the Great Crash Forever Changed American Finance* (Perino, 2010).

Even as Pecora prepared for his first committee hearing, the economy took a new plunge as a run on the banks led to a wave of closures. This crisis put renewed pressure on the committee to deliver both an explanation for and a solution to the problem. Pecora made news, not only for the information he gathered in the hearings he organized but also for the prosecutorial style he evinced in handling men who, during the previous decade, had been the lords of the financial universe.

Pecora made the National City Bank the first target of his hearings and its chairman, Charles "Sunshine Charley" Mitchell, his first witness. The National City Bank (now Citibank) was the second largest bank in the United States. It had grown since Mitchell had become its chairman, in large part by engaging in activities far beyond the usual commercial banking model – taking deposits from investors and making loans to businesses – and becoming deeply involved in underwriting stocks and bonds.

National City began to underwrite entire securities offerings, on the gamble that it could make a profit by selling them to investors (Hoffmann, 2001, 113). Its depositors, whose deposits were uninsured, were in effect taking the gamble as well. In carrying out this strategy, Mitchell showed a preference for high-return investments even though they also inevitably carried more risk. In 1929, Carter Glass, then a Democratic senator from Virginia, described Mitchell as being "more than any 50 men" responsible for the stock crash (Appelbaum, 2009). In exchanges with his first witness, Pecora got Mitchell to admit that National City Bank used cash bonuses to incentivize traders without regard to the risk passed on to those buying the stocks and bonds – who were not fully aware of the risk the instruments carried (Conti-Brown, 2011; Perino, 2010). As one investor wrote to Pecora,

I am writing this from McGrath's Funeral Parlor [in Brooklyn]. My wife is laying in her casket in the next division. She died of pneumonia. Had I hoarded my $10,000, I could have taken her to the South for the winter.... When you see Mr. Mitchell, you might ask him if it comes within your jurisdiction, why his Company or Bank, so trusted, could palm off such poor stuff on an old retiring teacher. (Perino, 2010, 136)

Inevitably, some of the riskiest offerings proved to be losers, and many of his investors lost everything in National City's investments; however, the bank was still in good shape, having unloaded much of its risk to its depositors, while charging brokers' fees and commissions. Mitchell himself continued to prosper, admitting that his income in the disastrous year of 1929 had been more than $1.2 million (United States Senate, 2014).

As more evidence came out, other of the bank's practices looked even more predatory. National City issued bank stocks and then secretly transferred money from them to stake a lucrative, but risky, position in Cuban sugar interests – a position Mitchell had to acknowledge as "bad" loans. The press covered the hearings extensively, and in 1933 National City's president resigned just six days after Pecora launched his investigation.

Other witnesses brought even more attention to Pecora's investigation, including J. P. Morgan, who was popularly thought to be at the center of the "money trust." Morgan's revelations were astounding. Pecora got Morgan to admit that he had not paid any income taxes in 1930, 1931, or 1932. Morgan also admitted that he had made loans to 60 other bankers and, with other financiers, had helped set up stock pools that had been able to move stock prices. Pecora was also able to trace the connecting directorships that gave Morgan control of many strategic industries. In a notable comment, Senator Glass complained that the investigation was "having a circus, and the only things lacking now are peanuts and colored lemonade" (Dennis, 2009) – a complaint that led a Ringling Brothers publicist to place a midget on Morgan's lap with the pronouncement, "The smallest lady in the world wants to meet the richest man in the world!" (Schlesinger, 2003, 437). The resulting photo covered the front pages of major newspapers, perhaps subliminally signaling that even the most powerful could be brought down to size.

The public controversy grew even larger through the 1930s. In 1937, the new district attorney of Manhattan, a Republican prosecutor named Thomas Dewey, went after Richard Whitney. Whitney had been one of the targets of the early hearings, and he was still in a leadership position on the board of the New York Stock Exchange and the leading opponent of regulation. In 1938, Dewey established that Whitney had been embezzling his clients and others. Sunshine Charlie was indicted by a grand Jury and sent to Sing Sing prison to serve a term of 5 to 10 years.

The public's rage supported the passage of historic new legislation to do something about the financial industry, especially so because some of the most questionable actions were legal under current law. The questions (for lawmakers in 1933 and echoed in recent debates as well) were as follows. What kind of correction was called for? Should Congress grant itself more power to supervise the agencies that were already in existence (like the FTC)? Should the president's cabinet-level departments (such as the Treasury) be given new regulatory assignments? Should new laws be passed making it easier to sue executives in court? Should new agencies be created, working on a short leash under presidential or congressional direction? Should Congress itself decide the exact regulatory solution for the financial industry?

Instead, the responsibility to resurrect the financial industry during the 1930s went in large part to new agencies like the SEC and a newly reorganized Federal Reserve. These agencies were given a remarkably autonomous role to play, either by explicit grant or implicitly, as the result of conflicting preferences existing among political principals. And as argued earlier, the relative autonomy of these agencies played a positive role in creating a Northian credible commitment to a stable system of property rights and contract enforcement. The system served to avoid politicization by screening out forms of moral hazard on the part of public figures. As a result, investors, bankers, stockbrokers, corporate executives, labor, and others were able to count on a stable (if not always level) playing field. For decades to follow, the role of professional expertise was unyielding and unresponsive, in the interest of stability. The bureaucracies were so predictable and unresponsive to political pressure that interest groups did not bother to lobby on many questions; the small likelihood of changing bureaucratic dictates by lobbying (say, the Fed's open market decisions) did not justify the cost of hiring lobbyists. Overall, a significant degree of bureaucratic autonomy contributed to a half-century of financial stability.

GLASS-STEAGALL AND BANKING REGULATION

In June 1933, Congress passed legislation in response to the revelations of bank depositors losing their deposits as the banks they trusted used their money to finance the riskiest of gambles. Just a few months after his inauguration, Roosevelt signed the Banking Act of 1933, which developed a regulatory structure not only for the following years of depression and war but also for the later decades of peace and economic expansion.

Deposit Pyramids

In 1913, Carter Glass, as a Democratic member of the House of Representatives, had been a central force behind the creation of the Fed. By 1933, he was in the Senate and chair of the Appropriations Committee, and he still remained concerned about keeping the nation's financial capital out of the control of Wall Street speculators. He was convinced that measures he had incorporated into the 1913 legislation had been circumvented, resulting in the 1929 crash. He was determined to get it right in 1933.

Glass's primary concern was the "pyramiding" of bank deposits, which was the means by which Wall Street speculators such as Mitchell had come to control large pools of capital. Local banks across the country had to protect depositors by keeping money in reserve. Small local banks might deposit their reserves with larger regional banks, which might in turn place their deposits in the nation's largest Wall Street institutions. The largest banks directed the money to the stock market as a way of generating earnings on reserves deposited with them (Hoffmann, 2001, 112).

Carter Glass had hoped in 1913 that the creation of regional Federal Reserve Banks would deter pyramiding by requiring banks to deposit their reserves in the new Federal Reserve Banks: "Instead of the pyramiding arrangement that effectively channeled money to New York, banks would deposit their required reserves in the new Federal Reserve Banks. This arrangement would break the money trust by preventing the movement of money's control to New York" (Hoffmann, 2001, 122). Glass considered the creation of the Reserve banks to be the most important feature of the 1913 legislation.

Twenty years later, it seemed that Glass's hopes had been dashed, because New York's privately owned banks had offered high interest on demand deposits as a way of attracting funds. So the first item that Glass inserted into the legislation was a prohibition, called Regulation Q, on interest for deposits (Hoffmann, 2001, 127–129). Banks could no longer take risky investments in order to compete for checking accounts. Glass hoped that this prohibition would stop Wall Street security firms from once again gaining control of too much of the nation's capital.

1933 Monetary Policy

Another issue that was crucial to Glass was the regulation of monetary policy. He believed that a correct structure for commercial finance would implement a self-regulating monetary policy based on short-term commercial assets; when more money was needed, banks would increase their assets and then reduce them when the need decreased.

Having a correct structure was important to Glass because it would then be unnecessary to put discretionary authority in the hands either of bankers or politicians, neither of whom he trusted. He felt that it had been a mistake to give the presidency a key role, in part through appointments to the Board of Governors. Once again, he hoped that the 1913 legislation would have created such a mechanism, restricting discretionary policy from whatever source. Again, he was disappointed and felt it necessary in 1933 to try again.

The 1913 legislation had forbidden the Fed's member banks from borrowing money for speculation in the stock market. However, money is fungible, and the member banks were able to easily evade that prohibition (Hoffmann, 2001, 129). Therefore Glass introduced in 1933 a structural feature that he hoped would quash such conscious manipulation of the money supply: he prohibited regional banks from such activities and placed responsibility for monetary policy in a new Federal Open Market Committee (FOMC), under the supervisory control of the Federal Reserve Board, which he presumed was less susceptible to such schemes. "The board was given more authority over reserve banks so that it could stop them from exercising discretionary monetary policy, not so that it could exercise monetary policy in their place" (131). Specifically, the Fed was given the authority to keep regional banks from letting capital get into the hands of Wall Street. "To keep the government from seizing control, the Federal Reserve Board was moved physically out of Treasury's building, and the terms of the board members were lengthened from 10 to 12 years" (131). Congress hoped that the Fed's physical location, separated from the Treasury Department and the Wall Street influences at Treasury, would encourage the FOMC to regulate monetary policy on behalf of the public.

Ironically, the new structure – the FOMC – that was intended to stop discretionary monetary policy making became the most important vehicle for that policy. Just as ironically, the actions that were intended to keep politicians and bankers from having discretion ended up providing the basis for a discretionary Fed.

Deposit Insurance for Commercial Banks

Not everyone had the same priorities as Glass. Representative Henry Steagall, chair of the House Banking Committee, demanded deposit insurance as the price for his support for the 1933 bill (Calomiris & White, 1994). Considering the terrifying wave of bank failures of the previous year, it is not surprising that one of the most central innovations of this bill was the creation of the Federal Deposit Insurance Corporation (FDIC). The FDIC was the means by which the federal government insured bank depositors. It was designed to pay for itself by charging the banks fees – and many banks were more than willing to pay for the machinery of regulation, because, as specified in the law, it brought with it the prospect of deposit insurance.

Deposit insurance largely eliminated bank runs overnight. Depositors no longer had to try to discern which banks were safe and which were not. In previous years, rumors had been sufficient to start a bank run, as shown in Frank Capra's classic film *It's a Wonderful Life*, and even sound banks could go broke following a bank run. Commercial banks, as well as their investors, benefited from the security of investors protected by deposit insurance.

In exchange for deposit insurance, which prevented bank runs, banks were required to support the FDIC financially. More importantly, the explicit tradeoff was safety for regulation. Commercial banks benefited from deposit insurance, and in return they had to submit to regulation – regulation that protected the taxpayers from having to pay out for deposit insurance. The FDIC insured banks' viability when its examiners audited their books to certify safety and soundness. Banks thus accepted regulation in exchange for protection from bank runs. This trade – regulation for protection – became the basis for a half-century of financial stability in commercial banking.

Banks had to choose between being an investment bank or a commercial bank, knowing that commercial banking would be safer and more regulated, whereas investment banking would be less regulated and riskier. Some firms such J. P. Morgan split into two entities. Investors, too, had a choice: they could invest in commercial banks with their savings guaranteed, or they could seek higher interest rates in riskier opportunities supplied by the investment banks.

The negotiation between Glass and Steagall gave each side what it most wanted. Glass got the prohibition on interest for reserve deposits, the constraints on the regional banks, the creation of the FOMC, and longer terms of office for Fed governors. Steagall fought hard for deposit insurance, forcing Glass "to compromise with the populist outcroppings of the moment and accept the FDIC" (Hoffmann, 2001, 132). The 1933 Banking Bill, also known as the Glass-Steagall Act, became a bulwark of the New Deal economic reform, although it did not always resemble the Fed that was originally envisioned by the participants.

1935 Banking Bill: More Compromise on Monetary Policy and the Fed

The Banking Act of 1935 featured an energetic debate between Carter Glass and FDR's choice for the Fed chairman, Mariner Eccles. The two clashed precisely on the question of agency. Glass argued in favor of a decentralized Fed, believing that neither bankers nor politicians could be trusted with monetary policy. The 1933 Banking Bill reinforced the original vision of the Fed as one in which the money supply would regulate itself automatically if the correct structures were in place.

Eccles, on the other hand, believed that monetary policy could not be managed efficiently by any self-correcting market-based mechanism. He "explicitly rejected the view that the economy was a natural phenomenon and could be counted on to correct itself" (Hoffmann, 2001, 134). So Eccles argued for a re-creation of the Fed as a means for conscious intervention in the money supply.

Eccles sought legislative recognition of what have become the three modern tools of monetary policy: the discount rate, reserve requirements, and open market operations. After negotiations with Glass, he obtained for the Fed a constrained power to set reserve rates and the discount rate. Most interesting, the 1935 bill created the modern structure of the Federal Open Market Committee, which was legally recognized for the first time in 1933. Although Eccles wanted to vest open market operations in the Board of Governors alone, with advice from 5 board members, he got as a compromise a board with 12 members that included 5 rotating Fed presidents. This compromise also guaranteed that decisions of the FOMC bound all reserve banks. Eccles again received most of what he wanted.

However, Eccles was unable to gain the power for the president to fire the Fed chairman, in the face of Glass's strong opposition. Inter-institutional jealousy once again had the effect of increasing the independence of the Fed. Glass also succeeded in depriving two key presidential appointees – the Treasury Secretary and the Comptroller of the Currency – seats on the Fed Board of Governors. The size of the board decreased from eight to seven, and the length of office increased from 12 to 14 years. These longer terms of office helped shore up the independence of the Fed Board, as Eccles proceeded to determine monetary policy with a toolbox filled with more tools and more discretionary authority in the use of them.

Compensation, Growth, and Culture in the Stable Years

In the decades after World War II, a bank's managers had to be particularly obtuse to allow a bank to go belly up. Commercial bankers' regulations kept the industry "boring" – fixed interest rates guaranteed a modest profit margin and plenty of time to enjoy it. Compensation packages for those in the financial industry were in line with those of managers in other industries (Crotty, 2012; Johnson & Kwak, 2010). More importantly, the financial services industry offered no incentives that put managers at odds with their clients. Investment bankers saw themselves as serving the capital needs of the industrial firms that were their clients. The sharp conflict of interest between the financial industry and its clients did not come about until later – with the advent of proprietary trading.

The limits on external competition reflected the situation inside the banking firms: they did not have a particularly competitive environment. Commercial banks and thrifts, in which engaging in price competition to attract depositors was constrained, competed on the basis of personalized service. The same held true for investment bankers. Investment banks had a corporate culture based on meticulous care for their clients. If General Motors needed capital, investors at Salomon Brothers or elsewhere were there to help supply it. Personal relationships were important in maintaining this business, and a reputation for integrity was key.

Shareholders were constrained from pushing aggressive profit-maximizing policies by a collective action problem: there were just too many of them in most firms to be able to speak authoritatively to their firm's managers. Perhaps economists and others worried that shareholder passivity meant they were being exploited by managers, but even if managers were in complete control of their firms, they apparently were not very greedy. They did not own large numbers of shares in the firms they managed, and their compensation was not routinely linked with the share price; the norm was for executives to be compensated by an annual salary, as were managers in industrial and other firms in the era. Nor did financial managers' earnings stand out; until the late 1970s, their real average annual compensation tracked that in the private sector almost perfectly (Johnson & Kwak, 2010, 115). And throughout the half-century after 1933, very little of the compensation package for employers was linked to the performance of the firm (M. C. Jensen & Murphy, 1990a).

Executive salaries were healthy, to be sure, but they were laughably small by today's standards. The ratio of CEO salary to the average worker's salary was 45 in 1973, far less than the ratio in 2002, when the CEO earned 140 times the earnings of his average worker's salary (Cassidy, 2009). As M. C. Jensen and Murphy (1990b) demonstrated (disapprovingly), executives typically had "low intensity" compensation. With a weak ownership structure, the managers might be more interested in gross revenues than in profits: it was the "size" of the firm (more than its profits) that indicated both higher status and a justification for a higher annual salary.

The financial firms did not particularly value risk during these stable decades. "Historically, and continuing through the 1960s and most of the 1970s, the big firms and partnerships that dominated Wall Street employed a business model that was decidedly low risk, focusing mainly on selling advice to investors and large companies" (Gasparino, 2009, 14). The Fed's Regulation Q prohibited financial rent-seeking by eliminating competition among demand deposits. Glass-Steagall required banks to decide whether they were (more risky) investment banks or (less risky) commercial banks. Together, these regulatory institutions provided the basis for protected rent-seeking by financial firms, in which they took their rents in the form of security and stability – not excess profits.

Thus the half-century after the New Deal was characterized by weak shareholders in firms, the lack of outcome-contingent managerial compensation, the lack of direct accountability by managers to shareholders, and the strong position of economic regulators monitoring securities, banking, and labor markets. Despite (or perhaps because of) these characteristics, the United States performed strongly through this period. Fueled by consumer demand and investor confidence, the economy was strong. The gross national product rose from $200 billion in 1940 to $300 billion in 1950, and to more than $500 billion in 1960. The expansion during the Kennedy-Johnson years was just as strong. This growth spread generously, causing an expansion in the middle class. The SEC, purposely insulated from executive control, was able to turn its insulation into a reputation for keeping the playing field level. At the Fed, William McChesney Martin periodically "took the punchbowl away just as the party" was heating up, and so inflation was under control. These and other administrative professionals may not have been responsible for the economic development of these decades, but they exercised a form of administrative discretion that was manifestly consistent with that growth.

Politics of Professionalism

Other factors also supported the persistence of professionalism in financial regulation. One was the mutual blocking of political forces throughout this era, which led to little accountability being required on the part of professionals. It was not only the Fed where political stalemate placed fewer constraints on bureaucrats; similar situations existed at the NLRB, the SEC, FHLBB, and the FDIC. These agencies tended to maintain agency policy persistence – to the benefit of the industrial and financial worlds.

Firms and their regulators made an implicit bargain. Regulators needed information, but firms were afraid that regulators would use any information they could gather to harm the firms. However, this left room for cooperation between firms and regulators: the firm could share information in the expectation that long-term relationships were sustainable. That the regulators were long-term, culture-bound professionals helped build the agencies' credibility.

COMPETITION, RISK TAKING, AND CORPORATE GOVERNANCE

Beginning in the 1980s, the transformation of investment banking initiated a series of connected institutional changes.

John Gutfreund and Howie Rubin

The traditional culture at investment banking partnerships such as Salomon Brothers was staid and reserved. Each partner was supposed to keep a large amount of his capital in the firm to encourage loyalty and a shared concern for the firm's best interests. Handling a major client – say a major manufacturer wanting to raise capital by issuing bonds – required a team effort, knowledge of the client, and diplomacy. Employees underwent a long apprenticeship, and senior partners got both respect and the lion's share of the earnings.

Further, as members of a private partnership, the partners knew that it was their own money that would be funding any risks to be taken. As a result, the culture did not encourage risk taking. Most money earned was in the form of commissions for putting deals together and for giving advice. Neither of those activities carried much risk.

That culture changed in 1981 when the first of the large investment partnerships – Salomon Brothers – went public, a decision made by John Gutfreund, who had risen to managing partner in 1978 by assuring traditionalists that he would not take the firm public.

Gutfreund made millions by taking the firm public, but not surprisingly, the traditionalists were not pleased. Retired partner William Salomon said, "I was disgusted by his [Gutfreund's] materialism." But Gutfreund had resisted the pressure of tradition and "lifted a giant middle finger in the direction of the moral disapproval of his fellow Wall Street CEOs" (M. Lewis, 2010, 257). Over lunch with writer Michael Lewis, Gutfreund said, "They – the heads of the other Wall Street firms – all said what an awful thing it was to go public and how could they do such a thing. But when the temptation rose, they all gave in to it" (263). Gutfreund may have taken the first big Wall Street investment partnership public, but he was not the last to do so. "By the mid-1980s Wall Street's private partnerships were a dying breed; one by one, the big Wall Street private partnerships became public companies that grew in size by issuing stock to public shareholders, and with that they began gambling not with the house money but with public shareholders' money. The once-staid Wall Street business model with it modest leverage was now an anachronism, and with Salomon...the risk-taking took off" (Gasparino, 2009, 29).

The change in culture that followed occurred almost instantaneously. "As the big Wall Street firms converged from private partnerships to public companies in the 1980s, they were gambling no longer with their own money but with that of public shareholders, and literally overnight the bets got bigger and the use of borrowed funds, known as leverage, grew and grew" (14).

The trading wing of Salomon began to bring in a lot of money and to carry a lot of power. Trading did not require team effort – indeed, trading seemed to inspire competitive, even combative relationships on the trading floor. The quiet, reserved diplomats who had helped corporate executives with bond offerings clashed with the brassy, boastful traders. Political power in the firm continued to flow to the units that made the firm profits, and by 1985 those were the trading sections.

By 1985, Salomon was making a lot of money trading the newly devised mortgage bonds. Unlike the traditional "deals" put together by the investment banking side of Salomon, the trading of mortgage bonds allowed individual traders to keep track of how much they made for the firm – and for themselves. The kind of person who succeeded in the trading room was decidedly more open to risk. "The best traders...are more like bookmakers – they use information to lay odds on favorites and underdogs. They arrange odds in their favor based on information that you can't get anywhere else.... They were successful because they were smart of course. But they had something else going for them: the will...to take risks and gamble. Most of it was with other people's money, which made the losses more palatable" (Gasparino, 2009, 11–14). The "other people" were the firm's own shareholders.

A bond trader named Howie Rubin exemplified these traders' activities. Rubin had a Harvard MBA and a gift for trading mortgage bonds. In his first year, when he had a salary of $9,000, Rubin's trading earnings were $25 million. The second year he was paid $175,000 (the most possible under Salomon's rules that year) and made $30 million for the company. As Lewis writes, Rubin's unprecedented trading success raised the question, "Who really made that money, Howie Rubin or Salomon Brothers?" (M. Lewis, 1989, 126). Gutfreund maintained that Salomon, the firm, had made Rubin's trades possible, because of its reputation and position on Wall Street. Rubin felt he could produce profits for any firm that would give him a place on a trading floor. Gutfreund was now clearly uncomfortable with the new culture of the trading floor brought about by his taking the firm public.

Despite a strong emotional attachment to Salomon, Rubin quit the firm and moved to Merrill Lynch for a guaranteed minimum salary of $1 million a year for three years, plus a percentage of trading gains. This move signaled an end to the traditional culture of loyalty to the firm and reinforced a culture of competitiveness at Salomon. If Rubin could make $1 million by moving, others wanted to leave with even higher offers in hand. "The Howie Rubin legend grew into mortgage trading people who planned to leave just as soon as they got their three-million-dollar contracts elsewhere. A whole new attitude toward working at Salomon Brothers was born: Hit and run. And that is how Salomon Brothers, and the mortgage trading desk in particular, became a nursery for the rest of Wall Street" (M. Lewis, 1989, 128). Mortgage traders felt that their compensation demands were justified by what they produced, whereas traders of government and corporate bonds felt that they had been denied the opportunity to make as much money as the more profitable traders. And Gutfreund thought it ridiculous to pay out so much to traders: they were, after all, just employees. Pointing to employees on the trading floor, he told a journalist, "I don't understand what goes on in their pointy little heads" (127). Of course, he could have looked back just four years earlier to his own decision to go public to help understand Rubin's greed.

The combined examples of Gutfreund's and Rubin's actions encouraged an aggressive attitude toward compensation on the part of firm directors and their employees. All realized that they could maximize short-term compensation by taking high-reward risks – claiming part of the return – and leaving the downside of the risk to the shareholders.

Rubin accepted the lucrative offer from Merrill Lynch at a time when it was striving to be a major presence in the new markets that Salomon and other investment banks dominated. High-flying thrifts were trying to unload conventional mortgages that paid little interest, and the investment banks began to package them in a promising innovation – the mortgage-backed bond. These bonds packaged a variety of bonds in ways that allowed investors to buy more or less risky segments of them. The bonds were then sold to investors (including the thrifts themselves), who liked the high returns that the riskier segments of the bonds promised.

Incidentally, Howie Rubin became famous for his fate at Merrill Lynch. Two years after he left Salomon, Rubin refused to back out of a bet he had made that interest rates would stay low. The increase in the interest rate was reducing the value of his $900 million portfolio. Instead of backing out, Rubin bought an additional $800 million in derivatives betting on the interest rate. The result was a loss of $377 million for his employer; although that is a relatively small amount in today's terms, it was the largest one-day loss on Wall Street at that time. Merrill Lynch fired him; he was then hired at Bear Stearns, a firm that was evidently not concerned either by Rubin's losses or by the fact that he made those losses on unauthorized and hidden trades (Gasparino, 2009, 63). Rubin's new employer, Bear Stearns, was the first to succumb to the crisis in 2008.

Gutfreund was to have a more serious run-in with regulators. Salomon was legally prohibited from having more than 30% of funds under its control be in the form of bonds. Some of his government bond traders arranged, with the cooperation of their clients, to have more than the legal limit of 30%. With this market power, they were able to squeeze traders who needed to buy bonds to complete their short-sale transactions. Salomon's buyers were able to make very large amounts of money, but discovery of their flouting of the law resulted in the forced resignation of the traders' supervisors, up to and including Gutfreund.

The examples of Rubin and Gutfreund suggested that not all would go smoothly in the aftermath of the investment firms going public and the resulting expansion of trading. Not only would there be greater risk taking, more internal competition, and leverage but also the competition for compensation would create an aggressive business posture that required more leeway from the traditional financial regulators. Each regulatory concession increased the scope of the market and the ferocity of the competition – as well as the perceived need for further grants of discretion from regulators. Regulators were either in support of this deregulatory "snowball" (Hammond & Knott, 1988) or were sidetracked and rendered ineffective.

Increased Risk Taking and Leverage

As mentioned earlier, the result of these changes was a new culture at Salomon and on Wall Street as a whole. The investment bankers had historically looked down on the bond traders at Salomon as pedestrian and crass. The traders then adopted a culture that emphasized their crassness, but made the rest of the firm appreciate it because of the new techniques they discovered for making money (M. Lewis, 1989). In fact, they showed that financial investment banks could make more profits by trading than through traditional corporate bond underwriting.

In addition to the transformation of private partnerships, such as Salomon Brothers, into publicly held firms, another cause of the increased risk taking was that the stable, service-oriented business strategy of the earlier decades had been adversely affected by the SEC's recent deregulation of services (Weingast, 1984). This deregulation allowed more competition among service providers, which meant a collapse in the profits generated by trading commissions. Brokers, investment bankers, and other financial service providers could no longer afford the luxury of implicit understandings that dulled their competitive edge. The deregulation of commissions encouraged firms to move to a model in which leveraged position-taking commanded the profits and supported the claims of brokers for larger shares of those profits.

Yet another key reason for increased risk taking was the return of low interest rates after Volcker attempted to rein in inflation. Low interest rates made it cheap to leverage the bets taken by the new breed of Wall Street brokers. It was also cheaper for homeowners to mortgage or refinance their homes. And these low rates meant that investors were constantly on the lookout for financial products that promised higher returns on their investment – such as the new mortgage bonds and junk bonds. More than anything else, perhaps, it was the insatiable demand for these new products by both institutional and individual investors that paved the way for Wall Street's cultural transformation. "And just like that, Wall Street's business model had shifted from giving advice to taking on risk" (Gasparino, 2009, 16).

The abandonment of the old business model and the new willingness of financial firms to embrace risk changed the corporate culture of the firms. In 2008 Fareed Zakaria quoted Boykin Curry, managing director of Eagle Capital, as saying,

For 20 years, the DNA of nearly every financial institution had morphed dangerously. Each time someone at the table pressed for more leverage and more risk, the next few years proved them "right." These people were emboldened, they were promoted and they gained control of ever more capital. Meanwhile, anyone in power who hesitated, who argued for caution, was proved "wrong." The cautious types were increasingly intimidated, passed over for promotion. They lost their hold on capital. This happened every day in almost every financial institution over and over, until we ended up with a very specific kind of person running things. (Zakaria, 2008)

These and other innovations fundamentally changed the nature of the financial services industry. In recent years, it has become popular to point to the rise of "shadow banking" – and other ways of describing credit intermediation that happened outside of traditional, regulated banks and depository institutions – as a key driver in the Great Recession. For instance, Fed Chairman Bernanke noted in a 2012 speech that a "key vulnerability" in the crisis was how short-term "wholesale" funding fueled shadow banking (Bernanke, 2012). For some, though, shadow banking is a parallel system that complements the traditional banking system (Noeth & Sengupta, 2011), and although its roots and consequences for financial stability are complex (e.g., Chinn & Frieden, 2011), the financial innovations associated with this time period and their effects on the old business model clearly have been important for our understanding of prudential regulation. One of their most important effects has been to change the relative returns to financial innovation.[1]

Compensation and Corporate Culture

Economists, who in the 1980s increasingly voiced concern about the relatively weak position of shareholders, had come to support an "alignment" of managerial and shareholder interests in an attempt to put shareholders in the driver's seat (M. C. Jensen & Murphy, 1990b). From the perspective of principal-agency theory, this outcome could be achieved most easily by abandoning traditional compensation schemes in favor of stock options. Many senior executives in the decades after World War II regarded stock options as "too risky" (Cassidy, 2009, 68), but that was just the point from the perspective of principal-agency theory. Granted an opportunity to buy stock at the present time, the option was worthless unless the price were to go up – an outcome presumably beneficial to the shareholders as well as the manager. But such an arrangement did not always benefit firm performance in the long run. Consider the case of "Chainsaw Al."

On June 8, 1998, the financial magazine *Barrons*, in its article "Dangerous Games: Did 'Chainsaw Al' Manufacture Sunbeam's Earnings Last Year?," wrote, "Deconstructing Al Dunlap is a daunting task. But to save our gentle readers the effort, our total estimate of artificial profit boosters in 1997 came to around $120 million compared with the $109.4 million profit the company actually reported" (Laing, 1998). This was the very public beginning of the end for Al Dunlap's tenure as Sunbeam's chief executive officer, which began only two years earlier when he was hired as a famous "turnaround specialist."

Al Dunlap may be a singular example of the potential dark side of incentives-based compensation practices, yet, his story provides a unique and powerful lens on how compensation shapes organizational outcomes. Dunlap came to Sunbeam, manufacturer of household appliances and other products, from Scott Paper when that company merged with Kimberly-Clark. At Scott, his total

---

[1] An important question in policy debates about shadow banking is whether actions by regulators responded to or caused these innovations. The truth is probably more complicated. A number of key changes in the competitive environment of banks (including technological change, access to high-speed computing, etc.) shaped the behavior of financial intermediaries both among regulated depository institutions and within the shadow-banking world (Fein, 2013). Yet, at key points regulators pursued changes to the rules to increase flexibility for institutions (both inside and outside traditional banking spaces), the results of which were undoubtedly to spur activity in the shadow-banking sector; see, for instance, Robert Clarke's views on bank deregulation and how they affected the OCC's activities (e.g., R. L. Clarke, 1987). Our focus in this chapter and the next, though, is not on shadow banking as an enterprise, except to the extent that specific deregulatory events happened to lay the foundation for the risk taking that became endemic in the sector during the early 2000s.

compensation was largely due to gains in stock value: "My $100 million was less than 2 percent of the wealth I created for all Scott shareholders. Did I earn that? Damn right I did. I'm a superstar in my field, much like Michael Jordan in basketball and Bruce Springsteen in rock 'n roll" (Dunlap & Andelman, 1996, 21).

Dunlap's approach was rooted in the view that shareholders mattered most: "That's why executive compensation must be tied to shareholder return. If boards will always align it with shareholder gains...the boards need no further justification. But if you reward failing executives who have no stock, what do they have at risk? Nothing" (Dunlap & Andelman, 1996, 178). He pursued shareholder value by ruthlessly cutting costs and often personnel. He laid off 11,200 employees at Scott; at Sunbeam, he sought to cut 6,000 of 12,000 employees and 18 of 26 factories (Clikeman, 2009, 213–215). These tactics helped him become known as "Chainsaw Al" or even "Rambo in Pinstripes," famously appearing on the cover of *USA Today* with a black bandanna, ammunition bandoleers, and pistols.

Throughout the organizational hierarchy of Sunbeam, shares were used to motivate and obtain compliance. Because Dunlap thought "money is very important as motivation" (Dunlap & Andelman, 1996, 183), he "took the options deeper into the organization and gave key people more of them" (185).

At Sunbeam, most of Dunlap's own compensation was in stock options. By 1997, he was ready to arrange its sale to a bigger company, and had he found a buyer, he would have walked away with $100 million or more in profits (Clikeman, 2009, 216). However, after several acquisitions in 1998, Sunbeam's performance came into question, centering on serious allegations of accounting irregularities that indicated that the books were cooked to support higher share prices. The Barron's story pointed to "inventory stuffing," "mother's little helpers," and other accounting strategies to shift sales forward in time, inflate earnings, and give the impression of profitability (Laing, 1998) – activities now called the "Live for Today" strategy (Koch & Wall, 2000).

Clikeman points directly to compensation schemes as having contributed to the culture facilitating the committing of accounting irregularities to support higher share prices. He notes that "no Sunbeam employees have publicly accused Dunlap of ordering or even approving improper accounting," yet

employee stock options created another powerful incentive for Sunbeam's aggressive accounting....Sunbeam's top managers worked at the company and tolerated Dunlap's abuse only because they thought they could make a lot of money quickly. All the senior managers knew that if Sunbeam failed to meet the analysts' forecasts, their work and suffering would be for naught. (Clikeman, 2009, 220–221)

Board members also faced these pressures to meet the forecasts (J. Hill, 1999). As a competitor said after Dunlap was fired, "He is the logical extreme of an executive who has no values, no honor, no loyalty, and no ethics. And yet he was held up as a corporate god in our culture" (Byrne, 1998, 59).

In Chainsaw Al's case, the simple task of incentivizing executives for the good of the whole turned out to be trickier than it might have seemed – even when everyone agreed that shareholder profits were a natural and justified measure of the executive's worth. Because stock prices were influenced by profits, anything that increased the price of a share was then thought worth doing – even if the effect was only temporary. Similarly, IBM, Xerox, and Procter & Gamble fired tens of thousands of workers; whether or not those workers represented a long-run asset for their firms, their CEOs benefited when the price of a share rose higher than the designated strike price. The executive with a stock option might well discover that it was easier to alter the accounting data than the reality of firm profitability. As stock options expanded in the 1990s, so did episodes of reporting irregularities. In other words, the compensation bonuses were more like a pool of shareholder profits, except the "rainmakers" got first chance at it.

Executives as First Claimants on Profits

In contrast to the stable half-century since the Depression, compensation for financial executives became noticeably higher than that for executives in other industries in the late 1980s and 1990s. Bonuses soared as the trading model took over in these financial houses. Nor were mortgage bonds the only basis for prosperity in the financial industry. For most of the 20th century, the financial sector had tracked exactly the average profits of the nonfinancial sector. By the 1980s, however, the financial sector far outstripped the nonfinancial industries in real corporate profits (Johnson & Kwak, 2010, 61): "From 1980 until 2005, financial sector profits grew by 800 percent" (60), compared to 250% for nonfinancial sector profits. The difference was very often the result of the diversion of profits to executive salaries that were out of line with other industries.

Beginning in the 1990s, an unprecedented development occurred in the financial industry. Whereas large bonuses were originally justified as motivating executive commitment to shareholder profit, the 1990s saw a growing disconnect between the compensation to top executives and the returns to shareholders. A person who bought stock in the top five investment firms in 1998 would have lost 77% of that investment, in real terms, by 2009 (Crotty, 2009, 17). During that same period, however, corporate executives and program managers were earning larger and larger bonuses. Not only were bonuses large but also they were no longer contingent on an outstanding individual or organizational outcome. Bonuses were high when the bank's earnings went up, and they were high when the bank's earnings went down.

Bear Stearns's earnings illustrated this pattern. By 2006, it had a decade-long record of allocating more money in bonuses than it left for the shareholders in net earning – but at least earnings were going in the right direction. Then, in 2007, net earnings dropped from more than $2 trillion to less than

$250 million – but the amount of money allocated to bonuses remained over $2 trillion (Crotty, 2009, 66). The losses to investors were the direct result of the size of the bonuses to the executives.

This pattern was not limited to Bears Stearns, however, New York Attorney General Andrew Cuomo investigated the compensation practices of the largest banks, documenting that, at Goldman Sachs, Morgan Stanley, and J. P. Morgan Chase, bonuses in 2008 were greater than the banks' net income. Goldman Sachs, for example, earned $2.3 billion and paid out $4.8 billion in bonuses (Crotty, 2009, 66).

Bank of America's net income rose from $10 to $18 billion in the four years leading up to 2006, which may have justified a compensation package in that year of $18 billion – the compensation package claimed one dollar for every dollar in net income. However, when net income dropped to only $4 billion in 2008, the compensation package remained at $18 billion (Cuomo, 2009, 2). Clearly, the compensation package did not force Bank of America officials to share the pain in bad times.

Increasingly, the top executives and bankers at the biggest banks regarded themselves as having a prior claim to the earnings of their banks – a claim that had nothing to do with a successful performance. Not only that, but the bonuses they paid themselves had higher priority than the claims of shareholders: a loss of revenue meant a decrease in net income, but did not imply a significant decrease in compensation bonuses. Bankers took theirs off the top. The firms were "run by rainmakers for rainmakers; these firms seek maximum rainmaker compensation, not minimum cost" (Crotty, 2009, 60).

As Eswaran and Kotwal (1984) showed in their paper, "The Moral Hazard of Budget-Breaking," it is bad news for a firm when its key decision makers are also the residual claimants. Residual claimants inevitably have incentives to maximize their share of the residual, and those incentives are inconsistent with those that would maximize the overall size of the pie.

In the Great Recession, it is easy to see the link between the financial executives' first claim on earnings and the incentives for inefficiency. Executives directed their firms' efforts toward high returns, while minimizing the risk of a collapse of the housing market. They were especially inclined to underweight this risk if they felt that the government would bail out their firms. To the extent that their compensation was linked to accounting numbers, they had every incentive to manipulate those figures with off-the-record entities and outright misrepresentation. And when their bonuses and golden parachutes were measured in the tens of millions, they could ride the mortgage bond frenzy with little concern for the long-run consequences. As Crotty notes, "Since they do not have to return their bubble-year bonuses when the inevitable crisis occurs, and since they continue to receive substantial bonuses even in the crisis, they have a powerful incentive to pursue high-risk, high-leverage strategies. In recent years at least, these perverse incentives caused rainmakers to make decisions that helped create the global financial crisis" (Crotty, 2009, 11).

POLITICIZING FINANCIAL REGULATION

As the financial industry reoriented itself around trading and risk taking, instead of providing services to investors and corporations, financial executives increasingly saw the familiar machinery of postwar regulation as an obstacle to lucrative ventures and full exploitation of the trading markets. Objecting to regulations placed on them by independent regulatory agencies, they sought political intervention to reduce those constraints of regulation. The object of the increased political activism by the financial industry was bureaucratic politicization – the opening up of the regulatory personnel and their decision-making processes to pressure from politicians friendly to the financial industry.

Each of the most effective financial regulation agencies became the focus of demands to soften or eliminate its regulatory constraints on the financial industry. These demands were effective, minimizing the effectiveness of the regulatory agencies that might have been expected to blow the whistle on the excessive risk taking, consumer abuse, and leverage that led to events like the Enron accounting scandal and ultimately the crisis of 2008.

Deregulatory Unanimity among Multiple Principals

We argued in Chapter 5 that self-interested politicians will grant autonomy to the bureaucracy when they are in conflict with each other. The natural compromise in the face of stalemate is delegation to experts in bureaucracy. The converse of that claim is that unanimity among politicians leads to a decline in bureaucratic autonomy and more effective direct control of the agency. We argue that politicians of many stripes came together in the last three decades around a deregulatory philosophy and that this unanimity resulted in the erosion of bureaucratic autonomy and an inability of agencies to control the destructive practices that led to the crisis of 2008.

We offer four reasons for the increased unanimity of politicians vis-à-vis regulators: (1) academic support for deregulation, (2) unprecedented political contributions made possible by the burgeoning profits of the financial industry, (3) unified government under six years of the George W. Bush administration, and (4) the logic of partisan conflict that led Democrats to mount an effective strategy of competing with Republicans for the support of business interests in general and Wall Street in particular.

The Power of Ideas

A distinguished academic tradition supported deregulation, high-powered incentives, and principal-agency theory. Since the success of deregulation in transportation in the 1970s, the pendulum had swung hard in that direction. Deregulation of the financial industry seemed like the next natural step in an inevitable freeing of the marketplace. When advocated by members of Congress, key executive figures like Larry Summers, and even the chairman of the Fed (a faithful disciple of Ayn Rand), deregulation became a powerful unifier of previously disparate interests. Indeed, after the success of airline, trucking, and train deregulation in the 1970s (e.g., Biederman, 1982; A. E. Brown, 1987; Dempsey & Goetz, 1992; Derthick & Quirk, 1985; Noll & Owen, 1983), it was hard to find anyone in the mainstream skeptical of deregulation.

Financial Contributions

The expanding scale of Wall Street activities, the growing availability of ready cash from trading activities, and the profits increasingly earned by financial firms made lobbying an attractive option. Financial firms quickly went to the top of the lists of political contributors. McCarty (2012, 212) documents an increase in campaign contributions from the financial sector of more than 300% from 1990 to 2008, with the greatest parts of that increase coming from the insurance and securities and investment subsectors. As McCarty notes, "This growth exceeds that of all of the industrial sectors tracked by the Center for Responsive Politics with the exception of the legal profession" (211).

One important element creating this state of affairs was the significant returns to human capital for those working in finance. As Philippon and Reshef (2012) document, workers in the financial industry did about as well as other workers until 1990 (as measured in terms of earned education-adjusted wages), but after 2006, the wage premium those in finance received was (on average) 50% higher than the wages of similar workers; the wage premium for top executives was 250% higher. They show that about half of the increase in the average wage premium was likely due to changes in earnings risk. This finding clearly indicates the stakes for those in the industry. Employees in finance were not only increasingly able to afford political contributions but also were confident that the right connections would reduce the risk normally associated with their expected returns.

Unified Government

During the six critical years of deregulation – the first six years of Bush's tenure – Republicans controlled both Congress and the White House for much of that time (his first five months in office and also the time period between the 2002 and 2006 midterm elections). Although social conservatives and pro-business Republicans had their differences, they shared the same attitude toward regulation. Both sides of the Republican Party agreed that less regulation was inevitably an improvement and that cutting back on the resources for agencies was fiscal wisdom. This unity among principals greatly constrained the policy, staffing, and structural autonomy of the economic regulatory agencies; the agencies became increasingly accountable to their political masters, which diminished their capacity to guarantee a level playing field or stability. In fact, we argue that there is a direct link between increased accountability and the failure of the regulatory agencies to anticipate or respond to the mounting fiscal crises from the S&L crisis, through the dot-com bubble and the Enron/accounting scandal, to the crisis of 2008.

Democrats might try to divide the Republicans with wedge issues such as immigration, but these wedge issues were never regulatory in nature. On the contrary, Democrats joined with Republicans in support of many aspects of deregulation. The sheer volume of campaign contributions from accounting and financial firms made it imperative that Democrats find a way to earn a share of that cash.

Bipartisan Deregulation

Because of partisan shifts the Democratic Party was no longer an automatic check on the political pressure that Wall Street exerted on the GOP. The realignment that had created the Reagan "big tent" Republican coalition resulted in an opening for Democrats. With social conservatives increasingly dominating the Republican Party, pro-business Republicans (many with social liberal proclivities) were an unstable element of the Reagan coalition. A rapprochement between Democrats and pro-business social liberals became a distinct possibility (Miller & Schofield, 2003).

President Clinton, for example, knew that Democrats had a lock on social liberal votes. He also knew that a number of traditional fiscal-conservative Republicans were increasingly dissatisfied with the growing role of evangelical Christians and other social conservatives within the ranks of their party.

He took advantage of this opportunity in 1996 with a "triangulating" presidential campaign emphasizing welfare reform, free trade, and fiscal constraint (leading to actual fiscal surpluses by the time he left office). Many pro-business Republicans liked that package better than the anti-abortion, anti-evolution, anti-immigration social policies of their own party.

The result was that Democrats, in pursuit of an understanding with business interests, were no longer a reliable check on Republican pro-business policies (Knott, 2012; see also McCarty, Poole, & Rosenthal, 2013). Both parties converged on a deregulatory philosophy that pleased Wall Street, which combined with the growing campaign contributions of interest groups and the persuasive academic philosophy in favor of deregulation. There was, in fact, very little in the way of challenges to that philosophy, and most of those challenges came from within the agencies, as agency professionals found their discretion being increasingly cut back.

As a result of these forces, financial regulators faced a political environment that was unified in its perspective and gave them very little leverage. The result was increased responsiveness of these agencies to the deregulatory demands of financial enterprises, mediated through the electoral ambitions of politicians. This responsiveness can be seen most clearly in thrift supervision, the Commodity Futures Trading Commission (CFTC), and the SEC. In all these cases, resources for effective regulation were cut back, and key political appointees in leadership positions were committed to a radical deregulation that demotivated or confused lower level professionals.

Many have offered explanations for the Great Recession, but perhaps Chinn and Frieden put the situation best in their book, *Lost Decades*:

> No one factor on its own could have caused a crisis of this magnitude. The capital inflow might have been managed more effectively; the borrowed funds could have been used more productively; financiers may have had reasons to behave more prudently; regulators should have realized the implications of the risks they were allowing banks to take. (Chinn & Frieden, 2011, 27)

Frieden and Chinn document how global capital flows set the stage for increased risk taking by financiers in the United States and how political pressure exacerbated this problem. We agree that capital flows shaped the nature of the regulatory environment, just as political interventions limited the relative independence of regulators charged with managing that environment.

However, our position throughout this chapter and the next focuses on the moral hazard of politicians and the relative independence of bureaucrats. Our claim is that the delegation of policy-making authority to professionalized bureaucrats can be a fragile equilibrium. We see strong parallels between the recent recession and earlier events both in and outside the United States, but the problem remains acute for market economies such as that of the United States: how to balance the relative costs of potentially disordered markets with the costs that come with intervention by the state.

FROM FHLBB TO OTS

The savings and loan crisis of the 1980s was a kind of "model" for the financial crises that were to come. As in later crises, the thrifts then had every reason to take on risk. The regulatory agency, the Federal Home Loan Bank Board (FHLBB), was in many ways unprepared for the changes in the savings and loan industry. They needed more resources to manage more problematic thrifts, but got less.

The attacks on the FHLBB came in a variety of forms. First were the budgetary and personnel restrictions. It needed more than 679 bank examiners to monitor the increasingly risky activities of more than three thousand thrifts. Its plans to increase the number of examiners ran afoul of Reagan's promise to reduce the size and impact of the bureaucracy. In response, Edwin Gray, the FHLBB head, privatized the examiners. He fired them in a Reduction in Force (RIF), placed the open positions in the twelve semi-private Federal Home Loan district banks, and finally ordered the district banks to hire 700 additional bank examiners.

The FHLBB also was concerned that the Federal Savings and Loan Insurance Corporation's capital reserves available to cover deposits for bankrupt thrifts were inadequate. As the number of weak and risky thrifts grew, the FHLBB realized its ability to close down crooked or broke thrifts was limited by the number of depositors the FSLIC could repay. The FHLBB asked Congress for a recapitalization bill, but an obstacle was Speaker Jim Wright of Texas – a state with a large number of dubious thrifts. One of them, Vernon Savings and Loan, was known as the single most fraudulent thrift, whose owner used Ponzi schemes to make money and hired prostitutes to keep his political and business allies in line (Kleinfield, 1991).

Despite strong support in the House, Wright kept the recapitalization bill from coming up for a vote. Wright also tried to get the supervisor of the FHLBB district bank in Dallas fired, spreading rumors of his involvement in a "homosexual ring" (Black, 2005, 110). Wright's protection of the Vernon thrift was one of the revelations in the press that later led to his forced resignation on ethics charges in June 1989.

Yet another form of political undermining of an independent agency was through statutory limitations. This occurred in 1987 when Congress passed by a wide margin a very weak recapitalization bill with a forbearance clause. The forbearance clause, supported by the thrift lobby, prohibited the FHLBB from closing down weak thrifts that had net worth as little as 0.5% of liabilities (White, 1991).

The pressure from political figures – from Speaker Wright, to the Keating Five, to the White House – was always in the direction of leniency and laxness, despite the fact that hundreds of millions of taxpayer-protected deposits were increasingly at risk. No politician came forward to defend Gray and his doughty band of thrift inspectors. Political responsiveness meant only one thing – allowing the politically connected thrift owners to take more risks while paying themselves exorbitant salaries and then sharing the largesse as campaign contributions.

The FHLBB had demonstrated both its ability to identify an enormous threat to the general public and also its willingness to use its independent status in the face of threats and blandishments of elected officials and their staffs. The Keating Five, Speaker Wright, and other politicians were burdened with a compelling form of political moral hazard: their calculation of their political advantage made them allies of frauds and felons whose actions were inevitably adding costs to the bill held by the U.S. taxpayers. Even worse, the willingness of politicians to prostitute themselves had to create the kind of investor uncertainty that would discourage future development.

If Gray and the FHLBB had not closed the fraudulent thrifts that they did manage to close in 1986 and 1987, then the $200 billion cost to the taxpayers would have been immensely greater (Black, 2005, 61).

Competitive Regulation

The lesson taken from the FHLBB's actions might well have been "provide the FHLBB with the examiners, the resources, and the statutory authority to protect taxpayer dollars from the risks taken on by the thrifts." Instead, politicians made the FHLBB and their staff the scapegoats for the crisis. The lesson applied was that bureaucrats needed to be more accountable to politicians like Speaker Wright and, through them, to financiers like Charles Keating: to these regulators, thrift supervision required more accountability, not more autonomy. In 1989 Congress passed a law eliminating the FHLBB and replacing it with the Office of Thrift Supervision. The OTS was housed in the Treasury Department, not positioned as an independent regulatory agency. A single executive headed the OTS rather than multiple commissioners. The OTS director had no fixed term, but was completely accountable to the president, who could fire him or her at will.

After assuming office in 2001, George W. Bush appointed James Gilleran to head the OTS. Gilleran articulated an anti-regulatory ideology that was consistent with Bush's own statements: "Our goal is to allow thrifts to operate with a wide breadth of freedom from regulatory intrusion" (Johnson & Kwak, 2010, 95). Why anyone would think that a greater "breadth of freedom" was preferable for the industry, in the light of the events of the 1980s, is a mystery. The nation suffered during the S&L crisis from the unified deregulatory ideology of the OTS. How well did this new, more accountable OTS perform in subsequent financial crises?

OTS employees did not have the resources available to blow the whistle on a politically favored client, as William Black blew the whistle on Keating. Black, a law professor by the time the Bush administration came to office, kept close watch on the altered incarnation of his former employer; he said, "The reputation of the Office of Thrift Supervision was that it was the weakest, and the laxest [of the financial regulatory agencies], and it was indeed outright friendly to the worst of the non-prime lending" (Johnson & Kwak, 2010, 96). By the time of Great Recession, anecdotal evidence had accumulated that the OTS – the "smallest of the financial regulators and dependent" – was "regulating with a particularly light touch," that it "had grown especially close to the financial industry" (Donelson & Zaring, 2010–2011, 1792).

The effects of a regulatory gap and of the OTS lax regulatory style were magnified by the fact that, in the face of overlapping regulatory jurisdiction, firms with multiple possible overseers were permitted to pick their regulator! AIG, an insurance firm, was regulated by the OTS, even though the OTS did not have the resources to effectively supervise the firm's far-flung insurance and derivative activities (Sjostrum, 2009). In 2005, Countrywide (a major lender of subprime mortgages) had a meeting to consider moving from the Office of the Controller of the Currency (OCC) to the Office of Thrift Supervision (Appelbaum & Nakashima, 2008). Because both the OCC and OTS were funded by fees paid by the regulated firms, the recruitment incentive for the regulators was to "race for the bottom" by promising the lax regulation sought by Countrywide and other firms. The OTS was the winner of the competition with the OCC when, in 2007, Countrywide officially changed its structure to that of a thrift and paid its fees to the OTS. In addition, the OTS was also responsible for regulating Washington Mutual, another firm that was to collapse during the subprime mortgage crisis (Dam, 2009–2010).

One view on this competition among agencies – among the OTS, the OCC, and other possible regulators – is that it had little impact on instability or firm performance (Donelson & Zaring, 2010–2011). Another is that OTS and OCC engaged in a destructive "race to the bottom" in terms of enforcing regulations (Levitin, 2014; Provost, 2010). Yet, the primary long-term consequence of deregulation at the OTS, driven by political responsiveness, was the loss of belief in the agency's willingness and ability to make professional decisions. The four largest charters of OTS failed in a single year (2008) – events that supported a perception the agency was practicing "abject, fee-chasing behavior" (Kwak, 2014, 254), resulting in its dissolution in 2011.

UNDERMINING THE SEC

The professionalized SEC, described in Chapter 7, was one of the building blocks of a stable financial regulatory regime. Investors gradually returned to the stock market in the post–World War II era, providing low-cost capital for an economic expansion like none ever seen before.

Most of the time, members of Congress were content with largely symbolic representation of their interests to the SEC. Given the imbalance in expertise, there was a downside to too much interference: "No politician wants to be associated with a downturn in the markets or worse, a downturn in the economy.... [T]o the extent that issues are technical...and the outcome of a policy is uncertain, any attempt by committee members to influence or dictate agency decision making is checked by the need to defer to an 'expert'" (Khademian, 1992, 12). As a result, the SEC believed not only that it was viewed in a nonpartisan perspective but also that this posture advanced its ability to serve the public; "in dealing with people on the Hill, the SEC was never political.... [Committee members] had the view they could trust the agency. It was fair, aggressive, and it put the public interest on top of anything we did. It was rare confidence on the Hill" (129).

The leading legal historian of the SEC, Joel Seligman, argues that the relationship of legislators to the SEC was one of benign neglect: "It is a fair generalization that Congress in the first twenty post-World War II years had no great interest in the work of the Commission" (Seligman, 2003, 350). During those years, presidents could see no great advantage to intervening in the SEC one way or the other. The SEC stuck to its primary responsibility – enforcement of disclosure rules – and developed a reputation as a nonpartisan protector of the levelness of the playing field.

One immediate impact of the expansion of risk taking on Wall Street was that regulating Wall Street became more challenging. It took more personnel with more expertise to keep track of the continual innovations in the products being traded. At the same time, the likelihood that regulatory agencies could claim the resources necessary for that regulation decreased as the political strength of the deregulatory movement developed apace.

The chief architect of the SEC, James Landis, believed that the SEC's record justified the innovation of the independent regulatory agency. He felt that Congress had trouble reconciling the different factions interested in economic regulation and did so only "by the use of vague phraseology" (Seligman, 2003, 2), leaving room for the expert to emerge as a force. The appropriate role for Congress was "to define the agency's area of expertise and recite the appropriate problems for it to solve, leaving it broad discretion as to means" (3).

Although the SEC earned early respect, it did not always get uniform levels of funding. According to Seligman the SEC got its highest levels of funding during times of economic troubles. Bull markets led to a rapid reduction in support for the SEC, evidently on the theory that, just as roof repairs are not needed when the sun shines, the SEC regulatory function could be cut back during a bull market. Yet, it is during good economic times when a rising market tends to result in more fraud and the SEC could do the most good. The pattern, however, was set for less support for SEC enforcement during a rising market, which could result in more fraud and less ability to investigate it (Seligman, 2003).

This same pattern held true during the boom times of the 1990s. The Clinton administration cut back on funding and staffing for the SEC (Seligman, 2003, 4). Salaries were also an issue, because SEC lawyers and accountants earned less than their peers in the Fed and other agencies. In the face of impossible workloads and submarket pay, morale dropped, and turnover rose rapidly. When SEC chairman Levitt testified before Congress in 1999, he told them that from 1980 to 1994, the number of SEC-authorized positions increased by 35%, as "the assets under control of investment companies and investment advisers increased 964 percent and 2082 percent respectively," but that since 1995 staffing growth had been flat (6). The extra positions and cash that Congress gave the SEC after this time were "too little, too late," doing little to reduce turnover of SEC attorneys; the SEC lost 25% of its attorneys between 1998 and 2000 (7). The turnover made it hard to provide the same level of promptness and service; checking financial statements, answering complaints, and running investigations were all done more slowly and handled often by new staff just learning the ropes. What the investing public saw was an agency whose efficiency seemed limited by red tape.

Levitt felt that the answer to the ill-timed bull-market cuts in SEC funding was to insulate the SEC from the vagaries of congressional budgeting by instituting self-funding, as with the Fed or the FDIC. In addition to making money on its open market operations (much of it returned to the Treasury), the Fed charged assessments from member banks that pay for the Fed's regulatory functions. As Seligman notes,

A significant practical advantage of the Fed approach to SEC budgeting would be to avoid periodic atrophy of SEC staff during boom economies. Just as it has historically been regarded as essential to insulate the Federal Reserve Board from political pressures

to protect its independent judgment on questions of monetary policy, it is also wise to insulate the SEC from staff size declines during market surges....An independent budgetary process would be more effective in adjusting the size of the SEC staff to the Agency's regulatory needs during the good times, which ironically are when the SEC is more vulnerable to a lack of budgetary support. (Seligman, 2003, 11–12)

Looking back, Levitt felt his advocacy for self-funding was naïve. In any case, the pattern repeated itself during the housing boom. A tide of financial deals increased the SEC's workload, undermined staff morale, and reduced the level of financial support for SEC enforcement. The result was another round of fraud, including Bernie Madoff's pyramid scheme, which was repeatedly brought to the attention of the SEC but failed to produce agency action.

The SEC and Compensation

Trading was the heart of Enron's business by the late 1990s – about 5,000 of its 18,000 employees were traders (McLean & Elkind, 2003, 125–126). Just as Salomon made money through its knowledge of the bond market, Enron did likewise because of its knowledge of the energy markets (Gasparino, 2009, 359): both used this knowledge to occasionally manipulate the market for greater trading profits. As with Salomon, Enron floor traders created a macho culture within the firm because of the money they brought to the firm – a culture magnified by their own compensation arrangements. Throughout the financial industry, traders who were compensated on an "eat what you kill" basis increasingly dominated the politics of firms. At Enron, Ken Rice made it clear that "[i]f you really worked hard and delivered results, you could make a lot of money" (quoted in Swartz, 2001); a gas trader with a couple of years of experience could make a $1 million annual bonus.

In a series of financial crises from the Reagan to the Obama administration, the same pattern held true. Financial firms wanted to take risky strategies that increased bankers' short-term wealth. Elected politicians proved open to the blandishments of the financial firms, and the objections of an independent regulatory agency proved to be the primary obstacle to the plans of the financial firms.

Before deregulation, these short-term demands of the financial firms were largely stifled and concealed by the system of checks and balances and the existence of the independent agency. That is, one constituency (such as a pension fund) might go to a legislator and complain about the Fed's monetary policy or the constraints of the SEC's accounting rules. In the normal course of events, the member of Congress, or even the president, could express sympathy and support and promise a symbolic speech or even an investigation, but both sides knew that actually changing the policy was beyond the powers of any legislator or (generally) the president. As also noted by Krause (1999), responding to an independent agency like the SEC required the coordinated action of politicians holding multiple veto points. Our claim, though, is that some of those actors would normally be responsive to a constituency with interests in maintaining the status quo, rather than change. As a result, the politician would have to pay very little electoral cost for his powerlessness with the independent agency; in general, the constituency interest would spend more time trying to accommodate to a stable set of rules than trying to change it.

This scenario, however interesting, provides very little evidence in favor of the theory advanced here. We would not be able to observe the morally hazardous inclinations of politicians, because they would be checked before they became visible. Consequently, we would not be able to see the actions of the agency as checking that morally hazardous behavior.

As a result, it is only in times of disequilibrium that evidence of political moral hazard is visible, as politicians see an opportunity to form a coalition, including all the potential veto players, in favor of a shared or powerful constituency. Such disequilibrium arguably occurred in the 1990s with regard to the accounting profession.

One issue was executive compensation. The stakes had grown as executive compensation grew by leaps and bounds. As in the case of Chainsaw Al, granting stock options was increasingly popular and their size increasingly large, even though they had the effect of diluting the value of other shareholders' stock. The Financial Accounting Standards (FASB) had proposed a requirement that stock options granted after 1996 be treated as an expense. The requirement would have guaranteed more meaningful accounting statements, but it also would have reduced earnings reports and therefore the share price of the company. As Seligman notes, "Accounting is one thing. Politics is quite another. Hell hath no fury like a corporate chief executive officer whose pay package is threatened" (Seligman, 2003, 715). Treating stock options as an expense also would have been a more transparent way of revealing their cost to investors, who then would presumably not be pleased.

Chairman Levitt recalled, "I spent nearly one-third of my first year at the commission meeting with business leaders who opposed" the new requirement (Seligman, 2003, 715). These leaders not only lobbied Levitt but they also broke precedent by heavily lobbying Congress: "they flooded Capitol Hill and own the support of lawmakers who didn't take the time to understand the complexities of the issue and the proposed solution" (716). Ultimately, congressional pressure forced Levitt to back down, a decision he later characterized as "my single biggest mistake during my years of service" (716). Pressure from Congress did more than bring the SEC to heel; it generated enormous benefits in the form of campaign contributions from newly flush accounting firms and from corporations headed by grateful CEOs. At the same time, it was a disservice to investors trying to navigate the stock market in the high-rolling 1990s, because it muddied the information available in accounting reports and increased investor uncertainty.

Why did Levitt yield to the pressure? He said that the reason was the November 1994 election, in which Republicans took power in Congress:

It appeared the country had taken a sharp turn to the right, and regulation of any sort, even accounting rules proposed by a private-sector body [FASB] would come under close scrutiny. I came to the conclusion that the FASB rule would not survive in this atmosphere. I worried that, if the group continued to push for the stock-option rule, disgruntled companies would press Congress to end the FASB's role as a standard-setter. To me, that would have been worse than going without the stock-option rule. (Levitt, 2002, 109–110)

In other words, Levitt's concerns about the traditional independence of the SEC from Congress caused him to make a strategic compromise. The SEC was no longer as independent as it had been, political opportunism was unloosed, and the stock market investor paid the price. In fact, FASB's retraction of the proposed rule led to an expansion of stock options, which by 2001 were a part of 80% of management compensation packages; "the options craze created an environment that rewarded executives for managing the share price, not for managing the business.... [B]etween 1995 and 2000, the average earnings growth of the companies in the Standard & Poor's 500 index would have been 9.4 percent, not the 12 percent they reported, had they expensed stock options" (Seligman, 2003, 717).

The successful circumvention of the SEC by congressional lobbying created a change in expectations: Congress, rather than the SEC, became the venue for resolving issues within the accounting profession. This would have enormous implications for the neutrality of the accounting profession and for the independence of the SEC.

In the 1990s, accounting lobbyists for accounting firms began to provide consulting services along with their auditing services. The consulting services proved to be more lucrative than the core auditing business, but SEC constraints limited their ability to compete to provide consulting services to firms for which they were also providing accounting services. The fear was that accounting firms' motivation for providing investors with fair and unbiased auditing information (which was tenuous at the best of times) would be trumped by the motivation to please the businesses being audited with favorable but unrealistic auditing results. Levitt, a defender of professionalism in accounting, began to worry publicly about the deteriorating integrity of the auditing system. "Too many corporate managers, auditors, and analysts are participants in a game of nods and winks. In the zeal to satisfy consensus earnings estimates and project a smooth earnings path, wishful thinking may be winning the day over faithful representation; ... integrity may be losing out to illusion" (Seligman, 2003, 719).

By 1999, consulting generated 51% of accounting firm revenues (Seligman, 2003, 723). Levitt proposed a new rule that would restrict the ability of auditors to provide other services such as consulting to firms, in the interest of neutral auditing. As quoted in Seligman, Levitt recalled, "Within a month of issuing the proposed rule, I received negative letters from forty-six members of Congress, including two-thirds of the Senate Banking Committee's Securities Subcommittee.... They questioned the SEC's authority to regulate accounting firms, and some threatened to cut the agency's funding" (725). The incentives available to the SEC's principal were invoked to make the agency responsive to the electoral aspirations of key members of Congress. The 2000 election campaign was financed in large part by accounting firms trying to get Congress to revoke the SEC's independence. Millions of dollars from accounting firms went to hundreds of members of Congress, and "each of the Big Five accounting firms also was on the list of President Bush's top twenty contributors" (725). Enron, with its "eat what you kill" culture, was Bush's largest campaign contributor.

Once again, Levitt negotiated away some SEC independence in an attempt to retain the rest; he recalled, "Most of all, I feared retribution in the form of a funding cut for the agency. Never before had the SEC faced such a threat to its independence" (Seligman, 2003, 727). Congressional pressure and pressure from the incoming president prevailed shortly after the 2000 election. Over the objections of the staff, Levitt compromised, allowing firms to offer consulting in addition to accounting services, in a way that Seligman characterizes as a "capitulation" (728). The historic independence of the SEC was diminished.

As it turned out, the impact of that compromise was dramatic for everyone who had invested in the stock market or had a retirement portfolio. The Anderson/Enron scandal began with admissions that previous financial statements were incorrect. Similar revelations from a number of other major firms followed. Investors were shaken in their belief that the SEC was in a position to protect the neutrality of the financial reporting system. The inevitable result was a sharp drop in the stock market. One source reported in the *New York Times* a multi-trillion dollar decrease in aggregate equity prices, as a result of investor uncertainty caused by the auditing crisis (Feaster, 2002).

Congressmen who had accepted campaign contributions and pressured Levitt before the Enron crisis now used Levitt and the SEC as a scapegoat. With investor confidence shaken, Congress, with the support of the president, passed the Sarbanes-Oxley Act of 2002, which mandated reforms to enhance corporate responsibility and financial disclosures, to reduce corporate and accounting fraud, and to create the "Public Company Accounting Oversight Board" to oversee the activities of the auditing profession (Fass, 2003).[2] In addition, it

---

[2] Sanders (1936) notes that the early SEC also played a role in establishing uniform accounting standards through its disclosure rules. This fed into the growing social role of accounting, as evidenced in SEC Chairman James J. Caffrey's comments in 1947: "In any given situation the exercise of an accountant's judgment may vitally affect the ownership interests of one competing group of security holders against another" (quoted in Grady (1948, 270)). For perspectives on how the SEC exercises a "veto" over accounting standards, see also Werntz (1953), Newman (1981), and Melumad and Shibano (1994).

gave separate financing to the Financial Accounting Standards Board to promote its independence from firms donating funding for its operations.

After years of relative privation, the SEC received a large budgetary infusion in 2003, enabling it to increase its staff by 25%, specifically more lawyers, accountants, and investigators, within a year (Labaton, 2003). Despite the budgetary infusion, the message from political appointees was that too much regulatory enforcement was not good. The leading advocate of this position at the SEC was Commissioner Paul S. Atkins, appointed in 2002. Atkins criticized then-SEC chairman Donaldson for his efforts to regulate hedge funds, and he lobbied for lighter penalties when wrongdoing was found (Borrus, 2005). When two Democrats resigned from the SEC, Atkins and Kathleen Casey held veto power over the more moderate chairman Christopher Cox during the critical months between the Bear Stearns crisis and the Lehman crisis.

The effect was striking: the SEC had historically kept leverage-to-asset ratios at financial firms to 12 during the period from 1975 to 2003. In 2004, however, in response to pressure from Goldman Sachs chief Henry Paulson, the SEC unanimously agreed to increase the approved leverage rate to 40 and made enforcement voluntary.

The loosening of capital requirements enhanced the ability of Lehman Brothers under Dick Fuld to take on more leverage in pursuit of high (but risky) return. The increasingly unregulated market did nothing to discourage this strategy by Lehman Brothers (Gasparino, 2009, 211). When Lehman's own risk assessor told Fuld that the firm was taking on too many risky, leveraged positions, he was fired (211). With the SEC stepping aside, and internal dissenters silenced or fired, there was nothing to prevent Lehman Brothers from leading the herd over the precipice.

CFTC: MORTGAGE BONDS AGAIN, WITH DERIVATIVES

The Commodity Futures Trading Commission (CFTC) is another independent agency, like the FHLBB, whose independence was crushed as a result of political pressure from the financial industry and its political allies – including this time figures in the Clinton administration.

Beginning in 1921, the Department of Agriculture regulated commodity grain futures contracts. The CFTC, created as a result of bipartisan legislation passed by a Democratic Congress and signed by Gerald Ford, took over this regulatory function in 1974. The new agency had the classic Progressive Era structural features for independence: a five-member commission, including a chair, with long five-year terms. Terms are staggered, so that one term runs out each year. No more than three commissioners may be of the same party, and they are named by the president and ratified by the Senate.

In 1997, Brooksley Born was head of the CFTC. Born was a distinguished lawyer with a history of working in derivatives law. Clinton had nominated her for the chair's position in 1996.

As Scheer (2009) and Johnson and Kwak (2010) document, Born began to get a sense that the volume of over-the-counter derivatives trading was increasing at an unknown rate – unknown because there were no record-keeping requirements for these trades, unlike other market transactions. Furthermore, the variety of types of derivatives seemed to be proliferating rapidly.

Born began to worry about the possible outcomes from all this trading. She let it be known that she was going to issue a "concept release" – a report outlining the possibility of rule changes. The response was overwhelmingly negative, especially by the other three principals of the President's Working Group on Financial Management – Fed chair Alan Greenspan, Secretary of the Treasury Robert Rubin, and SEC Commissioner Arthur Leavitt. All three argued that signaling the possibility of rulemaking on derivatives could cause an adverse reaction among investors and lead to the destabilization of the major firms that were increasingly involved in the derivatives markets. When Born objected that the CFTC did not even have the means to find out how deeply involved the firms were in the markets, she was told that the markets would work it all out efficiently, without government interference. Alan Greenspan, especially, was vocal in his advocacy of a laissez-faire position. Born did not comment on the irony that he, Greenspan, arguably carried more authority, capacity, and will to interfere in the market than anyone else in the economy and that his responsibility as chair of the Fed included to intervene in the public's interest when the markets failed.

Despite this strong opposition, Born issued the "concept release." As a chastisement for her independence, she was called to testify before Congress. There she was subject to attack by Republican House members. She might have expected protection from Democrats in Congress and the White House, but her toughest detractors included Secretary of the Treasury (ex-Goldman Sachs chairman) Rubin and his deputy secretary, Larry Summers. Summers had already accused Born of risking catastrophe: "I have thirteen bankers in my office, and they say if you go forward with this you will cause the worst financial crisis since World War II" (Johnson & Kwak, 2010, 9). Fed chairman Greenspan also joined in the collective demand for legislation protecting the derivatives industry from any kind of regulation. In a private meeting with Born, he told her that there would never be agreement between the two, because "[y]ou probably will always believe there should be laws against fraud, and I don't think there is any need for a law against fraud" (Scheer, 2009, 99). The nation's leading regulator felt that markets would spot and correct fraud without help from regulators.

A few months after testifying in 1997, Born's action was apparently vindicated by the crisis surrounding the hedge fund, Long-Term Capital Management (LTCM). LTCM had been founded and managed by John Merriwether, a successful Salomon bond trader, with two Nobel Prize-winning economists to help with the mathematical modeling. Despite the hedge fund's early success using arbitrage strategies based on converging bond prices, LTCM fell apart in the face of the market's rush from investing in defaulting Russian bonds to buying U.S. treasuries.

As the case of the CFTC showed, there was a direct connection between the risk-taking preferences of the financial institutions and political encroachments on bureaucratic autonomy. By working through Congress and the presidency, financial firms were able to force their risk preferences on increasingly responsive regulatory agencies.

The Commodity Futures Modernization Act (CFMA) of 2000 was not the result of the normal separation-of-powers conflict, stalemate, and ultimate compromise. Instead, everybody (except a few regulators) seemed to be reading from the same page. The leading Wall Street firms were unanimous in believing that regulation of derivatives was a bad idea. Merely gathering information about derivatives was a bad idea; even talking about the regulation of derivatives could be a dangerous signal to the world of high finance. Even the outcome of the Long Term Crisis Management (LTCM) did not lead to possible concerns about a need for enhanced regulation in a high-risk future. Although those like Brooksley Born feared the consequences of unregulated derivatives markets, the CFMA prevented her from using her position as chair of the Commodity Futures Trading Commission to regulate or even gather information about derivatives trading.

The accounting firms, mortgage companies, bond-rating agencies, and housing industry – all reinforced the deregulatory message. They were making profits at every stage of the process from mortgage origination, to packaging bundles of mortgages in mortgage-backed securities, to selling the securities to the eager investing public, to making bets on how those mortgage bonds would do in the future. Profits in the financial industry were unprecedented, and much of this money found its way as contributions to politicians. There seemed to be no downside to climbing on board the deregulation bandwagon. The legislation seemed to be the next logical step in the deregulatory process. And the unanimity of the financial world meant that politicians could support the legislation without political cost.

Alan Greenspan, head of the Fed, supported the CFMA and took a strong position in favor of self-regulation in the derivative industry; he opposed federal regulations for mortgage fraud and for the same reason: the market was capable of sorting out and rewarding the non-fraudulent mortgage companies. What is more, he kept interest rates low to encourage expansion in the housing market.

Even the Democratic White House was playing a lead role in favor of deregulation. Larry Summers, chair of Clinton's Council of Economic Advisors, had taken an aggressive position in silencing doubters from within the bureaucracy. Clinton had made history, seeing opportunity for himself and his party by moving toward pro-business conservatives who were uncomfortable with the increasing social conservatism of the Republican Party – a party more concerned about stopping abortion, immigration, teaching of evolution, and stem cell research. By passing NAFTA, a crime bill, welfare reform, and, most of all, by balancing the budget, Clinton made it respectable for many economic conservatives to vote Democratic. Clinton's support, along with the support of both Republican houses of Congress, made it happen.

CONCLUSION: AUTONOMY IN REGULATION

The theme of this chapter is that the autonomous bureaucracy, buttressed by a separation of powers and conflicts of interest, can be the vehicle of effective financial regulation. The economic agencies of the New Deal and those created after it benefited from a spirited clash of interests – institutional, partisan, and interest group based. The conflict of interests in the five decades after the Depression had allowed regulatory agencies to establish positions of autonomy.

The deregulatory movement changed the configuration of interests by establishing a unity among key political actors on the key questions of bureaucrats' role in managing the economy. This unity deprived bureaucratic regulators of much of the autonomy they had grown accustomed to wielding in the financial world. The establishment of bureaucratic autonomy in the mid-twentieth century to its erosion in its last decades of that century took just roughly 65 years.

Unification of political principals made bureaucracies more accountable – more accountable to members of Congress who wanted to cut back on the SEC's regulatory enforcement machinery; to key administration figures who wanted to prevent the CFTC from establishing any regulatory stance toward derivatives; to accounting firms that wanted to expand the scope of accountants' services, even at the expense of audit neutrality; to the financial industry, which opposed regulatory constraints on lucrative risk taking. In short, the bureaucracies were more accountable to politicians and firms who had a shared interest in prohibiting public bureaucracies from reining in the excesses of the housing and credit bubble.

In the next chapter, we examine the consequences of weakening the SEC, prohibiting the CFTC from regulating derivatives, politicizing Fannie Mae and Freddie Mac, and allowing bank regulators to compete with laxity. We address how the separation of powers and professionalism contributed to the Great Recession.

9

The Financial Crisis and Reregulation

The only case for an independent central bank in a democracy is that it can take a longer-term view and do what is in the interest of the people in ways that elected politicians cannot.

– Wessel (2009, 271)

"It's laissez faire until you get in deep shit"

– Gutfreund quoted in M. Lewis (2010, 264)

MERRILL LYNCH

Merrill Lynch was a financial firm known for its "thundering herd" of brokers – a herd of up to 15,000 brokers that made Merrill Lynch the brokerage firm for the general public. These brokers allowed Merrill Lynch to sell directly to the public the stock offerings that it underwrote. As an organization, it also had a strong "family-style" culture that helped keep its large work force motivated and loyal.

As the largest brokerage, it could also make risk-free money through financial advice and commissions. Unfortunately, when it did take risk, it generally seemed to fail. It had gambled on trader Howie Rubin and almost went broke when Rubin lost hundreds of millions of dollars on mortgage bonds (Gasparino, 2009, 177). It convinced Orange County to buy mortgage bonds in 1994, and Orange County went bankrupt. It lost more hundreds of millions with the failure of Long Term Capital Management (LTCM), the elite firm that relied on Nobel Prize-winning economists, mathematical models, and a lot of leverage. "In all of these cases, the firm's response was to drastically scale back on risk and miss out on the subsequent bond market rally, only to get back into the market near its top, when the bubble was about to burst once again" (177).

By 2003, Merrill Lynch still had a family-style culture, and it had one of the lowest leverage rates on Wall Street, with just $16 in borrowed funds for every dollar of its own (Gasparino, 2009, 178). In that year, however, change came to Merrill Lynch in the form of Stanley O'Neal, CEO and chair. O'Neal set out to transform Merrill Lynch into another Goldman Sachs, complete with a large trading desk of its own, a willingness to take big risks in pursuit of high-reward investments, and a greatly expanded leverage rate. To do this, O'Neal fired a large number of employees, and instilled a much more hard-driving, competitive culture. His rule was increasingly autocratic; he made it clear that he did not want to hear dissenting opinions. He trusted his own judgment and paid himself accordingly – $48 million in 2006 and $46 million a year later (235–6).

What O'Neal did demand was more risk and the reward that went with it. To magnify the profits from those risks, he rapidly increased borrowing. He created and later expanded trading operations, and Merrill's mortgage under-writing business became the most profitable on Wall Street within a few years (Gasparino, 2009, 179). To compete for investors, Merrill had to offer mortgage bonds with higher returns – which came, as usual, with higher risks. To guaran-tee a steady supply of mortgages to securitize for hungry investors, Merrill, like other Wall Street firms, began in 2003 to purchase its own mortgage origination firms. Merrill bought First Franklin, the nation's second largest mortgage orig-ination firm, applying intense pressure on it to generate subprime mortgages – with their generous returns and risks (168).

At some level, all of the participants knew that greater risk accompanied the higher rate of return on low-quality mortgage bonds. However, they had a story that allowed them to rationalize their purchases. The story was that, although an individual subprime loan might be risky, the packaging of these bonds (usu-ally through slicing the package into tranches reflecting different risks) meant that the few mortgages that did go bad in one region would be balanced by other safe mortgages from various regions of the country and different types of mortgagors.[1]

This story made sense as long as the subprime mortgages did not all go delinquent at the same time. However, by 2008, delinquencies on the mortgages had increased all across the nation, and Merrill was bleeding money.

---

[1] The development of special investment vehicles such as those used in mortgage-backed securi-ties and collateralized debt obligations has been widely discussed (C. R. Morris, 2008). Morris documents how the development of collateralized mortgage obligations in the 1980s first saved homeowners billions of dollars in interest per year, but as their complexity increased, such instru-ments inevitably lead to instability as ignorant purchasers were caught with investments with too much risk (39–41). By 2006, it was clear to regulators that some financial actors were holding too much risk in the form of the riskiest tranches (127), the consequence of which was that those actors were holding significant amounts of invisible leverage. As Morris notes, for an equity bond with "a face value of, say, 3 percent of the total portfolio face," for which the actor was "at risk for the first 3 percent of losses," the "securities' embedded leverage would therefore be 33-to-1 – so a 3 percent portfolio loss wipes out the entire tranche" (149). Most asset books, though, failed to accurately report this invisible leverage.

Merrill lost $8 billion in August and September 2008. It would go bankrupt if it did not find a buyer. Ultimately, Merrill Lynch had to accede to a purchase agreement facilitated by Fed chair Ben Bernanke and the Fed: Bank of America bought Merrill Lynch on September 15, the same day that Lehman went bankrupt. This was in the midst of a disastrous year that began when the Fed had to arrange an acquisition of Bear Stearns by JP Morgan in March.

THE PERFECT STORM OF DEREGULATION: THE FINANCIAL CRISIS OF 2008

At the root of the financial crisis that upended Merrill Lynch was a regulatory regime that had been weakened, sidetracked, demoralized, and/or subjugated by the political demands of politicians. The politicization of regulatory agencies enabled the perfect storm: the financial crisis of 2008. It would not have happened if any one of a variety of deregulatory actions had not taken place. If the OTS had been incentivized to regulate Washington Mutual (WaMu) and similar institutions, those firms' financial problems might have been revealed in time to minimize the loss. If the CFTC had not been so soundly restrained by the deregulatory troika of Greenspan, Rubin, and Summers and then by Congress, investors might have had more information – and more doubts – about the risks associated with high-return derivatives. If the Bush-era SEC commissioners had not actively pulled back the regulatory enforcement wing of the SEC, then that agency might have been empowered to blow the whistle in a more timely way.

The systematic elimination of regulatory options from the repertoire of regulatory agencies reduced their capacity to limit the risk-seeking activities of the financial industry, just as its lobbyists had demanded. The constraints on the SEC and the CFTC, and the structural weakness of the OTS and the FDIC, meant that managing the financial crisis would be more difficult when it came and that the responsibility for dealing with the crisis would be all the more focused on one agency that had largely managed to keep its independence – the Fed.

And Then There Was One: The Fed

After Greenspan's appointment, the Fed had not actively pursued fraud in the marketplace or advanced consumer protection in the mortgage industry. Under Greenspan, it abandoned the possibilities for a more active regime of regulation out of a faith in the power of the market to self-regulate. He argued that the marketplace would value subprime mortgages appropriately (Cassidy, 2009, 254). He assumed that fraudulent mortgage originators would earn a negative reputation and be punished appropriately in the marketplace. He not only encouraged the development of derivatives and other new financial instruments but he also actively opposed regulation that required transparency in derivative markets, even when the failure of LTCM revealed a "major failure of counter-party surveillance" (254).

By the time the crisis hit in 2008, Greenspan admitted problems with his worldview in his testimony before Congress. "To exist, you need an ideology. The question is whether it is accurate or not." Looking at the evidence one month after the failure of Lehmann Brothers, Greenspan said, "I found a flaw in the model that I perceived as the critical functioning structure that defines how the world works....I was shocked. Because I had been going forty years, or more, with considerable evidence that it was working exceptionally well" (Cassidy, 2009, 6).

Although Greenspan's deregulatory ideology had limited the Fed's ability to have an impact on the run-up to the crisis, its control over monetary policy was still intact. Greenspan's replacement, Ben Bernanke, was committed to using this monetary policy to the extent necessary.

THE FED AND THE FINANCIAL CRISIS

The monetarist Milton Friedman had argued that the Fed, by not pouring enough money into the economy to prevent a contraction, was responsible for the depths of the Great Depression. At a 2002 University of Chicago conference held in honor of Milton Friedman, Bernanke, who was both a leading scholar of the Depression and a new governor of the Federal Reserve, referenced Friedman in accepting the Fed's responsibility for the Depression: "Regarding the Great Depression. You're right, we did it. We're very sorry. But thanks to you, we won't do it again" (Wessel, 2009, 48). Bernanke's resolve was strong to do what had to be done as the banker of last resort.

In 2008, Bernanke, who had become the Fed chair in 2006, and the Fed were not in a position to undo all of the harmful effects of deregulation; however, it could address the magnitude of the impact on the overall economy. Said Bernanke, "I believed that a failure of a major institution in the midst of a financial crisis would not only create contagion through effects on counterparties, but would likely have a tremendous negative effect on broader market confidence" (Wessel, 2009, 21). Although Bernanke did not escape criticism for the actions he chose for the Fed, he did demonstrate that it could attack the psychological and economic forces behind the economic panic, even when the political institutions that called for "accountability" from the Fed were stalemated and unresponsive.

A Spreading Liquidity Crisis

By 2008, the basic problem was a classic liquidity crisis. Banks in trouble were trying to call in their debts, which forced other institutions to call in their debts as well. As housing prices went down everywhere, the value of mortgage bonds dropped below what most had thought possible. As a result, the firms, large and small, that were holding mortgage bonds – or derivatives based on mortgage bonds – were going broke.

In the spring of 2008, Moody downgraded the debt of one of the Big Five investment banks – Bear Stearns. This was the first warning of serious liquidity problems, and it generated a closer look at Bear by a variety of Wall Street firms, including its rivals. That close look revealed that Bear Stearns' investors were losing money on mortgage-backed securities.

As the crisis mounted, Bear Stearns followed a classic "bigger gamble" strategy, investing in more mortgage-backed securities in the desperate hope that they would turn around, with the realization that if they did not, it was sunk anyhow. An emergency loan from the Fed was insufficient to keep Bear Stearns afloat, and in a frenzied weekend in March 2008, the Fed offered JP Morgan a subsidized purchase of Bear Stearns. It was an unprecedented form of intervention in the economy, but it did prevent the immediate chain reaction that would have occurred among Bear Stearns' creditors – and its creditors' creditors – if it had just been allowed to go under.

Unfortunately, Bear Stearns was not the only firm that had placed losing bets on mortgage-based securities. By the summer of 2008, Fannie Mae and Freddie Mac, holding billions in mortgage-backed securities, were showing signs of collapsing from the bursting of the housing bubble. The chairmen of these entities resisted, but the Fed, working with Treasury Secretary Henry Paulson, placed them into receivership. The two organizations' preferred shareholders lost their investment entirely, but the bondholders were protected. The operation went smoothly, given that it was another rushed weekend job and that they were playing with the destruction of the financial system as one of the possible outcomes.

Lehman Brothers: September 15, 2008

As quickly cobbled together as the Fannie Mae and Freddie Mac conservatorships were, they bought Paulson and Bernanke no time. In September, the entire financial system was again threatened, but this time it was by the potential bankruptcy of two more of the Big Five firms: Merrill Lynch and Lehman Brothers. Both of these major financial institutions were on the verge of going broke, and again their holdings in the mortgage-backed securities and derivatives were the cause of the problem. What had been the implicit risk associated with those investments was now very explicit.

At the same moment that Merrill Lynch was negotiating a purchase by Bank of America, Lehman was going under. Lehman was regarded as the weakest of the remaining investment banks, and as "rumors emerged that Lehman was short on cash,…those rumors quickly became self-fulfilling" as Lehman's creditors demanded payment (Johnson & Kwak, 2010, 162). Given Lehman's astronomical leverage rates, meeting all its creditors' demands was not a possibility. Nor were there any enthusiastic buyers for Lehman, especially when potential buyers realized that the Lehman books exaggerated the value of its real estate assets. It had a large position in subprime mortgages, and its investors were leaving rapidly. Tim Geithner, then the president of the Federal Bank of New York and soon to be Treasury Secretary, observed, "There is no political will for a federal bailout" (162). Lehman was allowed to go bankrupt, and the effects cascaded throughout the economy – from financial firms to manufacturers, from Wall Street to Main Street. Everyone needed to sell their assets to meet their debt obligations, and there were no buyers on the other side of the market. According to Bernanke, this was the point at which "[w]e came very, very close to a global financial meltdown" (Wessel, 2009, 3).

The Fed's Independence – and Innovation

With the bankruptcy of Lehmann, Bernanke and Paulson were concerned about the real possibility of a nationwide run on the banks. Within a week, Paulson and Bernanke went to Congress to request $500 billion to prevent a meltdown. Paulson anticipated trouble: "They'll kill me up there. I'll be hung out to dry" (Wessel, 2009, 203). Bernanke told Congress that the financial system was only days from meltdown. Without major action, "you can expect another Great Depression, and this is going to be worse" (204). Majority Leader Harry Reid warned Bernanke, "We're elected. You're not. This needs hearings....I know the Senate. It takes two weeks to pass a bill to flush the toilet" (205). The original plan was rejected by a September vote of 228–205 (226).

The failure of the bailout vote in September dramatized an important lesson about the Fed. Whereas the Treasury was fundamentally limited by presidential and congressional constraints, "[t]he Fed, it was clear, could and would act when the political system was frozen" (Wessel, 2009, 269). In fact, the Fed was arguably *more* empowered when the political system was frozen.

The Fed's ability to chart an independent course in the face of political stalemate was a major contributor to finding the way out of the crisis of 2008. It helped that Bernanke was known to be "a serious academic who has devoted much of his career to analyzing central bank behavior during the Great Depression" (I. L. Morris, 2002, 106).

The Fed's actions included a variety of innovations – which had the effect of convincing many actors in the economy that the Fed, at least, was not so constrained by political pressure that it could not resist the destabilizing influence of presidential elections, hostile congressional committee chairs, and lobbying. Although contributions from the financial industry necessarily influence some members of Congress, large amounts of money fail to impress the agency that prints it.

Bernanke repeatedly showed his willingness to innovate in the interest of financial stability. Starting in 2007, a year before Wall Street acknowledged the dangerous situation it was in, Bernanke changed the structure of the Fed's balance sheet to give a boost to liquidity. As Bernanke had established in an earlier Fed study, the Fed should theoretically be able to establish the price of an asset like a Treasury security by buying enough at the target price. But could the Fed control the price of other assets in the same way? In December 2007, Bernanke set about to support the price of illiquid collateralized debt obligations (CDOs) and other assets of now-dubious value. This resulted in a balance sheet that was unique for the Fed, with a lower proportion of Treasury securities and a much larger proportion of more dubious assets than ever before.

Bernanke began his effort to support the price of CDOs by buying them from Federal Reserve banks. A never-before-used clause in the Federal Reserve Act allowed the Fed to loan to anyone in "unusual and exigent circumstances."[2] In 2008, the Fed used this power for the first time to lend to "broker dealers" and then to AIG – an insurance corporation. Bernanke extended the "volume and the range of targeted securities he would lend against, including subprime mortgage CDOs" (Morgan, 2008, 108).

While Bernanke's efforts to extend liquidity were helping some firms (Appelbaum & McGinty, 2011), the two remaining Big Five investment firms (Goldman Sachs and Morgan Stanley) seemed to be in danger of going the same way as Bear Stearns, Merrill Lynch, and Lehman – either to a takeover or a bankruptcy. In the days after Lehman's bankruptcy, Goldman and Morgan saw their clients leaving the firms, their share prices diving, and their creditors looking askance at them (Sorkin, 2009). Rather than letting these last two major investment banks go under, their CEOs and Bernanke agreed on an entirely new architecture for the postcrisis financial world: the two firms would give up their status as investment banks and submit to more regulation as bank holding companies. With their new status, they could avail themselves of the Fed's discount window for loans, using the wider array of collateral available to commercial banks.

In addition, the firms would also be subject to more regulation: they would have to lower their leverage rates markedly – from $20 or $30 of loans per dollar of capital reserve, down to something closer to the Bank of America's $11 leverage ratio. Less leverage would make their investments safer, even as it diminished the profits available to them (Sorkin, 2009). (By May 2011, average ratios were $13.50 and $17.00 at Goldman and Morgan Stanley, respectively.) They would also be subject to more disclosure to regulators.

The Fed's actions showed its ability to operate when political forces were stalemated. Overall, the new arrangement achieved success in its foremost goal: it averted any further speculation about these two firms going the way of Bear Stearns or Lehman and thereby helped stem the tide of panic. More fundamentally, the Fed's agreement effectively returned "Wall Street to the way it was

---

[2] Federal Reserve Act. Section 13. Powers of Federal Reserve Banks. 12 USC 342. As amended by act of Sept. 7, 1916 (39 Stat. 752), which completely revised this section; June 21, 1917 (40 Stat. 234); and March 31, 1980 (94 Stat. 139). Available at www.federalreserve.gov/aboutthefed/section13.htm

structured before Congress passed...the Glass-Steagall Act" (Sorkin & Bajaj, 2008, A1).

As late as early October 2008, the Fed's efforts were still in the imaginable range. After Congress turned down the first asset relief proposal, however, the Fed increased its assets from $890 billion to $2 trillion by the end of October. Nearly all of this increase occurred during the period that Congress was considering the revised Troubled Asset Relief Program (TARP). Only about $269 billion was in traditional Treasury securities; the remaining assets were in a variety of debt instruments (Morgan, 2008, 108–109).

The period after the initial failure of the TARP bailout bill in September 2008 illustrates dramatically the thesis of Chapter 5 – that stalemate among other political actors endows an agency with greater autonomy. In a few weeks' time, Bernanke changed the composition of the Fed balance sheet, used a forgotten clause in the Federal Reserve Act to loan massive amounts of money to nonbanks, extended the scope of its lending, and restructured the last two remaining investment banks of the Big Five so as to increase its regulatory oversight. In other words, in the weeks that Congress took to consider the nature and cause of the crisis, Bernanke unilaterally transformed the Fed!

FINANCIAL REREGULATION AND BUREAUCRATIC INSULATION

The financial collapse led to a mounting parade of attacks on the financial regulatory agencies and raised the question: is there a future for bureaucratic autonomy? Republican senator Richard Shelby of Alabama did not hesitate to blame the crisis on regulators: "In light of the S.E.C.'s questionable record, Congress must maintain some authority over the agency's budget. Ceding that authority would make the S.E.C. unaccountable to the American people" (Sorkin, 2011). Everywhere, bureaucratic agencies were criticized for their lack of "accountability" – often by the very members of Congress who had demanded, largely successfully, deregulatory structures and policies that enabled financial firms to take the risks they wanted without interference from regulatory agencies. The question became whether political actors would press for accountability to the point that economic actors would feel no protection against the policy vagaries of electoral cycles in the White House, partisan realignment within the public, majority-rule instability in Congress, and the mutability of majority rule.

The first postcrisis agency to be held accountable was the Fed, and the occasion was the reappointment of Fed chairman Ben Bernanke.

Restructuring the Fed and Reaffirming Autonomy

During the financial crisis and in its aftermath, the Fed came in for a good deal of criticism from a variety of sources. Many legislators either refused to see the possibility of the systemic risk that the Fed was addressing, or they felt the threat of a global meltdown was exaggerated in this case. In contrast, liberal academics like Krugman and Stiglitz argued that the Fed failed to take advantage of the opportunity to break the cycle of risk seeking, leverage, and bailout that had plagued the financial industry since the junk bond/S&L crisis of the 1980s (e.g., Stiglitz, 2010). The Tea Party activists aimed yet another populist critique at the Fed.

As always during difficult economic times, the criticisms of the Fed led to calls for a change in its charter that would make it more accountable to Congress and/or the president. These calls were particularly loud in the winter of 2009–10 when Congress was both considering Bernanke's renomination as Fed chair and debating financial reform legislation that could either restrict or expand the Fed's autonomy. And criticism came from both the right and the left: "Among the senators who say they intend to use their filibuster powers to try to rein in the Fed are Senator Bernard Sanders, Vermont independent and one of the Senate's most liberal members, and Senator Jim DeMint, South Carolina Republican and one of the chamber's most conservative members" (P. Hill, 2009).

Nevertheless, the political logic of independent central banking reasserted itself, as public officials realized that the alternatives were to place the responsibility of oversight with members of Congress or the President; neither institution wanted to see that much power in the other's hands. The president was warning against politicians exercising undo influence over the Fed, and a jealous Congress was sure to object to presidential intrusions: the lobbying impact of the financial industry on Congress was palpable, and the power of the financial industry was internalized in the White House in the form of Geithner and other Wall Street insiders. Recognizing that ambitions to control the Fed would always be blocked by opponents, partisans of every stripe agreed that delegation to experts was better than risking giving power to their opponents. Delegation, as always, offered a politically viable strategy: turn the critical decisions over to experts, experts with a fighting chance of having informational equity with the financial industry itself. And then if things went very wrong, the regulators could always be scapegoated.

Investors, too, expressed concern about the politicization of the Fed. The *Washington Times* reported, "Investors are increasingly worried by threats in Congress to ... meddle in the Federal Reserve's decisions on interest rates, fearing a politicization of the agency with the greatest reach over the economy and markets" (P. Hill, 2009). Some top executives joined the White House in lobbying for Bernanke's reappointment.

In January 2010, the Senate confirmed Bernanke's reappointment with a 70–30 vote, with 18 Republicans joining 11 Democrats and one independent in voting against it. Although it was a record number of votes against a Fed chairman's appointment (the previous high total was 16 votes against Volcker in 1983), the support of a bilateral coalition nevertheless restored the authority of the Fed.

AN INEVITABLE ROLE FOR BUREAUS

Just as with Bernanke's reappointment, we argue that, in another key moment, the traditional arguments for agency independence reasserted themselves in the construction of the postcrisis world. Despite the continued expressions of concern about the accountability of the Fed and other financial agencies, the Dodd–Frank Wall Street Reform and Consumer Protection Act[3] (commonly known as Dodd-Frank) that President Obama signed on July 21, 2010, modified the structure of these agencies in a way that guaranteed a great range of freedom in writing the regulations that would give substance to financial reform. Congressional deliberations over financial regulatory agencies were very complex, and the bill only passed due to a combination of careful compromises and deliberate ambiguity. As usual, these characteristics resulted in the maintenance or even expansion of bureaucratic insulation – not its elimination (Moe, 1989).

Structural Change in Financial Regulation

The first structural change imposed by Dodd-Frank was the elimination of the Office of Thrift Supervision. It had been created after the S&L crisis and located in the Treasury Department on the theory that as a cabinet agency it would be more accountable to the president and that accountability to the president would produce better thrift regulation.

It had not worked out that way in practice. The structural move had indeed made the OTC responsive to administration forces, but this had facilitated a destructive politicization that undermined its motivation and ability to regulate the thrifts. The OTS competed with the Office of the Comptroller to get firms to adopt a charter that would put them under its own regulatory regime. The competition was based on which regulator would adopt the most laissez-faire approach to regulation. With the collapse of WaMu and other OTS-regulated firms, the OTC became the scapegoat for regulatory laxity and failure, and it followed its predecessor, the Federal Home Loan Bank Board, into oblivion.

Dodd-Frank also created the Financial Stability Oversight Council (FSOC), charged with identifying systemic threats to the financial industry and headed by the Treasury Secretary. Another voting member, also from the Treasury Department, is the Comptroller of the Currency, who has a five-year term and a degree of independence in the department. In addition to the Treasury Secretary and the Comptroller, eight other voting members of the FSOC contribute to the autonomy of the Council. These include the chairs of five established independent regulatory agencies – the Fed, the SEC, the CFTC, the FDIC, and the National Credit Union Administration Board. Three additional members are from newly created positions: the director of the Federal Housing Finance

---

[3] Public Law 111–203. Located at www.gpo.gov/fdsys/pkg/PLAW-111publ203/html/PLAW-111publ203.htm

Agency, created in 2008 as the independent regulator and conservator of Fannie Mae and Freddie Mac; an expert on insurance appointed for a six-year term (as of 2014 it was Roy Woodall, former insurance commissioner of Kentucky); and the director of the Bureau of Consumer Financial Protection Bureau (CFPB).

One of the bitterest aspects of the fight for reform was how to prevent home-owners from getting in over their heads in financing their homes. The Consumer Financial Protection Bureau was created by the Dodd-Frank act and charged with regulating the marketing of financial products, with the goal of minimizing the abuses that went into the marketing of subprime mortgages. As its first director, Elizabeth Warren, a Harvard academic, focused attention on consumer fraud in the form of misleading information such as "liars' loans" and other high-risk strategies that drew consumers into the housing market. The CFPB operates within but independently of the Fed. Richard Cordray, director as of 2014, has a five-year term of office.

The effective executive director of the umbrella Financial Stability Oversight Council (FSOC) is the director of the Office of Financial Research, which gathers technical information and provides other support services for the FSOC. This director (Richard Berner, as of 2014) has a position in the Treasury Department, but a six-year term of office. With the support of the Office of Financial Research, the FSOC has far-reaching authority to monitor and investigate firms in the financial industry. It can require information about financial condition and transactions of any financial firm with assets greater than $50 billion.

The Dodd-Frank legislation also authorized a number of other changes to the financial regulation ecosystem (Acharya, Cooley, Richardson, & Walter, 2010). It finally provided for the regulation of the derivatives markets (e.g., central clearing, market transparency, swap margins) that had previously been placed congressionally out of bounds in the aftermath of the Born investigation. It reinstated a limited form of Glass-Steagall in the Volcker Rule. This rule was suggested by the former Fed chairman in his capacity as president of Obama's Economic Recovery Advisory Board, created in February 2009. While it was trading that drove the risk taking in search of huge profits, the Volcker Rule prohibits a bank from proprietary trading. It was denied a vote in the Senate, but was passed in the House. It was reinstated in a modified form in the conference committee and then included in the final legislation. In addition, Dodd-Frank created new mortgage standards and rules and reduced bank leverage ratios to no more than 20:1 of assets to equity (with possibly higher equity requirements).

Unsurprisingly given the stakes of Dodd-Frank, there were soon calls to reform it. Worries about "too big to fail" have loomed large in debates about changes to Dodd-Frank – from arguments that the act has been a success but that more reform is needed (Krugman, 2014), to ambiguous evidence about whether "too big to fail" has been resolved (Morgensen, 2014; United States Government Accountability Office, 2014), to complaints that the act has over-whelmed agencies and stifled growth (Wallison, 2014). There may be merit to the complaints that specific rules in the act are conflicting, unwieldy, or difficult to perfect via rulemaking; Congress was not in the position to specify the best way to reduce systemic risk. Our central point remains, however: the expansion of authority for the purpose of devising institutional rules to reduce risk was a return to an older era of delegation to independent, professionalized bureaus. Structural changes, at least, are difficult to unwind.

AMBIGUOUS COMMITMENTS

The concern about the lack of effective regulation was one of the causes of what some called "the lost generation" – a generation of investors who left the stock market soon after the financial panic. "Said one investor, 'I'm sitting on an uncomfortable amount of cash. Until things get better, I'm not putting any more money into stocks.'…Another one-time avid stock investor said that his 'distrust of market regulators and the belief that they don't protect individual investors are the top reasons for his anti-stock stance.' The same investor said: 'What would bring me back? Show me that the SEC is back to protecting the little guy'" (Shell, 2009, B2).

Consider one of the SEC's most important early attempts to avert the crisis – FAS 157, the Financial Accounting Standards Board's mark-to-market rule. It required firms to evaluate assets by their market price, rather than their historic book value. The new rule, which went into effect in November 2007, undermined the ability of financial firms to exaggerate the value of their mortgage-based bonds. Every time a transaction took place at a given price, that information was no longer hidden, which required firms to evaluate their own similar assets in terms of that hard, market-based data. It is interesting to speculate whether an earlier imposition of FAS 157 might have put a stop to the mortgage debt bubble earlier and in a less devastating way. But as of 2007, investors began to have a basis for making more realistic evaluations of their options in the bond market, though this rule was insufficient to sustain investor confidence.

In Chapter 5, we argued that the separation of powers played a role in the creation of independent agencies, particularly because the president has a distinct information advantage vis-à-vis Congress. The only recourse for Congress to counter that information advantage is to impose reporting requirements that will keep it informed and in the game.

Yet Congress is often criticized for leaving too many key decisions to regulators. One firm estimated that Dodd-Frank explicitly required 398 new regulations and that the SEC had missed 45% of congressional deadlines in implementing them four years after its passage (Wallison, 2014). When the bill was criticized "for leaving so many critical decisions to federal regulators," Senator Dodd responded," It's the dumbest argument I've ever heard. What do they expect me to write, a 100,000-page bill? This is far beyond the capacity, the expertise, the knowledge of a Congress" (Dennis, 2010, A01). For Congress, an important question is whether it should intervene in the independent operation of SEC's enforcement functions.

The Direction of Enforcement

Despite budget cuts, personnel turnover, and rumors of its demise, the SEC had never quite given up on enforcing the financial disclosure requirements that were its main responsibility.

In 2008, for instance, it brought charges against Ralph Cioffi, a hedge fund manager at Bear Stearns. The SEC charge, based in part on emails, was that Cioffi and colleagues knew about the coming disaster with subprime mortgages even as they praised the viability of the subprime debt to clients who were considering pulling their money from Cioffi's fund (U.S. Securities and Exchange Commission, 2012).

One of Mary Schapiro's goals when she became the new head of the SEC in January 2009 was to give more strength and authority to the professional staff at the Enforcement Division, after years of decreasing morale under Cox. To this end, she named Robert Khuzami to head the division. It would be difficult to name someone with better credentials for that job. Khuzami had been general counsel for Deutsche Bank, so he knew Wall Street. In 1991, President Bush appointed him U.S. Attorney for the Southern District of New York, covering Wall Street. He not only helped prosecute the 1993 World Trade Center bombers but he also took on white-collar crime. It was probably not coincidental that in 1999 he had successfully prosecuted the largest Ponzi scheme to that time. Appointing him as head of the SEC had to be a signal that the agency meant to overcome the embarrassment of failing to uncover the Madoff ponzi scheme under the previous administration. In fiscal 2011, under Khuzami's leadership, the Enforcement Division brought a record 735 actions (McKenna, 2012).

It was probably also not a coincidence that Khuzami's Enforcement Division tackled, among other "big" cases, Goldman Sachs – the largest, most profitable, and most politically influential firm on Wall Street. The SEC imposed a $500,000,000 fine on Goldman for fraudulently creating a complex derivative, called Abacus 2007-AC1, that it was confident would only decrease in value. It was so confident because Abacus was designed to hinge on the performance of subprime mortgage-backed bonds, at a time in 2007 when Goldman was increasingly aware of the problems with subprimes. By convincing someone else to buy it, Goldman Sachs could make money by selling it short. So it was essential to keep from the buyer the knowledge that the hedge fund that had helped Goldman construct the CDO was also selling it short. In one view, the action against Goldman could hardly have been a more eloquent statement of political independence. As Khuzami noted at the time, "Half a billion dollars is the largest penalty ever assessed against a financial services firm in the history of the SEC. This settlement is a stark lesson to Wall Street firms that no product is too complex, and no investor too sophisticated, to avoid a heavy price if a firm violates the fundamental principles of honest treatment and fair dealing" (quoted in U.S. Securities and Exchange Commission, 2010).

The value of that lesson was later undermined by an analysis conducted by *The American Lawyer* of several thousand pages of SEC documents about the Goldman case obtained under the auspices of the Freedom of Information Act (Beck, 2014). Its report focused on the case of James Kidney, an SEC lawyer who retired in April 2014 and on his retirement speech. In that speech, Kidney called out SEC leaders for focusing on too many small violators to increase enforcement statistics and of turning a blind eye to the actions of those in the C-suite. Specifically, the SEC case against Goldman had focused on 28-year-old trader Fabrice Toure.

Kidney was one of 30 SEC lawyers who testified in front of SECs' inspector general about the case in 2010. He had said, "When I got in, the staff, particularly the assistant director, seemed to pretty much feel that the investigation was over, which shocked me. There were obvious holes in the investigation.... It was not a case where there was only one low-level vice president involved" (Beck, 2014, 18). He noted the reluctance of higher SEC officials to pursue Toure's manager. In his 2014 retirement speech, Kidney argued that such choices were routine: "I have had bosses, and bosses of my bosses, whose names we all know, who made little secret that they were here to punch their ticket. They mouthed serious regard for the mission of the commission, but their actions were tentative and fearful in many instances. The revolving door doesn't push the agency's enforcement envelope very often or very far" (18).

Inside financial regulatory agencies, the interests of professional employees with long time horizons can come into conflict with the short-term interests of those who may soon leave for partnerships in law firms or industry positions. Thus the tactic of targeting employees of firms instead of those in the executive suite is unsurprisingly common (Garrett, 2014). During this period of enforcement after the Great Recession, stories continue to emerge about the resignations of professionalized bureaucrats whose hands were tied by the decisions of their superiors to forgo launching prosecutions at the higher levels of corporations. Because this problem is so fundamental to our claim about independent agencies and professionalized bureaucrats, in the next chapter we consider the intriguing cases of Gary Aguirre and other whistleblowers.

Self-Funding at the SEC

Holding an agency accountable by cutting its funding is a "self-fulfilling prophecy.... Without the extra money to help police the markets and make long-term investments in the department, the S.E.C. faces the increased probability of weak enforcement and lax oversight" (Sorkin, 2011). One way to protect the critical enforcement and other functions of the SEC from budgetary cuts that lead to "weak enforcement and lax oversight" is self-funding.

Like the Fed and the FDIC, the SEC generates its own revenue. Unlike those two agencies, however, the SEC does not get to decide for itself how to allocate the money it collects; instead, Congress determines its budget, just as it does with other agencies that are not self-funding. After the financial crisis, some support emerged for self-funding, as a way to protect the professional agency from political interference. Forty-one Wall Street securities lawyers, many of them "revolving door" attorneys who had left the SEC for their current positions, have since lobbied Congress not only for more funding for the SEC but also for self-funding (Sorkin, 2011) – claiming that Wall Street needs an effective SEC for its own well-being. Essentially, the issue is not just more or less money for the SEC but rather its independence as a market watchdog (Seligman, 2003–2004). Political forces can change drastically with any election, and a weak SEC can change in response to those forces. Compare the SEC with the CFPB, which, for all its warts and controversy over its mission, is self-funded (Khademian, 2011). The more effective that politicians like Senator Shelby are in imposing "accountability" over the SEC, the more the investing public has to assume that property rights and contract enforcement on Wall Street are subject to changing coalitional prospects from liberal Democrats, traditional Republicans, Tea Party advocates, and whoever may control Congress after the next election – which is always less than two years away.

Double Delegation in the Regulation of Public Auditors

Attacks on bureaucratic independence, and especially the SEC, also came through the courts. The Supreme Court's decision in *Free Enterprise Fund* v. *Public Company Accounting Oversight Board* was particularly noteworthy. The Sarbanes-Oxley Act of 2002 created the Public Company Accounting Oversight Board (PCAOB) to monitor public auditors in the interest of promoting full disclosure for investors.[4] It is formally a private, nonprofit organization, governed by a five-member board, whose members are appointed to staggered five-year terms by the SEC. The members of the PCAOB, like the SEC itself, can only be fired for cause, and only the SEC can do that firing, just as only the president can fire SEC members for cause.

Notice that these appointment rules render the PCAOB doubly protected from political pressure. The Free Enterprise Fund, a 501(c)(4) organization advocating for limited government, sued the PCAOB on constitutional grounds. The claim was that the president was unable to do his constitutional duty as chief executive, because he could not fire the members of the PCAOB.

The members of the Supreme Court were unanimous that the PCAOB was legally established and appointed. However, on a 5–4 vote, the majority of the Supreme Court voted that there must not be two levels of for-cause protection between the president and the members of the PCAOB. One level, however,

4 130 S. Ct. 3138 (2010).

was commonplace. So the court allowed the SEC (not the president!) to have the power to fire members of the PCAOB at will. It was sufficient that the president's power over the PCAOB consist of the SEC's enhanced power to fire PCAOB board members.

The irony is that, in providing for greater accountability of the PCAOB, the Court also strengthened the discretion of the SEC itself – the question remaining being the degree to which the president is willing to live with an independent SEC.

MORAL HAZARD AND "NO BAILOUT" POLICIES

In the aftermath of 2008, although no one is certain that a similar crisis could not happen again, some make a stronger assertion – it can and will happen again. Competition among financial firms will encourage a search for high-return investment opportunities, and these will come with high risk. However, for the "too big to fail" firms at least, the risk will be discounted because of the near certainty of bailout.

In a classic credible commitment game, a financial firm (e.g., JPMorgan Chase) has to decide whether to play it safe or take risks that promise high returns. The latter strategy eventually results in the possibility of bankruptcy, which will occur unless the government offers a bailout. Knowing this, the firm can assume that the government will offer a bailout in the long run, making bailout the subgame perfect equilibrium of the game. This is the moral hazard resulting from the revelation that some banks have, in the opinion of government, reached a "too big to fail" size. The government would like to discourage the high-risk strategies that result in bailout, but can only do so by changing the game in some way.

The question that determines our financial future is this: how can government make a credible commitment to a no-bailout policy? The answer, we assert, must involve independent, professionalized regulatory authorities that politicians allow to be insulated from pressure emerging from the financial industry and transmitted through the inevitably yielding elected public officials. Anything less risks becoming a guarantee of sorts for a bailout, for as Proverbs 6:1-2 warns, "My son, if you have become a surety for neighbor, have given your pledge for a stranger, you are snared in the utterance of your lips" (Pollock, 2014).

A case in point is Sheila Bair, former head of the FDIC (Suskind, 2011, 204–208). She was the only major regulator to warn before 2008 that failing mortgage bonds were going to cause havoc in the financial world. When she was proven right, she weighed in on behalf of the taxpayer, rather than the bondholder. She managed to get through the crisis without a run on any of the FDIC banks. She funded the FDIC Deposit Insurance Fund by placing assessments on member banks. As banks got into financial trouble, she resolved the crises by working out their purchases by healthier banks.

She strongly preferred the FDIC resolution practice to bailouts, which used taxpayer funds to help the bondholders and executives of bankrupt banks. She felt these resolution practices, referred to as "FDIC receivership authority," could be extended to bank holding companies and investment firms.

She fought to use Dodd-Frank to "tie the hands" of future governments so that they could not yield to political and economic pressure to save bankrupt firms. In addition to extending receivership authority, Dodd-Frank ended up creating a high bureaucratic bar for receivership – a two-thirds vote of the governors of the Federal Reserve and the FDIC boards. Dodd-Frank bans federal bailouts of all sorts unless the firm is in receivership.

Dodd-Frank also addresses the funding of receiverships. Ex-post funding would mean dealing with Congress, and "[r]equiring the receiver to go to Congress for an appropriation would be disastrous" (Engel & McCoy, 2011, 241). Dodd-Frank therefore gives FDIC the authority to fund receivership by selling obligations to the Treasury Department, thereby insulating the funding for FDIC receivership.

Once Dodd-Frank issued its bans on bailouts, Sheila Bair hoped to convince the financial firms that the new rules were credible. After all, "[j]ust as Congress could enact TARP, it could repeal the no-bailout provisions in Dodd-Frank" (Engel & McCoy, 2011, 242). If both houses of Congress and the president at some future time agree that bailouts are a good idea, then they have the authority to enact such legislation. Delegating receivership to bureaucracies is made more credible by the unlikelihood of such agreement across veto points.

CONCLUSION: THE RESULTS OF POLITICIZATION

Our separation of powers is supposed to make it difficult for "factions" to use the power of government for their own benefit. Something clearly went wrong leading up to the financial crisis of 2008.

The pattern in financial regulation from the Federal Reserve Act of 1915 through the Reagan administration was for different political interests – Democrats versus Republicans, labor supporters versus capitalists, White House versus Congress – to check each other's most ambitious aspirations. This led to a stalemate in which the ultimate outcome was the delegation of disputed authority to professional regulators. It was the bureaucrats who prevented any particular faction from undermining the government's credible commitment to contract enforcement and property rights.

This situation was changed when the multiple factions in financial policy joined ranks behind a deregulatory philosophy. When Enron, Citigroup, and Goldman Sachs offered legislation to deregulate banking and prohibit the regulation of derivatives, the actors one would have expected to oppose this action instead signed on to it. The Clinton White House and a large proportion of the Democrats in Congress joined the Republicans in passing the Financial Services Modernization Act (1999) and the Commodities Futures Modernization

Act (2000). Within the year, the newly formed Citigroup was investing heavily in mortgage-backed derivatives; Citi was the textbook case of "too big to fail" (Suskind, 2011, 208).

As a result of spreading deregulation, the economic regulators were left with few tools to defend against fraud and abuse and fewer reasons to take the task seriously. As Geithner and Summers wrote in the *Washington Post* in 2009, "the crisis was in part due to basic failures in financial supervision and regulation....In recent years, the pace of innovation in the financial sector has outstripped the pace of regulatory modernization, leaving entire markets and market participants largely unregulated" (Geithner & Summers, 2009). This is the kind of cautionary note that might have done some good if articulated by the Democratic White House 10 years earlier, but unfortunately, on that earlier occasion, the same Larry Summers had been a bulldozer, burying Brooksley Born's opposition to the deregulatory legislation signed by Clinton with Summers' emphatic recommendation. It was an arrangement that came about as part of "the 'we're in this all together' bond built across three decades between Washington and Wall Street" (Suskind, 2011, 207).

Virtually every report on the 2008 crisis includes an account of the regulators' responsibility in bringing about this disaster, and we agree with that assessment. But let us be clear that the actions taken by regulators were largely the result of a damaged bureaucracy in which professionalization was subjugated to a culture that gave elected deregulators what they wanted. The elected deregulators eliminated the independent FHLBB and replaced it with the pliant OTS. The CFTC's attempts to provide a foundation for the regulation of derivatives were quashed first by officials of the Clinton administration and then by congressional legislation. The SEC was transformed by the deregulatory rhetoric of its 21st-century commissioners, who put the staff on a short leash. And even the Fed, led by a heartfelt deregulator, was absent without leave in several of its crucial banking and consumer protection regulatory responsibilities.

And in this culture of risk taking, regulators could hardly resist effectively – at least after 1994, when Democrats and Republicans, legislators and executives, and interest group lobbyists of all stripes agreed that markets corrected themselves. Stalemate had nurtured regulatory independence since at least the creation of the SEC (when Roosevelt's opponents succeeded in imposing a new, more independent SEC in place of the New Deal-friendly Federal Trade Commission as the regulator of the new securities exchanges); this stalemate disappeared under a new deregulatory consensus. Bureaucracies really do not live in a vacuum. "Independent" bureaucracies are only approximated when the separation of powers creates the conditions for stalemate. When the environment is uniformly hostile, Weberian expertise alone is not sufficient to stand up to those political forces.

Now, in the wake of the worst economic crisis since 1929, political stalemate and compromise have resulted in a new institutional legislative structure – Dodd-Frank. Dodd-Frank, like most regulatory legislation written in the immediate aftermath of crises, based on disparate legislative opinions about appropriate correctives, is ambiguous and unclear. The legislation is not so much a regulatory regime as an invitation to regulatory agencies to create a new regime through the rulemaking process.

Giving significant authority in the rulemaking process to the agencies could have several advantages. One could be insulation from lobbying. Insofar as the agencies are writing the rules for the new financial world, at least they will be at one remove from the lobbying and campaign contributions that keep congressional candidates responsive to the financial industry.

An informational advantage could be just as important. The knowledge of experts provides much more leverage in the presence of divisions of opinion than in the face of multiple, unanimous principles. As was the case with the Keating Five, at least five financial crises ago, the bureaucrats will have an informational advantage over members of Congress in dealing with firms from Wall Street.

In this sense, the crisis of 2008 had one very significant result: it restored conflict and stalemate to the ranks of elected politicians. As was the case before 1994, there are now serious differences of opinion in place of deregulatory unanimity. The head of the House Banking Committee would like to see the Fed eliminated; others believe the Fed should be given additional responsibilities to protect banking consumers. Some think the SEC should be reined in; others would allow the SEC to budget for itself out of the fees it generates. This is the historic form of conflict that has been behind the emergence of autonomous regulatory agencies since the Progressive Era. With the resurgence of political stalemate, will regulatory agencies once again be a source of policy making that is at one remove from electoral and coalitional instability? And is it possible that a reassertion of professionalism will re-create the right conditions for credible commitment in financial regulation?

10

Conclusion

The Unraveling of Dodd-Frank

> *Dodd-Frank is full of imperfections – "no bill is ever perfect," as Senator Dodd put it. Its principal authors revealed their own imperfections as they steered their versions of regulatory reform toward final passage. Their huge "piece of legislation"…will have unintended consequences – every big bill does. The effects of many of its provisions won't be known until regulatory agencies write and apply "rules" under which they will enforce the law. Those rules will be challenged in court and altered in practice. Eventually Dodd-Frank will be amended by additional legislation. Only the next big financial crisis will fully test the new law, if it remains in effect when that crisis arrives. In Washington, nothing is forever, no argument is ever finally resolved.*
>
> – Kaiser (2013, xviii)

Section 716 of Dodd-Frank prohibited federal government bailouts of financial entities involved in the business of credit default "swaps." These were the complex instruments that in 2002 investor Warren Buffett had presaged as being "financial weapons of mass destruction, carrying dangers that, while now latent, are potentially lethal" (Berkshire Hathaway Inc., 2002, 15). Swaps involving complex arrangements were often the main problem in the crises engulfing so many financial entities during this time period. AIG, for instance, guaranteed the coverage of losses for many banks or funds that had invested in mortgage-backed securities, often of the subprime variant.

As Kaiser notes about the negotiations over Section 716, "regulating derivatives in some fashion was part of the broad consensus on the need for regulatory reform" (Kaiser, 2013, 169). But certain financial institutions challenged the "broad consensus" on regulatory reform and sought to weaken Section 716 in particular, so that they could take higher risks with federal funds covering those risks.

The debates over Section 716 were especially divisive, often pitting representatives from the same party against one another. The stakes had everything to do with all of those bailouts of the large firms, because the problem was how to cordon off risk in banks to ensure that there was no federal backstop for this highly risky market segment. Many considered one early position, pushed by Senator Blanche Lincoln, the new chairman of the Senate Agriculture Committee, to be too soft on derivatives. Facing a primary challenge, she later offered a new proposal that many, including the Treasury Department, judged as being too strong: it would require all banks to "push out" or spin off any operations related to derivatives trading. Debates ensued about the toughness of competing proposals, often centering on worries that pushing out all derivatives trading to new, unregulated entities would instead create a different set of problems (Kaiser, 2013, 293).

Section 716 prohibited financial assistance in the forms of advances from federal credit facilities, loans, purchased obligations or stock, guaranteed debt, tax breaks, or other "bailouts" for any swaps entity (except for banks involved in situations of "normal" derivatives such as hedging foreign currency). In negotiating the final Dodd-Frank bill, with its multiple constituencies in both chambers and incorporating elements of legislation originating in several committees, Congressman Dodd argued that Section 716 was "the most complex title in the bill" and that "this one is profoundly important – that we get it right" (quoted in Kaiser, 2013, 351). Although the final legislation allowed banks to take advantage of swaps, many believed it made derivatives markets more transparent and regulated and at least limited the likelihood of another major federal bailout of the banks.

The debate over Section 716 became even more politicized after the 2014 midterm elections when the Republican Party won enough seats to control both the House and the Senate. Yet both parties seemed eager to resolve past contentious debates about the budget. In 2013, an inability to agree on spending had led to a federal government shutdown; after doing business by short-term continuing resolutions for such a long time, both parties wanted to fund the government through 2015. Looking to mitigate the label of "most do-nothingest Congress" (Eldridge, 2014), in December 2014, Congress passed a trillion-dollar "CRomnibus" (continuing resolution omnibus spending bill) that also fundamentally reversed Section 716: it eliminated the prohibition on bailouts for banks engaging in derivatives trading for securities and other restricted assets.

This rollback of the Dodd-Frank financial regulation came thanks to the hard work of Representative Kevin Yoder (R-KS). In June 2014, during committee deliberations on the appropriations bill, Yoder attached technical changes to Section 716 that were taken from a bill that the House had passed in 2013 on a 292–122 vote. Yoder's proposal passed the committee without a recorded vote (Weisman, 2014). Democrats, as the minority, spoke out against this proposal, but were unable to block it; yet, they did not ask for a recorded vote on its inclusion.

The Senate had ignored the House legislation when it passed in 2013, but they could not ignore it after Yoder effectively attached an entire financial reform bill to a single appropriations bill, the CRomnibus – which joined all the appropriations bills together and, as mentioned earlier, was passed at the beginning of December. By failing to strip out roughly two pages of text added by Yoder, the Congress had gutted Section 716, the prohibition of derivatives and swaps trading by banks insured by the federal government.

Of course, those in favor of Dodd-Frank such as Senator Elizabeth Warren argued that this was a full-on assault of financial regulation – that the measure "would let derivatives traders on Wall Street gamble with taxpayer money and get bailed out by the government when their risky bets threaten to blow up our financial system" (Helling, 2014). To his constituents, Yoder argued, "Without this change, small regional banks would be in danger of being unable to serve the lending needs of their customers. Ultimately, farmers, manufacturers, and other Main Street businesses would be harmed the most" (Shelly, 2014). To Wall Street, he claimed, "We have a created a model.... This bipartisan success shows a pathway to solving other issues in the financial services area" (Wasson, 2014).

Campaign finance data show that Yoder received $62,500 in the last election cycle from commercial banking interests (Helling, 2014), and "[s]ince the beginning of 2013, he's received $29,000 from the political action committees of Citigroup, Goldman Sachs, Bank of America and JPMorgan Chase, which represent more than 90 percent of the swaps market" (Shelly, 2014).

Although politicians were the means for gutting Section 716, the banks stood to gain the most. For the big firms, the stakes were especially high:

Just five accounted for 95% of the total notional derivatives of $302 trillion. They are: J.P. Morgan, Citigroup, Goldman Sachs Group, Bank of America and Morgan Stanley. Of vital importance, especially for Citi, is where the derivatives are legally housed.... The bank subsidiaries, with implicit government backing, are considered less risky than parent holding companies. Being seen as a less-risky counterparty gives banks an advantage in pricing and collateralization of derivatives. (J. Carney, 2014)

Citigroup had drafted Yoder's 2013 bill "nearly word for word" (Weisman, 2014, B2); "Citigroup's recommendations were reflected in more than 70 lines of the House committee's 85-line bill" (Lipton & Protess, 2013, A1). The financial industry lobbied for that bill at a rate of 15 to 1 compared to the activities of other interest groups (Citigroup was the single most active lobbying entity on the measure; Drutman, 2014). Later, a delegation of bankers lobbied Treasury after the June 2014 vote that attached the Section 716 rollback to the CRomnibus (T. P. Carney, 2014). Jamie Dimon, CEO of JPMorgan Chase, personally called legislators to urge them to pass the CRomnibus, Section 716 rollback included (J. Carney, 2014; T. P. Carney, 2014). Representative Maxine Waters (D-CA) noted, "I know that the president was whipping and he was supporting this bill and I know that Jamie Dimon was whipping. That's an odd combination" (Hopkins & Brush, 2014).

As Bair said in 2013, "Since Dodd-Frank, unfortunately, the trend has been to move this activity [swaps] from the investment banking affiliates, which do not use insured deposits, into the banks where the activity can be funded with cheap, FDIC backed deposits. Section 716 would at least keep certain credit default swaps outside of insured banks" (Konczal, 2013). That is no longer the case. With relative ease and a paltry financial contribution from the banks, special interests had undermined Section 716 and decreased the transparency of the financial system.

OUR ARGUMENT

In Chapter 1, our description of Charles Keating's lobbying of five Senators to push off the efforts of FHLBB regulators served as an introduction to our broader argument about the role of credible commitment in polities and markets. We see clear parallels between events at the FHLBB in the 1980s and these recent changes to Dodd-Frank. In both cases, market actors sought profits by betting on risky investments. In both cases, those actors sought to subsidize that risk by backstopping their losses with taxpayer-subsidized deposits. In both cases, when faced with the prospects of regulation to limit their ability to backstop those losses – and when they saw the impact of such a "risk shift" on their firms' ability to chase outsized profits without also eating the very large downside risk that accompanied that chase – those market actors sought via the political process to remove the regulatory hurdle.

In the case of the FHLBB, however, the hurdle was a bunch of bureaucrats who, once confronted, stuck to their guns and argued that such regulation was necessary to protect the public good. In contrast, in the Dodd-Frank case, market actors sought and obtained removal of the regulatory burden by going directly to Congress, by taking advantage of a situation where political preferences were aligned (for passing a spending bill), and by activating specific politicians to obtain the outcomes they wanted – literally, by transcribing the preferences of Citigroup.

Our argument in this book centers on four observations. First, government is integral for long-term economic growth and stability in markets. Second, given time-inconsistent preferences, politicians' promises are often not credible. They are expected not to intervene on behalf of specific market actors adversely affected by government's actions in the markets via regulation or management of the money supply. Third, regulatory agencies are central to understanding the relationship between government and markets because delegation from politicians to bureaus solves a broader problem of credible commitment – but only if bureaus (like politicians) "tie their own hands."

Our last claim is that this implicit agreement is two-sided: politicians can violate this agreement by intervening in the markets – by pushing bureaus to take actions that do not advance social welfare or by acting in ways to circumvent the actions of bureaus. Likewise, bureaus can violate this agreement if they use their positions for ill, for the good of the bureau alone, or for the good of specific market actors. With regard to these restrictions on bureaus, we argue that professionalism is a form of social delegation to groups – for example, economists, engineers, lawyers, or doctors – that are bound by agreements to serve "higher goods."

Our claims are not about any "universal good" or any "unavoidable equilibrium." Rather, as with Djankov et al. (2003), we see this agreement as a kind of tradeoff – as a possible outcome that results from a dilemma about minimizing both the social costs of disorder and the social costs of dictatorship. The benefit of having independent regulators and central banks staffed by professionalized bureaucrats is an outcome that was largely unanticipated by their designers. Indeed, as noted in Chapter 1, debates in political science and public administration about accountability and responsibility mostly focus on the role of hierarchical control by elected political principals of their unelected bureaucratic agents. We believe our focus on both the "principal's problem" and the "bureaucrat's burden" presents political science and public administration with an opportunity to help answer questions asked by economists like Estache and Wren-Lewis (2009) when they observe regulatory independence and credible commitment in market settings around the world; for example, "Which [mechanisms] are likely to be more important and which are likely to have the greatest risks?"

Our purpose in this conclusion is to elaborate on some of the inherent risks in a "delegation to professionals" arrangement. We recognize that there are no perfect mechanisms – that all management strategies and all organizational arrangements are themselves a set of interlocking dilemmas (Miller, 1992). We offer here two vignettes to help illuminate some of these inherent risks and tradeoffs. First, we describe the intriguing cases of the SEC's Gary Aguirre and those of other whistleblowers as a way of considering whether bureaucrats are trustworthy, a question we raised in Chapter 1. Then we describe the seizure of assets from and blacklisting of Hermitage Capital Management, a hedge fund doing business in Russia, as a "corner case" of the lack of professionalization.

BLOWING THE WHISTLE

We cannot control ourselves. You have to step in and control the Street.
– John Mack, CEO of Morgan Stanley (Moore, 2009)

On September 1, 2005, the SEC fired Gary Aguirre. Aguirre, a lawyer, had practiced in California since the 1960s, but had decided to go back to school, earning an LLM in securities law at the Georgetown Law Center in 2003. He was hired in the SEC's Enforcement Division in September 2004.

His firing in September 2005, toward the end of but still within his one-year probationary period, followed his receipt of positive performance reviews in June, which led to a merit pay increase. Mark Kreitman, Assistant Director of the Division of Enforcement, even awarded Aguirre with a "Perry

Mason Award" for his diligence in detecting the deep structure of financial crimes.

In 2010, on the orders of a judge from the Merit Systems Protection Board, the SEC paid Aguirre $755,000 to settle a wrongful termination lawsuit he filed as a whistleblower reprisal action (Morgensen, 2010). As a 2007 report from the Minority Staff of the Senate Committee on Finance and the Committee on the Judiciary describes, Aguirre was caught between his professional obligations to pursue a case that he thought was justified and pressure from above not to bring cases against important constituents.

It all started in 2001 with the acquisition by GE Capital, General Electric's financial services subsidiary, of Heller Financial for $5.3 billion. Twenty-eight days before the deal closed, Arthur Samberg, CEO of Pequot Financial Management, initiated large purchases of Heller stock and shorted GE stock. After the deal was announced on July 30, 2001, Pequot sold its Heller share and covered its shorts on GE, earning a profit of $18 million in a matter of weeks. Within six months, the New York Stock Exchange began an investigation of the Heller trades.

After Aguirre was hired at the SEC, the agency opened an investigation of Pequot and its involvement with Heller and GE shares; Aguirre was assigned to the case. After a meeting between Pequot's legal counsel and the SEC's Director of Enforcement, Aguirre was told to concentrate on only the two or three most promising leads (of the 17 original potential referrals; Minority Staff of the Committee on Finance, 2007, 17). The missing piece to be discovered in the investigation centered on information. How was it that Pequot came to learn about the potential deal between GE and Heller? Who tipped them off?

Both Morgan Stanley and Credit Suisse First Boston had advised GE on the deal. In 2005, Aguirre developed the theory that the information about the potential deal came from John Mack, who had been the CEO of Morgan Stanley but had left in March 2001. After leaving, he invested substantial sums with Pequot. In July 2001, just before the deal was announced, Mack was hired as CEO of Credit Suisse First Boston. Robert Hanson, Aguirre's SEC branch chief, wrote to him in June 2005 that "Mack is another bad guy [in my view]" (Minority Staff of the Committee on Finance, 2007, 58). In 2005, Debevoise & Plimpton, a law firm, sought out Aguirre on behalf of Morgan Stanley to ask if he would be pursuing Mack. When he asked Hanson if he could proceed with the subpoena, Aguirre says he was told that "this would be very difficult, Mack had very powerful political connections" (51 fn. 120). The Minority Staff report continues, "Morgan Stanley's Board of Directors hired former U.S. Attorney Mary Jo White to determine whether prospective CEO John Mack had any exposure in the Pequot investigation. White contacted Director of Enforcement Linda Thomsen directly, and other Morgan Stanley officials contacted Associate Director Paul Berger. Soon afterward, SEC managers prohibited the staff from asking John Mack about his communications with Arthur Samberg at Pequot" (5). In June 2005, Mack returned to Morgan Stanley as its CEO.

Aguirre alleged to Berger that Hanson had blocked the Mack subpoena because of Mack's connections. Hanson told Berger that Aguirre and another attorney were "looking to raise trouble" (Minority Staff of the Committee on Finance, 2007, 69). In response, Berger told Hanson to do an additional performance evaluation of Aguirre (after the positive one Aguirre had received). Unsurprisingly, Aguirre received a special "negative re-evaluation outside the SEC's ordinary performance appraisal process" in August (Minority Staff of the Committee on Finance, 2007, 6).

The SEC fired Aguirre on September 1, 2005, and from that point until June 2006 the SEC effectively abandoned its investigation of John Mack's involvement with Pequot. As the Minority Staff report describes the situation: "When the SEC finally did take Mack's testimony on August 1, 2006, it did so five days *after* the statute of limitations period applicable to civil and criminal penalties expired" (Minority Staff of the Committee on Finance, 2007, 41 emphasis included). Mack was never charged with any involvement in these events surrounding Pequot. Pequot closed its doors later and paid a fine for its involvement with a different case relating to Microsoft shares.

In the end, Pequot was fined and closed its doors, and Aguirre was compensated for the four years he would have worked had he not been fired for blowing the whistle on the SEC's unwillingness to fully prosecute this case. Yet John Mack won too. He no longer was subject to financial and legal penalties from his possible wrongdoing, and his involvement in the case was limited by the SEC's delay in taking his testimony regarding the GE-Heller deal. Later, as Morgan Stanley CEO, he was able to advocate for strong regulation in the wake of the financial collapse: "We cannot control ourselves. You have to step in and control the Street" (Moore, 2009).

In June 2006, Berger became a partner at Debevoise & Plimpton, the firm that had inquired, on behalf of Morgan Stanley, about John Mack's exposure in the Pequot case. Records show that Berger began a conversation with this firm about partnership opportunities just days after Aguirre was fired. As the report notes, "Although Robert Hanson testified that the SEC took Mack's testimony, 'as soon as we could,' it appears that the SEC did very little to investigate Mack's potential role in the period between Aguirre's firing in September 2005 and Berger leaving the Commission in the spring of 2006" (Minority Staff of the Committee on Finance, 2007, 46).

Protections against "revolving door" employment agreements are meant to reduce the likelihood that bureaucrats will subjugate their agency's and society's long-term interests in managing markets to their own short-term preferences about wages. On the one hand, Berger's landing at Debevoise & Plimpton and the delay in taking Mack's testimony indicate that institutional improvements are needed. On the other hand, Gary Aguirre's experience over several years and the publicity of this case show the power of individual professionals to push agencies to make decisions based on longer term views of the public good.

Of course, much depends on the roles played by culture and leadership as discussed in Chapter 6. Indeed, President Obama's selection for the chair of the

SEC in 2013 was Mary Jo White, the lead counsel for Debevoise & Plimpton (the firm that offered Berger a partnership) and the person who spoke directly to the SEC's enforcement chief during negotiations over the matter of John Mack. Such appointments call into question the credibility of the professionals who implement policy.

We want to be clear that Aguirre is just one of many professionals asked to carry out their responsibilities within agencies where not all employees feel bound by an agreement to be "above politics." For instance, in September 2014, public radio show *This American Life* and website ProPublica covered 46 hours of tape recordings made by Carmen Segarra, a former bank examiner in the New York Federal Reserve Bank, that documented decisions made by the bank with regard to enforcement actions against Goldman (J. Bernstein, 2014; *This American Life*, 2014). Our understanding of Segarra's experiences at the Fed continues to evolve, but Michael Lewis, who reviewed the evidence from Segarra's tapes, captured this anecdote: "in one meeting a Goldman employee expressed the view that 'once clients are wealthy enough certain consumer laws don't apply to them.' After that meeting, Segarra turned to a fellow Fed regulator and said how surprised she was by that statement – to which the regulator replied, 'You didn't hear that'" (M. Lewis, 2014).

Or consider the example of James Kidney from Chapter 9, the longtime trial lawyer at the SEC who retired in March 2014 and at his retirement party offered extended remarks about what he saw as capitulation by the agency to not make busts that affected the powerful and connected. His direct involvement in the Goldman Sachs Abacus case speaks to wider concerns about the relative role and influence of professionals in these settings.

Aguirre fought and won, though it had little direct effect on the case he cared about most. Segarra fought and lost (though her wrongful dismissal case is currently under appeal), but the extent of the publicity from her revelations is remarkable for a professional like a bank examiner. Kidney fought from the inside, but had "his day" when his retirement speech was important enough to make headlines in journals like *The American Lawyer*. But in each of these cases, there were also bureaucrats, some even professionals, who chose to suppress professional obligations for short-term gains. This is part of the nature of the tenuous agreement we highlight in this book: sometimes the political forces acting on a bureaucracy can undermine its autonomy and weaken the commitment of the regime to professional independence.

A DICTATORSHIP OF LAW

> *But democracy means a dictatorship of the law and not of the people whose job is to uphold the law.... The police and the Prosecutor's Office must serve the law rather than trying to "privatise" their authorities for their own benefit ... It is time to clearly determine who owns what in Russia.*
>
> – Vladimir Putin (2000)

In 2005, the Russian government denied William Browder entrance to the country. Browder, CEO of Hermitage Capital Management, was labeled a threat to Russian national security, which was striking since at that point Hermitage Capital was the single largest foreign investor in the country ("An Enemy of the People," 2006; Hope, 2006). As Russia's largest equity fund, Hermitage had more than $4 billion in managed assets (Hamilton, 2007).

But the size of this investment, its importance to the future of the country, was not the only reason why outsiders were troubled by the decision to bar Browder from entry. Browder, who had served as Hermitage's chief executive since its creation in 1996, was often seen as a "loyal Putinista," having defended the prosecution of Mikhail Khodorkovsky on tax evasion charges and the eventual (effective) nationalization of Yukos Oil Company ("An Enemy of the People," 2006). As a "vocal cheerleader," some saw Browder as central to Moscow's interests; one investor, Red Star Asset Management partner James Fenkner, described it this way: "It's hard to find any other investors who have done more to bring money into Russia than Bill" (Hope, 2006).

Of course, Browder's involvement was not always positive for Russia's political elite, but this was natural given the nature of his investments and the fund's fiduciary responsibility to its shareholders. For instance, Browder had often pointed to "corporate governance issues" in his advocacy of shareholder rights (Aldrick, 2008; Hope, 2006). Targets included government-sponsored enterprises such as Gazprom and Surgutneftgaz ("An Enemy of the People," 2006; Hope, 2006). The decision to bar his entrance probably involved his "scrutiny of Russia's murky corporate governance" ("Dancing with the Bear," 2007).

The response was striking in that outside political interests saw this decision as a blow to the conditions under which foreign capital competed in markets like Russia. In notable statements, Foreign Secretary Jack Straw of the United Kingdom appealed to Foreign Minister Sergei Lavrov of Russia to overturn this decision, and Clara Furse, head of the London Stock Exchange, told the Putin administration that the event "could have a negative impact on Russia's image as a country that welcomes foreign investment, on the ability of Russian companies to raise capital outside Russia" ("LSE Warns Russia on Investor Ban," 2006). She saw it as a message to investors: "If the single largest investor in the Russian market can be arbitrarily denied entry into the country, that would send a very negative signal to other parties seeking to invest in Russian companies" ("LSE Warns Russia on Investor Ban," 2006).

Russia's Interior Ministry upped the ante in 2007 when three of Hermitage's Russian subsidiaries were investigated for roughly $44 million in unpaid taxes (Aldrick, 2008; Hamilton, 2007). Shortly after this, the ministry confiscated computers and documents in raids on the offices of both Hermitage and Firestone Duncan, its legal firm (Hamilton, 2007). At this point, Hermitage essentially was operating only outside Russia, with few "legal" legs to stand on in its fight with the Russian government. It disputed the charges, claiming, "In this case, the Interior Ministry leapfrogged the whole process, which is both illegal and strange" (H. Brown, 2007). Notably, three agencies inside Russia – the Ministry of Finance, the Federal Tax Service, and the Tax Authority Number 7 – agreed with Hermitage in stating that the firm had complied with all requirements in the tax code (Aldrick, 2008).

But it appears that the Russian government ignored this support, because in October 2007, the firm found out that it owed a company called Logos Plus nearly $376 million in fees (Aldrick, 2008). A judge had ruled that Hermitage owed this money to the firm after attorneys, who claimed to represent Hermitage, pled guilty to six charges filed against three Hermitage subsidiaries. Browder and Hermitage argued that in the June 2007 office raids, officials had obtained documents for use in changing ownership details for the holding companies (Aldrick, 2008). In response, Browder and Hermitage sought legal protection by filing complaints against those officials of the law enforcement organizations that had carried out the actual raids.

Hermitage's legal representative in these matters was a Russian attorney, associated with Firestone Duncan, named Sergei Magnitsky. In January 2009, Russian officials arrested Magnitsky just before he was scheduled to provide an investigating prosecutor with what Hermitage said was crucial testimony (Matthews, 2009). In November 2009, Magnitsky died in jail having been denied medical treatment for 11 months. A later report by a Russian presidential advisor said Magnitsky's death may have been the result of a beating (A. E. Kramer, 2011). There are reports that a bribe of $6 million was paid to keep Magnitsky in prison; the arresting officers were later awarded medals for good service (Ledeneva, 2013, 165 fn. 19).

In the wake of Magnitsky's death, President Dmitry Medvedev offered law-enforcement reforms and pushed out several heads of agencies as activist organizations urged formal inquiries ("Activists Urge Prosecution in Russian Prison Death," 2010; Cahill, 2010). By 2011, in a telling sign of the way outsiders saw the events and the lack of resolution, the Obama administration blocked entrance to the United States of dozens of Russian officials who had been connected to the detention and death of Magnitsky. As Andrew Kramer noted in the *New York Times*, "While accounts of human rights abuses are rife in Russia, Mr. Magnitsky's case stood out because of the brazenness of the abuse, the scale of the venality and because this victim, unlike most, had powerful friends outside of Russia" (A. E. Kramer, 2011, A7). Browder welcomed the ban, but continued to push for passage of what became known as the "Sergei Magnitsky Rule of Law Accountability Act." That act, which was signed into law in 2012, froze the assets in the United States of those Russian officials banned from entering the country.

This case may be regarded as what engineers call a "corner" case, in which two environmental conditions are simultaneously at extreme levels – in this situation, strong interventions by politicians and low professionalism within the bureau. Our focus, given the principal's moral hazard, is on the lack of professionalism on the part of those public bureaucrats who carried out these activities against Hermitage and Magnitsky.

Despite Putin's call for a "dictatorship of the law," events in Russia over the last 15 years indicate the reverse – a preference for dictatorship over "rules for all." Browder has argued that "property rights and the rule of law don't exist in Russia" (B. D. Taylor, 2011, 107), but it is more likely his complaint is really about the low level of professionalism of Russian law enforcement. As B. D. Taylor (2011, 197) describes in great detail, "the gap between modern professional law enforcement standards and actual Russian practice has gotten worse since the Soviet collapse, not better." The problems involve low-quality workers, low pay and benefits, and poor training; "professional civil service standards for promotion and for protecting workers from unwarranted dismissal are absent." Structures are not present to transmit professional values from older cadres to younger ones. Instead of training in professional practices, "new officers are now introduced into the aprofessional practices of predation, such as corruption, violence, and arbitrary despotism" (198).

This problem is only enhanced by the lack of professionalization within the Procuracy, the main arm for prosecution in Russia. Formally, the Procuracy is neither part of the executive nor judicial branches; headed by the Prosecutor-General, it employs 54,000 people. Effectively, it operates as a source of power for politicians in Russia: "It's a service organized with a military hierarchy and uniforms and so forth" (Peter Maggs quoted in B. D. Taylor, 2011, 51).

Outside observers have been quick to highlight the importance of the Procuracy to the *siloviki* (politicians from the security or military forces). It is this close relationship that has defined much of the conflict between Putin (and his cohort) and the oligarchs, such as Khodorkovsky (Goldman, 2004). In 2003, columnist William Safire characterized the great struggle in Russia as "siloviki versus oligarchs": "[t]he K.G.B.'s Putin came to power by making a deal: we of the siloviki run the country, and you oligarchs can keep your ill-gotten gains – provided you cut us in on some of the money and stay out of politics" (Safire, 2003, A25). That agreement fell apart over time, perhaps due to presumptions on the part of the siloviki that the division of the spoils with the oligarchs was too one-sided.

The Procuracy was a natural tool for a politician wishing to wield the force of the law in the interests of gaining more of the spoils. Over time, the Procuracy has become second in stature only to the Federal Security Service (FSB), and even though there have been efforts to enhance its independence, "it still largely takes its direction from the president, just as it did the Party during the Soviet period" (B. D. Taylor, 2011, 69). It has been described as "a guard dog of the new regime.... The president's warning was clear: No one had immunity anymore, and his critics could find themselves in an extremely unhappy situation" (Shvetsova, 2005, 107). Some make the point more strongly: "The Procuracy played an indispensable role in this *de facto* coup" (Burger & Holland, 2008, 144). Many have argued that the rule of law in Russia and, indeed, the development of the Russian legal profession itself were damaged by earlier Soviet use of the law as a tool or instrument of political power (Hendley,

2006). Thus legal processes and the legal profession as an independent force in a system of democratic representation were necessarily underdeveloped.

In practice, the impact of lawyers qua lawyers – as a professional body – within the Procuracy is limited. Instead, although on paper procurators seem independent and professional, they remain dependent on the state (and increasingly the president) for the definition of their roles, rights, and responsibilities as lawyers working in government. The bar itself was a closed institution during Soviet times; during subsequent periods of liberalization, with little regulation of the training of lawyers and even of the practice of the law, the development of an infrastructure for professional regulation was not in place until 2002 (Shabelnikov, 2008).

In Russia, most lawyers (the *advokatura*, or "advocates") are neither strongly self-regulated nor regulated by the state. Similarly, the procurators who carry out the work of the Procuracy are not regulated. Only the primary code of professional ethics – a limited source of professional self-regulation – applies to advocates alone. While civil law countries like France also separate lawyers into different professions, the lack of a professional identity outside the Procuracy itself is made even more difficult when the Procuracy is a politicized agency.

The nationalization of the Yukos Oil Company shows directly how this plays out in practice. A new criminal code adopted in 2002 was intended to regularize the procedures requiring the police to obtain warrants for investigations and limiting circumstances for the pretrial detention of the accused. Khodorkovsky, like Magitsky later, was jailed while awaiting trial despite not meeting the conditions of the code, showing that "the rules regarding pretrial detention can and will be disregarded when inconvenient for the Kremlin" (Hendley, 2006, 361).

Politicians might "tie their hands" and professionalized bureaucrats might pursue the public good. Some politicians choose not to tie their hands. When that happens, bureaus without professionals are at sea.

BUREAUS: AID TO REGIME CORRUPTION OR CREDIBLE COMMITMENT?

Nothing in this book dispels a healthy skepticism about bureaucracy. Our point is not that all professional bureaucrats use their expertise to establish the healthy basis of credible commitment. Nor do we claim the opposite – that all bureaucrats use their expertise to provide the basis for a corrupt regime of capture and extraction.

The question we have explored is why is bureaucracy sometimes successful in applying professional expertise to society's benefit, while other times it is the servant of special interests.

Do we have the theoretical tools to understand bureaucrats who provide a prop for corrupt regimes? At the same time, can we understand bureaucracy as an autonomous check on democratic institutions?

As we noted at the beginning of this chapter, the tension here is between the bureau as professional and autonomous versus the bureau as beholden to powerful special interests. In North's view, institutional leaders in many settings can use their influence to define self-serving institutional rules; for instance, creating personally favorable property rights and corrupt contract enforcement. But sometimes, societies deploy more benign legal and institutional rules that produce, over time, benefits for society writ large. We see this same process at play in our research on bureaucratic independence.

As with rules that support contract enforcement and stable property rights, bureaus can counterbalance normal majority-rule politics (such as bargaining over distributive policies) and contribute to stability and economic development, but only if they are insulated from unstable politics. Independent bureaus limit the influence of captive politicians.

What keeps the bureaucrats from being more abusive than elected officials? A separation-of-powers stalemate creates the possibility for bureaucratic autonomy. Autonomy also can result from hierarchical negotiation that, when successful, typically binds subordinate bureaucrats to a cooperative exchange of effort for autonomy. Professionalism goes even further to extend autonomy by embedding its practitioners in professional norms and cultures.

This view of the world is fragile and tentative, shifting and ad hoc. The pieces of our argument do not allow us to claim that "professionalism inevitably wins" or "capture will out." Rather, it allows us to strike a balance – to portray how an agency with significant autonomy can use that autonomy as the basis of credible commitment. The captive bureaucrat is always a risk, but social mechanisms such as professionalism help us better understand the multiple reasons why some agencies will be captured by dominant interest groups and others will serve as bulwarks.

THE CAMPAIGN AGAINST BUREAUCRATS

> *If this guy prints more money between now and the election, I dunno what y'all would do to him in Iowa but we would treat him pretty ugly down in Texas. Printing more money to play politics at this particular time in American history is almost treasonous in my opinion – Governor Rick Perry on Chairman Bernanke.*
> – quoted in Benen (2011)

Whistleblowers needing protection but not being able to reverse the protection of the wealthy and connected or law enforcers capriciously imprisoning people and raiding corporations – why should we trust bureaucrats? The answer, in our view, is that it is better *in the long run* to have professionals managing the Fed, the SEC, or even the Procuracy. This is the nature of the credible commitment problem. In the long run, professionals are more credible than their political overseers.

Of course, smart politicians probably know this; thus, the incentive for "bureau-bashing." The campaign against bureaucrats is by no means new. As H. Kaufman (1981b) reminds us, hostility toward "unelected bureaucrats" has been present throughout much of history. The colonists had distaste for the king's "placemen" who soaked up revenue for negligible productive activity. President Andrew Jackson felt that many public officials (assessors, sheriffs, judges) should be elected; the result was the "long ballot." The point of Jackson's initiatives was clear: those who were not elected should be made responsive to the electoral majority through the spoils system.

The Progressives were unusual in arguing that accountability to politicians (in the form of party bosses and machine henchmen) was a danger in itself (Knott & Miller, 1987). Their criticism of bureaucrats was inseparable from their criticism of the party machines that the spoils system made possible. As mentioned earlier, Progressives, allied with professionals and technicians, supported the creation of agencies staffed by these types and insulated from too much political interference.

But consider the incentives for politicians in such a system. With the waning of the New Deal, the more populist critique of bureaucrats (based on their elitism, incompetence, laziness, and power hunger) reasserted itself, with a larger number of targets given the newly expanded number and size of the executive agencies. As social conservatives broke away from the New Deal coalition, any remaining patience with the bureaucracy seemed to disappear. George Wallace, in his northern primary races in 1964, tried out a campaign based on resentment of elites, especially college professors, Supreme Court justices, and pointy-headed bureaucrats.

As social conservatives entered Reagan's big-tent Republican coalition, one thing that united them with traditional pro-business Rockefeller Republicans was an antipathy for regulation and for bureaucrats, an antipathy fed by Reagan himself. Reagan attacked "fraud, waste, and abuse" and the bureaucrats who benefited. Many politicians have followed Reagan down this path, but it is hard to imagine a more telling example than Michele Bachman, at the beginning of her 2012 presidential campaign, who made this accusation of the Obama administration: "the number of federal limousines for bureaucrats [has] increased 73 percent in two years. I can't think of anything more reprehensible than seeing bureaucrats on their cell phones in the back" (L. Madison, 2011). This image combines the underlying fear and loathing of privilege and elites, who are making irresponsible decisions in the back seat of a limo.

Even more ominous was Governor Rick Perry's attack on Fed independence, in which he castigates Chairman Bernanke's monetary policy as "treason" and threatened Bernanke with an "ugly" situation if he should be so bold as to come to Texas. A more striking example of why bureaucrats need independence from political masters is hard to imagine.

In all of these cases, a legitimate concern for bureaucratic accountability is transformed into a belittling of bureaucratic professionalism and expertise combined with hostility toward bureaucratic independence and the bureaucrats themselves. Bureaucrats are always going to create enemies. These enemies can always use the incompleteness of bureaucratic solutions as evidence supporting an anti-bureaucratic political stance: "bureaucrats are inept but power-hungry; don't give them the autonomy they desire."

This criticism would be of little concern, except that this kind of politicized attack on bureaucracies deprives them of the independence that allows them to contribute to the credible commitment of the state to the kind of economic conditions that are requisites for economic development. The fear is that attacks on the Fed, the SEC, the NLRB, or perhaps even the EPA all will encourage politicized decision making: monetary policy enacted by whichever political party captures control of Congress, encouragement of financial interests to invest in political campaigns in the knowledge that elected officials can continue to block regulations, and majority-rule instability casting doubt over the durability of every possible government regulation.

WICKED PROBLEMS, SELF-FULFILLING PROPHECIES, AND THE FEDERALIST STALEMATE

Given the public's responsiveness to political attacks on bureaucracy, it is easy to see the potential for a downward spiral. Politicians castigate bureaucrats as both acquisitive and incompetent – and most of all elitist. If bureaucrats are evil, then the product of their efforts is worthless or contrary to the nation's interests. The EPA's success in saving lives by controlling air pollution is challenged. The overwhelming numbers of scientists who raise the issue of global warming are thought to be just playing for public attention to save their jobs and their federal grants. Economists who agree that cutting state and local employment is a bad way to get out of a recession are advancing a partisan agenda and are not to be believed. This political response makes it imperative for politicians to follow through on these conclusions by cutting bureaucratic funds, staff, and authority. Otherwise, "we're just encouraging them."

However well bureaucrats were doing before the attacks, they inevitably do worse with less funds, staffing, and support. This leads to further attacks, further diminishment of support, and more unsatisfactory consequences for everyone.

As was the case with the control paradox in Chapter 6, with close and hostile scrutiny from the public and politicians, bureaucrats will work to rule – they will provide the most defensible minimum of effort and initiative. They will wrap themselves in specified procedure and routine to justify their actions.

The problem is worse when bureaucrats are charged with solving technical problems for which ultimate resolution is unlikely or impossible. One thinks readily of global warming, guiding the economy through a financial panic, or even teaching third grade. All of these missions are of sufficient complexity and subtlety that they cannot be articulated on a bumper sticker or lawn sign, where politicians feel most comfortable.

The Federalist Stalemate Counters Political Loathing

In view of the anti-bureaucratic sentiment in the nation, it is curious that bureaucracies exist at all and have the discretion that they do have. It is not enough to say that delegation of monetary policy (for example) exists because it is a good idea. Lots of good ideas are not enacted, and plenty of bad policies are implemented with a will.

This book's explanation for the discretion and autonomy granted to bureaucracy is based not on the best-laid plans (or altruism!) of politicians; it is based on political stalemate. Bureaucracies are not created and given independent authority because some politician thinks of a benevolent purpose they could serve and then convinces a majority of Congress and the president. Autonomous bureaucracies exist because different political constituencies demand inconsistent things of government, and elected officials resort to symbolic responses and vague generalities that bureaucracies must interpret. The Interstate Commerce Act was the result of a stalemate between long-haul shippers, railroads, and others – and the compromise was an independent bureaucracy. As we saw with Dodd-Frank's Section 716, a lack of stalemate reduces the power of agencies to make decisions based on "state of the art" knowledge in a technical domain.

The Rules of the Game

A more disturbing situation occurs when large parts of society draw what we think is exactly the wrong conclusion – that "experts" are the problem and that the less we support them, listen to them, or defer to them, the better off society will be. But North's views still apply: economic development requires a level playing field in the form of contract enforcement and transparency in property rights. We fail to imagine how majority-rule politicians with short-term election goals can supply these requirements.

Political opposition to Dodd-Frank rulemaking is an example of the kind of political response that can diminish the confidence of economic actors in the stability of the rules. Over and over again in American history, financial, commercial, and industrial interests have all at one time or another acknowledged that implementing any of a wide range of stable regulatory regimes is better than the uncertainty of not knowing. If anti-regulatory forces have their way in the long run, hiring, manufacturing, and inventory decisions will be negatively affected. This in turn will affect the value of land in different regions and how different firms raise capital. It will increase some share prices and decrease others.

All of the planning that would result from a confident long-distance time horizon would be mitigated by the uncertain political factors that inevitably surround majority-rule coalition formation in democratic legislatures – including the simple fact that (in general) every possible outcome can be replaced by a different coalition wanting something else. Under a new political regime, businesses may find that certain land purchases, certain technological innovations, and certain financial investments are all worth less because of a political coalition that effectively reneged on political assurances from the previous regime. Businesses wisely hedge their bets when they bet on legislative commitment to a particular regime of property rights and contract enforcement.

If professionalized bureaucracies were just as volatile as legislative politics, then there would be no reason to write this book. However, there are good reasons to think that decision making is different in professionalized bureaucracies than in political institutions. Most decisions are not subject to majority-rule instability. Elections change the bureaucrat's environment, but with an impact that is muted by layers of hierarchy and rules that go back to the Progressive Era. Lobbyists can be a forceful presence in a bureaucracy, but bureaucrats do not solicit, accept, or need campaign contributions. Experts from regulated business have experts, but effective bureaucracies have their own experts and a reputation that leverages that expertise (Carpenter, 2001, 2010).

This does not mean that bureaucratic decision making is untouched by the politics of legislatures and politicized members of the executive branch. But it does mean that bureaucratic decisions are often different than they would be if made on the floor of Congress or in a presidential cabinet meeting, for instance. And the differences are not biased so much toward business, as toward a stability that comes from expertise itself. As long as the body of knowledge supporting (say) an EPA rule on greenhouse gases does not change, then businesses can make long-run plans based on a rule regime that is as stable as the science itself.

"Above Politics"

Effective regulators are not, of course, "above politics." But they do use the image of being "above politics" to play the political hand they are dealt. Although it is ironic that being "above politics" increases their political effectiveness, the goal of professionals engaged in bureaucratic politics is to minimize the extent to which they are at the mercy of changing and unstable political demands from elected officials. Playing the "above politics" card can give them room to commit to regulatory policies that are at least stable.

Might we see a reassertion of bureaucratic independence in the United States, of the sort exercised over the decades after the 1940s? The forces that protect bureaucratic independence are still in place, as represented by the Dodd-Frank legislation, in which the necessity of legislating was blocked by conflict over what to legislate. Yet professionalized bureaucracies, even when given formal rulemaking authority, may be punished by budgetary limitations and challenges to authority, as when Congress attempted to deny EPA the power to regulate climate change gases.

What is the alternative? The alternative is government by politicians alone – politicians who have at every opportunity shown themselves to be responsive to powerful electoral forces. The prospects of monetary policy making by legislative committee, or regulation of credit default swaps by the partisan process in Congress, illustrate the dangers of trying to imagine a world without a professionalized bureaucracy.

And if we are to have bureaucracies, it is no use running endless pogroms against them. The bad effects of the politicization of financial regulation are still evident – in the absence of many potential but worried (especially younger) investors from the stock market, in the long-term damage done to many families by the chaos surrounding backlogged mortgage foreclosures, in the simmering resentment toward executive compensation excesses. Fundamentally, at risk are the very concerns of North: clarity of property rights and transparency of contract enforcement. These can never be guaranteed by a political system with politicians so profoundly beholden to substantial economic interests with a taste for risky bets and a preference for a safety net. Credible commitment requires professionalized bureaucracies with enough resources and respect to get their job done.

Works Cited

Acharya, V. V., Cooley, T. F., Richardson, M. P., & Walter, I. (Eds.). (2010). *Regulating Wall Street: The Dodd-Frank Act and the New Architecture of Global Finance*. New York: Wiley.

Ackerman, B. (1981). *Clean Coal/Dirty Air: Or How the Clean Air Act Became a Multibillion-Dollar Bail-Out for High-Sulfur Coal Producers*. New Haven, CT: Yale University Press.

Activists Urge Prosecution in Russian Prison Death. (2010, April 22, 2010). *Reuters*. Retrieved from www.reuters.com/article/2010/04/22/russia-magnitsky-idUSLDE63 LoZD20100422

Adams, J. R. (1989). *The Big Fix: Inside the S&L Scandal: How an Unholy Alliance of Politics and Money Destroyed America's Banking System*. New York: Wiley.

Akerlof, G. A. (1970). The Market for "Lemons": Quality Uncertainty and the Market Mechanism. *Quarterly Journal of Economics*, 84(3), 488–500.

Akerlof, G. A. (1982). Labor Contracts as Partial Gift Exchange. *Quarterly Journal of Economics*, 97(4), 543–569.

Aldrick, P. (2008, April 4, 2008). Exposing Russia's Corporate "Corruption." *The Telegraph*. Retrieved from www.telegraph.co.uk/finance/markets/2787471/Exposing-Russias-corporate-corruption.html

Allen, F. L. (1931). *Only Yesterday: An Informal History of the 1920s*. New York: Harper & Row.

Appelbaum, B. (2009, March 11). Citi's Long History of Overreach, then Rescue. *Washington Post*, p. D1. Retrieved from www.washingtonpost.com/wp-dyn/content/article/2009/03/10/AR2009031003391_pf.html

Appelbaum, B., & McGinty, J. C. (2011, March 31). The Fed's Crisis Lending: A Billion Here, a Thousand There. *New York Times*, p. B1. Retrieved from www.nytimes.com/2011/04/01/business/economy/01fed.html

Appelbaum, B., & Nakashima, E. (2008, November 23). Banking Regulator Played Advocate over Enforcer. *Washington Post*, p. A1. Retrieved from www.washington post.com/wp-dyn/content/article/2008/11/22/AR2008112202213.html?sid=ST2008 122202386

Ariely, D. (2012). *The (Honest) Truth about Dishonesty: How We Lie to Everyone – Especially Ourselves*. New York: Harper.

Arnold, R. D. (1979). *Congress and the Bureaucracy*. New Haven, CT: Yale University Press.

Arrow, K. J. (1963). *Social Choice and Individual Values* (2d ed.). New York: Wiley.

Arrow, K. J., & Debreu, G. (1954). Existence of an Equilibrium for a Competitive Economy. *Econometrica*, 22(3), 265–290.

ASA & Associates. (2012). A Brief Report on Telecom Sector in India. New Delhi, India.

Axelrod, R. (1984). *The Evolution of Cooperation*. New York: Basic Books.

Baker, G., Gibbons, R., & Murphy, K. J. (1994). Subjective Performance Measures in Optimal Incentive Contracts. *Quarterly Journal of Economics*, 109(4), 1125–1156.

Bar-Isaac, H., & Hörner, J. (2014). Specialized Careers. *Journal of Economics & Management Strategy*, 23(3), 601–627.

Barro, R. J., & Gordon, D. B. (1983a). A Positive Theory of Monetary Policy in a Natural Rate Model. *Journal of Political Economy*, 91(4), 589–610.

Barro, R. J., & Gordon, D. B. (1983b). Rules, Discretion and Reputation in a Model of Monetary Policy. *Journal of Monetary Economics*, 12(1), 101–121.

Barry, J. M. (1989). *The Ambition and the Power*. New York: Viking.

Bawn, K. (1995). Political Control versus Expertise: Congressional Choices about Administrative Procedures. *American Political Science Review*, 89(01), 62–73.

Beck, S. (2014). Going after Goldman: A Veteran SEC Lawyer Urged the Agency to be More Aggressive in its Abacus Probe. *American Lawyer*, 36(5), 17.

Beckner, S. K. (1996). *Back from the Brink: The Greenspan Years*. New York: Wiley.

Bendor, J., Glazer, A., & Hammond, T. H. (2001). Theories of Delegation. *Annual Review of Political Science*, 4(1), 235–269.

Benen, S. (2011). Top White House Aides Welcome Confrontation. Retrieved from www.washingtonmonthly.com/political-animal/2011_08/top_white_house_aides_welcome031548.php

Berkshire Hathaway Inc. (2002). 2002 Annual Report of Berkshire Hathaway, Inc. Omaha, NE.

Bernanke, B. S. (1983). Nonmonetary Effects of the Financial Crisis in the Propagation of the Great Depression. *American Economic Review*, 73(3), 257–276.

Bernanke, B. S. (2012). Some Reflections on the Crisis and the Policy Response. A Speech at the Russell Sage Foundation and the Century Foundation Conference on "Rethinking Finance," New York, April 13. Washington, DC: Retrieved from www.federalreserve.gov/newsevents/speech/bernanke20120413a.htm

Bernheim, B. D., & Whinston, M. D. (1986). Common Agency. *Econometrica*, 54(4), 923–942.

Bernstein, J. (2014). Inside the New York Fed: Secret Recordings and a Culture Clash. Retrieved from www.propublica.org/article/carmen-segarras-secret-recordings-from-inside-new-york-fed

Bernstein, M. H. (1955). *Regulating Business by Independent Commission*. Princeton, NJ: Princeton University Press.

Bertelli, A. M. (2012). *The Political Economy of Public Sector Governance*. New York: Cambridge University Press.

Bertelli, A. M., & Whitford, A. B. (2009). Perceiving Credible Commitments: How Independent Regulators Shape Elite Perceptions of Regulatory Quality. *British Journal of Political Science*, 39(3), 517–537.

Biederman, P. (1982). *The U.S. Airline Industry: End of an Era.* New York: Praeger.

Black, W. K. (2005). *The Best Way to Rob a Bank Is to Own One: How Corporate Executives and Politicians Looted the S&L Industry.* Austin: University of Texas Press.

Blasi, J., Conte, M., & Kruse, D. (1996). Employee Stock Ownership and Corporate Performance among Public Companies. *Industrial and Labor Relations Review*, 60(1), 60–79.

Blau, P. M. (1963). *The Dynamics of Bureaucracy: A Study of Interpersonal Relations in Two Government Agencies.* Chicago: University of Chicago Press.

Borrus, A. (2005, February 13). Dr. No Digs in at SEC. *BusinessWeek*, 3920, 76–79.

Bottom, W. P., Holloway, J., Miller, G. J., Mislin, A., & Whitford, A. (2006). Building a Pathway to Cooperation: Negotiation and Social Exchange between Principal and Agent. *Administrative Science Quarterly*, 51(1), 29–58.

Bowen, M. (2008). *Censoring Science: Inside the Political Attack on Dr. James Hansen and the Truth of Global Warming.* New York: Dutton.

Box, G. E. P., & Draper, N. A. (1987). *Empirical Model-Building and Response Surfaces.* New York: Wiley.

Brams, S. J., & Taylor, A. D. (1996). *Fair Division: From Cake-Cutting to Dispute Resolution.* Cambridge: Cambridge University Press.

Brehm, J., & Gates, S. (1999). *Working, Shirking, and Sabotage: Bureaucratic Response to a Democratic Public.* Ann Arbor: University of Michigan Press.

Bridewell, D. A. (1938). *The Federal Home Loan Bank Board and its Agencies.* Washington, DC: Federal Home Loan Bank Board.

Brown, A. E. (1987). *The Politics of Airline Deregulation.* Knoxville: University of Tennessee Press.

Brown, H. (2007, June 14). Russia Goes after Hermitage Client. *Forbes.*

Brown, J. S., & Duguid, P. (1991). Organizational Learning and Communities-of-Practice: Toward a Unified View of Working, Learning, and Innovation. *Organization Science*, 2(1), 40–57.

Broz, J. L. (1997). *The International Origins of the Federal Reserve System.* Ithaca, NY: Cornell University Press.

Burger, E. S., & Holland, M. (2008). Law as Politics: The Russian Procuracy and Its Investigative Committee. *Columbia Journal of East European Law*, 2(2), 143–194.

Burnham, W., Maggs, P. B., & Danilenko, G. M. (2012). *Law and Legal System of the Russian Federation* (5th ed.). New York: Juris Publishing.

Byrne, J. A. (1998, July 6). How Al Dunlap Self-Destructed. *BusinessWeek*, 3585, 58–65.

Cahill, T. (2010, February 17). Firestone Flees Moscow "Mafia" Police as Browder Affair Widens. Bloomberg.com. Retrieved from www.bloomberg.com/apps/news?pid=newsarchive&sid=a75BfbH3Vyhw

Callahan, R. E. (1962). *Education and the Cult of Efficiency: A Study of the Social Forces that Have Shaped the Administration of the Public Schools.* Chicago: University of Chicago Press.

Callow, A. B. (1966). *The Tweed Ring.* New York: Oxford University Press.

Calomiris, C. W., & White, E. N. (1994). The Origins of Federal Deposit Insurance. In C. Goldin & G. D. Libecap (Eds.), *The Regulated Economy: A Historical Approach to Political Economy* (pp. 145–188). Chicago: University of Chicago Press.

Carney, J. (2014). Ratings Game behind Big Banks' Derivatives Play. *Wall Street Journal.* Retrieved from www.wsj.com/articles/ratings-game-behind-big-banks-derivatives-play-heard-on-the-street-1418417119

Carney, T. P. (2014, December 16). The True Story of the Financial Deregulation Provision in the Cromnibus. *Washington Examiner*. Retrieved from www.washingtonexaminer.com/the-true-story-of-the-financial-deregulation-provision-in-the-cromnibus/article/2557482

Caro, R. A. (1974). *The Power Broker: Robert Moses and the Fall of New York*. New York: Knopf.

Carpenter, D. P. (1996). Adaptive Signal Processing, Hierarchy, and Budgetary Control in Federal Regulation. *American Political Science Review*, 90(2), 283–302.

Carpenter, D. P. (2001). *The Forging of Bureaucratic Autonomy: Reputations, Networks, and Policy Innovation in Executive Agencies, 1862–1928*. Princeton, NJ: Princeton University Press.

Carpenter, D. P. (2010). *Reputation and Power: Organizational Image and Pharmaceutical Regulation at the FDA*. Princeton, NJ: Princeton University Press.

Carpenter, Daniel C. (2011, December 14). Free the F.D.A. New York Times, p. A35.

Carter, D. T. (1995). *The Politics of Rage: George Wallace, the Origins of the New Conservatism, and the Transformation of American Politics*. New York: Simon & Schuster.

Cassidy, J. (2009). *How Markets Fail: The Logic of Economic Calamities*. New York: Farrar, Straus, and Giroux.

Chandrasekaran, R. (2006). *Imperial Life in the Emerald City: Inside Iraq's Green Zone*. New York: Alfred A. Knopf.

Chang, K. H. (2003). *Appointing Central Bankers: The Politics of Monetary Policy in the United States and the European Monetary Union*. New York: Cambridge University Press.

Chase, W. G., & Simon, H. A. (1973). Perception in Chess. *Cognitive Psychology*, 4(1), 55–81.

Chinn, M. D., & Frieden, J. A. (2011). *Lost Decades: The Making of America's Debt Crisis and the Long Recovery*. New York: W. W. Norton.

Chubb, J. E., & Moe, T. M. (1988). Politics, Markets, and the Organization of Schools. *American Political Science Review*, 82(4), 1066–1087.

Chwe, M. S.-Y. (1998). Culture, Circles, and Commercials: Publicity, Common Knowledge, and Social Coordination. *Rationality and Society*, 10(1), 47–75.

Chwe, M. S.-Y. (2001). *Rational Ritual: Culture, Coordination, and Common Knowledge*. Princeton, NJ: Princeton University Press.

Clarke, E. H. (1971). Multipart Pricing of Public Goods. *Public Choice*, 11(1), 17–33.

Clarke, R. L. (1987). The Limits of Bank Regulation. *American Review of Banking Law*, 6, 227–233.

Clikeman, P. M. (2009). *Called to Account: Fourteen Financial Frauds that Shaped the American Accounting Profession*. New York: Routledge.

CNN. (2005). Lawmakers Scramble to Save Bases: Pentagon Recommends Closing 30-Plus Major Facilities. Retrieved from www.cnn.com/2005/POLITICS/05/13/base.closings/

Coase, R. H. (1937). The Nature of the Firm. *Economica*, 4(16), 386–405.

Collins, H., & Evans, R. (2007). *Rethinking Expertise*. Chicago: University of Chicago Press.

Comptroller and Auditor General of India. (2010). *Performance Audit Report on the Issue of Licences and Allocation of 2G Spectrum by the Department of Telecommunications Ministry of Communications and Information Technology*. Comptroller and Auditor General of India.

Conti-Brown, P. (2011). The Accidental History of the Federal Securities and Banking Laws: A Review of Michael Perino's *Hellhound of Wall Street: How Ferdinand Pecora's Investigation of the Great Crash Forever Changed American Finance*. *Securities Regulation Law Journal*, 39(1), 45–53.

Cooke, W. N., & Gautschi, F. H., III. (1982). Political Bias in NLRB Unfair Labor Practice Decisions. *Industrial and Labor Relations Review*, 35(4), 539–549.

Cooke, W. N., Mishra, A. K., Spreitzer, G. M., & Tschirhart, M. (1995). The Determinants of NLRB Decision-Making Revisited. *Industrial and Labor Relations Review*, 48(2), 237–257.

Cooper, R., & Ross, T. W. (1985). Product Warranties and Double Moral Hazard. *RAND Journal of Economics*, 16(1), 103–113.

Crotty, J. (2009). *The Bonus-Driven "Rainmaker" Financial Firm: How These Firms Enrich Top Employees, Destroy Shareholder Value and Create Systemic Financial Instability*. PERI Working Paper Series. Political Economy Research Institute, University of Massachusetts Amherst. Retrieved from www.peri.umass.edu/fileadmin/pdf/working_papers/working_papers_201-250/WP209.pdf

Crotty, J. (2012). How Bonus-Driven "Rainmaker" Financial Firms Enrich Top Employees, Destroy Shareholder Value, and Create Systemic Financial Instability. In B. Z. Cynamon, S. Fazzari, M. Setterfield, & R. Kuttner (Eds.), *After the Great Recession: The Struggle for Economic Recovery and Growth* (pp. 104–126). New York: Cambridge University Press.

Cuomo, A. (2009). *No Rhyme or Reason: The 'Heads I Win, Tails You Lose' Bank Bonus Culture*. Albany: Office of the Attorney General, State of New York.

Dahlberg, J. S. (1966). *The New York Bureau of Municipal Research: Pioneer in Government Administration*. New York: New York University Press.

Dal Bó, E. (2008). Regulatory Capture: A Review. *Oxford Review of Economic Policy*, 22(2), 203–225.

Dam, K. W. (2009–2010). The Subprime Crisis and Financial Regulation: International and Comparative Perspectives. *Chicago Journal of International Law*, 10, 581–638.

Dancing with the Bear. (2007, February 3). *The Economist*, 382, 63–64.

Davies, G. (2014). Shackling the Fed with the Taylor Rule. Retrieved from blogs.ft.com/gavyndavies/2014/07/13/shackling-the-fed-with-the-taylor-rule/?

Debreu, G. (1959). *Theory of Value; An Axiomatic Analysis of Economic Equilibrium*. New Haven, CT: Yale University Press.

De Groot, A. D. (1965). *Thought and Choice in Chess*. New York: Basic Books.

De Groot, H. L. F., Linders, G.-J., Rietveld, P., & Subramanian, U. (2004). The Institutional Determinants of Bilateral Trade Patterns. *Kyklos*, 57(1), 103–123.

Dempsey, P. S., & Goetz, A. R. (1992). *Airline Deregulation and Laissez-Faire Mythology*. Westport, CT: Quorum Books.

Demski, J. S., & Sappington, D. E. M. (1991). Resolving Double Moral Hazard Problems with Buyout Agreements. *RAND Journal of Economics*, 22(2), 232–240.

Dennis, B. (2009, September 16). Ferdinand Pecora Ushered In Wall Street Regulation after 1929 Crash. *The Washington Post*. Retrieved from www.washingtonpost.com/wp-dyn/content/article/2009/09/15/AR2009091501936.html

Dennis, B. (2010, July 16). Congress Passes Financial Reform Bill. *Washington Post*, p. A01. Retrieved from www.washingtonpost.com/wp-dyn/content/article/2010/07/15/AR2010071500464.html

Derthick, M., & Quirk, P. J. (1985). *The Politics of Deregulation*. Washington, DC: Brookings Institution.

DiIulio, J. D., Jr. (1994). Principled Agents: The Cultural Bases of Behavior in a Federal Government Bureaucracy. *Journal of Public Administration Research and Theory*, 4(3), 277–318.

DiMaggio, P. J., & Powell, W. W. (1983). The Iron Cage Revisited: Institutional Isomorphism and Collective Rationality in Organizational Fields. *American Sociological Review*, 48(2), 147–160.

Dixit, A. K., & Nalebuff, B. (1991). *Thinking Strategically: The Competitive Edge in Business, Politics, and Everyday Life*. New York: W. W. Norton.

Djankov, S., Glaeser, E., La Porta, R., Lopez-de-Silanes, F., & Shleifer, A. (2003). The New Comparative Economics. *Journal of Comparative Economics*, 31(4), 595–619.

Dodd, L. C., & Schott, R. L. (1979). *Congress and the Administrative State*. New York: Wiley.

Donelson, D. C., & Zaring, D. (2010–2011). Requiem for a Regulator: The Office of Thrift Supervision's Performance during the Financial Crisis. *North Carolina Law Review*, 89, 1777–1811.

Drutman, L. (2014). How Did Swaps Regulation Get into the CRomnibus? Ask this Army of Lobbyists. Retrieved from www.vox.com/2014/12/17/7405307/swaps-lobbying

Dunlap, A. J., & Andelman, B. (1996). *Mean Business: How I Save Bad Companies and Make Good Companies Great*. New York: Fireside.

Dybvig, P. H., & Lutz, N. A. (1993). Warranties, Durability, and Maintenance: Two-Sided Moral Hazard in a Continuous-Time Model. *Review of Economic Studies*, 60(3), 575–597.

Eggertsson, T. (1990). *Economic Behavior and Institutions*. New York: Cambridge University Press.

Eisner, M. A., & Meier, K. J. (1990). Presidential Control versus Bureaucratic Power: Explaining the Reagan Revolution in Antitrust. *American Journal of Political Science*, 34(1), 269–287.

Eldridge, D. (2014). Do-Nothing Congress' Rewrites Legacy with "Cromnibus." Retrieved from blogs.rollcall.com/218/do-nothing-congress-not-so-fast/?dcz=

Elster, J. (1983). *Sour Grapes: Studies in the Subversion of Rationality*. New York: Cambridge University Press.

An Enemy of the People. (2006, March 25). *The Economist*, 378, 70.

Engel, K. C., & McCoy, P. A. (2011). *The Subprime Virus: Reckless Credit, Regulatory Failure, and Next Steps*. New York: Oxford University Press.

Epstein, D., & O'Halloran, S. (1999). *Delegating Powers: A Transaction Cost Politics Approach to Policy Making under Separate Powers*. New York: Cambridge University Press.

Estache, A., & Wren-Lewis, L. (2009). Toward a Theory of Regulation for Developing Countries: Following Jean-Jacques Laffont's Lead. *Journal of Economic Literature*, 47(3), 729–770.

Eswaran, M., & Kotwal, A. (1984). The Moral Hazard of Budget-Breaking. *RAND Journal of Economics*, 15(4), 578–581.

Falaschetti, D. (2002). Golden Parachutes: Credible Commitments or Evidence of Shirking? *Journal of Corporate Finance*, 8(2), 159–178.

Falaschetti, D. (2009). *Democratic Governance and Economic Performance: How Accountability Can Go Too Far in Politics, Law, and Business*. New York: Springer.

Fass, A. (2003, July 7). One Year Later, The Impact of Sarbanes-Oxley. *Forbes.*

Feaster, S. W. (2002, July 21). The Incredibly Shrinking Stock Market. *New York Times,* Section 4, p. 14.

Fehr, E., & Falk, A. (1999). Wage Rigidity in a Competitive Incomplete Contract Market. *Journal of Political Economy,* 107(1), 106–134.

Fein, M. L. (2013). *The Shadow Banking Charade.* Fein Law Offices. Retrieved from papers.ssrn.com/sol3/papers.cfm?abstract_id=2218812

Fenno, R. F. (1973). *Congressmen in Committees.* Boston: Little, Brown.

Ferejohn, J., & Shipan, C. (1990). Congressional Influence on Bureaucracy. *Journal of Law, Economics, & Organization,* 6, 1–20.

Finer, H. (1941). Administrative Responsibility in Democratic Government. *Public Administration Review,* 1(4), 335–350.

Fisher, E. M. (1950). Changing Institutional Patterns of Mortgage Lending. *Journal of Finance,* 5(4), 307–315.

Fisk, C. L., & Malamud, D. C. (2009). The NLRB in Administrative Law Exile: Problems with Its Structure and Function and Suggestions for Reform. *Duke Law Journal,* 58, 2013–2085.

Flynn, J. (2000a). "Expertness for What?" The Gould Years at the NLRB and the Irrepressible Myth of the "Independent" Agency. *Administrative Law Review,* 52(2), 465–545.

Flynn, J. (2000b). A Quiet Revolution at the Labor Board: The Transformation of the NLRB. *Ohio State Law Journal,* 61, 1361–1455.

Fogelson, R. M. (1977). *Big City Police: An Urban Institute Study.* Cambridge, MA: Harvard University Press.

Fournier, V. (1999). The Appeal to "Professionalism" as a Disciplinary Mechanism. *Sociological Review,* 47(2), 280–307.

Frankel, M. S. (1989). Professional Codes: Why, How, and with What Impact? *Journal of Business Ethics,* 8(2–3), 109–115.

Frant, H. (1993). Rules and Governance in the Public Sector: The Case of Civil Service. *American Journal of Political Science,* 37(4), 990–1007.

Franzese, R. J. (1999). Partially Independent Central Banks, Politically Responsive Governments, and Inflation. *American Journal of Political Science,* 43(3), 681–706.

Freidson, E. (2001). *Professionalism, the Third Logic: On the Practice of Knowledge.* Chicago: University of Chicago Press.

Friedman, J. W. (1971). A Non-Cooperative Equilibrium for Supergames. *Review of Economic Studies,* 38(1), 1–12.

Friedrich, C. J. (1940). Public Policy and the Nature of Administrative Responsibility. In C. J. Friedrich & E. S. Mason (Eds.), Public Policy: A Yearbook of the Graduate School of Public Administration, Harvard University, 1940 (pp. 3–24). Cambridge, MA: Harvard University Press.

Friedrich, C. J. (1958). Authority, Reason, and Discretion. In C. J. Friedrich (Ed.), *Authority* (pp. 28–48). Cambridge, MA: Harvard University Press.

Frohlich, N., & Oppenheimer, J. (1978). *Modern Political Economy.* New York: Prentice-Hall.

Gailmard, S. (2010). Politics, Principal–Agent Problems, and Public Service Motivation. *International Public Management Journal,* 13(1), 35–45.

Gailmard, S., & Patty, J. W. (2007). Slackers and Zealots: Civil Service, Policy Discretion, and Bureaucratic Expertise. *American Journal of Political Science,* 51(4), 873–889.

Gailmard, S., & Patty, J. W. (2013). *Learning while Governing: Expertise and Accountability in the Executive Branch.* Chicago: University of Chicago Press.

Garrett, B. L. (2014). *Too Big to Jail: How Prosecutors Compromise with Corporations.* Cambridge, MA: Harvard University Press.

Garten, J. (2005, June 20). The Dangerous Silence of Business Leaders. *Business Week,* 28.

Gasparino, C. (2009). *The Sellout: How Three Decades of Wall Street Greed and Government Mismanagement Destroyed the Global Financial System.* New York: Harper-Business.

Gaus, J. M. (1936). In J. M. Gaus, L. D. White, & M. E. Dimock (Eds.), *The Responsibility of Public Administration* (pp. 26–44). Chicago: University of Chicago Press.

Gazley, B. (2014). Good Governance Practices in Professional Associations for Public Employees: Evidence of a Public Service Ethos? *Public Administration Review,* 74(6), 736–747.

Geithner, T., & Summers, L. (2009, June 15). The Case for Financial Regulatory Reform. *Washington Post.* Retrieved from www.washingtonpost.com/wp-dyn/content/article/2009/06/14/AR2009061402443.html

Gibbard, A. (1973). Manipulation of Voting Schemes: A General Result. *Econometrica,* 41(4), 587–601.

Gilardi, F. (2008). *Delegation in the Regulatory State: Independent Regulatory Agencies in Western Europe.* Northampton, MA: Edward Elgar.

Gjerstad, S., & Smith, V. L. (2009). Monetary Policy, Credit Extension, and Housing Bubbles: 2008 and 1929. *Critical Review,* 21(2), 269–300.

Globerman, S., & Shapiro, D. (2003). Governance Infrastructure and U.S. Foreign Direct Investment. *Journal of International Business Studies,* 34(1), 19–39.

Goldberg, M. J. (2002). Inside Baseball at the NLRB: Chairman Gould and His Critics. *Stanford Law Review,* 55(3), 1045–1066.

Goldin, M. (Writer). (1990). Other People's Money [DVD]. In M. Goldin (Producer), *Frontline.* WGBH.

Goldman, M. I. (2004). Putin and the Oligarchs. *Foreign Affairs,* 83(6), 33–44.

Goldstein, J. (1989). The Impact of Ideas on Trade Policy: The Origins of U.S. Agricultural and Manufacturing Policies. *International Organization,* 43(01), 31–71.

Golosinski, D., & West, D. S. (1995). Double Moral Hazard and Shopping Center Similarity in Canada. *Journal of Law, Economics, & Organization,* 11(2), 456–478.

Gonzalez, N. (2008, June 3). Stafford Teachers Band Together to Protest School Board Decisions on Wages. *Fredericksburg Free-Lance Star.* Retrieved from fredericksburg.com/News/FLS/2008/062008/06032008/383904

Gordon, R. A. (1974). *Economic Instability and Growth: The American Record.* New York: Harper & Row.

Gould, W. B., IV. (2000). *Labored Relations: Law, Politics, and the NLRB, A Memoir.* Cambridge, MA: MIT Press.

Gould, W. B., IV. (2005). The NLRB at Age 70: Some Reflections on the Clinton Board and the Bush II Aftermath. *Berkeley Journal of Employment and Labor Law,* 26(September), 309–318.

Gouldner, A. W. (1954). *Patterns of Industrial Bureaucracy.* Glencoe, IL: Free Press.

Grady, P. (1948). The Increasing Emphasis on Accounting as a Social Force. *Accounting Review,* 23(3), 266–275.

Greenwald, B. C., & Stiglitz, J. E. (1986). Externalities in Economies with Imperfect Information and Incomplete Markets. *Quarterly Journal of Economics*, 101(2), 229–264.

Greider, W. (1989). *Secrets of the Temple: How the Federal Reserve Runs the Country*. New York: Simon & Schuster.

Gross, E. (1967). When Occupations Meet: Professions in Trouble. *Hospital Administration*, 12(3), 40–59.

Grossman, S., & Stiglitz, J. E. (1982). On the Impossibility of Informationally Efficient Markets: Reply. *American Economic Review*, 72(4), 875.

Groves, T., & Loeb, M. (1975). Incentives and Public Inputs. *Journal of Political Economy*, 4(3), 211–226.

Haber, S. (1964). *Efficiency and Uplift: Scientific Management in the Progressive Era, 1890–1920*. Chicago: University of Chicago Press.

Hahn, R. W., & Hester, G. L. (1989). Marketable Permits: Lessons for Theory and Practice. *Ecology Law Quarterly*, 16, 361.

Halac, M. (2012). Relational Contracts and the Value of Relationships. *American Economic Review*, 102(2), 750–779.

Halberstam, D. (1986). *The Reckoning*. New York: Morrow.

Hall, R. E., & Jones, C. I. (1999). Why Do Some Countries Produce So Much More Output per Worker than Others? *Quarterly Journal of Economics*, 114(1), 83–116.

Hall, R. H. (1967). Some Organizational Considerations in the Professional-Organizational Relationship. *Administrative Science Quarterly*, 12(3), 461–478.

Hall, R. H. (1968). Professionalization and Bureaucratization. *American Sociological Review*, 33(1), 92–104.

Hamilton, D. (2007, July 17). Hermitage Fund Still Invests in Russia. *Reuters*. Retrieved from uk.reuters.com/article/2007/07/17/funds-hermitage-idUKNOA 62580220070717

Hammond, T. H. (1986). Agenda Control, Organizational Structure, and Bureaucratic Politics. *American Journal of Political Science*, 30(2), 379–420.

Hammond, T. H., & Knott, J. H. (1988). The Deregulatory Snowball: Explaining Deregulation in the Financial Industry. *Journal of Politics*, 50(1), 3–30.

Hammond, T. H., & Knott, J. H. (1996). Who Controls the Bureaucracy? Presidential Power, Congressional Dominance, Legal Constraints, and Bureaucratic Autonomy in a Model of Multi-Institutional Policy-Making. *Journal of Law, Economics, and Organization*, 12(1), 119–166.

Hammond, T. H., & Miller, G. J. (1985). A Social Choice Perspective on Expertise and Authority in Bureaucracy. *American Journal of Political Science*, 29(1), 1–28.

Hammond, T. H., & Miller, G. J. (1987). The Core of the Constitution. *American Political Science Review*, 81(4), 1155–1174.

Hardin, R. (1971). Collective Action as an Agreeable n-Prisoners' Dilemma. *Behavioral Science*, 16(5), 472–481.

Harris, M. (1989). *Our Kind: Who We Are, Where We Came From, Where We Are Going*. New York: Harper & Row.

Harris, M., & Raviv, A. (1979). Optimal Incentive Contracts with Imperfect Information. *Journal of Economic Theory*, 20(2), 231–259.

Helling, D. (2014, December 17). U.S. Rep. Kevin Yoder of Kansas Defends Measure Relaxing Banking Rules. *Kansas City Star*. Retrieved from www.kansascity.com/news/government-politics/article4539005.html

Hendley, K. (2006). Assessing the Rule of Law in Russia. *Cardozo Journal of International and Comparative Law*, 14, 347–391.

Herring, E. P. (1938). The Experts on Five Federal Commissions. *American Political Science Review*, 32(1), 86–93.

Hetzel, R. L., & Leach, R. F. (2001). The Treasury-Fed Accord: A New Narrative Account. *Federal Reserve Bank of Richmond Economic Quarterly*, 87(1), 33–55.

Hill, J. (1999). Deconstructing Sunbeam – Contemporary Issues in Corporate Governance. *University of Cincinnati Law Review*, 67(4), 1099–1128.

Hill, P. (2009, December 30). Congress Takes Aim at Fed's Autonomy. *Washington Times*. Retrieved from www.washingtontimes.com/news/2009/dec/30/bernanke-seat-pits-congress-wall-street/?page=all

Hoffmann, S. (2001). *Politics and Banking: Ideas, Public Policy, and the Creation of Financial Institutions*. Baltimore, MD: Johns Hopkins University Press.

Holmström, B. (1979). Moral Hazard and Observability. *Bell Journal of Economics*, 10(1), 74–91.

Holmström, B. (1982). Moral Hazard in Teams. *Bell Journal of Economics*, 13(2), 324–340.

Holmström, B., & Milgrom, P. (1991). Multitask Principal-Agent Analyses: Incentive Contracts, Asset Ownership, and Job Design. *Journal of Law, Economics, & Organization*, 7, 24–52.

Holmström, B., & Milgrom, P. (1994). The Firm as an Incentive System. *American Economic Review*, 84(4), 972–991.

Homans, G. C. (1954). The Cash Posters: A Study of a Group of Working Girls. *American Sociological Review*, 19(6), 724–733.

Hope, C. (2006, March 18). UK Investor Barred by Russia. *The Telegraph*. Retrieved from www.telegraph.co.uk/finance/2934561/UK-investor-barred-by-Russia.html

Hopkins, C., & Brush, S. (2014, December 12). Wall Street's Win on Swaps Rule Shows Washington Resurgence. Bloomberg.com. Retrieved from www.bloomberg.com/news/2014-12-12/wall-street-s-win-on-swaps-rule-shows-resurgence-in-washington.html

Horn, M. J. (1995). *The Political Economy of Public Administration: Institutional Choice in the Public Sector*. New York: Cambridge University Press.

Huntington, S. P. (1952). The Marasmus of the ICC: The Commission, The Railroads, and the Public Interest. *Yale Law Journal*, 61(4), 467–509.

Jain, R. S. (2001). Spectrum Auctions in India: Lessons from Experience. *Telecommunications Policy*, 25(10), 671–688.

Jensen, H. (1997). Credibility of Optimal Monetary Delegation. *American Economic Review*, 87(5), 911–920.

Jensen, M. C., & Meckling, W. H. (1976). Theory of the Firm: Managerial Behavior, Agency Costs, and Ownership Structure. *Journal of Financial Economics*, 3, 305–360.

Jensen, M. C., & Murphy, K. J. (1990a). CEO incentives: It's Not How Much You Pay, but How. *Harvard Business Review*, 68(3), 138–149.

Jensen, M. C., & Murphy, K. J. (1990b). Performance Pay and Top Management Incentives. *Journal of Political Economy*, 98(2), 225–254.

Johnson, S., & Kwak, J. (2010). *13 Bankers: The Wall Street Takeover and the Next Financial Meltdown*. New York: Pantheon.

Kaiser, R. G. (2013). *Act of Congress: How America's Essential Institution Works, and How It Doesn't*. New York: Alfred A. Knopf.

Katzmann, R. A. (1980). *Federal Trade Commission*. In J. Q. Wilson (Ed.), *The Politics of Regulation* (pp. 152–187). New York: Basic Books.

Kaufman, D., Kraay, A., & Zoido-Lobatón, P. (2002). *Governance Matters II: Updated Indicators for 2000–01*. Washington, DC: World Bank.

Kaufman, H. (1960). *The Forest Ranger, A Study in Administrative Behavior*. Baltimore, MD: Johns Hopkins University Press.

Kaufman, H. (1981a). *The Administrative Behavior of Federal Bureau Chiefs*. Washington, DC: Brookings Institution.

Kaufman, H. (1981b). Fear of Bureaucracy: A Raging Pandemic. *Public Administration Review*, 41(1), 1–9.

Keefer, P., & Stasavage, D. (2003). The Limits of Delegation: Veto Players, Central Bank Independence, and the Credibility of Monetary Policy. *American Political Science Review*, 97(3), 407–423.

Kerr, S. (1975). On the Folly of Rewarding A while Hoping for B. *Academy of Management Journal*, 18(4), 769–783.

Khademian, A. M. (1992). *The SEC and Capital Market Regulation: The Politics of Expertise*. Pittsburgh: University of Pittsburgh Press.

Khademian, A. M. (2002). The Securities and Exchange Commission: A Small Regulatory Agency with a Gargantuan Challenge. *Public Administration Review*, 62(5), 515–526.

Khademian, A. M. (2011). The Financial Crisis: A Retrospective. *Public Administration Review*, 71(6), 841–849.

Kilberg, W. J., Schwartz, J., & Chadwick, J. (2009). A Measured Approach: Employment and Labor Law during the George W. Bush Years. *Harvard Journal of Law and Public Policy*, 32, 997–1013.

Kleinfield, N. R. (1991, March 17). He Had Money, Women, an S.&L. Now Don Dixon Has Jail. *New York Times*, p. C7.

Klemperer, P. (2002). What Really Matters in Auction Design. *Journal of Economic Perspectives*, 16(1), 169–189.

Klock, M. S., Mansi, S. A., & Maxwell, W. F. (2005). Does Corporate Governance Matter to Bondholders? *Journal of Financial and Quantitative Analysis*, 40(04), 693–719.

Knez, M., & Simester, D. (2001). Firm-Wide Incentives and Mutual Monitoring at Continental Airlines. *Journal of Labor Economics*, 19(4), 743–772.

Knott, J. H. (1986). The Ambiguous Role of Professionals in Public Policy Making. *Knowledge: Creation, Dissemination, Utilization*, 8(1), 131–153.

Knott, J. H. (2012). The President, Congress, and the Financial Crisis: Ideology and Moral Hazard in Economic Governance. *Presidential Studies Quarterly*, 42(1), 81–100.

Knott, J. H., & Miller, G. J. (1987). *Reforming Bureaucracy: The Politics of Insitutional Choice*. Englewood Cliffs, NJ: Prentice-Hall.

Knott, J. H., & Miller, G. J. (2008). When Ambition Checks Ambition: Bureaucratic Trustees and the Separation of Powers. *American Review of Public Administration*, 38(4), 387–411.

Koch, T. W., & Wall, L. D. (2000). *The Use of Accruals to Manage Reported Earnings: Theory and Evidence*. Federal Reserve Bank of Atlanta Working Paper Series. Federal Reserve Bank of Atlanta.

Kolko, G. (1963). *The Triumph of Conservatism: A Re-Interpretation of American History, 1900–1916*. New York: Free Press of Glencoe.

Konczal, M. (2013, May 18). Sheila Bair: Dodd-Frank Really Did End Tax-payer Bailouts. *Washington Post*. Retrieved from www.washingtonpost.com/blogs/wonkblog/wp/2013/05/18/sheila-bair-dodd-frank-really-did-end-taxpayer-bailouts/

Konrad, R. (2000). IBM and Microsoft: Antitrust Then and Now. *cnet*. Retrieved from news.cnet.com/2100-1001-241565.html

Koremenos, B. (2005). Leadership and Bureaucracy: The Folk Theorem and Real Folks. *Rationality and Society*, 17(1), 35–79.

Kramer, A. E. (2011, July 7). Russians Linked to Jail Death Are Barred from U.S. *New York Times*, p. A7. Retrieved from www.nytimes.com/2011/07/27/world/europe/27russia.html?_r=0

Kramer, R. M. (1969). *Participation of the Poor: Comparative Case Studies in the War on Poverty*. Englewood Cliffs, NJ: Prentice-Hall.

Krause, G. A. (1999). *A Two-Way Street: The Institutional Dynamics of the Modern Administrative State*. Pittsburgh, PA: University of Pittsburgh Press.

Kreps, D. M. (1990). Corporate Culture and Economic Theory. In J. E. Alt & K. A. Shepsle (Eds.), *Perspectives on Positive Political Economy*. New York: Cambridge University Press.

Kreps, D. M. (1996). Corporate Culture and Economic Theory. In P. Buckley, J. Michie, & R. Coase (Eds.), *Firms, Organizations, and Contracts: A Reader in Industrial Organization* (pp. 221–275). New York: Oxford University Press.

Kreps, D. M., & Wilson, R. (1982). Reputation and Imperfect Information. *Journal of Economic Theory*, 27(2), 253–279.

Krugman, P. (2010, January 14). Bankers without a Clue. *New York Times*, p. A27.

Krugman, P. (2014, August 4). Obama's Other Success: Dodd-Frank Financial Reform Is Working. *New York Times*, p. A21. Retrieved from www.nytimes.com/2014/08/04/opinion/paul-krugman-dodd-frank-financial-reform-is-working.html?_r=0

Kwak, J. (2014). Incentives and Ideology. *Harvard Law Review*, 127, 253–258.

Kydland, F. E., & Prescott, E. C. (1977). Rules Rather than Discretion: The Inconsistency of Optimal Plans. *Journal of Political Economy*, 85(3), 473–491.

Labaton, S. (2003, March 14). S.E.C. Chief Says Fixing the Agency Will Take Time. *New York Times*, p. C5. Retrieved from www.nytimes.com/2003/03/14/business/sec-chief-says-fixing-the-agency-will-take-time.html

Laffont, J.-J., & Martimort, D. (2002). *The Theory of Incentives: The Principal-Agent Model*. Princeton, NJ: Princeton University Press.

Laffont, J.-J., & Tirole, J. (1993). *A Theory of Incentives in Procurement and Regulation*. Cambridge, MA: MIT Press.

Laing, J. R. (1998, June 8). Dangerous Games: Did "Chainsaw Al" Manufacture Sunbeam's Earnings Last Year? *Barron's*, 78, 17–19.

Lanoie, P. (1991). Occupational Safety and Health: A Problem of Double or Single Moral Hazard. *Journal of Risk and Insurance*, 58(1), 80–100.

Lapuente, V. (2010). A Tale of Two Cities: Bureaucratisation in Mayor-Council and Council-Manager Municipalities. *Local Government Studies*, 36(6), 739–757.

Law, M. T., & Kim, S. (2005). Specialization and Regulation: The Rise of Professionals and the Emergence of Occupational Licensing Regulation. *Journal of Economic History*, 65(3), 723–756.

Law, M. T., & Tonon, J. M. (2006). The Strange Budgetary Politics of Agricultural Research Earmarks. *Public Budgeting & Finance*, 26(3), 1–21.

Law, M. T., Tonon, J. M., & Miller, G. J. (2008). Earmarked: The Political Economy of Agricultural Research Appropriations. *Applied Economic Perspectives and Policy*, 30(2), 194–213.

Ledeneva, A. V. (2013). *Can Russia Modernise? Sistema, Power Networks, and Informal Governance*. New York: Cambridge University Press.

Leland, H. E. (1979). Quacks, Lemons, and Licensing: A Theory of Minimum Quality Standards. *Journal of Political Economy*, 87(6), 1328–1346.

Levinthal, D. A., & March, J. G. (1993). The Myopia of Learning. *Strategic Management Journal*, 14, 95–112.

Levitin, A. J. (2014). The Politics of Financial Regulation and the Regulation of Financial Politics. *Harvard Law Review*, 127, 1991–2068.

Levitt, A. (2002). *Take on the Street: What Wall St. and Corporate America Don't Want You to Know / What You Can Do to Fight Back*. New York: Knopf Doubleday.

Lewis, D. E. (2003). *Presidents and the Politics of Agency Design: Political Insulation in the United States Government, 1946–1997*. Stanford, CA: Stanford University Press.

Lewis, D. E. (2008). *The Politics of Presidential Appointments: Political Control and Bureaucratic Performance*. Princeton, NJ: Princeton University Press.

Lewis, E. (1980). *Public Entrepreneurship: Toward a Theory of Bureaucratic Political Power: The Organizational Lives of Hyman Rickover, J. Edgar Hoover, and Robert Moses*. Bloomington: Indiana University Press.

Lewis, M. (1989). *Liar's Poker: Rising through the Wreckage on Wall Street*. New York: W. W. Norton.

Lewis, M. (1997, May 25). A Question of Honor. *New York Times Magazine*.

Lewis, M. (2010). *The Big Short: Inside the Doomsday Machine*. New York: W. W. Norton.

Lewis, M. (2014, September 26). The Secret Goldman Sachs Tapes. Bloomberg .com. Retrieved from www.bloombergview.com/articles/2014-09-26/the-secret-goldman-sachs-tapes

Lipton, E., & Protess, B. (2013, May 23). Banks' Lobbyists Help in Drafting Financial Bills. *New York Times*, p. A1. Retrieved from dealbook.nytimes.com/2013/05/23/banks-lobbyists-help-in-drafting-financial-bills/?_r=0

Litwak, E. (1961). Models of Bureaucracy Which Permit Conflict. *American Journal of Sociology*, 67(2), 177–184.

Lohmann, S. (1992). Optimal Commitment in Monetary Policy: Credibility versus Flexibility. *American Economic Review*, 82(1), 273–286.

LSE Warns Russia on Investor Ban. (2006, April 27). *BBC News*. Retrieved from news .bbc.co.uk/2/hi/business/4950374.stm

Lubove, R. (1965). *The Professional Altruist: The Emergence of Social Work as a Career, 1880–1930*. Cambridge, MA: Harvard University Press.

Lucia, J. L. (1983). Allan Sproul and the Treasury-Federal Reserve Accord, 1951. *History of Political Economy*, 15(1), 106–121.

Madison, J. (1788). *Federalist No. 51*. New York: Signet Classics.

Madison, L. (2011, June 26). Bachmann Says Obama Upped Gov't Limos by 73%. *CBSNews.com*. Retrieved from www.cbsnews.com/news/bachmann-says-obama-upped-govt-limos-by-73/

Majone, G. (1997). From the Positive to the Regulatory State: Causes and Consequences of Changes in the Mode of Governance. *Journal of Public Policy*, 17(2), 139–167.

Mann, D. P., & Wissink, J. P. (1988). Money-Back Contracts with Double Moral Hazard. *RAND Journal of Economics*, 19(2), 285–292.

Marschak, J. (1955). Elements for a Theory of Teams. *Management Science*, 1(2), 127–137.

Mason, D. L. (2004). *From Buildings and Loans to Bail-Outs: A History of the American Savings and Loan Industry, 1831–1995*. New York: Cambridge University Press.

Matthews, O. (2009, October 16). Hermitage and Russia's Vulture Capitalism. *Newsweek*.

Maxwell, R. S. (1956). *La Follette and the Rise of the Progressives in Wisconsin*. Madison: State Historical Society of Wisconsin.

Mayer, K. R. (1995). Electoral Cycles in Federal Government Prime Contract Awards: State-Level Evidence from the 1988 and 1992 Presidential Elections. *American Journal of Political Science*, 39(1), 162–185.

McCarty, N. (2012). The Politics of the Pop: The U.S. Response to the Financial Crisis and the Great Recession. In N. Bermeo & J. Pontusson (Eds.), *Coping with Crisis: Government Reactions to the Great Recession* (pp. 201–232). New York: Russell Sage Foundation.

McCarty, N., Poole, K. T., & Rosenthal, H. (2013). *Political Bubbles: Financial Crises and the Failure of American Democracy*. Princeton, NJ: Princeton University Press.

McCraw, T. K. (1975). Regulation in America: A Review Article. *Business History Review*, 49(2), 159–183.

McCraw, T. K. (1984). *Prophets of Regulation: Charles Francis Adams, Louis D. Brandeis, James M. Landis, Alfred E. Kahn*. Cambridge, MA: Belknap Press of Harvard University Press.

McCubbins, M. D., Noll, R. G., & Weingast, B. R. (1987). Administrative Procedures as Instruments of Political Control. *Journal of Law, Economics, and Organization*, 3(2), 243–277.

McCubbins, M. D., & Schwartz, T. (1984). Congressional Oversight Overlooked: Police Patrols versus Fire Alarms. *American Journal of Political Science*, 28(1), 165–179.

McDonough, J. E. (1934). The Federal Home Loan Bank System. *American Economic Review*, 24(4), 668–685.

McGregor, D. (1960). *The Human Side of Enterprise*. New York: McGraw-Hill.

McKelvey, R. D. (1976). Intransitivities in Multidimensional Voting Models and Some Implications for Agenda Control. *Journal of Economic Theory*, 12(3), 472–482.

McKenna, F. (2012, November 12). Is The SEC's Ponzi Crusade Enabling Companies to Cook the Books, Enron-Style? *Forbes*.

McLean, B., & Elkind, P. (2003). *The Smartest Guys in the Room: The Amazing Rise and Scandalous Fall of Enron*. New York: Penguin.

Meier, K. J., Polinard, J. L., & Wrinkle, R. D. (2000). Bureaucracy and Organizational Performance: Causality Arguments about Public Schools. *American Journal of Political Science*, 44(3), 590–602.

Meier, K. J., Stewart, J., Jr., & England, R. E. (1991). The Politics of Bureaucratic Discretion: Educational Access as an Urban Service. *American Journal of Political Science*, 35(1), 155–177.

Melumad, N. D., & Shibano, T. (1994). The Securities and Exchange Commission and the Financial Accounting Standards Board: Regulation through Veto-based Delegation. *Journal of Accounting Research*, 32(1), 1–37.

Merton, R. K. (1957). *Social Theory and Social Structure* (Rev. and enl. ed.). Glencoe, IL: Free Press.

Miller, G. J. (1992). *Managerial Dilemmas: The Political Economy of Hierarchy*. New York: Cambridge University Press.

Miller, G. J. (2000). Above Politics: Credible Commitment and Efficiency in the Design of Public Agencies. *Journal of Public Administration Research and Theory*, 10(2), 289–328.

Miller, G. J. (2001). Why is Trust Necessary in Organizations? The Moral Hazard of Profit Maximization. In K. Cook (Ed.), *Trust in Society* (pp. 307–331). New York: Russell Sage Foundation.

Miller, G. J. (2004). Monitoring, Rules, and the Control Paradox: Can the Good Soldier Švejk Be Trusted? In R. M. Kramer & K. S. Cook (Eds.), *Trust and Distrust in Organizations: Dilemmas and Approaches* (pp. 99–126). New York: Russell Sage Foundation.

Miller, G. J., & Schofield, N. (2003). Activists and Partisan Realignment in the United States. *American Political Science Review*, 97(2), 245–260.

Miller, G. J., & Whitford, A. B. (2002). Trust and Incentives in Principal-Agent Negotiations: The "Insurance/Incentive Trade-Off." *Journal of Theoretical Politics*, 14(2), 231–267.

Miller, G. J., & Whitford, A. B. (2007). The Principal's Moral Hazard: Constraints on the Use of Incentives in Hierarchy. *Journal of Public Administration Research and Theory*, 17(2), 213–233.

Milner, H. V., & Rosendorff, B. P. (1997). Democratic Politics and International Trade Negotiations: Elections and Divided Government as Constraints on Trade Liberalization. *Journal of Conflict Resolution*, 41(1), 117–146.

Minority Staff of the Committee on Finance. (2007). *The Firing of an SEC Attorney and the Investigation of Pequot Capital Management*. Washington, DC: U.S. Government Printing Office.

Moe, T. M. (1985). Control and Feedback in Economic Regulation: The Case of the NLRB. *American Political Science Review*, 79(4), 1094–1116.

Moe, T. M. (1987). Interests, Institutions, and Positive Theory: The Politics of the NLRB. *Studies in American Political Development*, 2(Spring), 236–299.

Moe, T. M. (1989). The Politics of Bureaucratic Structure. In J. Chubb & P. Peterson (Eds.), *Can the Government Govern?* (pp. 267–329). Washington, DC: Brookings Institution.

Moore, M. J. (2009, November 19). Morgan Stanley's Mack Welcomes Regulation by Fed. Bloomberg.com. Retrieved from www.bloomberg.com/apps/news?pid=newsarchive&sid=aWrIZEzc5yNc

Morgan, C. (2008). *The Two Trillion Meltdown*. New York: Public Affairs.

Morgensen, G. (2010, June 30). SEC Pays Settlement to Staff Lawyer It Fired. *New York Times*, p. B3.

Morgensen, G. (2014, August 2, 2014). Big Banks Still a Risk. *New York Times*, p. BU1. Retrieved from www.nytimes.com/2014/08/03/business/big-banks-still-a-risk.html

Morris, C. R. (2008). *The Two Trillion Dollar Meltdown: Easy Money, High Rollers, and the Great Credit Crash*. New York: PublicAffairs.

Morris, I. L. (2002). *Congress, the President, and the Federal Reserve: The Politics of American Monetary Policy-Making*. Ann Arbor: University of Michigan Press.

Mosher, F. C. (1968). *Democracy and the Public Service.* New York: Oxford University Press.

Mowry, G. E. (1951). *The California Progressives.* Berkeley: University of California Press.

Murphy, K. J. (2012). Executive Compensation: Where We Are, and How We Got There. In G. M. Constantinides, M. Harris, & R. M. Stulz (Eds.), *Handbook of the Economics of Finance* (pp. 211–356). Oxford: North-Holland.

Nash, N. C. (1989, July 9). Showdown Time for Danny Wall. *New York Times.*

Nelson, D. (1975). *Managers and Workers: Origins of the New Factory System in the United States, 1880–1920.* Madison: University of Wisconsin Press.

Newman, D. P. (1981). The SEC's Influence on Accounting Standards: The Power of the Veto. *Journal of Accounting Research,* 19, 134–156.

Nikolsko-Rzhevskyy, A., Papell, D. H., & Prodan, R. (2014). *Deviations from Rules-Based Policy and Their Effects.* Social Science Research Network. Retrieved from papers.ssrn.com/sol3/papers.cfm?abstract_id=2463781

Noeth, B. J., & Sengupta, R. (2011). Is Shadow Banking Really Banking? *Regional Economist,* 19(4), 8–13.

Noll, R. G., & Owen, B. M. (1983). *The Political Economy of Deregulation: Interest Groups in the Regulatory Process.* Washington, DC: American Enterprise Institute for Public Policy Research.

North, D. C. (1979). A Framework for Analyzing the State in Economic History. *Explorations in Economic History,* 16(3), 249–259.

North, D. C. (1981). *Structure and Change in Economic History.* New York: W. W Norton.

North, D. C., & Weingast, B. R. (1989). Constitutions and Commitment: The Evolution of Institutions Governing Public Choice in Seventeenth-Century England. *Journal of Economic History,* 49(4), 803–832.

Novak, W. J. (2014). A Revisionist of Regulatory Capture. In D. P. Carpenter & D. A. Moss (Eds.), *Preventing Regulatory Capture: Special Interest Influence and How to Limit It.* New York: Cambridge University Press.

O'Brien, M. (2014). Republicans Want to Control, not End, the Fed. Retrieved from www.washingtonpost.com/blogs/wonkblog/wp/2014/07/18/republicans-want-to-control-not-end-the-fed/

Olson, M. (1965). *The Logic of Collective Action: Public Goods and the Theory of Groups.* Cambridge, MA: Harvard University Press.

Oppenheimer, J. (1975). Some Political Implications of "Vote Trading and the Voting Paradox: A Proof of Logical Equivalence": A Comment. *American Political Science Review,* 69(3), 963–966.

Peltzman, S. (1976). Toward a More General Theory of Regulation. *Journal of Law and Economics,* 19(2), 211–240. doi: 10.2307/725163

Perino, M. (2010). *The Hellhound of Wall Street: How Ferdinand Pecora's Investigation of the Great Crash Forever Changed American Finance.* New York: Penguin Press.

Perry, J. L., & Wise, L. R. (1990). The Motivational Bases of Public Service. *Public Administration Review,* 50(3), 367–373.

Philippon, T., & Reshef, A. (2012). Wages and Human Capital in the U.S. Finance Industry: 1909–2006. *Quarterly Journal of Economics,* 127(4), 1551–1609.

Pizzo, S., Fricker, M., & Muolo, P. (1989). *Inside Job: The Looting of America's Savings and Loans.* New York: McGraw-Hill.

Polanyi, M. (1958). *Personal Knowledge: Towards a Post-Critical Philosophy*. Chicago: University of Chicago Press.

Polanyi, M. (1966). *The Tacit Dimension*. Garden City, NY: Doubleday Anchor Books.

Pollock, A. J. (2014, December 1). A Federal Guarantee Is Sure to Go Broke. *Wall Street Journal*, p. A15.

Prendergast, C. (1999). The Provision of Incentives in Firms. *Journal of Economic Literature*, 37(1), 7–63.

Press Trust of India. (2011). Raja, Behura, Chandolia Are Core Sector of 2G Conspiracy: CBI. *Business Standard*. Retrieved from www.business-standard .com/article/economy-policy/raja-behura-chandolia-are-core-sector-of-2g-conspiracy-cbi-111113000168_1.html

Provost, C. (2010). *Another Race to the Bottom? Venue Shopping for Regulators in the American Financial System*. University College London, School of Public Policy. Retrieved from http://www.regulation.upf.edu/dublin-10-papers/7A3.pdf

Putin, V. (2000). Open Letter to Voters. Published in the newspapers Izvestia, Kommersant, and Komsomolskaya Pravda. [Press release]. Retrieved from http://eng.kremlin .ru/transcripts/8587

Qi, B., Zysman, G., & Menkes, H. (2001). Wireless Mobile Communications at the Start of the 21st Century. *Communications Magazine, IEEE*, 39(1), 110–116.

Radner, R. (1985). Repeated Principal-Agent Games with Discounting. *Econometrica*, 53(5), 1173–1198.

Rauch, J. E. (1995). Bureaucracy, Infrastructure, and Economic Growth: Evidence from US Cities during the Progressive Era. *American Economic Review*, 85(4), 968–979.

Riccucci, N. (1995). *Unsung Heroes: Federal Execucrats Making a Difference*. Washington, DC: Georgetown University Press.

Ricks, T. E. (2006). *Fiasco: The American Military Adventure in Iraq*. New York: Penguin Press.

Riker, W. H. (1980). Implications from the Disequilibrium of Majority Rule for the Study of Institutions. *American Political Science Review*, 74(2), 432–446.

Riker, W. H. (1982). *Liberalism against Populism: A Confrontation between the Theory of Democracy and the Theory of Social Choice*. San Francisco: W. H. Freeman.

Rogin, J. (2011). McCain and Graham Spell Out How They'll Get around the "Supercommittee." Retrieved from thecable.foreignpolicy.com/posts/2011/11/09/mccain_and_graham_spell_out_how_they_ll_get_around_the_supercommittee

Rogoff, K. (1985). The Optimal Degree of Commitment to an Intermediate Monetary Target. *Quarterly Journal of Economics*, 100(4), 1169–1189.

Root, H. L. (1989). Tying the King's Hands. *Rationality and Society*, 1(2), 240–258.

Rothschild, M., & Stiglitz, J. E. (1975). Equilbrium in Competitive Insurance Markets. (Vol. Technical Report No. 170).?

Rourke, F. E. (1984). *Bureaucracy, Politics, and Public Policy* (3rd ed.). Boston: Little, Brown.

Safire, W. (2003, November 5, 2003). Siloviki versus Oligarchy. *New York Times*, p. A25. Retrieved from http://www.nytimes.com/2003/11/05/opinion/siloviki-versus-oligarchy.html

Safire, W. (2008). *Safire's Political Dictionary* (updated and expanded ed.). New York: Oxford University Press.

Salanie, B. (2005). *The Economics of Contracts* (2nd ed.). Cambridge, MA: MIT Press.

Salop, J., & Salop, S. (1976). Self-Selection and Turnover in the Labor Market. *Quarterly Journal of Economics*, 90(4), 619–627.

Sanders, T. H. (1936). Influence of the Securities and Exchange Commission upon Accounting Principles. *Accounting Review*, 11(1), 66–74.

Sappington, D. E. M. (1991). Incentives in Principal-Agent Relationships. *Journal of Economic Perspectives*, 5(2), 45–66.

Satterthwaite, M. A. (1975). Strategy-Proofness and Arrow's Conditions: Existence and Correspondence Theorems for Voting Procedures and Social Welfare Functions. *Journal of Economic Theory*, 10(2), 187–217.

Schattschneider, E. E. (1935). *Politics, Pressures and the Tariff*. New York: Prentice-Hall.

Scheer, R. (2009). *The Great American Stickup: How Reagan Republicans and Clinton Democrats Enriched Wall Street while Mugging Main Street*. New York: Nation Books.

Schelling, T. C. (1960). *The Strategy of Conflict*. Cambridge, MA: Harvard University Press.

Schiesl, M. J. (1977). *The Politics of Efficiency: Municipal Administration and Reform in America, 1800–1920*. Berkeley: University of California Press.

Schlesinger, A. M. (2003). *The Coming of the New Deal: 1933–1935, The Age of Roosevelt* (Vol. 2). New York: Houghton Mifflin Harcourt.

Schmidt, D. E. (1994). NLRB Regional Office Decision Making: Independence, Partisanship, and Caseloads. *American Review of Public Administration*, 24(2), 133–148.

Schmidt, D. E. (1995). The Presidential Appointment Process, Task Environment Pressures, and Regional Office Case Processing. *Political Research Quarterly*, 48(2), 381–401.

Schmidt, D. E. (2002). Politicization and Responsiveness in the Regional Offices of the NLRB. *American Review of Public Administration*, 32(2), 188–215.

Schumpeter, J. A. (1950). *Capitalism, Socialism, and Democracy* (3rd ed.). New York: Harper.

Schumpeter, J. A., & Schumpeter, E. B. (1954). *History of Economic Analysis*. New York: Oxford University Press.

Schwartz, T. (1981). The Universal-Instability Theorem. *Public Choice*, 37(3), 487–501.

Scott, W. R. (1965). Reactions to Supervision in a Heteronomous Professional Organization. *Administrative Science Quarterly*, 10(1), 65–81.

Scott, W. R. (1969). Professional Employees in a Bureaucratic Structure: Social Work. In A. Etzioni (Ed.), *The Semi-Professions and Their Organization*. New York: Free Press.

Securities and Exchange Commission. (1999). Testimony of Arthur Levitt, Chairman of the U.S. Securities and Exchange Commission, Concerning Loan Loss Allowances, Before the Subcommittee on Securities Committee on Banking, Housing and Urban Affairs, United States Senate, July 29, 1999.

Seidman, H. (1970). *Politics, Position, and Power: The Dynamics of Federal Organization*. New York: Oxford University Press.

Seligman, J. (2003). *The Transformation of Wall Street: A History of the Securities and Exchange Commission and Modern Corporate Finance*. New York: Aspen Publishers.

Seligman, J. (2003–2004). Self-Funding for the Securities and Exchange Commission. *Nova Law Review*, 28, 233–259.

Shabelnikov, D. (2008). *The Legal Profession in the Russian Federation*. Moscow, Russia: Organization for Security and Co-operation in Europe and the Public Interest Law Institute.

Shaked, A., & Sutton, J. (1981). The Self-Regulating Profession. *Review of Economic Studies*, 48(2), 217–234.

Shapiro, S. P. (1984). *Wayward Capitalists: Target of the Securities and Exchange Commission*. New Haven, CT: Yale University Press.

Shavell, S. (1979). On Moral Hazard and Insurance. *Quarterly Journal of Economics*, 93(4), 541–562.

Shell, A. (2009, September 1). Could Investors Fleeing Stocks Become a Lost Generation? *USA Today*, p. B2. Retrieved from usatoday30.usatoday.com/money/perfi/stocks/2010-09-02-lostgeneration02_CV_N.htm

Shelly, B. (2014, December 16). Elizabeth Warren Squashes Kevin Yoder's Sorry Rationale for Unraveling Taxpayer Protection. *Kansas City Star*. Retrieved from www.kansascity.com/opinion/opn-columns-blogs/barbara-shelly/article4535487.html

Shvetsova, L. (2005). *Putin's Russia* (revised and expanded ed.). Washington, DC: Carnegie Endowment for International Peace.

Sjostrum, W. K. (2009). The AIG Bailout. *Washington and Lee Law Review*, 66(3), 943–991.

Smith, A. (1776). *An Inquiry into the Nature and Causes of the Wealth of Nations*. London: Printed for W. Strahan, and T. Cadell.

Snyder, S. K., & Weingast, B. R. (2000). The American System of Shared Powers: The President, Congress, and the NLRB. *Journal of Law, Economics, and Organization*, 16(2), 269–305.

Sorkin, A. R. (2009). *Too Big to Fail: Inside the Battle to Save Wall Street*. New York: Viking.

Sorkin, A. R. (2011, February 7). Dealbook: Wall St. Joins S.E.C. in Plea for Bigger Budget. *New York Times*. Retrieved from dealbook.nytimes.com/2011/02/07/wall-st-joins-s-e-c-in-plea-for-bigger-budget/

Sorkin, A. R., & Bajaj, V. (2008, September 21, 2008). Shift for Goldman and Morgan Marks the End of an Era. *New York Times*, p. A1. Retrieved from www.nytimes.com/2008/09/22/business/22bank.html?_r=0

Spulber, D. F., & Besanko, D. (1992). Delegation, Commitment, and the Regulatory Mandate. *Journal of Law, Economics, & Organization*, 8(1), 126–154.

Stasavage, D. (2002). Credible Commitment in Early Modern Europe: North and Weingast Revisited. *Journal of Law, Economics, & Organization*, 18(1), 155–186.

Steffens, L. (1904). *The Shame of the Cities*. New York: McClure, Phillips & Company.

Stein, H. (1984). *Presidential Economics: The Making of Economic Policy from Roosevelt to Reagan and Beyond*. New York: Simon & Schuster.

Stein, M. A. (2001). Hardball, Politics, and the NLRB. *Berkeley Journal of Employment and Labor Law*, 22, 507–515.

Stigler, G. J. (1971). The Theory of Economic Regulation. *Bell Journal of Economics and Management Science*, 2(1), 3–21. doi: 10.2307/3003160

Stiglitz, J. E. (1974). Incentives and Risk Sharing in Sharecropping. *Review of Economic Studies*, 41(2), 219–255.

Stiglitz, J. E. (2002). Information and the Change in the Paradigm in Economics. In T. Frängsmyr (Ed.), *Les Prix Nobel: The Nobel Prizes 2001*. Stockholm: Nobel Foundation.

Stiglitz, J. E. (2010). *Freefall: Free Markets and the Sinking of the Global Economy*. New York: W. W. Norton & Company.

Stone, H. A., Price, D. K., & Stone, K. H. (1940). *City Manager Government in the United States: A Review After Twenty-five Years (Vol. XII)*. Chicago: Committee on Public Administration of the Social Science Research Council by Public Administration Service.

Suskind, R. (2011). *Confidence Men: Wall Street, Washington, and the Education of a President*. New York: Harper.

Swartz, M. (2001). How Enron Blew It. *Texas Monthly*, 136–147.

Tarbell, I. M. (1904). *The History of the Standard Oil Company (Vol. 1–2)*. New York: McClure, Phillips & Company.

Taylor, B. D. (2011). *State Building in Putin's Russia: Policing and Coercion after Communism*. New York: Cambridge University Press.

Taylor, J. B. (1993). Discretion versus Policy Rules in Practice. *Carnegie-Rochester Conference Series on Public Policy*, 39, 195–214.

Teodoro, M. P. (2011). *Bureaucratic Ambition: Careers, Motives, and the Innovative Administrator*. Baltimore, MD: Johns Hopkins University Press.

Teodoro, M. P. (2014). When Professionals Lead: Executive Management, Normative Isomorphism, and Policy Implementation. *Journal of Public Administration Research and Theory*, 24(4), 983–1004.

This American Life. (2014, September 26). 536: The Secret Recordings of Carmen Segarra, September 26, 2014. Retrieved from www.thisamericanlife.org/radio-archives/episode/536/the-secret-recordings-of-carmen-segarra

Thompson, V. A. (1961). Hierarchy, Specialization, and Organizational Conflict. *Administrative Science Quarterly*, 5(4), 485–521.

Thoreau, H. D., & Shepard, O. (1927). *The Heart of Thoreau's Journals*. Boston: Houghton Mifflin.

Tideman, T. N., & Tullock, G. (1976). A New and Superior Process for Making Social Choices. *Journal of Political Economy*, 84(6), 1145–1159.

Tietenberg, T. H. (1990). Economic Instruments for Environmental Regulation. *Oxford Review of Economic Policy*, 6(1), 17–33.

Timberlake, R. H. (1978). *The Origins of Central Banking in the United States*. Cambridge, MA: Harvard University Press.

Tirole, J. (1986). Hierarchies and Bureaucracies: On the Role of Collusion in Organizations. *Journal of Law, Economics, & Organization*, 2(2), 181–214.

Tonon, J. M. (2008). The Costs of Speaking Truth to Power: How Professionalism Facilitates Credible Communication. *Journal of Public Administration Research and Theory*, 18(2), 275–295.

Tyack, D. (1974). *The One Best System: A History of American Urban Education*. Cambridge, MA: Harvard University Press.

U.S. Securities and Exchange Commission. (2010). Goldman Sachs to Pay Record $550 Million to Settle SEC Charges Related to Subprime Mortgage CDO: Firm Acknowledges CDO Marketing Materials Were Incomplete and Should Have Revealed Paulson's Role [Press release]. Retrieved from www.sec.gov/news/press/2010/2010-123.htm

U.S. Securities and Exchange Commission. (2012). Litigation Release No. 22398 / June 25, 2012, SEC *v.* Ralph R. Cioffi and Matthew M. Tannin, Civil Action No. 08

2457 (FB) (E.D.N.Y.). Washington, DC: U.S. Securities and Exchange Commission Retrieved from www.sec.gov/litigation/litreleases/2012/lr22398.htm.

United States Government Accountability Office. (2014). *Large Bank Holding Companies: Expectations of Gogvernment Support. Testimony before the Subcommittee on Financial Institutions and Consumer Protection, Committee on Banking, Housing and Urban Affairs, U.S. Senate. Statement of Lawrance L. Evans, Jr., PhD, Director Financial Markets and Community Investment. (GAO-14-809T)*. Washington, DC: United States Government Accountability Office Retrieved from www.gao.gov/assets/670/665167.pdf.

United States Senate. (2014). Subcommittee on Senate Resolutions 84 and 234 (The Pecora Committee). Retrieved from www.senate.gov/artandhistory/history/common/investigations/Pecora.htm

Vickers, J. (1985). Delegation and the Theory of the Firm. *Economic Journal, 95*, 138–147.

Vickrey, W. (1960). Utility, Strategy, and Social Decision Rules. *Quarterly Journal of Economics, 74*(4), 507–535.

Walker, S. (1977). *A Critical History of Police Reform*. Lexington, MA: D. C. Heath.

Wallison, P. J. (2014, July 20). Four Years of Dodd-Frank Damage. *Wall Street Journal*. Retrieved from online.wsj.com/articles/peter-wallison-four-years-of-dodd-frank-damage-1405893333

Walras, L. (1954). *Elements of Pure Economics; or, The Theory of Social Wealth*. Homewood, IL: American Economic Association and the Royal Economic Society.

Warburg, P. M. (1930). *The Federal Reserve System, Its Origin and Growth; Reflections and Recollections*. New York: Macmillan.

Warwick, D. P. (1975). *A Theory of Public Bureaucracy: Politics, Personality, and Organization in the State Department*. Cambridge, MA: Harvard University Press.

Wasson, E. (2014, December 19). GOP to Warren: That Dodd-Frank Rollback Was Just the Appetizer. Bloomberg.com. Retrieved from www.bloomberg.com/politics/articles/2014-12-19/gop-to-warren-that-doddfrank-rollback-was-just-the-appetizer

Watson, J. (2002). *Strategy: An Introduction to Game Theory*. New York: W.W. Norton.

Weaver, S. (1977). *Decision to Prosecute: Organization and Public Policy in the Antitrust Division*. Cambridge, MA: MIT Press.

Weaver, S. (1980). Antitrust Division of the Department of Justice. In J. Q. Wilson (Ed.), *The Politics of Regulation* (pp. 123–151). New York: Basic Books.

Weber, M., Gerth, H. H., & Mills, C. W. (1958). *From Max Weber: Essays in Sociology*. New York: Oxford University Press.

Weingast, B. R. (1984). The Congressional-Bureaucratic System: A Principal-Agent Perspective (with Applications to the SEC). *Public Choice, 44*(1), 147–191.

Weingast, B. R., & Moran, M. J. (1983). Bureaucratic Discretion or Congressional Control? Regulatory Policymaking by the Federal Trade Commission. *Journal of Political Economy, 91*(5), 765–800.

Weisman, J. (2014, December 17). A Window into Washington in an Effort to Undo a Dodd-Frank Rule. *New York Times*, p. B3. Retrieved from dealbook.nytimes.com/2014/12/15/in-push-out-provision-example-of-how-congress-does-its-job/

Werntz, W. W. (1953). The Impact of Federal Legislation upon Accounting. *Accounting Review, 28*(2), 159–169.

Wessel, D. (2009). *In Fed We Trust: Ben Bernanke's War on the Great Panic.* New York: Crown Business.

Wheelock, D. C. (2008). Changing the Rules: State Mortgage Foreclosure Moratoria during the Great Depression. *Federal Reserve Bank of St. Louis Review,* 90(6), 569–583.

White, L. J. (1991). The S&L Debacle. *Fordham Law Review,* 59(6), S57-S270.

Whitford, A. B. (2002). Decentralization and Political Control of the Bureaucracy. *Journal of Theoretical Politics,* 14(2), 167–193.

Whitford, A. B., Bottom, W. P., & Miller, G. J. (2013). The (Negligible) Benefit of Moving First: Efficiency and Equity in Principal-Agent Negotiations. *Group Decision and Negotiation,* 22(3), 499–518.

Wilensky, H. L. (1964). The Professionalization of Everyone? *American Journal of Sociology,* 70(2), 137–158.

Williamson, O. E. (1983). Credible Commitments: Using Hostages to Support Exchange. *American Economic Review,* 73(4), 519–540.

Wilson, J. Q. (1980). *The Politics of Regulation.* New York: Basic Books.

Wilson, J. Q. (1989). *Bureaucracy: What Government Agencies Do and Why They Do It.* New York: Basic.

Woodward, B. (2000). *Maestro: Greenspan's Fed and the American Boom.* New York: Simon & Schuster.

Wooley, J. T. (1986). *Monetary Politics: The Federal Reserve and the Politics of Monetary Policy.* Cambridge: Cambridge University Press.

Zakaria, F. (2008, October 10). A More Disciplined America. *Newsweek.*

Index

Other books in the series (*Series List Continued from page ii*)

C. Mantzavinos, *Individuals, Institutions, and Markets*

Mathew D. McCubbins and Terry Sullivan, eds., *Congress: Structure and Policy*

Gary J. Miller, *Managerial Dilemmas: The Political Economy of Hierarchy*

Douglass C. North, *Institutions, Institutional Change, and Economic Performance*

Elinor Ostrom, *Governing the Commons: The Evolution of Institutions for Collective Action*

Daniel N. Posner, *Institutions and Ethnic Politics in Africa*

J. Mark Ramseyer, *Odd Markets in Japanese History: Law and Economic Growth*

J. Mark Ramseyer and Frances Rosenbluth, *The Politics of Oligarchy: Institutional Choice in Imperial Japan*

Jean-Laurent Rosenthal, *The Fruits of Revolution: Property Rights, Litigation, and French Agriculture, 1700–1860*

Michael L. Ross, *Timber Booms and Institutional Breakdown in Southeast Asia*

Shanker Satyanath, *Globalization, Politics, and Financial Turmoil: Asia's Banking Crisis*

Norman Schofield, *Architects of Political Change: Constitutional Quandaries and Social Choice Theory*

Norman Schofield and Itai Sened, *Multiparty Democracy: Elections and Legislative Politics*

Alberto Simpser, *Why Governments and Parties Manipulate Elections: Theory, Practice, and Implications*

Alastair Smith, *Election Timing*

Pablo T. Spiller and Mariano Tommasi, *The Institutional Foundations of Public Policy in Argentina: A Transactions Cost Approach*

David Stasavage, *Public Debt and the Birth of the Democratic State: France and Great Britain, 1688–1789*

Charles Stewart III, *Budget Reform Politics: The Design of the Appropriations Process in the House of Representatives, 1865–1921*

George Tsebelis and Jeannette Money, *Bicameralism*

Georg Vanberg, *The Politics of Constitutional Review in Germany*

Nicolas van de Walle, *African Economies and the Politics of Permanent Crisis, 1979–1999*

John Waterbury, *Exposed to Innumerable Delusions: Public Enterprise and State Power in Egypt, India, Mexico, and Turkey*

David L. Weimer, ed., *The Political Economy of Property Rights Institutional Change and Credibility in the Reform of Centrally Planned Economies*